THE COMPLETE BOOK OF

Garden Flowers

THE COMPLETE BOOK OF

Garden Flowers

How to grow over 300 of the best performing varieties

SERIES EDITOR   GRAHAM STRONG

WHITECAP
BOOKS

CONTENTS

GROWING ANNUALS

Annuals are perhaps the easiest plants you will ever grow. Yet their ease of growth in no way detracts from their ability to provide color in the yard, in some cases virtually all year around. Whether your yard is large, small, or you work within the confines of just a small courtyard, annuals are plants for you.

Miracles are happening in our gardens every day, but perhaps the greatest "miracle" in which we can take part is growing plants from seeds. Nothing is quite as amazing, or as humbling, as seeing a fully grown plant, that started life as a tiny seed, burst into flower and create a riot of color just a few months after it was sown. Some annuals need no more care than simply scattering the seeds over the surface of the ground and "raking" them in using your fingertips; others only demand that they are sown to the correct depth and then given space to grow as they develop. By their very nature, many annuals produce brilliant results, even in the poorest of soils. So get some seed catalogs, visit the local garden center, and start performing your own gardening miracles with the easiest plants on earth!

LEFT: Annuals like these purple violas and white-flowered lobularia (alyssum) can be sown directly into the soil where you want them to flower, in criss-crossing patterns as here.

ABOVE: Rudbeckia or coneflower is available in a wide range of sizes, and provides valuable color in late summer.

MANY ANNUALS THRIVE in some of the most inhospitable parts of the yard. These portulacas, or sun flowers, are perfectly at home growing on a rock garden with very little soil for their roots—and are just as suited to light, sandy soils and make good summer bedding plants.

WHAT ARE ANNUALS?

Virtually all annuals are raised by sowing seeds, either in the early spring under cover (in a heated greenhouse, conservatory, or on the kitchen windowsill), or directly into prepared soil outdoors. Some annuals are so adaptable that you only need sow them once—from then onward these so-called "self-seeders" regularly drop seeds into the soil which then "come up," or germinate, of their own accord. In many ways, these "hardy annuals" do a better job of sowing than we do, finding just the right spot for perfect growth, often in places we might never dream of sowing seeds, such as in cracks in the sidewalk and in the gravel of driveways.

At the other extreme are annuals that need to be started into growth long before the warmer days of spring arrive outdoors. The so-called "half-hardy" annuals are those plants that are damaged by frosts, but perform brilliantly during the summer months. For these you must be able to provide suitable growing conditions, especially at sowing time, when temperature is all-important for getting the seeds to come up. In some cases, such as with ricinus, the castor oil plant, it is grown as a half-hardy annual, even though it is by nature a shrub, which in its native habitat would, like the shrubs in our gardens, eventually form a large plant. Petunias are another example of a half-hardy annual that is really a perennial plant, and quite capable of surviving the winter if potted-up and kept protected in a cold but frost-free place over winter. It helps to understand what the terms mean when growing annuals, since you will come across them all the time in catalogs and on the back of seed packets.

HARDY ANNUALS

The easiest of all annuals to grow, sow hardy annuals exactly where you want the plants to flower. Many hardy annuals do not like root disturbance, so bear this in mind.

They are given their ideal planting distances by gradually "thinning out" as the young plants grow—all this means is carefully removing a few plants every few weeks in the spring, to give those left behind more room to develop. By early summer this thinning should be complete, and plants can be left to produce flowers. Hardy annuals are not affected by low temperatures, and many, like calendula, the pot marigold, are sown and germinate outdoors in September, for strong plants with earlier flowers the following spring. Most self-seeders belong to this group.

HALF-HARDY ANNUALS

As already mentioned, these plants are not able to withstand frost or freezing temperatures and must be raised from seed every season, often starting in late winter and very early spring. Many half-hardy annuals are actually perennials—plants that keep growing year after year, but which are better suited to our needs when grown as strong, young plants every season. Half-hardy annuals are only planted (or moved outdoors if grown in containers) when spring frosts are finished. The exact timing of this depends on the area you garden in, but this book gives sowing/planting times for average conditions. At the other end of the season, the first fall frosts will flatten most half-hardy annuals, and they can be removed for composting.

HARDY BIENNIALS

A biennial is simply a plant that straddles two growing seasons before it produces its show of flowers or foliage. A good example is cheiranthus, or wallflower, which is sown outdoors in early summer. The young leafy plants are grown on, then lifted and planted in October where you want the flowers to grow the following spring. Think of hardy biennials as annuals with a foot in two seasons—instead of producing their flowers or leaves all within what we think of as "summer," they get going in one season, spend the winter building up speed, then go all-out for flowering the next spring and summer. Biennials are especially useful for filling any gaps between late spring and early summer, and many, such as Sweet William, are easy and worthwhile plants for cut flowers.

BUYING SEEDS

Growing from seed is addictive—once you have sampled one seed catalog, you will certainly want more. You can buy annual seeds by sending for them via post or a home delivery service, by visiting garden centers or the gardening section of hardware stores, or, increasingly, by buying them with your other shopping at the supermarket.

The choice will always be greater in catalogs, but the more limited range that you may find in garden centers can actually be more helpful. The seed packets are guaranteed to be colorful, giving encouragement to the beginner. Some mail order seed companies pack their products in plain, information-only packets—this is no reflection on the quality of the seeds, but they do lack inspiration! Bright, colorful packets are a great help when planning a color-themed display with annuals, so do not be afraid to play around with a handful of packets until you get a good balance or contrast of colors just to your liking.

If you do buy seeds from garden centers and similar outlets, always avoid any packets that are faded, yellow, and have obviously been exposed to the sun, as the results are likely to be disappointing.

SEED PACKETS

Remember that seeds are alive, and need looking after to keep them in tiptop condition until sowing. Inside most seed packets you will find another, smaller packet made of foil. Seeds are sealed inside this inner packet in a kind of suspended animation that preserves them until the foil seal is broken. This is when the normal ageing process of the seed begins. Where this type of storage is not vital for success, seeds are simply found sealed within the outer paper packet. Foil packets should not be opened until the time of sowing, for best results. On most packets the inspiration on the front is backed by full growing instructions on the reverse. The better packets give sowing times, expected flowering period, and alternative sowing times in the fall. Keep seed packets after sowing—along with catalogs, they build up into an invaluable library that you can refer to as and when necessary. Always keep seeds in a cool, dry, frost-free place.

YOUNG PLANTS

Many half-hardy annuals included in this book can also be bought in the spring and summer as "young plants," and this is stated, where relevant, in the "features" paragraph for each of the 90 annuals covered. The term "young plant" covers anything from ready-germinated trays of small seedlings to a large plant, perhaps in flower, growing in a 3½in pot that you can find for sale in garden centers. Buying young plants simply means that a lot of the work in raising the plants from seed has been done for you by the grower—which has advantages and disadvantages. Young plants are a great help if you do not have facilities for raising seeds or enough space, and they are often delivered ready to go directly into containers. The range compared to the number of varieties available from seed is limited, although this is always improving. You pay for convenience: seed-raising is usually cheaper than buying in young plants.

WHAT CAN GO WRONG?

Yellow leaves
● Seedlings are being grown too cold in the early stages, or plants may have been planted outdoors too early.
● Plants may need feeding—water thoroughly with an all-purpose liquid or soluble plant food, wetting the leaves at the same time to act as a foliar feed.

Curled or distorted leaves
● Look for clusters of aphids attacking flower buds and the youngest leaves at the shoot tips. Rub them off with your fingers or use a spray containing permethrin.
● Drift from weedkillers can cause this problem, so take great care if you are treating a lawn for weeds using a hormone-based weedkiller. Avoid days when there is any breeze, and keep well away from bedding displays.

Holes and silvery trails on/in leaves
● Slugs and snails will eat most annual plants and are a particular threat in late spring and early summer, especially after rain, when the air is warm and moist. They leave silver slime trails on the soil and on plants where they have been feeding. Chemical slug pellets can be scattered sparingly among plants, or an unbroken ring of sharp grit 2in wide can be used as a physical deterrent on smaller areas. Another option is to check plants at night and pick off slugs and snails while they feed, dropping them into salty water.

White "powder" on leaves
● Powdery mildew affects many annuals, but usually not until late summer. This disease is not a serious threat and treatment is not needed.

Seedlings indoors suddenly collapse
● "Damping off" disease can attack annual seedlings, and is a particular problem if the compost becomes too wet. Always use clean pots for sowing and fresh compost. If it does attack, water lightly with a copper-based fungicide and resow to play safe.

Leaf edges chewed
● Various caterpillars will attack annuals and can soon strip leaves bare. Pick them off by hand or use a spray containing permethrin, wetting both sides of the leaves with a strong jet from a sprayer.

Plants cut off at ground level
● Cutworms can sever newly planted bedding plants outdoors, causing a sudden wilting and yellowing of plants under attack. Search around in the soil and the greenish-brown caterpillars are easily found and destroyed.

Creamy-white grubs eating roots
● Vine weevil grubs can cause severe damage to container plants. Never re-use old compost, and if you find grubs, treat all pots with biological control or a chemical based on phenols as a drench.

Orange marigolds, red and orange nasturtiums, asters, and brown-coned rudbeckia intermingle to form a color-coordinated annual border.

One of the wisest approaches is to decide carefully just what you feel you can achieve with your existing facilities. If your propagator (somewhere that plants are raised from seeds in the early stages) is just the kitchen windowsill, buying half-hardy annuals as young plants may be the best option. These small plug plants are delivered in mid-spring and can be potted up and grown on placed on the windowsill, or even next to the glass in an unheated conservatory. This eliminates the often tricky job of germinating the seeds to begin with, but means you can still grow the plants you really want. And of course, there is nothing to stop you sowing hardy annuals directly into the soil outdoors at the correct time.

If you are more restricted, say to just a small courtyard or balcony, young plants may be the whole solution—larger plants are delivered (or can be bought) in late spring and early summer, and these can be planted directly into containers and hanging baskets without growing on. Even then there is nothing to stop you scattering a few seeds of malcolmia, Virginian stock, in the top of your courtyard pots for some quick and scented flowers!

Most seed catalogs and specialist young plant suppliers carry extensive and informative sections on young plants, and they are well worth getting. Pay particular attention to "last order dates"—these are the cut-off points for placing your order for young plants and many start to appear as early as January and February.

ANNUALS IN CONTAINERS
A container in the broadest gardening sense is anything capable of holding compost and supporting plant growth—this could be anything from a 3½in-diameter plastic plant pot to a large terracotta trough or tub. Whatever you use, it must have some form of drainage, and this is usually through holes in the base. Molded plastic containers often have no preformed holes , so you must drill these before planting up. Waterlogged compost kills plant roots and the whole plant will soon die.

For most uses, a good "multipurpose" compost serves all of an annual plant's needs—from sowing to growing on, and finally being planted up. Most multipurpose composts are based on peat, with plant nutrients and other materials, such as water-storing granules and "wetters" (allowing dried-out compost to be re-wetted), already added. An increasing number of composts available are based on recycled materials, and the coir-based ones are improving constantly. A few specific plants prefer a soil-based compost, such as the "John Innes" types, both for sowing and growing—details of these are given under "growing method" sections of this book, where relevant. Always buy fresh bags of compost in spring, avoiding any that are over-heavy and wet, or split, with green algae growing in them, or faded and past their use-by date.

There is no reason why hardy annuals cannot be used for container growing—the fact that many are usually sown directly into the soil is not a problem. Simply sow them in small pots or multi-cell trays (plastic trays where the area is divided into individual units or "cells") at the same times as recommended for outdoor sowing, and plant into your containers during the spring. Where appropriate under each plant entry, varieties suited to containers are given—these are usually dwarfer versions of taller varieties, and the range is increasing all the time. Half-hardy annuals offer great scope for container growing, for the reasons already discussed.

SOWING ANNUALS

Annual seeds are sown indoors or outdoors. Those sown outdoors are the easiest—they need no extra warmth or heat, just sow them in a patch of well-prepared ground and thin them out to give space as they grow. Sowing depth will depend on the size of the seed, but it is essential to work the soil using a rake (or your fingers in a small area) so it is fine and crumbly to at least 1in deep.

Seed can then be simply scattered over the soil and raked in, or sown in seed drills—these are simply grooves made in the soil with the head of a rake, the edge of a piece of wood, a length of bamboo cane, or even the side of your hand. Whichever you use, just press the edge into the soil to make a groove of the correct depth. Then sprinkle the seeds thinly along the drill, by rubbing them between your finger and thumb. Once finished, soil is moved back over the seeds with a rake or by lightly brushing the flat of your hand over the sown area. Take care not to disturb the sown seeds, and label with the variety and date sown. If you are sowing a large area with a variety of hardy annuals, or planning a mixture of hardy and half-hardy varieties, mark the sown patches with boundaries of light-colored sand—a traditional but still effective way of seeing just where you have been! By sowing in short drills within these marked areas it is easy to tell the annuals from the weeds, because they come up in rows.

Indoors, half-hardy annuals are sown ideally in a heated propagator with temperature control, and this piece of equipment is virtually essential when raising plants like pelargoniums (bedding geraniums) and begonias, both of which need high, constant temperatures. Otherwise, a brightly lit windowsill in a warm kitchen will work miracles —many half-hardy annuals are very undemanding once they have come up, and if not kept over-wet will grow steadily, even in quite cool conditions.

Narrow "windowsill propagators" are available that have a heated base and allow you to move pots on and off as seedlings appear—these are invaluable if you plan to do a lot of seed-raising. For all the plants in this book, a 3½in-diameter pot is sufficient for the germination of an average packet of half-hardy annual seeds. If you raise half-hardy annuals, remember that they will not be able to go out until after the last spring frosts. You can sow many plants later than the ideal times—this book describes the optimum sowing times unless otherwise stated—and plan for a later display of flowers, with the advantage of them being easier to raise and care for a little later in the spring season.

SOIL PREPARATION

All that annuals need to grow well is soil that has had plenty of "organic matter" added before sowing or planting, and this is best done by digging it in thoroughly the previous fall or in early spring. Suppliers of manure take some tracking down these days, so using home-made compost (or leaf mold) is a better option.

Whatever you use, it must be dark, well-rotted, and thoroughly broken down. Organic matter is vital for improving the soil's ability to hold onto moisture at the height of summer, and also supplies some plant foods. To take proper care of feeding, scatter pelleted poultry manure over the area 2–3 weeks before sowing/planting and rake it in. This should provide ample nutrients for the rest of the summer.

THINNING OUT

"Thinning out" or "thinning" means allowing sufficient room for plants to develop fully. This is most important with hardy annuals—as young seedlings grow larger, some are gradually removed to leave room for those left behind. Make sure you put your fingers on the soil when pulling plants out, or there is a risk the plants you leave behind will be uprooted. Water well after thinning, to settle seedlings back in. Thinning can start when plants are just 1in tall and is usually finished by early summer. Fall-sown annuals should be thinned in the spring, in case some plants are lost during the winter months.

GROWING ON

Once seedlings have been transplanted (moved) to either individual pots or cell trays, they are "grown on." This stage lasts until they are finally hardened off before planting outdoors or in pots. During growing on, make sure plants do not dry out, spread them out (if pot-grown) as they develop, and keep a look out for pests and diseases. Some plants (like thunbergia, Black-eyed Susan) benefit from being potted on when their roots fill the pot.

HARDENING OFF

Toughening plants raised indoors ready for outdoor conditions is vital if they are not to suffer a growth check when you put them out. Few of us have (or have the room for) the traditional "cold frame," which was the classic way of hardening off. These days we can make use of garden fleece, which is much easier, and just as effective. From mid-May onward, plants can be stood outside on warm days, in a sunny spot. For the first week, bring them in at night, then leave them out, but covered with fleece at night. Gradually, unless frost is forecast, the fleece can be left off even at night, but replaced during frosty spells. By early June, plants will be hardened off and ready to plant.

PLANTING

Whether you are planting in beds or containers, water the pots/trays the previous night to soak the roots. Planting can be done with a trowel—or even by hand in light soils. Using your hands is certainly the best way of planting up containers and hanging baskets. Never plant the base of plants deeper than they were growing originally. Firm well, and water. Keep labels with the plants for future reference, and note the planting date on the label, too.

WATERING

Lack of water causes many hardy annuals to flower and then quickly die. When the soil feels dry, enough water should be given so that it gets down to the roots—the soil should feel moist at least 6in down. Use a trowel and check that this is happening. Containers need much more care, since they rely solely on you for their water. Choosing a compost that contains water-storing crystals provides the best insurance. Do not overwater early on or roots may rot, but check them at least every other day and never allow them to dry out.

FEEDING

By mixing slow-release fertilizer granules with the compost before planting, you can take care of feeding for the whole season—you just need to water the plants. Outdoors, bedding displays will benefit from liquid feeding every 2–4 weeks. Many hardy annuals need no extra feeding and actually thrive on poor, hungry soils.

USING ANNUALS IN YOUR GARDEN

With annuals, the sky really is the limit. You can choose to grow just hardy or half-hardy annuals, a mixture of both, or you can be more adventurous and put them to work for you in a wide range of yard situations. Or, of course, you could just leave them to do their own thing!

Once you have annuals in your yard, you will never want to be without them. Self-seeding annuals, like limnanthes and nigella, will want to do their own thing and grow where they fall, while others such as lavatera and ricinus are put to much better use by carefully planning where they will grow. You can find a spot for annuals in every yard, and sometimes they can even help you out of a tight corner! What better plants could you ask for?

ABOVE: The delicately veined flower of agrostemma, the corncockle, an easily grown hardy annual that is sown outdoors in spring where you want it to flower.

AS EDGING PLANTS these Begonia semperflorens *are a good choice. Being of even height, they are good for growing in line.*

BEDDING SCHEMES

We see annuals used in bedding schemes almost every day of our lives, on traffic islands, in public parks, and in each other's yards. The "scheme" part of the phrase comes from the fact that many of these impressive colorful displays are pre-planned, and in many ways made-to-measure. If that is the effect you are after, you must do your homework. The structure of a basic bedding scheme is quite simple—you have tall plants in the center of the bed, and the shortest plants around the edge. In between are plants in a range of sizes and with varying growth habits, which fill the space between the tallest and the shortest. Bedding schemes can be as simple, or as elaborate, as you choose. The key points to remember are to decide which plants are going where, how many you need, and of course, whether they are suited to being grown together.

HARDY ANNUAL SCHEMES

Creating a show using just hardy annuals is both very easy and tremendous fun. The sheer range of hardy annual varieties is enormous and it is easy to be spoiled for choice. You can go out and sow an entire bed with hardy annuals at one go, then sit back and wait for the seedlings to come up. Then all you need to do is keep down annual weeds (all perennial weeds should be removed before sowing), thin out every few weeks until early summer, push in twiggy supports for taller, straggly plants, and enjoy the show.

THIS SUMMER BEDDING SCHEME features zinnias in the centre of the bed (with variegated tradescantia creeping through) then scarlet salvias, dropping down to the pink fluffy heads of ageratum, the floss flower, below.

The best effect is from bold groups of color, so sow in patches at least 2ft across. Sow roughly circular areas as a foolproof guide, although interweaving shapes can create some dramatic effects, with different plants merging as they grow into each other. Take a tip from the traditions of the past and mark out the sown areas with sand, just so you know what is where, and label each patch, or mark the varieties clearly on a sketch plan, if you have one. Using just hardy annuals means there is no need for heating early in the season, and no crisis when growing space runs short. Many hardy annuals can also be sown in the fall, usually September, to grow through the winter and then give an early performance the following spring.

CARE-FREE HARDY ANNUALS
What could be better than a plant you only buy once, but will then always have many of? It sounds too good to be true, but that is just what you get with a great many hardy annuals—the self-seeders that arrive in a packet and then spread to all their favorite spots. We have to thank the origins of many of these plants for their valuable qualities. Agrostemma (corncockle), for example, was once a common weed of cornfields, and many other care-free annuals like it thrive on the poorest and hungriest of soils. These plants will tell you where they prefer growing by seeding themselves there, and they will need no more attention, other than being pulled out when they get too

dominant or invasive in areas set aside for more carefully planned activities. Calendula, centaurea, eschscholzia, papaver, and tropaeolum are all good examples of care-free annuals.

BORDER FILLERS
With the sudden loss of a favorite plant, your dreams of a "perfect" border can soon evaporate, and this is where annuals can get you out of a tight spot. Any spare patch of ground can be sown, or planted, with annuals, which will grow quickly to fill any gaps. You might even scatter seeds among perennial plants and let them get on with things. Lunaria (honesty), is quite at home growing among spring-flowering perennial euphorbias; the purple lunaria flowers make a good contrast with the pale yellow-green euphorbias. For a touch of the tropical, ricinus, the castor oil plant, is unbeatable, with its large, exotic-looking leaves in a range of colors. Sunflowers (helianthus) are always a good choice for some instant color when it's needed, and the newer dwarf varieties like "Pacino" are easy to grow in pots for planting out whenever their bright flowers are needed to perk up flagging borders.

ABUTILON
Flowering maple

ABUTILON has a distinct exotic look, with its hanging, bell-like flowers that are either single or bicolored, as seen here.

BEING A SHRUB, abutilon can be kept from year to year in a frost-free greenhouse and planted outdoors in mixed borders in the summer.

FEATURES

A deciduous tender shrub that is easy to raise from seed sown in the spring, with maple-like leaves and showy, hanging, bell-shaped flowers in a wide range of colors. Plants make bushy growth, and are useful in summer bedding schemes and for courtyard containers sited in a warm spot, but they must be protected from frost. Abutilon can be kept in a conservatory or frost-free greenhouse in the winter and will flower throughout spring and summer. Plants grow to 2–3ft tall. Varieties such as *Abutilon pictum* "Thompsonii," with variegated leaves, are available from garden centers as young plants in the spring; these can be potted up, grown on, and then planted outdoors after the last frosts.

ABUTILON AT A GLANCE

A deciduous shrub grown as a summer bedding and container plant, with bell-like flowers. Frost hardy to 23ºF (zone 9).

Jan	/
Feb	sow
Mar	pot up
Apr	pot on
May	harden off/plant
Jun	flowering
July	flowering
Aug	flowering
Sept	flowering
Oct	/
Nov	/
Dec	/

Recommended Varieties

Abutilon hybrids:
 "Large Flowered Mixed"
 "Mixed Colors"

CONDITIONS

Aspect   Grow in full sunlight in borders or on a south-facing courtyard. In southern areas, plants grown against a south-facing wall in well-drained soil will often survive mild winters outdoors without protection.

Site   Mix plenty of rotted manure/compost into soil before planting, and use multipurpose compost in containers. Soil should be well-drained but moisture-retentive for best results.

GROWING METHOD

Sowing   In February, sow in 3½in-diameter pots, cover seed with its own depth of multipurpose compost, and keep at 70ºF in light. Seedlings appear over 1–2 months, so check regularly. When plants are 2in tall, pot up into 3½in pots and grow on. Plant out in early June after the last frosts.

Feeding   Apply liquid feed weekly. Mix slow-release fertilizer granules with container compost.

Problems   Use sprays containing pirimicarb for aphids, malathion for mealy bugs, and bifenthrin for red spider mite, or, on plants growing in conservatories, use natural predators.

FLOWERING

Season   Flowers appear all summer outdoors, and some may appear year-around on indoor plants and those grown in southerly, mild areas, especially near the coast.

Cutting   Not suitable.

General   Plants can be potted up before frosts and kept indoors. Increase favorites by taking cuttings in spring, rooting them on a windowsill or in a heated propagator.

AGROSTEMMA
Corncockle

SOFT PINK "Milas" is one of the best known of the corncockle varieties. Pink and white varieties are also available.

GROW AGROSTEMMA in bold clumps in borders where the tall lanky, swaying plants help to give each other support.

FEATURES

A very easily grown hardy annual for use in cottage yards and borders where it self-seeds year after year. Plants are tall, growing 2–3ft tall, and carry pink, purple, or white trumpet-like blooms. The seeds are poisonous. Commonly known as corncockle.

CONDITIONS

Aspect   Grow in full sunlight.

AGROSTEMMA AT A GLANCE

A tall hardy annual grown for its pink, purple, or white flowers, which are ideal for cottage borders. Frost hardy to 5°F (zone 7).

		Recommended Varieties
Jan	/	
Feb	/	*Agrostemma githago:*
Mar	sow 👈	"Milas"
		"Ocean Pearl"
Apr	thin out 👈	"Purple Queen"
		"Rose of Heaven"
May	flowering 🖐	
Jun	flowering 🖐	
July	flowering 🖐	

Site   Succeeds on well-drained and even light, sandy soils that are quite "hungry" (it used to grow as a weed in cornfields). Excessive feeding may reduce the number of flowers.

GROWING METHOD

Sowing   Sow outdoors from March onward, when the soil is warming up, in patches or drills ½in deep where you want the plants to flower. Thin seedlings so they are eventually 6–12in apart. Do not transplant. Can also be sown in pots in the fall, overwintered in a sheltered spot, then potted up in spring for flowers in early summer.

Feeding   Extra feeding is unnecessary, but water occasionally but thoroughly in dry spells.

Problems   Agrostemma is a floppy plant and twiggy supports can be useful.

FLOWERING

Season   Summer onward, but earlier flowers are produced by fall sowing.

Cutting   Short-lived as a cut flower, and rather floppy.

AFTER FLOWERING

General   Dead-heading throughout summer will keep flowers coming, but always leave a few to ripen and set seeds. Plants will self-sow and germinate the following spring. Alternatively, collect seedheads in paper bags and store.

AMARANTHUS
Love-lies-bleeding

SOME AMARANTHUS produce masses of copper-crimson leaves in summer and red flower spikes. They make good pot plants.

"JOSEPH'S COAT," 2ft tall, has striking gold-and-crimson upper leaves and green-yellow lower leaves marked with brown.

FEATURES

Amaranthus is grown for its colorful, exotic-looking foliage and its spiky, erect or drooping tassels of blood-red, green, golden-brown, purple, or multi-colored flowers up to 18in long. Leaves can be red, bronze, yellow, brown, or green, depending on the variety grown. Size ranges from 15in to 4ft tall. Use plants as potted plants, in courtyard containers, and as dramatic centerpieces in summer bedding displays. Superb when used cut for fresh or dried flower arrangements indoors.

CONDITIONS

Aspect   Full sun and shelter is essential for success.
Site   Soil should be well-drained, with plenty of rotted compost or manure added. Varieties of ***Amaranthus caudatus*** will also succeed on thin, dry soils. Use multipurpose compost in containers and pots. In northern areas grow in 8–10in diameter pots in the greenhouse or conservatory. Tall-growing varieties may need staking.

GROWING METHOD

Sowing   Sow seeds in March at 70°F in 3½in-diameter pots of multipurpose compost, just covering the seed. Seeds germinate in 7–14 days or sooner, and should be transplanted into cell trays or 3½in-diameter pots of multipurpose compost. Plant outside after the last frosts in late May/early June, 1–3ft apart, and water.
Feeding   Feed weekly from early summer onward with general-purpose liquid feed. In containers, mix slow-release fertilizer with compost before planting, and also feed every two weeks with half-strength liquid feed.
Problems   Aphids can feed on the colorful leaves and build up into large colonies, unless caught early. Use a spray containing permethrin.

FLOWERING

Season   Foliage is colorful from early summer onward, and is joined by flowerheads and then colorful seedheads later on.
Cutting   Varieties grown for their flowers can be cut and used fresh, while seedheads can be left to develop, then cut and dried for indoor use.

AFTER FLOWERING

General   Remove plants when past their best.

AMARANTHUS AT A GLANCE

A half-hardy annual grown for its leaves and flowers for bedding, containers, and for drying. Frost hardy to 32°F (zone 10).

Month		Recommended Varieties
Jan	/	***Amaranthus caudatus:***
Feb	/	"Green Thumb"
Mar	sow 🌱	"Viridis"
Apr	transplant 🌱	***Amaranthus cruentus:***
		"Golden Giant"
May	transplant 🌱	"Split Personality"
		"Ruby Slippers"
Jun	flowering 🌿	***Amaranthus hybridus:***
		"Intense Purple"
July	flowering 🌿	***Amaranthus tricolor:***
		"Aurora Yellow"
		"Joseph's Coat"

ANTIRRHINUM
Snapdragon

OLDER VARIETIES *of snapdragon like this have flowers that* "snap" *when squeezed. This trick is not found in newer types.*

DWARF VARIETIES *reaching just 6in are colorful for bed edges and have bushy growth without the need for pinching out.*

FEATURES

Antirrhinums fall into three groups: tall varieties up to 4ft for cutting; intermediates for bedding, 18in; dwarf varieties for edging/containers, 12in. Color range is wide, and includes bicolors and doubles. Flowers of older varieties open when squeezed at the sides, hence the name "snapdragon." Grow as a half-hardy annual. Available as young plants.

CONDITIONS

Aspect Must be in full sunlight all day.
Site Soil must be very well-drained but have plenty

ANTIRRHINUM AT A GLANCE

A half-hardy annual grown for tubular flowers, used for containers, bedding displays, and cutting. Frost hardy to 32°F (zone 10).

Jan	/	Recommended Varieties
Feb	sow	*Antirrhinum majus:*
Mar	sow	**For containers**
		"Lipstick Silver"
		"Magic Carpet Mixed"
Apr	grow on	"Tom Thumb Mixed"
		For bedding
May	plant	"Brighton Rock Mixed"
		"Corona Mixed"
		"Sonnet Mixed"
Jun	flowering	**For cutting**
		"Liberty Mixed"
July	flowering	

of rotted compost or manure dug in before planting. In containers, use multipurpose compost and ensure good, free drainage.

GROWING METHOD

Sowing Sow in February/March and barely cover the very fine seed. Use 3½in pots of multipurpose compost and keep in light at 64°F. Seedlings appear after a week and can be transplanted to cell trays when two young leaves have developed. Plant outside after hardening off, following the last frosts, 6–18in apart, depending upon the variety. Those grown for bedding purposes should have the growing tip pinched out when 6in tall to encourage bushy growth.

Feeding Liquid-feed plants in beds with a handheld feeder fortnightly. Mix slow-release fertilizer with container compost before planting up.

Problems Seedlings are prone to "damping off," so water the pots with a copper-based fungicide. Plants suffer with rust disease. Grow a resistant variety such as "Monarch Mixed" or use a spray containing penconazole at regular intervals.

FLOWERING

Season Flowers appear all summer and should be removed as they fade to keep buds coming.
Cutting Tall varieties are excellent as cut spikes.

AFTER FLOWERING

General Pull plants up when they are over.

ARCTOTIS
African daisy

AFRICAN DAISIES should be pinched out when they are 5in tall to encourage branching and masses of summer flowers.

WHEN PLANTED in groups of 3–6 plants, arctotis will form spreading clumps in sunny, south-facing borders and on banks.

FEATURES

African daisy is a perennial grown as a half-hardy annual for its flowers in shades of pink, red, yellow, gold, white, and even blue, often with a darker center. Plants reach 18in in height and have attractive silvery leaves. Use in bedding or as a container plant. Flowers are good for cutting.

CONDITIONS

Aspect Must have full sunlight all day long for the flowers to stay open and give the best display, so choose a south-facing border, courtyard, or bank.

Site Soil must be well-drained but moisture-retentive, so work rotted compost in before planting. In containers, use multipurpose compost and ensure drainage by adding a 2in layer of gravel or polystyrene chunks.

GROWING METHOD

Sowing Sow in February/March in small pots of multipurpose compost, just covering the seed, and keep at 64°F. Seedlings appear in 2–3 weeks and are transplanted individually into 3½in pots. Grow on, harden off at the end of May before planting after frosts, spacing plants 12–18in apart.

Feeding Extra feeding is rarely necessary, but container-grown plants benefit from liquid feed every two weeks. Avoid getting the compost too wet, especially in cooler wet spells.

Problems Grows poorly on heavy, badly drained soils. Plants in containers must receive full sunlight.

FLOWERING

Season Flowers from early summer onward.
Cutting A useful but short-lived cut flower.

AFTER FLOWERING

General Pot up before frosts and keep dry and frost-free over winter. Take and root cuttings in spring.

ARCTOTIS AT A GLANCE

A half-hardy annual grown for its flowers, used in bedding, containers, and as a cut flower. Frost hardy to 32°F (zone 10).

Month		Recommended Varieties
Jan	/	
Feb	sow	*Arctotis hybrida:*
Mar	sow	"Harlequin"
Apr	transplant	"Special Hybrids Mixed"
May	transplant	"Treasure Chest"
Jun	flowering	"T&M Hybrids"
July	flowering	
Aug	flowering	*Arctotis hirsuta*
Sept	flowering	
Oct	/	*Arctotis venusta*
Nov	/	
Dec	/	

BEGONIA
Begonia

FOR BEDDING DISPLAYS *in partial shade, few plants can equal the mixed varieties of* Begonia semperflorens, *seen here.*

IN CONTAINERS *begonias give a show from early summer, and you can choose dark-leaved types for specific color schemes.*

FEATURES

Excellent for bedding and containers, begonias have fleshy green or bronze leaves and they flower in many colors, and are grown as half-hardy annuals. "Fibrous" rooted varieties of *Begonia semperflorens* grow up to 8in, have many small flowers, and perform well in shaded spots. "Tuberous" rooted types reach 10in tall with fewer but larger flowers up to 4in across. Trailing varieties are also available for hanging baskets, reaching 1–2ft. Flowers are in mixed or single colors. A wide range of all types are available as young plants.

CONDITIONS

Aspect   Will succeed best in partial shade with at least

BEGONIA AT A GLANCE

A half-hardy annual grown for flowers and green/bronze foliage, useful for bedding/containers. Frost hardy to 32°F (zone 10).

		Recommended Varieties
Jan	sow	***Begonia semperflorens:***
Feb	sow	"Ambassador Mixed"
Mar	transplant	"Cocktail Mixed"
Apr	grow on	"Pink Sundae"
May	harden off	**Tuberous varieties**
Jun	flowering	"Non-Stop Mixed"
July	flowering	"Non-Stop Appleblossom"
Aug	flowering	"Pin-Up"
Sept	flowering	**Trailing varieties**
Oct	/	"Illumination Mixed"
Nov	/	"Show Angels Mixed"
Dec	/	

some protection from direct, hot sun.

Site   Soil should be very well prepared, with plenty of rotted manure or compost mixed in. Begonias produce masses of fine feeding roots. Plants do not like very heavy clay soils that stay wet for long periods, so grow in containers, if necessary, using multipurpose compost when potting up in the spring.

GROWING METHOD

Sowing   Sow in January/February. Seed is as fine as dust, so mix with a little dry silver sand and sow on the surface of 3½in pots of seed compost based on peat or coir. Stand the pot in tepid water until the compost looks moist. Keep at 70°F in a heated propagator in a light spot, and carefully transplant seedlings to cell trays when they have produced several tiny leaves. Seed raising is a challenge, so consider growing from young plants. Plant outdoors after the last frosts in early June, 6–8in apart, depending on the variety.

Feeding   Water regularly in dry spells and liquid-feed bedding displays every 2–3 weeks, or mix slow-release fertilizer with compost first.

Problems   Overwatering causes root rot and death. Remove faded flowers, especially in wet spells.

FLOWERING

Season   Flowers from early summer until frost.
Cutting   Not suitable as a cut flower.

AFTER FLOWERING

General   Varieties that form round tubers can be potted up in the fall, dried off, and then grown again the following spring.

BELLIS
Daisy

VARIETIES OF BELLIS differ greatly. Some have small flowers with yellow centres, or the whole flower is a mass of fine petals.

AFTER THE SPRING SHOW is over bellis can be replanted on rock gardens where it will grow as a perennial in spreading clumps.

FEATURES

All varieties of bellis are related to garden daisies, and are perennials grown as hardy biennials. Use in spring bedding and containers, with bulbs like tulips. Plants are spreading, 4–8in high, with white, pink, red, or bicolored double or "eyed" flowers. Petals can be tubular, or fine and needle-like. Available as young plants.

CONDITIONS

Aspect Needs a sunny, warm spot to encourage early

Site flowers when grown for spring displays. Most soils are suitable, but adding well-rotted manure or compost before planting increases plant vigor and flower size. In containers, use multipurpose compost and make sure the container is very free-draining.

GROWING METHOD

Sowing Sow seed outdoors in May/June in fine soil in drills ½in deep. Keep well-watered and when plants are large enough, space small clumps out in rows, 4–6in apart. Alternatively, pot up into 3½in pots. Grow on during the summer, then water, lift carefully, and plant out in beds or containers in the fall, spacing 6–8in apart.

Feeding Liquid feed can be given every 2–3 weeks in the spring when growth starts, but avoid feeding in winter, and take special care not to overwater containers or plants will rot off.

Problems Bellis is trouble-free.

FLOWERING

Season Flowers appear from early spring into the summer. Removal of faded flowers helps prolong flowering and reduces self-seeding.

Cutting Can be used in small spring posies.

AFTER FLOWERING

General Plants are removed to make way for summer bedding and can either be discarded or replanted and left to grow as perennials.

BELLIS AT A GLANCE

A perennial grown as a biennial for spring bedding displays and used with bulbs in yard containers. Frost hardy to 5°F (zone 7).

		Recommended Varieties
Jan	/	
Feb	flowering	*Bellis perennis:*
Mar	flowering	Small flowers
		"Carpet Mixed"
Apr	flowering	"Medici Mixed"
		"Pomponette Mixed"
		"Pomponette Pink"
May	flowers/sow	"Buttons"
Jun	sow	Large flowers
July	grow on	"Blush"
		"Giant Flowered Mixed"
		"Goliath Mixed"
Aug	grow on	"Habanera Mixed"

BRACHYSCOME
Swan river daisy

SWAN RIVER DAISIES produce mounds of small, daisy-like flowers in profusion throughout the summer months.

FOR MIXED SHADES and "eyes" of different colors, choose an up-to-date variety of Brachyscome iberidifolia *such as "Bravo Mixed."*

FEATURES

Brachyscome is covered in mounds of daisy flowers, and is good in beds and in hanging baskets and courtyard containers. It makes an effective edging plant, where it can develop unhindered without being crowded out by more vigorous plants. Leaves are light green and feathery, with a delicate appearance. Plants grow 9in tall with a similar spread. Choose single colors or mixtures. Brachyscome can be planted in May before the last frosts, and will tolerate short dry spells. A half-hardy annual, also seen as "brachycome."

CONDITIONS

Aspect Choose a south-facing position in full sunlight.

BRACHYSCOME AT A GLANCE

A half-hardy annual grown for its daisy-like flowers, useful for bedding, baskets, and containers. Frost hardy to 32°F (zone 10)

JAN	/	
FEB	/	
MAR	sow 🖐	
APR	sow/transplant 🖐	
MAY	plant outdoors 🖐	
JUN	flowering 🌸	
JULY	flowering 🌸	
AUG	flowering 🌸	
SEPT	flowering 🌸	
OCT	/	
NOV	/	
DEC	/	

RECOMMENDED VARIETIES

Brachyscome iberidifolia:
  "Blue Star"
  "Bravo Mixed"
  "Mixed"
  "Purple Splendor"
  "White Splendor"

Site Choose a warm, sheltered spot away from wind. Brachyscome likes rich, well-drained soil, with plenty of rotted compost or manure added. Use multipurpose potting compost in containers.

GROWING METHOD

Sowing Sow in March and April in 3½in diameter pots, just covering the seeds, and germinate at 64°F. Seedlings emerge within three weeks. Transplant into cell trays of multipurpose compost, and plant out in beds, 9–12in apart.

Feeding Liquid-feed each week outdoors. Add slow-release fertilizer granules to container compost, and also liquid-feed every two weeks in the summer. Avoid overwatering, especially in dull, wet spells, or plants may rot off.

Problems Support floppy plants with small twigs. Avoid planting among large, vigorous container plants that will swamp low growers and cast them in shade at the height of summer. Control slugs with pellets or set slug traps in bedding displays.

FLOWERING

Season Flowers appear all summer and are faintly scented—this is best appreciated by growing them at nose height in hanging baskets, flower bags, and windowboxes.

Cutting Not suitable.

AFTER FLOWERING

General Remove when flowers are over and add to the compost heap or bin.

BRASSICA
Ornamental cabbage and kale

ORNAMENTAL KALES help pack a punch in the yard during the fall, with their bright leaves that deepen in color when the temperature falls below 50°F. Plants grown in containers should be kept in a sheltered spot during spells of severe winter weather.

FEATURES

Ornamental cabbages and kales are grown for colorful fall and winter foliage, growing 12–18in tall and wide. Use for bedding or large pots. Leaf color is pink, rose, or white, and improves with temperatures below 50°F. Damage is caused by severe frost. Available as young plants.

CONDITIONS

Aspect   Needs full sunlight to develop good color.

BRASSICA AT A GLANCE

A hardy annual grown for its brightly colored leaves that last from the fall until spring. Frost hardy to 5°F (zone 7).

JAN	leaves	
FEB	leaves	
MAR	leaves	
APR	leaves	
MAY	leaves	
JUN	sow	
JULY	sow	
AUG	grow-on	
SEPT	plant	
OCT	leaves	
NOV	leaves	
DEC	leaves	

RECOMMENDED VARIETIES

Cabbages
"Delight Mixed"
"Northern Lights"
"Ornamental Mixed"
"Tokyo Mixed"

Kales
"Nagoya Mixed"
"Red & White Peacock"
"Red Chidori"

Site   Enrich soil with rotted compost or manure ahead of planting. Adding lime will improve results in acid soils. Avoid places exposed to driving winter winds. Plant up containers using multipurpose compost, making sure pots and tubs are free-draining.

GROWING METHOD

Sowing   Seed is sown in June/July in 3½in pots of multipurpose compost and kept out of the sun. Large seedlings appear after a week and are transplanted to individual 3½in pots. Grow these on outdoors, watering frequently, and then plant out in beds or in containers in the early fall where the display is required.

Feeding   Give a high-potash liquid feed fortnightly throughout the summer months. Tomato food is suitable and encourages leaf color.

Problems   Cabbage caterpillars will also attack ornamental varieties and kales. Pick off by hand or use a spray containing permethrin.

FLOWERING

Season   Plants are at their best in the fall and early winter. Any surviving the winter will produce tall clusters of yellow flowers during spring.

Cutting   Whole heads makes a striking, unusual element in winter flower arrangements.

AFTER FLOWERING

General   Remove in the spring or if killed by frosts.

BROWALLIA

Bush violet

BROWALLIA FLOWERS *have an almost crystalline texture when lit by the sun. They appear in masses on rounded plants, and at the height of summer can almost completely hide the leaves. Seen here are the varieties "Blue Troll" and "White Troll."*

FEATURES

Browallia takes its common name from its violet-blue flowers, which have a pale "eye." White flowered varieties and mixtures are available. Plants grow up to 12in and are suitable for containers and baskets, and in warmer areas, bedding. Varieties of ***Browallia speciosa*** are grown as half-hardy annuals and can also be used as indoor potted plants.

CONDITIONS

Aspect   Needs a warm, sheltered spot in sunlight.

BROWALLIA AT A GLANCE

A half-hardy annual grown for its blue, white, or pink flowers, useful for bedding/container planting. Frost hardy to 32°F (zone 10).

		Recommended Varieties
Jan	/	
Feb	sow 🖐	***Browallia speciosa:***
Mar	sow 🖐	**Blue flowers**
		"Blue Troll"
		"Blue Bells"
Apr	grow on 🖐	"Starlight Blue"
May	plant 🖐	
		White flowers
		"White Troll"
Jun	flowering 🌿	
		Blue/pink/white flowers
July	flowering 🌿	"Jingle Bells"

Site   Browallia does not tolerate poor drainage, and on heavy soils should only be grown as a container plant, using multipurpose compost. Otherwise, mix in well-rotted compost or manure several weeks before planting out.

GROWING METHOD

Sowing   For summer bedding, sow the seed on the surface of 3½in pots of multipurpose compost in February/March. Keep at 64°F and do not let the surface dry out. Seedlings appear in 2–3 weeks and should be transplanted to individual cell trays or 3in pots. Harden off at the end of May and plant in early June. For flowering potted plants, seed can be sown in the same way until June.

Feeding   Give plants a liquid feed fortnightly or, in containers and windowboxes, mix slow-release fertilizer with the compost first.

Problems   Aphids sometimes attack the soft leaves, so use a spray containing permethrin if they appear.

FLOWERING

Season   Flowers appear from early summer onward and continue until the first frosts. Take off faded flowers regularly to encourage buds.

Cutting   Not suitable as a cut flower.

AFTER FLOWERING

General   Plants die when frosts arrive. Potted plants indoors can be kept alive indefinitely.

CALCEOLARIA
Slipper flower

THE HOT COLORS OF THE "SUNSET" strain of calceolaria excel outdoors and combine well with marigolds.

FEATURES

Only a few varieties of calceolaria are suitable for outdoors; these are different to the indoor potted type. Shrubs by nature, they are grown from seed each year as hardy annuals and are useful for bedding and containers. None grow more than 16in tall and wide.

CONDITIONS

Aspect   Needs full sunlight or part shade.

CALCEOLARIA AT A GLANCE

A half-hardy annual, calceolaria is used for bedding and containers, with bright flowers. Frost hardy to 32°F (zone 10).

Jan	sow	
Feb	sow	
Mar	transplant	
Apr	grow on	
May	harden off	
Jun	flowering	
July	flowering	
Aug	flowering	
Sepr	flowering	
Oct	/	
Nov	/	
Dec	/	

Recommended Varieties

Calceolaria hybrids:
  "Little Sweeties Mixed"
  "Midas"
  "Sunshine"
  "Sunset Mixed"

Site   Slipper flowers thrive in moist soil, where their roots stay as cool as possible. Mix in well-rotted compost or manure before planting and use a peat- or coir-based multipurpose compost for filling containers.

GROWING METHOD

Sowing   The fine seed can be sown on the surface of peat- or coir-based multipurpose compost in a 3½in pot, January to March, at a temperature of 64°F. Keep in a bright place. Seedlings appear in 2–3 weeks and can be transplanted to cell trays, then hardened off and planted after frosts, 6–12in apart, or used with other plants in containers.

Feeding   Liquid feed every 3–4 weeks or mix slow-release fertilizer with compost before planting.

Problems   Slugs will eat the leaves of young plants in wet spells during the early summer. Protect plants with a barrier of grit or eggshell or scatter slug pellets sparingly around plants.

FLOWERING

Season   Plants will flower from the early summer until frosts. Take off dead flowers weekly.

Cutting   A few stems can be taken but avoid damaging the overall shape and appearance of the plant.

AFTER FLOWERING

General   Remove plants in the fall when finished.

CALENDULA
Pot marigold

MIXED VARIETIES of calendula offer a wide color range, most commonly shades of orange and yellow, as seen here.

CALENDULA is a bushy plant producing masses of summer flowers —the edible petals can be scattered on summer salads.

FEATURES

Also known as English marigold, calendula is a fast-growing, hardy annual with daisy-type flowers in shades of yellow, orange, red, pinkish, and even green. Flowers can be fully double, while others have a distinct darker "eye." The edible petals can be used in salads. Perfect for a "cottage garden" bed or border, and very easy to grow, the large curled seeds are sown straight into the soil outdoors. Plant size ranges from 12 to 28in tall and wide.

CONDITIONS

Aspect Needs full sunlight to succeed.
Site Does well even in poor soil, which can increase the number of flowers. Add rotted organic matter to the soil ahead of planting time to improve results. Calendula does not do well on heavy, badly drained soils, so grow in containers under these conditions.

GROWING METHOD

Sowing March to May or August/September are the sowing periods. Sow the large seeds direct into finely raked moist soil where you want plants to flower, in drills ½in deep, and cover. Thin out as seedlings grow so that plants are eventually spaced 10–12in apart. Fall-sown plants flower earlier the following year. If flowers for cutting are required, sow seed thinly in long rows.
Feeding Liquid feed once a month to encourage larger blooms. Use a feed high in potash to encourage flowers rather than leafy growth—tomato fertilizers are a good choice.
Problems The leaves are prone to attack by aphids, causing twisting and damage. Use a spray containing permethrin, but avoid eating flowers. Powdery mildew can affect leaves in late summer, but is not worth treating—pick off the worst affected leaves and compost them.

FLOWERING

Season Flowers appear in late spring on plants sown the previous fall, and from early summer on spring-sown plants. Removal of faded blooms will keep up a succession of flowers.
Cutting Good as a cut flower—cutting helps to keep flowers coming. Cut when flowers are well formed but before petals open too far.

AFTER FLOWERING

General Pull up after flowering. Will self-seed if a few heads are left to ripen fully and shed seeds.

CALENDULA AT A GLANCE

A hardy annual for growing in beds and borders and a useful cut flower in many shades. Frost hardy to 5°F (zone 7).

		Recommended Varieties
Jan	/	
Feb	/	*Calendula officinalis:*
Mar	sow	"Art Shades Mixed"
Apr	sow	"Fiesta Gitana Mixed"
May	thin out	"Greenheart Orange"
Jun	flowering	"Kablouna Lemon Cream"
July	flowering	"Kablouna Mixed"
Aug	flowers/sow	"Orange King"
Sept	flowers/sow	"Pacific Beauty"
Oct	/	"Pink Surprise'
Nov	/	"Princess Mixed"
Dec	/	"Radio"
		"Touch of Red Mixed"

CALLISTEPHUS
China aster

CHINA ASTERS, with their large, showy, and often double flowers, can be used as summer bedding plants for massed displays.

AS A CUT FLOWER, callistephus is unrivalled for producing long-lasting blooms in late summer when other flowers are past their best.

FEATURES

China asters are half-hardy annuals and are not to be confused with the perennial asters or Michaelmas daisies. Grow as bedding, as cut flowers, and in large pots. Flowers come in a wide range, from narrow, quill-like petals to bicolors, and also single shades. Size ranges from 8 to 36in tall, depending on the variety. Available as young plants.

CONDITIONS

Aspect   Must have a warm spot in full sunlight all day.

CALLISTEPHUS AT A GLANCE		
A half-hardy annual grown for its flowers, used in bedding, container,s and as a cut flower. Frost hardy to 32°F (zone 10).			

		Recommended Varieties
Jan	/	
Feb	/	***Callistephus chinensis:***
Mar	sow	"Apricot Giant"
Apr	sow	"Dwarf Comet Mixed"
May	plant	"Matsumoto Mixed"
Jun	flowering	"Moraketa"
July	flowering	"Milady Mixed"
Aug	flowering	"Ostrich Plume Mixed"
Sept	flowering	"Red Ribbon"
Oct	flowering	"Teisa Stars Mixed"
Nov	/	
Dec	/	

Site   Plants need well-drained soil with added organic matter, such as rotted manure or compost, dug in before planting. If grown in containers, use multipurpose compost mixed with slow-release fertilizer granules.

GROWING METHOD

Sowing   Sow in March/April in 3½in pots of compost and keep at 61°F. Seedlings appear after a week and can be transplanted to cell trays and grown on. Planted in late May, plants are not damaged by the last frosts. Seed can also be sown direct into the ground in late April and May. Plant 8–24in apart.

Feeding   Water regularly and give plants in containers a general liquid feed every two weeks. In beds, feed when you water with a handheld feeder.

Problems   Aphids cause the leaves to distort, which can affect flowering. Use a spray containing dimethoate. If plants suddenly collapse and die, they are suffering from aster wilt and should be removed with the soil around their roots and put in the trashcan. Avoid growing asters in that spot and try "resistant" varieties.

FLOWERING

Season   Early summer to early fall.
Cutting   An excellent and long-lasting cut flower.

AFTER FLOWERING

General   Remove plants after flowering and compost any that do not show signs of wilt disease.

CAMPANULA
Canterbury bells

THE BELL-LIKE *flowers of* Campanula medium *give it its common name of Canterbury bells. It is seen here growing with ageratum.*

WHEN CANTERBURY BELLS *display this characteristic "saucer" behind the cup-shaped bloom, they simply ooze charm.*

FEATURES

Canterbury bells are best in massed plantings in mixed borders and are good for cutting. Dwarf varieties can be used for bedding and in containers. The large, bell-like single or double flowers are blue, pink, mauve, or white, on stems 2–3ft high, rising from large clumps. Usually grown as a hardy biennial, the dwarf variety "Chelsea Pink" is grown as an annual, flowering three months after sowing in February. Stake tall plants.

CONDITIONS

Aspect   Grow in an open spot in full sunlight.

CAMPANULA AT A GLANCE

A hardy biennial grown for bedding and for tall flower spikes that are ideal for cutting. Frost hardy to 5°F (zone 7).

Jan	/	Recommended Varieties
Feb	/	
Mar	/	*Campanula medium:*
		Tall varieties
Apr	sow	"Calycanthema Mixed"
May	sow	"Cup and Saucer Mixed"
Jun	flowers/sow	"Rosea"
		"Single Mixed"
July	flowering	
Aug	flowering	**Shorter/dwarf varieties**
Sept	flowering	"Bella Series"
Oct	plant	"Bells of Holland"
Nov	/	"Chelsea Pink"
Dec	/	"Russian Pink"

Site   Plenty of well-rotted manure or compost dug into the soil produces strong growth. Requires good drainage but the soil should retain moisture and not dry out completely. In containers, use multipurpose compost.

GROWING METHOD

Sowing   Sow the fine seed from April to June outdoors, or in small pots of multipurpose compost. Just cover the seed. Either transplant seedlings to 12in apart or pot up individually into 3½in pots. Grow on through the summer and plant during the fall in groups of 3–5, spacing plants 12in apart. Flowers will appear the following summer.

Feeding   Give a monthly liquid feed, starting a few weeks after transplanting or potting up, and make sure potted plants do not dry out. Scatter a general granular fertilizer over beds in spring to keep growth strong and encourage flowers.

Problems Slugs will eat the crowns of plants in early summer, especially after rain, so scatter slug pellets or use a physical barrier, like grit.

FLOWERING

Season   Flower spikes appear from early summer onward. A second "flush" of flowers is possible if all stems are cut to the ground when faded.

Cutting   Campanula are good cut flowers, so grow extra plants of a tall variety in rows just for cutting.

AFTER FLOWERING

General   Remove plants after the flowering season and add them to the compost heap or bin.

CATHARANTHUS
Madagascar periwinkle

THE FAMILIAR FLOWERS *of* Catharanthus roseus *look similar to those of its close relative, the hardy vinca.*

FOR BEDDING DISPLAYS, *catharanthus is available in mixed colors that often contain flowers with darker "eyes," as seen here.*

FEATURES

Varieties of **Catharanthus roseus** have pink/rose, mauve, or white flowers, often with a deeper center. These plants quickly spread, growing to 10–16in, and are suitable for massed bedding displays or pots indoors. Grow as a half-hardy annual.

CONDITIONS

Aspect Needs full sunlight to succeed outdoors.

CATHARANTHUS AT A GLANCE

A half-hardy annual grown for its bright flowers and ideal for use in containers on a warm sunny yard. Frost hardy to 32°F (zone 10).

Jan	/
Feb	/
Mar	sow
Apr	transplant
May	harden off/plant
Jun	flowering
July	flowering
Aug	flowering
Sept	flowering
Oct	/
Nov	/
Dec	/

Recommended Varieties

Catharanthus roseus:
"Apricot Delight"
"Pacifica Red"
"Peppermint Cooler"
"Pretty In… Mixed"
"Tropicana Mixed"
"Terrace Vermillion"

Site Needs good drainage, but enrich the soil with well-rotted manure or compost before planting. For containers, use multipurpose compost mixed with extra slow-release fertilizer before planting up.

GROWING METHOD

Sowing Sow seed in March/April in 3½in pots of multipurpose compost and lightly cover. Keep at 64°F in a light spot and transplant seedlings when they are 1in tall, into cell trays. Keep in a warm greenhouse or warm spot indoors and do not get the compost too wet. Harden off in late May and plant 8–12in apart in their final positions or use in containers.

Feeding In bedding displays, apply a liquid plant food monthly to keep plants growing vigorously throughout the summer months.

Problems Overwatering and wet soil/compost can lead to rotting. If red spider mite attacks the leaves, use a spray containing bifenthrin.

FLOWERING

Season Flowers appear throughout the summer.
Cutting Not suitable for cutting.

AFTER FLOWERING

General Remove plants after the first fall frosts and use for composting.

CELOSIA
Prince of Wales' feathers

THE FEATHERY FLOWERS of celosia are made up of masses of smaller flowers, and have a distinctive, plume-like shape.

THE BRILLIANT PLUMES of cockscomb always look best in court-yard pots and containers when planted together in groups of 4–6 plants.

FEATURES

Also known as Prince of Wales' feathers, celosia or cockscomb has plume-like or crested flowers (shown left), ranging in color from deep crimson to scarlet, orange, and yellow. Tall forms grow to 30in, the dwarf forms to 10–12in. Grow it as a half-hardy annual and use in bedding or as a striking plant for containers. Good for cutting.

CONDITIONS

Aspect   Must have a sunny, warm spot to do well.

CELOSIA AT A GLANCE	
A half-hardy annual grown for its feathery, plume-like flower-heads in a range of colors. Frost hardy to 32°F (zone 10).	
Jan /	Recommended Varieties
Feb sow	**Plumed**
Mar sow	***Celosia argentea:***
Apr pot on	"Kimono Mixed"
May harden off/plant	"Dwarf Geisha"
Jun flowering	"Century Mixed"
July flowering	"New Look"
Aug flowering	***Celosia spicata:***
Sept flowering	"Flamingo Feather"
Oct /	**Crested**
Nov /	***Celosia cristata:***
Dec /	"Jewel Box Mixed"

Site   Needs well-drained soil that has been enriched with well-rotted manure or compost. Good soil preparation is essential to ensure strong plants and large flowerheads. Plant up containers using multipurpose compost.

GROWING METHOD

Sowing   Celosias dislike having their roots disturbed, so sow 2–3 seeds per cell in a multi-cell tray using multipurpose compost, in February/March. Keep at 64°F and, when the seedlings appear after 2–3 weeks, remove all but the strongest. Carefully pot the young plants on into 3½in pots, then harden off for two weeks before planting after the last frosts. Plant without damaging the roots, 6–12in apart, and water.

Feeding   Feed bedding monthly with liquid feed. Mix slow-release fertilizer with the compost before planting up containers.

Problems   Wet, cold soil/compost can cause rotting of the roots, so avoid heavy soils and grow in pots.

FLOWERING

Season   Flowers appear throughout the summer.

Cutting   May be used as a cut flower for unusual indoor decoration. Cut some plumes and hang them upside-down in a dry, airy place for later use in dried flower arrangements.

AFTER FLOWERING

General   Remove plants after the first frosts of fall.

CENTAUREA
Cornflower

CORNFLOWERS should have pale, fading flowers removed regularly. For indoor use, cut the stems when the buds are still closed.

GROWN IN GROUPS like this, cornflowers will support each other quite naturally. In windy spots, push twigs in between plants.

FEATURES

Cornflower, *Centaurea cyanus*, is one of the easiest hardy annuals to grow and can be used in bedding, containers, and for cut flowers. Other than blue, there are mixtures available and single colors such as the "Florence" types in red, pink, and white, reaching 14in tall. Taller varieties like "Blue Diadem" are best for cutting. Regular removal of dead flowers is essential to prolong flowering and to stop plants from becoming shabby.

CENTAUREA AT A GLANCE

A hardy annual grown for its "cottage garden"-style flowers in various colors, useful for cutting. Frost hardy to 5°F (zone 7).

Jan	/	Recommended Varieties
Feb	/	
Mar	sow	*Centaurea cyanus:*
		Short varieties
Apr	thin out	"Florence Blue"
May	flowering	"Florence Mixed"
Jun	flowering	"Florence Pink"
July	flowering	"Florence Red"
Aug	flowering	"Florence White"
		"Midget Mixed"
Sept	flowers/sow	**Tall varieties**
Oct	/	"Blue Diadem"
Nov	/	"Black Ball"
Dec	/	

CONDITIONS

Aspect   Needs full sunlight all day.
Site   Must have very well-drained soil, but no special soil preparation is necessary. Staking is necessary when grown in windy situations, but the plants are self-supporting when they are planted in groups. For container growing, use multipurpose compost.

GROWING METHOD

Sowing   Sow seed in the spring where plants are to flower in short rows ½in deep and approximately 12in apart. Thin out so the plants are finally 3–6in apart. This can also be done in late September for stronger plants and earlier flowers, but leave thinning out until the following spring. Can also be sown in pots and transplanted to cell trays for plants to use in courtyard containers.

Feeding   Extra feeding is usually unnecessary.
Problems   White mildew affects leaves but is not serious.

FLOWERING

Season   Summer until early fall.
Cutting   Cut before the petals open too far.

AFTER FLOWERING

General   Remove plants once flowering is finished. Plants self-seed if they are left in the ground.

CHEIRANTHUS
Wallflower

THE INTENSE COLORS of wallflowers are only matched by their strong, lingering scent that is best on warm, still days.

"IVORY WHITE" is a useful single-colored variety of Cheiranthus cheiri *for bedding schemes that are color-themed.*

FEATURES

Wallflowers have fragrant flowers of yellow, brown, cream, red, and orange and are grown for their sweet spring scent. These hardy biennials grow between 8 and 18in, depending on the variety, and are available as mixed or single colors. Plants are used for bedding but may also be used in courtyard containers, where they can be moved near doors and windows when in bloom. Ready-grown plants can be bought in early fall.

CHEIRANTHUS AT A GLANCE

With its bright flowers and strong scent, this biennial is useful for spring bedding and for containers. Frost hardy to 5°F (zone 7).

Jan	/	Recommended Varieties
Feb	flowering	
Mar	flowering	*Cheiranthus cheiri:*
Apr	flowering	**Tall**
May	sow	"Blood Red"
		"Cloth of Gold"
Jun	sow	"Harlequin"
July	thin out	**Medium**
		"My Fair Lady Mixed"
Aug	grow on	"Vulcan Improved"
Sept	grow on	**Dwarf**
Oct	plant	"Prince Mixed"
Nov	/	"Tom Thumb Mixed"
Dec	/	

CONDITIONS

Aspect   Grow in full sunlight for the best scent.
Site   Must have very well-drained soil. Add lime before planting to reduce the effect of clubroot disease. Use multipurpose compost in containers and windowboxes. Avoid places exposed to winter winds and move containers to shelter during severe winter weather.

GROWING METHOD

Sowing   Sow May/June outdoors in rows 12in apart and ⅓in deep. As plants grow, thin them to 12in apart, and pinch when 3in tall to make growth bushy. Can also be sown in pots and transplanted into 3½in pots. Plant in October in beds or containers. When lifting plants, keep as much soil on the roots as possible.
Feeding   Give a liquid feed monthly during summer.
Problems   Avoid growing in soil known to be infected with clubroot disease, or raise plants in pots using multipurpose compost.

FLOWERING

Season   Late winter through to the spring.
Cutting   Cut stems last well in water.

AFTER FLOWERING

General   Remove plants in late spring after flowering.

CLEOME
Spider flower

SPIDER FLOWERS *are available as single colors or mixed. The popular "Color Fountains Mixed" is seen here in a summer border.*

THE EXOTIC FEEL *that cleome adds to the yard can be used to best effect on a warm courtyard where their scent lingers in still air.*

FEATURES

The spider-like flowers of **Cleome spinosa**, in pink, white, or rose, have narrow petals with long stamens. They appear all summer up and down the length of the stem. These large half-hardy annuals grow to 5ft tall with a single stem, and with lobed leaves. Plant at the back of borders or use them as central "dot" plants in large tubs for an "exotic" feel. Look out for the thorny stems and pungent leaves.

CONDITIONS

Aspect   Needs full sunlight and a sheltered position to achieve maximum height during the summer.

CLEOME AT A GLANCE

A half-hardy annual grown for its exotic flowers and ideal as a centerpiece for bedding/containers. Frost hardy to 32°F (zone 10).

Jan	/	Recommended Varieties
Feb	sow 🖐	
Mar	sow 🖐	*Cleome spinosa:*
		Mixed colors
Apr	grow on 🖐	"Color Fountain Mixed"
May	harden off/plant 🖐	
Jun	flowering 🌸	**Single colors**
July	flowering 🌸	"Cherry Queen"
Aug	flowering 🌸	"Helen Campbell"
Sept	flowering 🌸	"Pink Queen"
Oct	/	"Violet Queen"
Nov	/	
Dec	/	

Site   Needs good drainage but tolerates a wide range of soils. For best results, improve soil by digging in rotted manure or compost, and use multipurpose compost with slow-release fertilizer added when planting containers. Stems are generally strong enough that they can be grow without extra support.

GROWING METHOD

Sowing   Sow seeds in 3½in pots of multipurpose compost in February/March and keep at 64°F. Seedlings appear after two weeks and are transplanted to 3½in pots, grown on in a warm greenhouse or conservatory. Pot on into 5in containers in early May, and harden off before planting after the last frosts.

Feeding   Feed plants in beds fortnightly with liquid feed from a handheld applicator. Don't allow the compost in containers to become over-wet.

Problems   Aphids attack young plants and cause twisted growth. Check under the leaves regularly and use a spray with permethrin if necessary, making sure the spray gets under the leaves.

FLOWERING

Season   The long flowering period extends throughout summer and well into mild falls. The long thin seed pods give it a real "spidery" look.

Cutting   Useful as a cut flower, but watch the spines.

AFTER FLOWERING

General   Remove plants after flowering, but wear gloves for protection, since the stems are spiny.

CONSOLIDA
Larkspur

LARKSPUR IS DOUBLY useful as a cut flower, because the spikes can be dried and used for dried flower arrangements.

FINELY DIVIDED LEAVES are characteristic of Consolida ajacis, *while flowers can be single, as here, or double, in various colors.*

FEATURES

Consolida ajacis, larkspur, is related to delphinium but is not as tall and is grown as a hardy annual. Ideal for a "cottage garden" border, larkspur grows up to 3ft tall and has spikes of pink, white, red, blue, and violet single or double flowers, with finely cut leaves. Good for cutting. Seeds are poisonous.

CONDITIONS

Aspect   Grow in a sunny, open spot.

CONSOLIDA AT A GLANCE

A hardy annual grown for its spikes of bright flowers that are useful for borders and cutting. Frost hardy to 5°F (zone 7).

Jan	/
Feb	/
Mar	sow
Apr	thin out
May	thin/flowers
Jun	flowering
July	flowering
Aug	flowering
Sept	flowers/sow
Oct	/
Nov	/
Dec	/

Recommended Varieties

Consolida ajacis:
Tall, for cutting
 "Earl Grey"
 "Frosted Skies"
 "Giant Imperial Mixed"
 "Hyacinth Flowered Mixed"
Short, for bedding
 "Dwarf Hyacinth Flowered Mixed"
 "Dwarf Rocket Mixed"

Site   Soil can be enriched with manure or compost well ahead of planting, but it must be well-drained. Plants will also grow well on thin and hungry soils. Plants should support each other as they grow and not need artificial support. Use taller varieties at the rear of borders.

GROWING METHOD

Sowing   Sow direct where the plants are to grow for best results, in short rows ½in deep, in either March or September. Expect seedlings to appear in 2–3 weeks. Thin plants out as they grow so they are eventually 3–6in apart, depending on the variety.

Feeding   Extra feeding is not necessary.

Problems   Slugs eat young seedlings so scatter slug pellets around plants or protect them with a 2in wide barrier of sharp grit.

FLOWERING

Season   Flowers appear from spring onward on fall-sown plants, June onward from spring sowings. Removing faded flower spikes will encourage more flowers.

Cutting   An excellent cut flower. Cut long stems and scald ends before soaking in cool water.

AFTER FLOWERING

General   Leave a few plants to die down naturally and self-seed into the soil, otherwise pull up when finished and use for composting.

COREOPSIS
Tickseed

"EARLY SUNRISE" is a semi-double variety of coreopsis usually treated as an annual, growing 18in tall and good for cutting.

COREOPSIS CAN FORM *very large clumps. It gets its common name "tickseed" from seeds that look like small bugs.*

FEATURES

Coreopsis make good yard plants with single and double flowers in yellow, red, and mahogany tones, growing 10–36in tall, depending on the variety. Some bedding varieties are perennials but are best grown as hardy or half-hardy annuals from a spring sowing. Dwarf varieties are used in courtyard pots.

CONDITIONS

Aspect   For best results, grow in full sunlight.
Site   Tolerates poor soil, but soil that has been enriched with rotted manure/compost ahead of planting time will give stronger plants. In containers, use multipurpose compost. Taller varieties should not need support if planted in groups so plants support each other.

GROWING METHOD

Sowing   Sow seed in February/March in 3½in pots of multipurpose compost, just cover, and keep at 61°F. Transplant into cell trays, harden off for two weeks in late May, and plant out after the last frosts. Seed can also be sown directly outdoors in May/June but expect later flowers continuing into the fall.
Feeding   Should not need extra feeding if soil is well prepared. Add slow-release fertilizer to compost when planting up containers.
Problems   Slugs and snails will eat seedlings in spring during wet spells, so protect with slug pellets.

FLOWERING

Season   The flowering period lasts throughout summer, especially if spent flowers are regularly removed from the plants.
Cutting   Tall varieties can be used as cut flowers. Pick when flowers have opened fully but the petals still look fresh.

AFTER FLOWERING

General   Perennial varieties such as "Mayfield Giant" and "Sunrise" can be lifted in the fall and planted in permanent border positions.

COREOPSIS AT A GLANCE

A perennial grown as a hardy or half-hardy annual for its yellow-to-mahogany flowers. Frost hardy to 5°F (zone 7).

Month	Activity	
Jan	/	
Feb	sow	
Mar	sow	
Apr	transplant	
May	harden-off/plant	
Jun	grow on	
July	flowering	
Aug	flowering	
Sept	flowering	
Oct	flowering	
Nov	/	
Dec	/	

Recommended Varieties

Coreopsis tinctoria:
   "Mahogany Midget"
   "T&M Dwarf Mixed"
   "T&M Originals Mixed"

Coreopsis grandiflora:
   "Early Sunrise"
   "Gold Star"
   "Mayfield Giant"
   "Sunburst"

COSMOS
Cosmos

"SENSATION MIXED" is a tall-growing (3ft) cosmos with single flowers of red, pink, white, and shades in between.

DURING THE SUMMER, varieties of Cosmos bipinnatus *grown in borders form masses of feathery leaves topped by flowers.*

FEATURES

Cosmos, with their finely cut, feathery foliage and large daisy-type flowers grow up to 5ft tall, but shorter varieties are available and can be used in containers. Varieties of *Cosmos bipinnatus* have red, pink, purple, or white flowers, while yellow, orange, and scarlet are available in varieties of *Cosmos sulphureus*. Cosmos is grown as either a hardy or a half-hardy annual, and is an excellent choice for a cottage yard-style border. "Seashells" has tubular "fluted" petals, and the taller varieties such as "Sensation Mixed" are good for cutting.

COSMOS AT A GLANCE

A hardy or half-hardy annual grown for its large daisy-like flowers. For borders, pots, and cutting. Frost hardy to 32°F (zone 10).

Jan	/	Recommended Varieties
Feb	/	
Mar	sow	*Cosmos bipinnatus:*
Apr	sow/transplant	"Daydream"
May	sow/plant	"Gazebo"
Jun	flowering	"Picotee"
July	flowering	"Seashells/Sea Shells"
Aug	flowering	"Sensation Mixed"
Sept	flowering	"Sonata Mixed"
Oct	/	*Cosmos sulphureus:*
Nov	/	"Ladybird Mixed"
Dec	/	"Ladybird Scarlet"
		"Sunny Red"

CONDITIONS

Aspect Needs full sunlight to flourish.
Site Well-drained soil is essential for success, and good results are guaranteed on light and slightly hungry soils. Pea sticks or twiggy shoots may be needed for support in exposed spots. Any multipurpose compost will give good results in courtyard pots and containers.

GROWING METHOD

Sowing Raise plants by sowing in March at 61°F. Sow the long thin seeds in 3½in pots of multipurpose compost, then transplant to cell trays and grow on. Harden off at the end of May before planting after frosts, or sow in April/May directly into the ground where the plants are to grow. Final spacing between plants should be 6–18in, depending on the variety grown.
Feeding Generally not necessary.
Problems Slugs will eat young seedlings outdoors, so protect with slug pellets.

FLOWERING

Season Flowers appear from the early summer onward.
Cutting The taller varieties are ideal as cut flowers. Ensure regular removal of faded flowers.

AFTER FLOWERING

General Pull up plants when frosted, but leaving a few to die off will ensure some self-sown seedlings.

DAHLIA
Bedding dahlia

BEDDING DAHLIAS are usually available in mixed colors. By planting time you can usually separate plants by flower color.

"DOUBLE DELIGHT MIXED" is a popular bedding variety ideally suited for growing in courtyard containers, reaching 18in tall.

FEATURES

Seed-raised bedding dahlias are close cousins of the "border" dahlia grown from tubers. A wide range is available, the dwarfer types growing only 12in tall. Flower color is varied and some, like "Redskin," also have bronze leaves. Grow as half-hardy annuals, and use for bedding displays, courtyard containers, and even windowboxes. Choose from single, double, or decorative "collarette" flowers. Widely available as young plants.

CONDITIONS

Aspect Bedding dahlias need full sunlight all day.
Site Dig in large amounts of decayed manure or

compost at least two or three weeks before planting. Soil must be well-drained but moisture-retentive. For containers, use multipurpose compost with added slow-release fertilizer granules to keep growth strong through the summer months.

GROWING METHOD

Sowing Sow seed February/March in 3½in pots and just cover. Water and keep at 61°F in a light spot. Transplant seedlings when large enough to handle into individual 3½in pots and grow on. Harden off at the end of May and plant in early June, when all frosts are over, spacing plants 6–12in apart.
Feeding Water and liquid-feed once a week, depending on the soil and weather conditions. Continue watering regularly throughout the season.
Problems Dahlia leaves are eaten by slugs, so protect them with slug pellets. Flowers may be chewed by earwigs—to catch them, fill upturned pots with straw and support these on canes among the flowers. Powdery mildew can affect leaves in the late summer but is not serious.

FLOWERING

Season The main show is from midsummer onward, lasting well into fall until the first frosts.
Cutting Taller varieties of bedding dahlias make useful and long-lived cut flowers.

AFTER FLOWERING

General Remove plants when the leaves turn black and collapse. Fleshy tubers of favorite plants can be stored dry and frost-free over the winter.

DAHLIA AT A GLANCE

A half-hardy annual grown for its pretty flowers and an ideal summer bedding or container plant. Frost hardy to 32°F (zone 10).

		Recommended Varieties
Jan	/	**Dahlia hybrids:**
Feb	sow	**Taller varieties**
Mar	sow	"Collarette Dandy"
Apr	transplant/grow	"Coltness Hybrids Mixed"
		"Pompon Mixed"
May	harden off/plant	**Shorter varieties**
Jun	flowering	"Diablo Mixed"
July	flowering	"Dwarf Double Delight"
		"Dwarf Amore"
Aug	flowering	"Figaro Mixed"
		"Redskin"

DIANTHUS BARBATUS

Sweet William

THE IMPACT OF SWEET WILLIAMS comes from their massed heads of small flowers, which often have attractive "picotee" edges.

STRONG SCENT is a characteristic of Dianthus barbatus *varieties and makes this an ideal plant for cutting in bunches in early summer.*

FEATURES

Sweet Williams are varieties of *Dianthus barbatus* and have flowers in pink, white, red, burgundy, and bicolors, on large rounded heads. Individual flowers often have darker central "eyes." Plants have clumping growth up to 18in, while dwarf forms grow to just 6in. The flowers appear from the spring into early summer and are scented and ideal for cutting. They are easily grown from seed as a hardy biennial, and useful for bedding schemes and as blocks of spring color in mixed borders. Some less common varieties, like "Sooty," have dark, almost black flowers.

DIANTHUS AT A GLANCE

A summer-sown biennial grown for its large heads of scented flowers in spring and early summer. Frost hardy to 5°F (zone 7).

Month		Recommended Varieties
Jan	/	*Dianthus barbatus:*
Feb	/	**Tall varieties**
Mar	/	"Auricula-Eyed Mixed"
Apr	flowering	"Forerunner Mixed"
May	flowers/sow	"Gemstones"
Jun	flowers/sow	"Harlequin"
July	flowering	"Monarch Mixed"
Aug	grow on	**Dwarf varieties**
Sept	grow on	"Dwarf Mixed"
Oct	plant	"Indian Carpet Mixed"
Nov	/	
Dec	/	

CONDITIONS

Aspect   Grow Sweet Williams in full sunlight.
Site   Needs well-drained soil that has been limed before planting, and has had plenty of rotted compost mixed in several weeks before.

GROWING METHOD

Sowing   Sow the fine seed in rows outdoors, ½in deep and just cover, in May/June. Transplant the seedlings so they are in rows 6in apart and pinch out the growing tips to make them bushy. Water regularly throughout the summer months, and then lift and plant into their flowering positions in October, keeping the roots intact. For cut flowers only, the plants can be left growing in rows.
Feeding   Liquid-feed monthly during the summer.
Problems   Poor drainage during winter can kill plants. If leaves are attacked by rust disease, try a spray containing the fungicide penconazole.

FLOWERING

Season   Flowers appear from late spring to early summer, and it is possible to get a second "flush" if all the stalks are cut hard back after the first flowers have faded.
Cutting   An excellent cut flower, and ideal for making into a small, rounded bouquet.

AFTER FLOWERING

General   Pull plants up when they are past their best, or leave some to develop into bigger clumps.

DIANTHUS CHINENSIS
Chinese pink

AS CONTAINER PLANTS, Chinese pinks are perfect as tidy edging plants, all growing to the same height. They are also valuable as colorful fillers and effectively bridge the gap between taller plants in the center of large tubs and trailing plants falling over the edges.

FEATURES

Growing 8–12in high, varieties of **Dianthus chinensis** are suitable for massed planting, edging garden beds, or for use in troughs or pots. Chinese pink is grown as a half-hardy annual, although it is fully hardy outdoors. Flower are red, pink, or white, with only slight scent. Available as young plants.

CONDITIONS

Aspect   Needs full sunlight to flower at its best.

DIANTHUS AT A GLANCE

A hardy annual grown for its small brightly colored pink-type flowers, used in bedding/pots. Frost hardy to 5°F (zone 7).

		Recommended Varieties
Jan	/	
Feb	/	*Dianthus chinensis:*
Mar	sow	"Baby Doll Mixed"
Apr	transplant	"Black & White Minstrels"
May	harden off/plant	"Double Gaiety Mixed"
Jun	flowering	"Princess Mixed"
July	flowering	"Raspberry Parfait"
Aug	flowering	"Snowfire"
Sept	flowcring	"Strawberry Parfait"
Oct	/	"T&M Frosty Mixed"
Nov	/	
Dec	/	

Site

Needs well-drained soil, but dig in plenty of well-rotted manure or compost when preparing beds. Lime can be added to the soil before planting and raked in. Containers must have very good drainage.

GROWING METHOD

Sowing   Sow seeds in 3½in pots of multipurpose compost in March, just cover, and keep at 60°F in a light place. When seedlings are 1in tall, transplant to cell trays and grow on with some protection (a cold frame is suitable). Harden off at the end of May and plant out in beds or containers.

Feeding   Do not overwater—a good weekly watering should be sufficient—and add liquid feed every 2–3 weeks. Plants in containers need no extra feeding if slow-release fertilizer is added.

Problems   Overwatering will cause yellowing of the leaves and rotting off at soil/compost level.

FLOWERING

Season   Plants come into flower from early summer onward and will continue until the fall if dead flowerheads are removed regularly.

Cutting   Taller varieties can be used as cut flowers, but choose a variety known for its scent such as "Double Gaiety Mixed."

AFTER FLOWERING

General   Remove plants when finished and compost.

DOROTHEANTHUS
Mesembryanthemum or Livingstone daisy

LIVINGSTONE DAISIES set beds alight with color on bright sunny days when the flowers open fully. Planted 6in apart they soon knit together to create a tapestry of color, and look especially at home when creeping among pieces of stone on a sunny rock garden.

FEATURES

Mesembryanthemum, also known as Livingstone daisy, is ideal for planting on dry, sunny banks, on rock gardens, and in pots of free-draining compost. It has a spreading habit, but is only 6in tall at most. The fleshy leaves have a crystalline texture with bright, daisy-like flowers in many shades. Grow as a half-hardy annual. All varieties of *Dorotheanthus bellidiformis* have the habit of closing their flowers in dull and wet spells of weather, opening again in bright sunshine.

DOROTHEANTHUS AT A GLANCE

A half-hardy, spreading annual grown for its daisy-like flowers that open fully in sunshine. Frost hardy to 32°F (zone 10).

		Recommended Varieties
Jan	/	
Feb	/	*Dorotheanthus bellidi-formis:*
Mar	sow	
Apr	sow/transplant	"Gelato Pink"
May	plant/harden off	"Harlequin Mixed"
Jun	flowering	"Lunette" ("Yellow Ice")
July	flowering	"Magic Carpet Mixed"
Aug	flowering	"Sparkles"
Sept	flowering	
Oct	/	
Nov	/	
Dec	/	

CONDITIONS

Aspect Needs full direct sun all day and will perform even better on a south-facing sloping bank.

Site Needs very well drained soil, with no special soil preparation necessary, since plants grow better on light, sandy, and hungry soils. If grown in containers, used soil-based compost and mix with fifty percent grit for good drainage.

GROWING METHOD

Sowing Sow seed in a 3½in pot of soil-based seed compost in March and barely cover. Keep at 64°F in a light place. When seedlings are large enough, transplant to cell trays of soil-based potting compost and grow on. Harden off at the end of May for two weeks and plant after the last frosts 6in apart.

Feeding Extra feeding is unnecessary and produces leaves at the expense of flowers. Take care not to overwater in beds or pots, else plants will rot.

Problems Slugs will attack the fleshy young leaves so scatter slug pellets after planting out.

FLOWERING

Season Flowers appear from midsummer onward. Remove faded flowers to encourage more.

Cutting Not suitable for cutting.

AFTER FLOWERING

General Pull up and compost when finished.

ESCHSCHOLZIA
California poppy

FALL SOWING of eschscholzia will produce early spring flowers around the same time as this bright green Euphorbia polychroma.

DRY, HOT, SUN-BAKED banks are perfect for California poppies, where conditions are very like those of their native State.

FEATURES

The bright flowers and finely divided blue-green foliage of the California poppy are best in large drifts, although it grows well even in cracks in paving slabs and in gravel, and thrives on dry soils in full sun. Varieties of ***Eschscholzia californica*** have flowers in yellow, cream, pink/beige, apricot, and scarlet. They grow 12in tall and wide. Grow as a hardy annual, sowing where plants are to flower. Very easy to grow and quickly self-seeds.

CONDITIONS

Aspect   Eschscholzia thrives in hot, sun-baked spots

ESCHSCHOLZIA AT A GLANCE

A hardy annual grown for its bright poppy-like flowers and ideal for light, dry soils and along paths. Frost hardy to 5°F (zone 7).

Month	Activity		Recommended Varieties
Jan	/		***Eschscholzia californica:***
Feb	/		"Apricot Bush"
Mar	sow		"Apricot Chiffon"
Apr	thin out		"Apricot Flambeau"
May	thin out		"Dalli"
Jun	flowering		"Mission Bells Mixed"
July	flowering		"Prima Ballerina"
Aug	flowering		"Rose Bush"
Sept	flowers/sow		"Thai Silk Mixed"
Oct	/		***Eschscholzia lobbii:***
Nov	/		"Moonlight"
Dec	/		

where other annuals struggle to grow. Must have full sunlight and likes it hot.

Site   Poor, light soil often gives the best results, so long as drainage is good. No special soil preparation is necessary, and avoid adding compost or manure, which encourages leafy growth at the expense of flowers.

GROWING METHOD

Sowing   Sow in March or September outdoors where the plants are to flower, since it dislikes being transplanted. Spread seed thinly in short drills ½in deep and cover. Thin out the seedlings as they grow to allow 3–6in between plants. Water thoroughly after thinning to settle plants back in.

Feeding   Except in spells of drought, watering is not necessary, and extra feed is not required.

Problems   No particular problems.

FLOWERING

Season   Long flowering period through the spring and summer months if faded flowers are removed.

Cutting   Use as a cut flower, although flowers close at night. Cut long stems and place in water immediately to just below the flower buds.

AFTER FLOWERING

General   Often self-seeds, so seedlings can be expected the following season. These will appear in cracks in the sidewalk, along paths and drives, and in gravel, where they are perfectly at home in dry, poor soil conditions.

EUPHORBIA
Snow-on-the-mountain

THE COLOR of snow-on-the-mountain comes from its white-edged leaves; this becomes more intense near the tops of the plants.

WHEN GROWN IN POTS, Euphorbia marginata *can be planted in mixed borders in groups of 3–5 plants for cool splashes of color.*

FEATURES

Commonly known as snow-on-the-mountain, *Euphorbia marginata* is grown for its attractive leaves. The flowers are insignificant, but the leaves have an edging of white. Plants grow 2–3ft tall and are used in annual or mixed borders. Grow as a hardy annual. The milky sap is poisonous.

CONDITIONS

Aspect Needs to be grown in the open in full sun.

EUPHORBIA AT A GLANCE

A hardy annual grown for its attractive leaves, which are streaked and edged with white. Frost hardy to 23°F (zone 9).

Jan	/	Recommended Varieties
Feb	/	*Euphorbia marginata:*
Mar	sow 🖐	"Summer Icicle"
Apr	thin out 🖐	
May	thin out 🖐	
Jun	flowering 🌼	
July	flowering 🌼	
Aug	flowering 🌼	
Sept	flowering 🌼	
Oct	/	
Nov	/	
Dec	/	

Site Does not tolerate poor drainage and succeeds best in light and slightly hungry soils—sandy soils give good results. Add very well-rotted organic matter before planting to help retain soil moisture.

GROWING METHOD

Sowing Sow seed during March direct into the ground, where plants are to grow, which avoids root disturbance as they develop. Make short drills ½in deep and scatter seed thinly, then cover. Plants are gradually thinned out so that final spacing is 6–12in by early summer. In exposed yards, short twigs can be used as supports. Alternatively, sow in pots in a cold frame and transplant to cell trays, planting out in May.

Feeding Grows well without extra feeding.
Problems Trouble-free.

FLOWERING

Season From early summer onward.
Cutting Foliage may be used in arrangements but stems must be burnt or scalded to stop the milky sap bleeding. Wear gloves to avoid getting the irritant sap on skin.

AFTER FLOWERING

General Remove plants in late summer and fall when they are past their best, but leave a few to die down and self-seed into the soil.

GAZANIA
Gazania

GAZANIA *flowers often have striking darker markings toward their centers.*

IN MILD COASTAL YARDS *it is worth leaving gazanias out during the winter months, since they often survive unharmed and will give an early show of flowers in the following spring.*

FEATURES

Gazanias come in an amazing range of brilliant colors, from pastel pinks to cream, strong reds, and mahogany. Modern varieties with striped petals are very eye-catching. All have contrasting "eyes" to their flowers. Gazanias are grown as half-hardy annuals from spring-sown seeds and used in beds and courtyard pots. Flowers tend to close up in dull weather, but newer varieties like "Daybreak Bright Orange" stay open for longer. They grow up to 12in tall and wide and thrive in coastal yards.

CONDITIONS

Aspect   For the flowers to open reliably, gazanias must be grown where they get roasting sun all day.

GAZANIA AT A GLANCE

A half-hardy annual grown for its bright flowers that open fully in sun. Use in beds and containers. Frost hardy to 23°F (zone 9).

		Recommended Varieties
Jan	/	
Feb	/	*Gazania rigens:*
Mar	sow	"Chansonette"
Apr	transplant	"Chansonette Pink Shades"
May	harden off/plant	"Daybreak Bright Orange"
Jun	flowering	"Daybreak Red Stripe"
July	flowering	"Harlequin Hybrids"
Aug	flowering	"Mini Star Mixed"
Sept	flowcring	"Sundance Mixed"
Oct	/	"Talent"
Nov	/	
Dec	/	

Site   Needs well-drained soil that is not too rich or leafy growth is the result. Light sandy soils give the best results. If growing in courtyard containers, choose clay pots or troughs and use a soil-based compost with extra sharp grit mixed in to ensure good drainage at all times.

GROWING METHOD

Sowing   Seed is sown in March at 68°F in a heated propagator, in 3½in pots. Just cover the seeds and keep in a light place. Seedlings appear in 1–2 weeks and can be transplanted into cell trays, when large enough. Grow on in a greenhouse or conservatory, then harden off and plant in late May, spacing plants 12in apart. In mixed containers, make sure they are not shaded out by other plants growing nearby.

Feeding   Only water gazanias when the soil or compost is dry, and stand courtyard pots undercover during prolonged spells of summer rain.

Problems   No real problems, but slugs may attack leaves in wet weather, so protect with slug pellets.

FLOWERING

Season   The flowering period lasts throughout summer if dead flowers and their stalks are removed.

Cutting   Flowers are not suitable for cutting.

AFTER FLOWERING

General   Favorite plants can be lifted, potted up, and kept dry in a frost-free greenhouse over winter. Cuttings can be taken in the spring and new plants grown on for planting out.

GODETIA
Godetia

FOR A RAINBOW of summer color, sow a mixed variety of godetia that includes shades of rose, pink, and white flowers.

AT ITS PEAK, godetia is smothered in masses of bright flowers with large petals that have a texture similar to crepe paper.

FEATURES

Godetia is available in a wide range of varieties and many colors. This hardy annual can be spring- or fall-sown, the latter giving earlier flowers on bigger plants. Size ranges from 8 to 36in; the taller varieties are ideal for cutting. Don't labor over godetia—the best flowers are produced on slightly hungry, dry soils.

GODETIA AT A GLANCE

Grown for its bright single or double flowers, this hardy annual can be spring- or fall-sown. Frost hardy to 5°F (zone 7).

		Recommended Varieties
Jan	/	
Feb	/	**Godetia hybrids:**
Mar	sow	**Tall varieties**
Apr	sow	"Duke of York"
May	thin out	"Grace Mixed"
Jun	flowering	"Schamini Carmine"
July	flowering	"Sybil Sherwood"
Aug	flowering	**Dwarf varieties**
Sept	flowers/sow	"Charivari"
Oct	/	"Lilac Pixie"
Nov	/	"Precious Gems"
Dec	/	"Salmon Princess"

CONDITIONS

Aspect	Needs an open position in full sunlight.
Site	Needs perfect drainage, but not rich soil.

GROWING METHOD

Sowing	Sow where plants are to grow, just covering the seeds in shallow drills 6in apart during March/April, or during September. Thin out seedlings until they are 6–12in apart, depending on the variety. Do not thin fall-sown plants until the following spring, to allow for winter losses.
Feeding	Not needed, or excessive leafy growth results.
Problems	Overwatering quickly causes root rot, followed by collapse and death of plants.

FLOWERING

Season	Flowers appear from May onward on plants sown the previous fall. Spring-sown plants start flowering from June.
Cutting	An excellent cut flower, especially if the taller varieties such as "Schamini Carmine" and "Grace Mixed" are grown in rows.

AFTER FLOWERING

General	Remove plants when flowering is over. A few can be left to self-seed onto the soil.

GOMPHRENA
Globe amaranth

"STRAWBERRY FIELDS" is a large-growing variety of gomphrena with red flowers 2in across, on stems 30in tall.

GLOBE AMARANTH makes a good edging for paths—choose one of the lower-growing varieties such as "Gemini Mixed" at 2ft.

FEATURES

Also commonly known as bachelor's buttons, gomphrena is a half-hardy annual growing 12–30in tall, depending on the variety. Its rounded heads of purple, pink, white, red, and mauve flowers are used in bedding displays and for cutting and drying. "Strawberry Fields" has bright red flowers.

GOMPHRENA AT A GLANCE

A half-hardy annual grown for its clover-like flowerheads, used in bedding and for cutting. Frost hardy to 32°F (zone 10).

Jan	/	
Feb	/	
Mar	sow	
Apr	transplant	
May	harden off/plant	
Jun	flowering	
July	flowering	
Aug	flowering	
Sept	flowering	
Oct	/	
Nov	/	
Dec	/	

Recommended Varieties

Gomphrena globosa:
"Buddy"
"Full Series"
"Gemini Mixed"
"Globe Amaranth"
"Qis Mixed"

Gomphrena hybrid:
"Strawberry Fields"

CONDITIONS

Aspect   Must have a sunny spot.
Site   Needs well-drained soil enriched with rotted manure or compost.

GROWING METHOD

Sowing   Sow in March in 3½in pots of multipurpose compost, just covering the seeds (soaking for a few days before helps germination). Keep at 64°F in a warm, dark place such as an airing cupboard and check regularly—seedlings appear in approximately two weeks. Transplant into cell trays, grow on under cover, harden off in late May, and plant out after frosts, 10–12in apart.
Feeding   Give an all-purpose liquid feed monthly.
Problems   No special problems affect gomphrena.

FLOWERING

Season   Flowers appear from midsummer to fall.
Cutting   Used fresh as a cut flower, but can also be dried in late summer by hanging upside-down in a warm, dry, airy place.

AFTER FLOWERING

General   Pull up in the fall and use for composting.

GYPSOPHILA
Baby's breath

CLOUDS OF SMALL FLOWERS are produced on annual gypsophila all summer if a few seeds are sown at two-week intervals from April until early June. For cut flowers, grow plants in a spare corner because they look bare once you begin to regularly remove stems.

FEATURES

Hardy annual varieties of **Gypsophila elegans** grow up to 2ft tall and wide, with many-divided stems bearing small, dainty pink, white, or rose flowers. It is widely used in flower arranging and as a "foil" for other plants in summer bedding schemes. The dwarf- growing **Gypsophila muralis** "Garden Bride," at 6in, is ideal for baskets and containers.

CONDITIONS

Aspect   Grow gypsophila in full sunlight.

GYPSOPHILA AT A GLANCE

Gypsophila is a hardy annual grown for tall, much-branching stems of flowers, for beds/cutting. Frost hardy to 5°F (zone 7).

		Recommended Varieties
Jan	/	
Feb	/	*Gypsophila elegans:*
Mar	/	"Bright Rose"
Apr	sow	"Color Blend"
May	thin out	"Covent Garden"
Jun	flowering	"Kermesina"
July	flowering	"Monarch White"
Aug	flowering	"Rosea"
Sept	flowers/sow	"Snow Fountain"
Oct	/	"White Elephant"
Nov	/	*Gypsophila muralis:*
Dec	/	"Garden Bride"

Site   Rotted compost or manure should be dug in before planting, for strong plants and better flowers, but the soil must also be well-drained. Varieties grown in baskets and containers will succeed in any multipurpose compost.

GROWING METHOD

Sowing   Seeds can go directly into the ground, where plants will grow and flower. Sow in short drills ½in deep in April, then thin to finally leave plants 4–6in apart to give each other support and allow room to grow. September sowing produces stronger plants with earlier flowers the following spring—do not thin out until after winter.

Feeding   Feeding is not generally necessary if the soil has been well prepared beforehand. In dry spells, give the soil a thorough soaking, and do not let containers dry out.

Problems   Gypsophila is trouble-free, but young plants are prone to rotting off in heavy soils.

FLOWERING

Season   Flowers appear from June onward on spring-sown plants, several weeks earlier on those sown the previous fall.

Cutting   Excellent when cut and an ideal "filler" to marry together other flowers in a wide range of floral arrangements.

AFTER FLOWERING

General   Pull up plants and use for composting.

HELIANTHUS
Sunflower

SUNFLOWERS *have a central disk that eventually becomes the fat seedhead in the fall and makes useful food for wild birds.*

"PACINO" is a modern variety of Helianthus annuus, *small enough to be used in courtyard pots, growing to only 18in tall.*

FEATURES

Sunflowers range in height from 18in up to 15ft, depending on the variety grown. They can be used in bedding, in courtyard containers, as cut flowers, or can be grown as traditional "giants" to several feet tall. Plants produce single or multi-flowered heads and the color range is enormous. "Teddy Bear" has furry, double flowers. Annual sunflowers are fully hardy and flower from mid-summer onward. Certain varieties, such as "Prado Sun & Fire," have been bred to be pollen-free, and these are ideal for use as indoor cut flowers. Seedheads left in the yard in the fall provide food for wild birds.

CONDITIONS

Aspect   Must have an open position in full sunlight.

HELIANTHUS AT A GLANCE

A hardy annual grown for its large flowers on both dwarf and tall plants; some are ideal for cutting. Frost hardy to 5°F (zone 7).

		Recommended Varieties
Jan	/	*Helianthus annuus:*
Feb	/	**Tall varieties**
Mar	sow	"Italian White"
		"Pastiche"
Apr	thin out	"Velvet Queen"
		For containers
May	support	"Big Smile"
		"Pacino"
Jun	flowering	**Double flowers**
		"Orange Sun"
		"Sungold Double"
July	flowering	"Teddy Bear"

Site   Tolerates most soil conditions, but soil enriched with plenty of manure or compost makes growth both rapid and vigorous, producing the largest flowerheads. Plants grown in groups in borders tend to support each other, but in exposed positions tie tall varieties to a cane. Use multipurpose compost mixed with slow-release fertilizer for planting up courtyard containers and windowboxes.

GROWING METHOD

Sowing   The seeds are large and easy to handle. Sow three seeds outdoors in March, where plants are to grow, removing all but the strongest when 6in tall. Can also be sown three seeds to a 3½in pot of compost and treated in the same way. Pot-grown plants can be kept outdoors and planted when the roots fill the pot. Spacing depends on the variety grown.

Feeding   Extra feeding is not usually needed, but keep plants well watered in long dry spells.

Problems   Slugs and snails can attack young plants, cutting them off at ground level, so protect with slug pellets or a barrier of sharp grit.

FLOWERING

Season   Throughout summer and early autumn.

Cutting   A very good cut flower, but use a heavy vase or add some weight to the bottom of it to prevent it toppling over. Pollen-free varieties should be grown if allergies are a problem.

AFTER FLOWERING

General   Leave the seedheads as bird food during the fall and winter, and then dig out the extensive roots. Sunflower roots can help break up and loosen heavy, compacted soils.

HELICHRYSUM
Strawflower

FOR DRYING cut helichrysum before the flowers reach this stage, while the petals are still curved inward (bottom right).

PAPER DAISIES ARE APT to be rather leggy, but the range of flower colors can be stunning, as shown here.

FEATURES

Varieties of strawflower come from *Helichrysum bracteatum*, with plants growing 6–24in tall. They are among the easiest annuals to grow for dried flowers, with double blooms in many colors, and petals that feel straw-like. Dwarf varieties make long-lasting container plants. A half-hardy annual.

CONDITIONS

Aspect   Must have a warm spot in full sun.

HELICHRYSUM AT A GLANCE

A half-hardy annual grown for its long-lasting dried flowers, and also used in bedding and containers. Frost hardy to 32°F (zone 10).

Jan	/	**Recommended Varieties**
Feb	/	
Mar	sow 🖐	*Helichrysum bracteatum:*
Apr	transplant/grow 🖐	**Tall varieties**
May	harden off/plant 🖐	"Drakkar Pastel Mixed"
Jun	flowering 🌿	"Monstrosum Double Mixed"
July	flowering 🌿	
Aug	flowering 🌿	"Pastel Mixed"
Sept	flowers/cutting 🌿	"Swiss Giants"
Oct	flowers/cutting 🌿	**Dwarf varieties**
Nov	/	"Bright Bikini"
		"Chico Mixed"
Dec	/	"Hot Bikini"

Site

Needs very well-drained soil that has been enriched with rotted compost or manure. If growing in containers use multipurpose compost and add slow-release fertiliser. Tall varieties will need staking as they develop.

GROWING METHOD

Sowing   Sow seeds in March in 3½in pots of multipurpose compost and germinate at 64°F. Transplant seedlings to cell trays when large enough and grow on, then harden off at the end of May and plant 6–24in apart depending on the variety. Seed can also be sown direct into short drills in the soil during May and the young plants gradually thinned to the planting distances above. In containers pack 2–3 plants together in groups to get a good block of flower color.

Feeding   Helichrysum grows well without extra feeding, but water container-grown plants regularly.

Problems   By late summer the leaves are often attacked by mildew, but it is not worth treating.

FLOWERING

Season   Flowers appear from early to midsummer.

Cutting   Pick the flowers when the petals are still incurved. Hang the bunches upside down in a dry, airy place to dry out. Long-lasting.

AFTER FLOWERING

General   Cut what you want and then pull up.

HELIPTERUM
Everlasting daisy

WHEN PLANTS REACH this stage of growth the entire plant can be harvested and hung up to dry. Individual stems are then cut off.

THINNING PLANTS to 6–12in apart helps them support each other. The flowers have a distinct rustle in a breeze.

FEATURES

The papery flowers of everlasting daisies come mainly in pinks and white. They grow 12–18in tall, and can be used in bedding or cut for dried flower arrangements. In catalogs they are also found listed under acrolinium and rhodanthe. Hardy annual.

CONDITIONS

Aspect   These Australian natives need full sun.
Site   Helipterum must have perfectly drained soil

HELIPTERUM AT A GLANCE

A half–hardy annual grown for its pinkish, "papery" flowers that are good for cutting and drying. Frost hardy to 32ºF (zone 10).

Month		Recommended Varieties
Jan	/	
Feb	/	Helipterum hybrids:
Mar	/	"Bonny"
Apr	sow	"Double Mixed"
May	sow/thin	"Goliath"
Jun	flowering	"Pierrot"
July	flowering	"Special Mixed"
Aug	flowers/cutting	
Sept	flowers/cutting	
Oct	/	
Nov	/	
Dec	/	

and does not require special preparation—the best results are obtained on thin and hungry soils that mimic the plant's natural growing conditions. Sheltered hot-spots are best.

GROWING METHOD

Sowing   Sow seeds direct into the soil in short drills ½in deep and 6in apart in April and May. Thin the seedlings as they grow, so plants are eventually 6–12in apart by early summer. Water only during long dry spells, but this is not necessary when flower buds begin to appear.
Feeding   Do not feed.
Problems   Plants fail on heavy, wet soils that are slow to warm up in spring, so try growing them in raised beds which have better drainage.

FLOWERING

Season   Although the plants flower for only a brief spell the effect is long-lasting because of their "everlasting" nature.
Cutting   Ideal as cut, dried flower. For the best results cut off whole plants when most of the flowers are still just opening out, and hang upside down in a dry, airy place.

AFTER FLOWERING

General   Plants sometimes self-seed. Any plants not lifted for drying are pulled up in fall and added to the compost heap.

IBERIS
Candytuft

CANDYTUFT is available in a wide range of colorful mixtures. Each 2in-wide "flower" is actually a mass of smaller flowers.

ALL SORTS OF COLORS appear in varieties of Iberis umbellata, *including white as seen here. The flowers have a sweet fragrance.*

FEATURES

Very decorative plants that grow no more than 12in tall, varieties of *Iberis umbellata,* a hardy annual, have sweet-scented flowers in white, pink, mauve, red, and purple. They produce good results even in poor soils and quickly self-seed so you get new plants springing up every year, which are at home growing in-between paving and in gravel drives. The best plants with the most flowers come from sowing in early spring.

CONDITIONS

Aspect
Site
Iberis prefers an open spot in full sun. Although it is happy in poor soil, adding rotted manure or compost before planting will help keep moisture in and reduce the need for extra watering during summer.

IBERIS AT A GLANCE

Iberis is a hardy annual grown for its heads of bright, scented flowers which are used in bedding. Frost hardy to 5°F (zone 7).

		Recommended Varieties
Jan	/	
Feb	/	*Iberis umbellata:*
Mar	sow 🧤	"Dwarf Fairy Mixed"
Apr	sow 🧤	"Fantasia Mixed"
May	thin out 🧤	"Flash Mixed"
Jun	flowering ❀	"Spangles"
July	flowering ❀	
Aug	flowering ❀	
Sept	sow 🧤	
Oct	/	
Nov	/	
Dec	/	

GROWING METHOD

Sowing
Seed is sown outdoors in March/April where the plants are to flower. Mark out circular patches of ground with sand and make short parallel drills ½in deep inside the circle, spaced 6in apart. Sow the seeds thinly in these drills and cover with fine, raked soil. Seedlings appear in 2–3 weeks and should be thinned out so they are eventually 3–6in apart by early summer. Can also be sown in September for earlier flowers.

Feeding
Extra feeding is not necessary. Watering in early summer will stop plants flowering prematurely before they achieve a good size.

Problems
Being relatives of brassicas like cabbage, they can suffer from clubroot disease. Treatment is not worthwhile, but to continue to enjoy candytuft where clubroot is present, sow a pinch of seed in 3½in pots of multi-purpose compost in early spring and plant out clumps in early summer. Disease-free roots will support the plants and let them flower.

FLOWERING

Season
Flowers will appear from early summer.

Cutting
Good cut flower. Flowers that are well-formed but not over-mature should last well if picked early in the day and immediately plunged into water to soak before arranging.

AFTER FLOWERING

General
Plants can be cut down after flowering, given a good soak with liquid feed, and they will usually produce a second "flush" of flowerheads several weeks later. Candytuft self-seeds very easily so leave a few plants to die away naturally and scatter their seeds. Seed can also be collected for sowing the following spring.

IMPATIENS

Busy lizzie

VIGOROUS AND LARGE-FLOWERED, "Accent Mixed" will carpet the ground in borders or fill containers in sun or shade.

NEW GUINEA busy lizzies can be successfully combined with smaller flowered varieties like this delightful "Mosaic Lilac."

FEATURES

Impatiens perform well in sun or shade and a huge range is available. Use in bedding, tubs, windowboxes, hanging baskets, and flower bags. As well as busy lizzies, there are also the larger "New Guinea" types (12in), and the "balsams," with bushy growth (10in). Busy lizzies grow from 6–12in tall and wide depending on variety. All impatiens are half-hardy annuals, and raising from seed requires some care. Widely available as young plants by mail order, they can also be bought ready-grown in spring. Flowers can be single or double in mixed or various colors.

IMPATIENS AT A GLANCE

A half-hardy annual grown for its flowers for bedding, containers, and hanging planters. Frost hardy to 32°F (zone 10).

Jan	/	
Feb	sow 🖑	
Mar	sow 🖑	
Apr	grow on 🖑	
May	harden/plant 🖑	
Jun	flowering 🌸	
July	flowering 🌸	
Aug	flowering 🌸	
Sept	flowering 🌸	
Oct	flowering 🌸	
Nov	/	
Dec	/	

Recommended Varieties

Busy lizzies:
 "Accent Mixed"
 "Bruno"
 "Mosaic Rose"
 "Super Elfin Mixed"
New Guinea impatiens:
 "Firelake Mixed"
 "Spectra"
 "Tango"
Impatiens balsamifera:
 "Tom Thumb Mixed"

CONDITIONS

Aspect	Will succeed in full sun or moderate shade.
Site	Soil should have rotted manure or compost mixed in before planting, and should be well-drained. Avoid planting in windy spots. In containers and baskets use multipurpose compost with slow-release fertiliser added.

GROWING METHOD

Sowing	In late February/March sow seeds onto a fine layer of vermiculite in 3½in pots of seed compost. Tap to settle but do not cover. Seal in a clear plastic bag or put in a heated propagator, in a bright place at 70–75°F. Seedlings appear in 2–3 weeks and are transplanted to cell trays when 1in tall. Grow on, then harden off and plant out after frosts, 6–12in apart.
Feeding	Apply liquid feed weekly to beds or containers using a hand-held feeder.
Problems	Damping off disease attacks seedlings. Use clean pots, fresh compost, and treat with a copper-based fungicide if seedlings collapse.

FLOWERING

Season	Flowers appear on young plants before planting and then throughout summer. Take off dead flowers to keep new ones coming.
Cutting	Not suitable as a cut flower.

AFTER FLOWERING

General	Remove when plants are past their best.

IPOMOEA
Morning glory

"HEAVENLY BLUE" morning glory never looks better than when scrambling through a host plant like this apple.

FEATURES

Look under ipomoea or morning glory in seed catalogs to find varieties of this stunning climber. Most familiar is sky-blue flowered "Heavenly Blue," others are red, pink, white, mauve, chocolate, one is striped, and "Murasaki Jishi" is double-flowered. Average height is 10–12ft. Plants will climb fences and other plants. For patios grow 3–4 plants in a 12in pot up a wigwam of 5ft canes. A half-hardy annual with flowers mostly 3in across. Seeds are poisonous.

IPOMOEA AT A GLANCE

A half-hardy annual climber grown for its trumpet-shaped flowers that open in the morning. Frost hardy to 32°F (zone 10).

		Recommended Varieties
Jan	/	
Feb	/	**Ipomoea hybrids:**
Mar	/	"Cardinal"
Apr	sow	"Chocolate"
May	grow on	"Early Call Mixed"
Jun	plant	"Flying Saucers"
July	flowering	"Grandpa Otts"
Aug	flowering	"Heavenly Blue"
Sept	flowering	"Mini Sky–Blue"
Oct	/	"Murasaki Jishi"
Nov	/	"Platycodon Flowered
Dec	/	White"

CONDITIONS

Aspect Must have full sun all day.
Site Mix rotted compost with soil before planting. In containers use multipurpose compost with slow-release fertiliser added. All ipomoeas must have shelter from wind, and must have support for their twining stems.

GROWING METHOD

Sowing Soak the seeds in warm water the night before sowing, then sow one to a 3½in pot, 1in deep, in April. Keep in a temperature of at least 70°F and put in bright light when the big pink seedlings come up 1–2 weeks later. Keep warm and grow on, potting on into 5in pots when the roots fill the pot. Support shoots with short stakes. Gradually harden-off in late May, planting out or into containers in early June.

Feeding Feed monthly with a high-potash tomato food.
Problems Seedlings will turn yellow if they are kept too cold in the early stages. Red spider mite feeds on leaves—use a spray containing bifenthrin.

FLOWERING

Season Summer.
Cutting Unsuitable for cutting.

AFTER FLOWERING

General Use for composting when finished.

KOCHIA
Summer cypress

SUMMER CYPRESS *is so-called because it resembles a dwarf conifer in color and shape. In early fall plants turn bright red.*

KOCHIA MAKES *a bold plant for the focus of a bedding display— seen here with pink nicotianas and silver-leaved senecio.*

FEATURES

Summer cypress is a bushy half-hardy foliage annual that grows up to 3ft high with soft, light-green feathery foliage forming an upright cone- or dome-shape. "Trichophylla" has narrow leaves and looks similar to a dwarf conifer in summer, turning to a fiery bronze red in fall, hence its other common name of burning bush. Grow in groups of 2–3 or singly as the centerpiece of a bedding scheme.

KOCHIA AT A GLANCE

A half-hardy annual grown for its light-green leaves on bushy plants which turn red in fall. Frost hardy to 32°F (zone 10).

		Recommended Varieties
Jan	/	
Feb	sow ✍	*Kochia scoparia:*
Mar	sow ✍	"Trichophylla"
Apr	grow on ✍	
May	harden off/plant ✍	For all-green leaves
Jun	leaves ✿	"Evergreen"
July	leaves ✿	
Aug	leaves ✿	
Sept	leaves ✿	
Oct	leaves ✿	
Nov	/	
Dec	/	

CONDITIONS

Aspect   Needs full sun to get the best leaf color.
Site   Grows on most soils but must be well-drained. Add manure/compost before planting.

GROWING METHOD

Sowing   Sow February/March on the surface of a 3½in pot of moist multipurpose compost but do not cover. Keep at 61°F in a bright spot, and expect seedlings in 2–3 weeks. When large enough, transplant to 3½in pots of multipurpose compost and grow on, hardening off in late May and planting outdoors after the last frosts. Space plants at least 2ft apart to allow room for development. They can also be planted in rows as a temporary and unusual summer "hedge."

Feeding   Water thoroughly in early summer for 2–3 weeks after planting. Extra feeding is not essential to get good results.

Problems   No particular problems.

FLOWERING

Season   Not grown for flowers but leaves.
Cutting   Unsuitable for cutting.

AFTER FLOWERING

General   Pull up and compost in fall.

LATHYRUS
Sweet pea

SWEET PEAS are perhaps the easiest and most rewarding of cut flowers you can grow. Choose a variety known for its fragrance.

CLIMBING VARIETIES of Lathyrus odoratus *make useful "living screens" in summer with the added benefits of color and scent.*

FEATURES

Varieties of *Lathyrus odoratus*, or sweet pea, occupy several pages in seed catalogs, but there are two basic groups—the tall climbers reaching 6–8ft, used as cut flowers and for screening, and dwarf "patio" varieties reaching up to 3ft which are used in bedding, baskets, and containers. Not all sweet peas have good scent, so check before buying seeds, and choose a fragrant mixed variety for a range of flower colors, which can be white, pink, red, mauve, orange, or blue, as well as many with picotee and other patterns. Sweet peas are easily-grown hardy annuals.

CONDITIONS

Aspect   Grow in full sun.

LATHYRUS AT A GLANCE

A hardy annual climber producing often strongly-scented flowers which are ideal for cutting. Frost hardy to 5°F (zone 7).

Jan	/	
Feb	/	
Mar	sow	
Apr	grow on	
May	plant	
Jun	flowering	
July	flowering	
Aug	flowering	
Sept	flowering	
Oct	sow	
Nov	/	
Dec	/	

Recommended Varieties

Lathyrus odoratus:
Tall, fragrant varieties
  "Bouquet Mixed"
  "Great Expectations"
  "Old Fashioned Mixed"
  "Old Spice Mixed"
Dwarf/patio varieties
  "Explorer"
  "Fantasia Mixed"
  "Jet-Set Mixed"
  "Knee-High"

Site   Needs well-drained soil packed with organic matter. Add compost or rotted manure the fall before sowing or planting. Climbing varieties need canes, bean netting, fences, or other supports to grow through. Use multipurpose compost for planting up baskets and patio containers.

GROWING METHOD

Sowing   Seeds can be sown individually in 3½in pots in February/March and germinated in a coldframe, cold porch, or even outdoors in a spot sheltered from rain. Nick or file the tough seed coat until a pale "spot" appears, then sow 1in-deep in soil-based seed compost. Pinch out the growing tips when plants are 3in tall to encourage sideshoots to grow. Grow outside, then plant out in May, 12in apart for climbers, and 6–12in apart for patio varieties used in baskets and containers.

Feeding   Plants benefit from a monthly feed with liquid tomato food. Water thoroughly in dry spells.

Problems   Mice will dig young seedlings up so set traps. Powdery mildew can attack leaves in the summer—use a spray containing sulfur.

FLOWERING

Season   Seed can also be sown in October, and plants overwintered for flowers from early summer. Spring-sown plants flower from June.

Cutting   Cut when the first few flowers on the stalk are opening and stand up to their necks in water.

AFTER FLOWERING

General   Cut off at ground level in fall so the nitrogen-rich roots rot down in the soil.

LAVATERA
Annual mallow

"SILVER CUP" is one of the most popular varieties of annual mallow, with rose-pink flowers up to 5in across.

IN MIXED BORDERS annual mallow can be sown direct into open patches of soil, for mounds of color from mid to late summer.

FEATURES

White, rose, pink, and red flowers with a silky sheen are characteristic of annual mallow. Plants grow between 2–4ft depending on variety, and bloom continuously from mid-June onward. Use them as the centerpiece in summer bedding schemes or grow in large blocks in annual borders. An easily-grown hardy annual that is also useful as a cut flower.

LAVATERA AT A GLANCE

A hardy annual grown for its large, colorful summer flowers on bushy plants 2–4ft tall. Frost hardy to 5°F (zone 7).

Jan	/	**Recommended Varieties**
Feb	/	*Lavatera trimestris:*
Mar	sow	"Beauty Mixed"
Apr	sow/thin out	"Dwarf White Cherub"
May	sow/thin out	"Loveliness"
Jun	flowering	"Mont Blanc"
July	flowering	"Mont Rose"
Aug	flowering	"Parade Mixed"
Sept	flowering	"Pink Beauty"
Oct	/	"Ruby Regis"
Nov	/	"Silver Cup"
Dec	/	

CONDITIONS

Aspect Must have full sun all day.
Site Lavatera needs good drainage but not rich soil —plants flower better if the ground is hungry, making them good plants for light sandy soils. They do well in seaside gardens.

GROWING METHOD

Sowing Seed is sown outdoors March-May, and earlier sowings mean earlier flowers. Mark out circles 2ft or more across, then sow seed in short drills ½in deep. When seedlings appear thin them out gradually so they are 1–2ft apart by early summer. Growing this way creates a roughly circular block of color, which can be used as the centerpiece of a bedding scheme using annuals.
Feeding Feeding is not necessary. Water thoroughly in early summer during long dry spells.
Problems Sometimes killed suddenly by soil fungal diseases—grow in a new spot the next season.

FLOWERING

Season Summer.
Cutting Grow a few plants just for cut stems.

AFTER FLOWERING

General Leave a few plants to self-seed, then pull up.

LIMNANTHES
Poached egg flower

POACHED EGG FLOWER has 1in-wide flowers like tiny eggs in early summer, and attractive, divided, fern-like leaves.

THE SEEDS OF LIMNANTHES go everywhere after flowering and seem to enjoy spreading along path edges in particular.

FEATURES

Limnanthes douglasii has cup-shaped white flowers with bright yellow centers, which explains its common name of poached egg flower. Plants grow to 6–9in in height and have a spreading habit. A hardy annual, it self-seeds very easily and keeps on coming. Grow in annual beds, along path edges and among other plants in borders.

LIMNANTHES AT A GLANCE

A hardy annual that quickly self-seeds, producing masses of yellow/white flowers in summer. Frost hardy to 5°F (zone 7).

Jan	/	Recommended Varieties
Feb	/	*Limnanthes douglasii*
Mar	sow	
Apr	sow/thin	
May	sow/thin	
Jun	flowering	
July	flowering	
Aug	/	
Sept	sow	
Oct	/	
Nov	/	
Dec	/	

CONDITIONS

Aspect   Prefers full sun and an open situation.
Site   Needs moisture-retentive soil with rotted organic matter mixed in well ahead of sowing.

GROWING METHOD

Sowing   Spring or fall are the sowing times. Sow from March to May or in September. Either sow seed in short drills ½in deep or mark areas of soil, scatter the seed over the surface, and rake in. Seedlings appear after 1–2 weeks and should be thinned out so they are about 3–6in apart, although this is not too critical. If sowing in fall do not thin until spring in case of winter losses.
Feeding   Feeding is not necessary, but water thoroughly in dry spells during early summer.
Problems No special problems.

FLOWERING

Season   Overwintered plants flower from late spring depending on the weather, and are very attractive to bees and beneficial garden insects.
Cutting   Not suitable for cutting.

AFTER FLOWERING

General   Pull plants up as soon as they are over.

LIMONIUM
Statice

LONG AFTER *the small pale flowers have faded the colorful papery bracts are still going strong, and they keep their color when dried.*

"PURPLE MONARCH" is a classic strain of statice for cutting and drying. It grows to 24in.

FEATURES

Annual varieties of *Limonium sinuatum* grow up to 3ft tall and have peculiar winged stems. The actual flowers are small, but statice is grown for its papery bracts of purple, white, pink, apricot, yellow, rose, or blue, which persist all summer, and can be used as a cut and dried flower. A half-hardy annual that is used solely for cutting, or in the case of the short varieties as a bedding/container plant.

CONDITIONS

Aspect   Grow in full sun in an open position.

LIMONIUM AT A GLANCE

A half-hardy annual grown for its heads of brightly colored bracts used for bedding and drying. Frost hardy to 23°F (zone 9).

Jan	/	**Recommended Varieties**
Feb	sow 👈	
Mar	sow/transplant 👈	*Limonium sinuatum:*
Apr	grow on 👈	**Tall varieties**
May	grow on/harden 👈	"Art Shades Mixed"
Jun	plant/grow 👈	"Forever Mixed"
July	flowering 🌣	"Forever Moonlight"
Aug	flowers/cutting 🌣	"Sunburst Mixed"
Sept	flowers/cutting 🌣	"Sunset Mixed"
Oct	/	**Short varieties**
Nov	/	"Biedermeier Mixed"
Dec	/	"Petite Bouquet"

Site   Must have very well-drained soil, and is quite happy in sandy, light soils that are on the "hungry" side. If growing dwarf varieties for containers use multipurpose compost. Statice does exceedingly well in seaside gardens.

GROWING METHOD

Sowing   Sow seed in February/March in a 3½in pot of multipurpose compost and keep at 64°F. Transplant to cell trays, grow on, then harden off in late May and plant after the last frosts 6–18in apart. If growing for cut flowers, seed can be sown outdoors in rows from early May, ½in deep and thinned to similar spacings.

Feeding   Does not need regular feeding, but water well if dry straight after planting out.

Problems   Plants may rot on heavy, wet soils, and powdery mildew can attack the leaves in late summer, but this is rarely serious.

FLOWERING

Season   Long flowering period throughout summer.

Cutting   Ideal cut flower. Can be used fresh, or cut and dried by hanging bunches upside down in a dry airy place. Cut when the flowerheads are showing maximum color. Dried flowers retain their color well over a long period.

AFTER FLOWERING

General   Pull plants up and compost when all the flowers have been cut or have gone over.

LINARIA
Toadflax

WHEN SOWN IN BOLD PATCHES *varieties of* Linaria maroccana *soon knit together to produce a tapestry of color if one of the mixtures such as "Fairy Bouquet" is grown. Clumps can also be carefully lifted and planted into patio pots in late spring and early summer.*

FEATURES

Linaria is commonly known as toadflax and has dainty little flowers like tiny snapdragons in a wide color range including white, cream, yellow, red, blue, and pink. Plants grow 9–24in and are good massed in drifts in annual borders, or used as fillers in mixed border plantings. Most annual toadflax are varieties of *Linaria maroccana*. A hardy annual that can be sown direct outdoors.

LINARIA AT A GLANCE

A hardy annual grown for its spikes of pretty flowers like small snapdragons appearing in summer. Frost hardy to 5°F (zone 7).

Jan	/	Recommended Varieties
Feb	/	
Mar	sow	*Linaria anticaria*
Apr	sow/thin out	
May	sow/thin out	*Linaria maroccana:*
Jun	thin/flowers	"Fairy Bouquet"
July	flowering	"Fantasia Blue"
Aug	flowering	"Fantasia Mixed"
Sept	flowering	"Fantasia Pink"
Oct	/	"Northern Lights"
Nov	/	*Linaria reticulata:*
Dec	/	"Crown Jewels"

CONDITIONS

Aspect Needs a warm, sunny spot.
Site Well-drained soil enriched with manure or compost ahead of planting is essential. Very good plants can be grown on light, sandy soils.

GROWING METHOD

Sowing Seeds are best sown in short drills ½in deep March–May. Mark the sowing areas with a ring of light-colored sand and label if sowing more than one annual in the same bed. The seedlings will appear in rows and can be told from nearby weed seedlings quite easily. Thin the seedlings out so they are finally 4–6in apart by early summer. Alternatively, leave them to grow as small clumps of 4–6 plants every 12in or so.
Feeding Feeding is rarely needed but water well after the final thinning if the soil is dry.
Problems No special problems.

FLOWERING

Season Flowers appear early to mid summer.
Cutting Not usually used for cutting.

AFTER FLOWERING

General Leave a few plants to die down and self-seed. Others can be pulled up and composted.

LOBELIA
Lobelia

LOBELIA FLOWERS are tubular with a large lower "lip" divided into three rounded lobes. Dark flowers have pale throats.

IN THIS HANGING BASKET lobelias mingle with begonias and brachyscome, and bright red nasturtiums creep up from below.

FEATURES

Choose the bushier "edging" varieties for bedding schemes and the "trailers" for hanging baskets, flower bags, and containers. Flower color ranges from white through pink, mauve and white to blue, and striking two-toned varieties like "Riviera Blue Splash" are also available. Edgers grow 4–6in tall, trailers up to 18in long when well-fed, and plants have a similar spread. Varieties of *Lobelia erinus* are available as single or mixed colors, and modern coated seed makes sowing much easier. A range of varieties are available as young plants by mail order. Half-hardy.

LOBELIA AT A GLANCE

A half-hardy annual used as an edging plant or a trailing plant for baskets, with many small flowers. Frost hardy to 32ºF (zone 10).

		Recommended Varieties
Jan	sow 🖐	
Feb	sow/transplant 🖐	*Lobelia erinus:*
Mar	sow/transplant 🖐	**Edging varieties**
Apr	grow on 🖐	"Cambridge Blue"
May	harden off/plant 🖐	"Crystal Palace"
Jun	flowering 🌸	"Mrs Clibran Improved"
July	flowering 🌸	"Riviera Lilac"
Aug	flowering 🌸	**Trailing varieties**
Sept	flowering 🌸	"Cascade Mixed"
Oct	/	"Fountains Mixed"
Nov	/	"Regatta Mixed"
Dec	/	"String of Pearls Mixed"

CONDITIONS

Aspect Flowers best when grown in full sun.
Site Enrich soil with rotted compost or manure before planting. Drainage must be good, but lobelia must also have adequate moisture all through the season. For baskets and containers use multipurpose compost and add slow-release fertiliser granules before planting up.

GROWING METHOD

Sowing Sow January–March in a 3½in pot of multipurpose compost. Sow the tiny seeds evenly over the surface but do not cover, and put in a well-lit spot at 64ºF. When the seedlings form a green "mat," carefully tease them apart into small clumps of 4–6, and transplant each clump to one unit of a multi-cell tray. Grow on, harden off in late May and plant after frosts.
Feeding Feed fortnightly with high-potash liquid feed, and never allow the plants to dry out.
Problems Trouble-free, but if seedlings keel over in spring water with copper-based fungicide.

FLOWERING

Season Flowers appear from June onward.
Cutting Not suitable for cutting.

AFTER FLOWERING

General Go over plants with shears when they look untidy and water with liquid feed—this encourages more flowers. Compost in fall.

LOBULARIA
Alyssum

ALYSSUM IS COMPACT and this makes it the ideal edging plant to fill in between other summer bedders. Flowers smell of honey.

"CARPET OF SNOW" is used here in a bed to create living lines and patterns around slightly taller plants like these violas.

FEATURES

Lobularia maritima, alyssum, has masses of tiny flowers in various colors in round heads; white, pink, lavender, and purple. All varieties smell sweetly of honey, although you need to get up close. None grow more than 6in high, making alyssum ideal as an edging plant, but it is also useful for planting in pots, troughs, and hanging baskets.

CONDITIONS

Aspect Grow alyssum in a spot receiving full sun.
Site Must have well-drained soil and adding rotted

LOBULARIA AT A GLANCE

A low-growing hardy annual for edging summer bedding schemes, with honey-scented flowers. Frost hardy to 5°F (zone 7).

Jan	/	**Recommended Varieties**
Feb	sow ✍	
Mar	sow/transplant ✍	*Lobularia maritima :*
Apr	sow/grow on ✍	"Aphrodite"
May	sow/harden off ✍	"Creamery"
Jun	flowering 🌸	"Easter Basket Mixed"
July	flowering 🌸	"Easter Bonnet"
Aug	flowering 🌸	"Golf Mixed"
Sept	flowering 🌸	"Golf Rose"
Oct	/	"Little Dorrit"
Nov	/	"Rosie O'Day"
Dec	/	"Snow Carpet"
		"Snow Crystals"

---

organic matter helps retain soil moisture. For baskets and patio containers plant using multipurpose potting compost.

GROWING METHOD

Sowing Alyssum grown for bedding and containers is best raised in early spring. Sow a whole packet of seeds in February/March in a 3½in pot of multipurpose compost, and just cover. When seedlings are ½in tall split up into small clumps of 4–6 seedlings and transplant each to individual units of a multi-cell tray. This is especially useful to get a good spread of different flower colors when growing a mixed variety. Grow on and harden off in late May before planting out. Seeds can also be sown direct into the soil in an annual border during April/May ½in deep.
Feeding Extra feeding is unnecessary.
Problems Look out for slugs—they will attack newly-planted alyssum, especially after rain.

FLOWERING

Season Flowers often appear before planting and until late summer—clip them over with shears and water well to encourage a second flush.
Cutting Not suitable as a cut flower.

AFTER FLOWERING

General Seeds will self-sow very easily, and come up the following spring. Compost when finished.

LUNARIA
Honesty

THE SEEDHEADS *of* Lunaria annua *are sought after for dried flower arrangements. Here they are still in the green stages of growth.*

"ALBA VARIEGATA" has leaves splashed with creamy-white and also white flowers. It adds easy and quick color to spring borders.

FEATURES

Honesty, *Lunaria annua*, a hardy biennial is also known as the money plant because of its large circular, smooth, silvery seedheads that resemble coins. It grows up to 3ft tall and is a plant that is best left to do its own thing, self-seeding very quickly, and thriving under dry hedges where most plants will not grow, and will seed into mixed borders. Flowers are purple or white and appear in early spring, and variegated varieties are available.

LUNARIA AT A GLANCE

A hardy biennial grown for its pretty purple/white flowers followed by large silvery seedheads. Frost hardy to 5°F (zone 7).

		Recommended Varieties
Jan	/	
Feb	/	*Lunaria annua:*
Mar	sow/flowers 🖐️ 🌱	"Fine Mixed"
Apr	thin/flowers 🖐️ 🌱	"Mixed"
May	thin/flowers 🖐️ 🌱	
Jun	flowering 🌱	Variegated leaves
July	/	"Variegata"
Aug	/	
Sept	/	White flowers
Oct	/	"Alba Variegata"
Nov	/	
Dec	/	

CONDITIONS

Aspect Succeeds in sun or the shade cast by hedges and large shrubs.

Site Thriving in poor soils, plants grow larger still if they are sown into soil that has been improved with rotted manure or compost, and produce the best seedheads for drying.

GROWING METHOD

Sowing Mark out patches using sand and sow the large seeds 1in deep in short drills, with 2–3in between each seed in March. Seedlings are quick to appear and can be thinned or left to develop as they are. Next spring look out for seedlings and move them when small to where you want plants to grow.

Feeding Needs no extra feeding or watering.

FLOWERING

Season Flowers from early spring to early summer.

Cutting Can be cut for flowers but some must be left to set seed if you want the large, silvery heads.

AFTER FLOWERING

General Cut when the seedheads are mature and dry, on a warm day, and hang upside-down in a dry, airy place until you can carefully remove the outer skin of the pod. Leave a few plants to die down naturally and self-seed.

LUPINUS
Annual lupin

SHORTER AND SQUATTER than their perennial cousins, annual lupins can create a sea of color when sown in large drifts like this. As the flowers fade the spikes should be removed completely with pruning shears to divert energy into new flowers rather than seed pods.

FEATURES

By growing annual lupins from seed you can enjoy the features of their perennial relatives without giving up too much space in the yard. Annual lupins are smaller, growing between 1–3ft tall, but have very colorful spikes in mixed shades and also striking single colors such as the blue-flowered *Lupinus texensis*. Hardy annuals. Seeds and plants are poisonous if eaten.

LUPINUS AT A GLANCE

A hardy annual grown for its spikes of colorful and spicey-scented flowers during summer. Frost hardy to 5°F (zone 7).

Jan	/	Recommended Varieties
Feb	/	
Mar	/	Lupinus hybrids:
Apr	sow	"Biancaneve"
May	thin out	"New White"
Jun	flowering	"Pink Javelin"
July	flowering	"Pixie Delight"
Aug	flowering	"Sunrise"
Sept	flowering	Yellow flowers
Oct	/	*Lupinus luteus*
Nov	/	Blue flowers
Dec	/	*Lupinus texensis*
		Lupinus varius

CONDITIONS

Aspect Needs full sun.
Site Well-drained, light soil is best for annual lupins, but mix in rotted manure or compost.

GROWING METHOD

Sowing The large seeds can go straight into the ground in April, but to ensure germination the tough seed coat must be nicked with a sharp knife or rubbed down with a file until the pale inside just shows. Next, soak the seeds on wet tissue paper and sow when they have swollen up, 3–6in apart and 2in deep, where you want plants to grow. Thin seedlings to 6in apart when well established. To grow in pots do the same, sowing one seed to a 3½in pot, then plant out.
Feeding Lupins need no extra feeding.
Problems Fat green lupin aphids can kill entire plants, so use a spray containing permethrin.

FLOWERING

Season Flowers appear from midsummer.
Cutting Cut when some buds at the base of the flower spike are fully open.

AFTER FLOWERING

General Cut off to leave the nitrogen-rich roots to rot in the ground, and compost the tops.

MALCOLMIA
Virginian stock

PINK IS JUST *one of the colors found in Virginian stocks. Expect reds, yellows, and whites from a variety like "Fine Mixed."*

JUST FOUR WEEKS *after sowing plants will be in flower.* Malcolmia maritima *thrives in the thin light soils of seaside gardens.*

FEATURES

Keep a packet of Virginian stock, *Malcolmia maritima* seed to hand at all times and sow a pinch of seeds every two weeks in gaps and under windows—plants will flower just a month later. They grow 6–8in high with small, single, four-petalled, sweetly scented flowers in red, mauve, pink, yellow, and white from June–September. They can also be sown into patio tubs. Hardy annual.

MALCOLMIA AT A GLANCE

Hardy annual grown for its pink, red, yellow, or white flowers. Flowers a month after sowing. Frost hardy to 5°F (zone 7).

Jan	/	Recommended Varieties
Feb	/	*Malcolmia maritima:*
Mar	sow 🌱	"Fine Mixed"
Apr	sow/flowers 🌱🌼	"Mixed"
May	sow/flowers 🌱🌼	
Jun	sow/flowers 🌱🌼	
July	sow/flowers 🌱🌼	
Aug	sow/flowers 🌱🌼	
Sept	sow/flowers 🌱🌼	
Oct	sow 🌱	
Nov	/	
Dec	/	

CONDITIONS

Aspect	Prefers full sun but tolerates some shade.
Site	Will grow on most soils but needs good drainage to do well.

GROWING METHOD

Sowing	Seed can be scattered in small patches 12in across on the soil where you want flowers, and mixed in using your fingertips, or it is simply scattered along the cracks in paths and driveways, from March onward, and repeated every few weeks all through the summer. Mark sown areas in borders with a label or circle of light-colored sand. Seedlings soon come up and there is no need to bother with thinning. For early flowers the following spring sow in October.
Feeding	Not necessary.
Problems	Trouble-free.

FLOWERING

Season	Expect flowers all summer long with repeat sowings.
Cutting	Unsuitable as a cut flower.

AFTER FLOWERING

General	Pull up as soon as the plants are over, and resow. Self-sown seedlings soon appear.

MATTHIOLA

Brompton stock

WHEN BEDDED-OUT in spring Brompton stocks provide an early splash of color and fill the air with scent on warm days.

FLOWER COLOR varies, and it should be possible to see the color in the flower buds before you plant, ensuring an even display.

FEATURES

The sweetly scented flowers of Brompton stocks are held above the gray-green leaves on plants up to 18in tall. There is a full range of pastel colors with some stronger purples, crimson and magenta as well; the flowers are double. Derived from *Matthiola incana*, Brompton stocks are beautiful in massed spring plantings, giving off a delicious strong fragrance. They are grown as biennials.

CONDITIONS

Aspect   Need full sun and a sheltered position.
Site   Must have well-drained soil. Incorporate rotted manure or compost into the soil a few weeks before planting. Tall varieties will need short stakes to prevent their flowers flopping.

MATTHIOLA AT A GLANCE

A hardy biennial sown in summer for strongly-scented pink flowers the following spring. Frost hardy to 5°F (zone 7).

Jan	grow on	
Feb	plant	
Mar	plant	
Apr	flowering	**Recommended Varieties**
May	flowering	*Matthiola incana:*
Jun	sow	"Brompton Mixed"
July	sow/transplant	"Brompton Dwarf Mixed"
Aug	transplant	"Spring Flowering Mixed"
Sept	grow on	
Oct	grow on	
Nov	grow on	
Dec	grow on	

GROWING METHOD

Sowing   June/July is the time to sow seed, in a 3½in pot of multipurpose compost. When the seedlings are large enough, transplant one seedling to a 3½in pot of multipurpose compost, water well and grow on. Later, pot on into 5in pots. When the first frosts arrive take the young plants into a coldframe, cold greenhouse or porch, standing them outside during mild spells all through the winter months. Keep on the dry side and only water when they wilt. Plant out from February onward when the soil is workable, or pot on into large pots and grow in a cool conservatory or porch with canes for support.

Feeding   Do not feed until 2–3 weeks before planting out, then give a general purpose liquid feed.

Problems   Cabbage butterflies will lay eggs on the young plants in late summer and the caterpillars can strip leaves, so use a spray containing permethrin, or pick them off by hand.

FLOWERING

Season   Brompton stocks will fill beds and borders with color and scent during April and May, weather permitting. They perform best in calm, mild spells with plenty of sunshine. While most plants will have double flowers, there may be singles that can be put to one side, planted separately, and used for cutting.

Cutting   A good cut flower. Scald stems after picking and change vase water every couple of days.

AFTER FLOWERING

General   Dig plants up when the show is over and prepare the ground for summer bedding plants. Add to the compost heap/bin.

MIMULUS
Monkey flower

MONKEY FLOWERS *have blooms that are face-like and marked with intricate patterns and spotting. They are good for shade.*

PLANT MIMULUS *along the edges of a path. Monkey flowers will bloom in just nine weeks.*

FEATURES

Mimulus or monkey flower is grown as a half-hardy annual and is useful for summer bedding and containers, with bright flowers in a range of colors, mainly red and orange, on plants 12–18in tall and wide. It is very useful for growing in shaded and wet spots.

CONDITIONS

Aspect   Will grow in sun or shade.

MIMULUS AT A GLANCE

Grown as a half-hardy annual for bedding, windowboxes, and hanging baskets. Colorful flowers. Frost hardy to 5°F (zone 7).

		Recommended Varieties
Jan	/	
Feb	sow 🖐	**Mimulus hybrids:**
Mar	sow/transplant 🖐	"Calypso"
Apr	grow on 🖐	"Extra Choice Mixed"
May	grow on/harden 🖐	"Magic Ivory"
Jun	flowering 🌸	"Magic Pastels Mixed"
July	flowering 🌸	"Malibu"
Aug	flowering 🌸	"Malibu Orange"
Sept	flowering 🌸	"Malibu Sunshine"
Oct	/	"Queen's Prize Mixed"
Nov	/	"Sparkles"
Dec	/	"Viva"

Site   Needs moist soil so dig in plenty of rotted organic matter well-ahead of planting. Use a peat- or coir-based multipurpose compost for growing mimulus in containers. Add slow-release fertiliser granules when planting.

GROWING METHOD

Sowing   Sow in 3½in pots in February/March, barely covering the fine seed. Keep at 54°F in bright light and expect seedlings after about two weeks. When large enough transplant to cell trays and grow on until the end of May, then harden off and plant from mid-May onward, 6–12in apart, or in groups of 2–3 in troughs and pots.

Feeding   Feed monthly with liquid feed and ensure that containers never dry out or flowering will be reduced and plants damaged.

Problems   If slugs attack plants growing in shaded areas protect with slug pellets or scatter sharp grit to make a physical barrier. Container-grown plants suffer in excessive heat so move them to a position where they are out of midday sun.

FLOWERING

Season   Summer, from June onward.
Cutting   Not suitable for cutting.

AFTER FLOWERING

General   Pull up and compost when finished.

MOLUCCELLA

Bells of Ireland

THE FLOWERS OF Moluccella laevis *are actually small, pale, and found in the center of each of the showier bell-like bracts.*

MOLUCCELLA *is ideal for use in mixed borders to add a welcome touch of vivid green. Sow in patches 2ft across.*

FEATURES

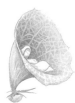

A half-hardy annual, also known as shell flower, moluccella is very lightly scented, and produces 2–3ft tall spikes in summer. It has small flowers surrounded by the more obvious and showy bell- or shell-like apple-green bracts. You can grow moluccella in flower beds and mixed borders, but its main value is as a cut flower, either fresh or dried. It is long-lasting when dried in late summer, the green spikes gradually fade from green to pale brown through fall and into winter.

CONDITIONS

Aspect   Needs an open spot in full sun.

MOLUCCELLA AT A GLANCE

A half-hardy annual grown for its tall spikes of green bracts that are used for drying. Frost hardy to 32°F (zone 10).

Jan	/	
Feb	sow 🌱	**Recommended Varieties**
Mar	sow 🌱	*Moluccella laevis*
Apr	transplant/grow 🌱	
May	plant/sow 🌱	
Jun	flowering 🌿	
July	flowering 🌿	
Aug	flowering 🌿	
Sept	flowers/cutting 🌿	
Oct	/	
Nov	/	
Dec	/	

Site   Must have good drainage, and working rotted manure or compost into the ground before sowing or planting helps. Avoid exposed, windy spots or the tall stems may be flattened.

GROWING METHOD

Sowing   Either sow seed in 3½in pots of multipurpose compost in February/March at 64°F, or sow directly in the soil where they are to grow in late April and May. Gradually thin out so plants are spaced 12–16in apart. Plants raised under cover are hardened off before being planted.

Feeding   If organic matter has already been added to the soil, extra feeding is not necessary, but keep plants well-watered during long dry spells.

Problems   Seeds can sometimes be slow and difficult to germinate, so put them in the bottom of a refrigerator for two weeks before you sow, to "chill" them, then sow in pots as described above and expect seedlings in 2–3 weeks.

FLOWERING

Season   Even after the actual flowers have faded the green bracts go on providing color and interest until they are cut for drying.

Cutting   Ideal as a cut flower, used fresh or dried. Cut when flowers are well-formed. Leaves can be removed to display the green bracts better. The stems dry to a light brown color.

AFTER FLOWERING

General   Remove roots when stems have been harvested, but leave a few behind to develop on the plant and finally shed seeds, which will self-sow.

MYOSOTIS
Forget-me-not

FORGET-ME-NOTS flower from early spring after growing slowly during the winter months. Flowers often have yellow "eyes."

"MONTE CARLO" early double tulips rising up through a haze of forget-me-nots is a springtime classic that is seldom bettered.

FEATURES

Forget-me-nots are useful spring bedding plants, producing swathes of pink, blue, or white flowers from April onward. They go well with bulbs like tulips which push up through the myosotis flowers. Grow as a hardy biennial and use shorter varieties such as "Blue Ball," reaching 6in, in winter and spring patio containers. None grow more than 12in tall, and these are the ideal choice for spring bedding displays. Available by mail order in fall as ready-grown young plants.

MYOSOTIS AT A GLANCE

A hardy biennial grown for its small flowers which appear in masses from early spring. Frost hardy to 5°F (zone 7).

		Recommended Varieties
Jan	/	
Feb	/	***Myosotis sylvatica:***
Mar	/	"Blue Ball"
Apr	flowering 🌱	"Carmine King"
May	flowers/sow 🌱🌱	"Compindi"
Jun	sow 🌱	"Indigo"
July	grow on 🌱	"Light Blue"
Aug	grow on 🌱	"Music"
Sept	grow on 🌱	"Rosylva"
Oct	plant 🌱	"Royal Blue"
Nov	/	"Spring Symphony Mxd"
Dec	/	"Victoria Mixed"

CONDITIONS

Aspect   Full or dappled sunlight is suitable.
Site   Responds well to soil with plenty of rotted compost or manure mixed in that holds plenty of moisture. When planting containers in fall ensure good drainage and use a multipurpose compost.

GROWING METHOD

Sowing   Seed is sown direct into the ground May–July, in drills ½in deep. Thin seedlings as they develop so plants are eventually 3–6in apart, keep weed free and water copiously in dry spells. Plant into their flowering positions/containers in October and water to settle in.
Feeding   Do not feed after planting in fall, but scatter a general granular fertiliser around plants in spring as they show signs of growth.
Problems   Powdery mildew can affect leaves but this is generally not worth treating.

FLOWERING

Season   From late winter to early summer.
Cutting   Not suitable for cutting.

AFTER FLOWERING

General   Remove plants to make way for summer bedding, but if you leave a few to die down they will self-sow into the soil.

NEMESIA

Nemesia

THE TWO-LIPPED FLOWERS *of nemesias come in an array of colors and they all have patterns deep in the flower's "throat."*

NEMESIAS CARRY THEIR *flowers in large, almost flat heads with individual flowers pointing off in all directions.*

FEATURES

No varieties of *Nemesia strumosa* grow more than 12in high making them ideal for beds and containers. Grown as a half-hardy annual, flowers can be single colors or bright and varied mixtures. Good as edging for troughs and windowboxes. Very easy to grow.

CONDITIONS

Aspect   Must have full sun to grow successfully.

NEMESIA AT A GLANCE

A half-hardy annual grown for its pretty lipped flowers, used for bedding and patio containers. Frost hardy to 32°F (zone 10).

Jan	/	Recommended Varieties
Feb	/	*Nemesia strumosa:*
Mar	sow 🌱	**Mixed colors**
Apr	sow/transplant 🌱	"Carnival Mixed"
May	harden off/plant 🌱	"Pastel Mixed"
Jun	flowering ❀	"Sparklers"
July	flowering ❀	"Tapestry"
Aug	flowering ❀	**Single colors**
Sept	flowering ❀	"Blue Gem"
Oct	/	"Fire King"
Nov	/	"KLM"
Dec	/	"National Ensign"

Site   In containers use multipurpose compost with slow-release fertiliser mixed well in. Soil with plenty of organic matter dug in well-ahead of planting gives good results, and must be well-drained.

GROWING METHOD

Sowing   Raise plants by sowing in small pots of soil-based seed compost starting in March/April (and repeating every few weeks for a succession of flowers), just covering the seeds. Keep at 60°F in a light place, and transplant to cell trays when seedlings are large enough to handle. Grow on and harden off in late May before planting after the last frosts, 6–12in apart. In containers make sure they are not swamped.

Feeding   Give a liquid feed to plants grown as bedding every two weeks, with a hand-held feeder. Regular watering in dry spells is vital.

Problems   Plants may rot off in heavy, wet soils.

FLOWERING

Season   For more flowerheads, pinch out growing tips of plants when they are 4in high.

Cutting   Not suited to cutting.

AFTER FLOWERING

General   Pull plants up when finished—this is quite often as they have a short flowering period.

NEMOPHILA
Baby blue eyes

NEMOPHILA MENZIESII *flowers are a brilliant sky-blue with a distinctive paler "eye," carried over bright green feathery leaves.*

NEMOPHILA *can be grown with other hardy annuals such as limnanthes, the poached egg flower, for a striking color combination.*

FEATURES

Nemophila is an easy annual sown in fall or spring. Flowers are sky-blue, white, or black/white. Plants grow to 8in high, with feathery leaves and a carpeting habit. Use them in borders, on rockeries, and around the edge of containers and windowboxes.

CONDITIONS

Aspect   Needs full sun or part shade to succeed.

NEMOPHILA AT A GLANCE

A hardy spreading annual grown for its flowers for beds, rockeries and container edges. Frost hardy to 5°F (zone 7).

Jan	/	Recommended Varieties
Feb	/	*Nemophila menziesii:*
Mar	/	(Also listed as *N.insignis*)
Apr	sow 🐾	"Baby Blue Eyes"
May	flowers/sow 🐾🐾	"Penny Black"
Jun	flowering 🐾	"Snowstorm"
July	flowering 🐾	
Aug	flowering 🐾	*Nemophila maculata:*
Sept	flowers/sow 🐾🐾	"Five Spot"
Oct	/	
Nov	/	
Dec	/	

Site   Needs well-drained soil, but mix in well-rotted organic matter before sowing to retain moisture. Nemophila will thrive in most multipurpose composts used in containers.

GROWING METHOD

Sowing   Sow seeds straight into the soil in fall or spring, in drills ½in deep. Seeds sown in fall will produce young plants that survive the winter and flower earlier. Gradually thin plants out so they are 3–6in apart as flowers appear.

Feeding   On well-prepared soil feeding is unnecessary, although large beds can be fed monthly with a general liquid feed applied through a hand-held feeder. Keep plants watered in dry spells or they may quickly die off.

Problems   Aphids can attack the soft leaves, so use a spray containing permethrin.

FLOWERING

Season   On fall-sown plants flowers appear from early spring to the first frosts, but appear slightly later on spring-sown plants.

Cutting   Not suitable for use as a cut flower.

AFTER FLOWERING

General   Leave plants to set seed and die back before removing—nemophila self-seeds and plants will appear on their own each spring.

NICOTIANA
Tobacco plant

"DOMINO SALMON PINK" is a popular variety of nicotiana because of its striking color and sheer flower power. Here in a bedding display it covers the ground and produces tubular, salmon-pink flowers non-stop through the summer. It is also useful for containers.

FEATURES

Not grown for tobacco but for their tubular flowers. Choose from dwarf modern varieties growing 1ft tall with upward-facing flowers, for bedding and containers, to *Nicotiana sylvestris* at 5ft for large borders—plant it behind other plants and especially against a dark evergreen background so that the large leaves as well as the flowers are shown off to best effect. Some release scent in the evening, so plant near doors and windows, or grow a few in large tubs that can be moved into the house or conservatory on a warm summer evening. Flowers can be pink to lime-green. A half-hardy annual. Widely available as young plants in a good selection of varieties.

NICOTIANA AT A GLANCE

A half-hardy annual grown for it colorful and often scented flowers, used in bedding/containers. Frost hardy to 32ºF (zone 10).

		Recommended Varieties
Jan	/	
Feb	/	***Nicotiana sanderae:***
Mar	sow 🖐	"Domino Mixed"
Apr	transplant/grow on 🖐	"Domino Salmon Pink"
May	harden off/plant 🖐	"Havana Appleblossom"
Jun	flowering 🌿	"Hippy Mixed"
July	flowering 🌿	"Lime Green"
Aug	flowering 🌿	"Merlin Peach"
Sept	flowering 🌿	
Oct	/	***Nicotiana langsdorfii***
Nov	/	
Dec	/	***Nicotiana sylvestris***

CONDITIONS

Aspect   Full sun or light shade. The flowers stay open longer in sun.

Site   Grow in well-drained, moisture-retentive soil with rotted manure/compost mixed in. For container growing use multipurpose compost.

GROWING METHOD

Sowing   Use 3½in diameter pots of multipurpose compost, sow the fine seed on the surface in March, but do not cover, and keep in a light place at 70ºF. Tiny seedlings emerge within three weeks. Transplant to cell trays of multipurpose compost or into 3½in diameter pots when each young plant has developed 3–4 small leaves. Grow on and harden off in late May, then plant after the last frosts in your area, 12–18in apart depending on the variety grown.

Feeding   Liquid feed weekly outdoors. Add slow-release fertiliser granules to container compost before planting.

Problems   Use a spray containing pirimicarb for aphids. Destroy plants attacked by virus, showing any puckered and mottled leaves

FLOWERING

Season   Flowers all summer. Nip off dead flowers.

Cutting   Not suitable.

AFTER FLOWERING

General   Remove plants after first frosts. It is possible to collect seed from *Nicotiana sylvestris* that can then be sown the following spring.

NIGELLA
Love-in-a-mist

"MISS JEKYLL" with semi-double blue flowers is a reliable variety of Nigella damascena. *Each flower has a feathery "collar."*

AFTER THE FLOWERS come the curiously attractive seedheads that give the plant its other common name, devil-in-a-bush.

FEATURES

Love-in-a-mist has fine, feathery leaves, with a fringe of foliage surrounding and slightly veiling each of the flowers, hence its common name. When the spiky seed pods appear it is also called devil-in-a-bush. Flowers are blue, pale and deep pink, white, or purple. Nigella grows 18in tall and is good for big drifts in beds or for cutting. Hardy annual. The variety "Transformer" has novel seed pods.

CONDITIONS

Aspect   Give it a sunny spot in an open position.

NIGELLA AT A GLANCE

A hardy annual grown for its flowers and its attractive, inflated seed pods which can be dried. Frost hardy to 5°F (zone 7).

		Recommended Varieties
Jan	/	
Feb	/	*Nigella damascena:*
Mar	sow ✍	"Dwarf Moody Blue"
Apr	flowers/thin 🌱✍	"Miss Jekyll"
May	flowering 🌱	"Miss Jekyll Alba"
Jun	flowering 🌱	"Mulberry Rose"
July	flowering 🌱	"Oxford Blue"
Aug	flowering 🌱	"Persian Jewels"
Sept	flowers/sow 🌱✍	"Shorty Blue"
Oct	/	
Nov	/	*Nigella orientalis:*
Dec	/	"Transformer"

Site   Needs good drainage but isn't too fussy about soils—rotted organic matter may be dug in ahead of planting, but this is not essential, and good results can be had on quite thin, poor soils as long as it is grown in full sun.

GROWING METHOD

Sowing   Sow in March or September, in short drills ½in deep. Thin plants as they grow so there is about 6–8in between them as they begin to produce flower buds. Leave thinning of fall-sown plants until spring in case there are winter losses. Plants can also be raised in cell trays, sowing 2–3 seeds per tray and removing all but the strongest seedling—nigella does not like disturbance.

Feeding   Does not need extra feeding during summer.

Problems   Plants are trouble free.

FLOWERING

Season   Fall-sown plants flower from late spring, spring-sown from early summer.

Cutting   Delightful cut flower. Remove foliage from lower part of stalk to prolong flower life.

AFTER FLOWERING

General   The inflated seed pods that form are useful in dried flower arrangements. Pick stems after pods have dried on the plant and hang upside-down in a warm, airy place. Nigella self-seeds prolifically and will produce masses of seedlings the following spring. Dead plants can be pulled up and composted.

OSTEOSPERMUM
Osteospermum

OSTEOSPERMUM *flowers are at their best in full sun in an open situation.*

CREATE A CARPET OF OSTEOSPERMUM BEDDING *in early summer that will continue to flower in flushes until the first frosts. Remember to propagate fresh plants each year.*

FEATURES

Many varieties of osteospermum can be bought in spring as young plants, but others can be grown from seed and treated as half-hardy annuals. Growing from seed is a cost-effective way of raising large numbers of plants quickly. Favorite plants can be potted-up in fall and kept in a well-lit frost-free place over winter, then increased by cuttings in spring. In mild areas plants will often survive the winter outdoors and carry on producing a few flowers except in severe spells. In some catalogs it is listed as dimorphotheca. Plants can grow 12–30in tall.

CONDITIONS

Aspect   Must have full, baking sun for best results.

OSTEOSPERMUM AT A GLANCE

A hardy/half-hardy annual grown for its brightly-colored daisy-like flowers that appear all summer. Frost hardy to 23°F (zone 9).

		Recommended Varieties
Jan	/	
Feb	/	Osteospermum hybrids:
Mar	sow	"Gaiety"
Apr	sow/transplant	"Giant Mixed"
May	harden off/plant	"Glistening White"
Jun	flowering	"Ink Spot"
July	flowering	"Potpourri"
Aug	flowering	"Salmon Queen"
Sept	flowering	"Starshine"
Oct	flowering	"Tetra Pole Star"
Nov	/	
Dec	/	

Site

Is not fussy about soil but it must be very well-drained. A sheltered spot with the sun beating down all day is ideal. Plants also perform well in containers and these should be sited in full sun facing south if possible. Use multipurpose compost.

GROWING METHOD

Sowing   March/April is the time to sow, sowing seed thinly in 3½in diameter pots of soil-based seed compost, and just covering. Germinate at 64°F in a bright spot. Seedlings are transplanted to cell trays or individual 3½in pots when large enough to handle. Harden off for two weeks and start planting from mid-May onward.

Feeding   Water well to establish and then water only in long spells of hot, dry weather. Extra feeding is unnecessary, but container-grown plants will benefit from occasional liquid feeds given for the benefit of other plants.

Problems   Aphids can attack the leaves, flower stalks and buds so choose a spray containing permethrin and wet both sides of the leaves.

FLOWERING

Season   Flowers appear from early summer onward with a peak later on when temperatures reach their highest.

Cutting   Flowers are unsuitable for cutting.

AFTER FLOWERING

General   After the main flowering give plants an overall clipping to tidy them up and maintain compact growth. Lift and pot favorite plants and keep frost-free over winter.

PAPAVER NUDICAULE
Iceland poppy

ICELAND POPPY has petals with the texture of crepe paper and a velvety sheen. The center of the flower is a mass of yellow stamens.

THEIR TALL STEMS mean the flowers of Papaver nudicaule *waft gently in the breeze, and look good like this, massed in bedding.*

FEATURES

Varieties of *Papaver nudicaule* are available in a wide range of colors and range from 10–30in tall depending on variety. They can be treated as either half-hardy annuals or hardy biennials sown in summer or fall. Tall varieties are used for cutting. Plants sown early flower from April onwards.

CONDITIONS

Aspect Can be grown in cool and warm areas.
Site Poppies need well-drained but moisture-retentive soil with plenty of rotted organic

matter added ahead of planting or sowing.

GROWING METHOD

Sowing Sow seed outdoors April-June or in September. Scatter the seed thinly along shallow drills ½in deep, and rake over with fine soil. Thin out when seedlings are 2in high, so that the spacing is ultimately at about 6–12in intervals by October. Do not disturb the fine roots when thinning out, and always water when finished to settle plants back in. Thin fall-sown poppies in spring in case of winter losses. For earlier flowers sow in pots at 60°F in February and grow in cell-trays, planting in late May.
Feeding Extra feeding not needed.
Problems Fall-sown plants may rot off in heavy soils, so sow in cell trays and keep dry in a coldframe over winter, planting out in spring.

FLOWERING

Season Flowers appear during early summer and should be picked off as they fade.
Cutting Excellent cut flower. Pick when buds are just opening. Singe stem ends before arranging.

AFTER FLOWERING

General Leave a few plants to self-seed, but otherwise pull up after the flowers are finished.

PAPAVER AT A GLANCE

A hardy biennial (or half-hardy annual) grown for its large showy flowers that appear in summer. Frost hardy to 5°F (zone 7).

Jan	/	Recommended Varieties
Feb	/	
Mar	/	*Papaver nudicaule:*
		Biennials
Apr	sow 🖐	"Large Flowered Special Mixture"
May	flowers/sow 🖐	
Jun	flowers/sow 🖐	"Meadow Pastels"
July	flowering 🌿	"Red Sails"
Aug	flowering 🌿	"Wonderland Mixed"
Sept	flowers/sow 🌿	
Oct	plant 🖐	**Half-hardy annuals**
Nov	/	"Summer Breeze"
Dec	/	

PAPAVER RHOEAS
Shirley poppy

THE UNOPENED BUDS of Shirley poppies gradually rise up from among the leaves before bursting open as the petals unfurl.

WHEN ALLOWED TO self-seed, poppies will come up among other plants. Unwanted plants are very easily pulled out.

FEATURES

Shirley poppies, varieties of *Papaver rhoeas*, generally grow to about 2ft high, have a very delicate appearance, and come in a wide range of colors including pastels. There are single or double varieties and they look effective in large drifts, but can also be sown in patches 1–2ft across and used as fillers in mixed borders. Each flower can be 3in across. A hardy annual.

PAPAVER AT A GLANCE

Shirley poppies are hardy annuals sown in spring or fall and grown for their large flowers. Frost hardy to 5°F (zone 7).

		Recommended Varieties
Jan	/	*Papaver rhoeas:*
Feb	/	"Angels Choir Mixed"
Mar	sow	"Angel Wings Mixed"
Apr	sow/thin	"Mother of Pearl"
May	flowers/sow	"Selected Single Mixed"
Jun	flowering	"Shirley Double Mixed"
July	flowering	"Shirley Single Mixed"
Aug	flowering	
Sept	flowers/sow	
Oct	/	
Nov	/	
Dec	/	

CONDITIONS

Aspect   Avoid any shade and grow in full sun.

Site   Must have very well-drained soil. Rotted compost or manure should be added to the soil a few weeks before sowing.

GROWING METHOD

Sowing   The fine seed can either be scattered on the soil and simply raked in, and the area marked with a circle of sand, or it can be sown in short ½in deep drills. March–May and September are the sowing times. Gradually thin out the seedlings until they are 12in apart, but avoid transplanting as they dislike disturbance. If sowing in fall leave thinning until the following spring in case of winter losses.

Feeding   Extra summer feeding is not required, but water thoroughly should plants start to wilt.

Problems   Trouble-free.

FLOWERING

Season   Fall-sown plants flower from late spring onward, while spring-sown flower in summer.

Cutting   Suitable as a cut flower if stems are scalded before arranging.

AFTER FLOWERING

General   Leave a few plants to die down and self-seed.

PELARGONIUM
Bedding geranium

DARK ZONED LEAVES and an enticing range of single and two-tone flower colors are characteristic of "Avanti Mixed."

YOU MAY BE SURPRISED to see an ivy-leaved geranium as good as "Summertime Lilac" coming true from seed.

FEATURES

Better known as geraniums, seed-raised pelargoniums are available with large bright flowerheads for bedding, and also as trailing "ivy-leaved" types. Seeds are sown January/February and need warmth to succeed, so consider buying them as young plants delivered ready-grown in spring. Varieties for bedding and patio containers grow no more than 1ft, while ivy-leaved types can spread and trail up to 2ft. Flowers may be single colors or mixtures—the new "ripple" varieties are eye-catching. Plant 1–2ft apart. All are half-hardy annuals.

PELARGONIUM AT A GLANCE

Half-hardy annuals grown for their flowers and also the attractive ivy-like foliage of some varieties. Frost hardy to 32°F (zone 10).

		Recommended Varieties
Jan	sow ✍	**Pelargonium hybrids:**
Feb	sow ✍	**For bedding**
Mar	transplant ✍	"Avanti Mixed"
Apr	pot on ✍	"Raspberry Ripple"
May	harden off/plant ✍	"Ripple Mixed"
Jun	flowering ✿	"Sensation Mixed"
July	flowering ✿	"Stardust Mixed"
Aug	flowering ✿	"Vidco Mixed"
Sept	flowering ✿	**Ivy-leaved varieties**
Oct	/	"Summertime Lilac"
Nov	/	"Summer Showers"
Dec	/	

CONDITIONS

Aspect   Must be grown in full sun.

Site   Well-prepared soil with rotted compost or manure mixed in gives best results. Soil must be well-drained, and when planting up containers use multipurpose compost with slow-release fertiliser mixed in. Bedding geraniums do well in terracotta containers.

GROWING METHOD

Sowing   Sow January/February in a heated propagator in a guaranteed temperature of 64°F. Seedlings appear in 2–3 weeks and can be transplanted to 3in pots or cell trays of multipurpose compost. Plants must have good light and a temperature of 61–64°F to grow well. Pot on into 4–5in diameter pots, harden off in late May, and plant out after the last frosts.

Feeding   Liquid feed bedding plants every 2–3 weeks.

Problems   Heavy wet soils can lead to rotting of the stems, so grow in containers. Snap off faded flowerheads to avoid grey mold.

FLOWERING

Season   Flowers appear from early summer onward.

Cutting   Not suitable.

AFTER FLOWERING

General   Pull up and compost. Favorite plants can be kept dry and frost-free over winter.

PETUNIA
Petunia

"FANTASY MIXED" is the latest in a new range of "milliflora" petunias with 1in flowers, ideal for containers and baskets.

MULTIFLORA PETUNIAS such as "Summer Morn Mixed" have 2in flowers and are suited to large patio tubs and bedding.

FEATURES

Petunias come in a wide range of different types depending on whether they are raised from seed or bought as young plants. Most petunias are perennials grown as half-hardy annuals. Seed-raised varieties fall into the following groups: Millifloras—small flowers 1in across on compact mounds, for containers and hanging baskets; Multifloras—plenty of 2in-wide flowers on bushy plants. For bedding and patio containers, with good weather resistance; Floribundas—intermediate in size between multifloras and grandifloras with 3in flowers; Grandifloras—large trumpet-like 5in flowers that can bruise in heavy rain and are best for containers in a sheltered position. These all grow 9-12in tall and can spread up to 2ft, and are also available as double-flowered varieties. Plant 9-12in apart. Flower color varies from single shades to striped, picotee, and other variations. Many seed-raised varieties are also widely available as young plants. An increasing number of petunias are only available as young plants, setting no seed. These are suited to container growing, and include many large double-flowered "patio" varieties such as "Able Mabel" and the vigorous Surfinias which can trail to 4–5ft—see page 78.

PETUNIA AT A GLANCE

A half-hardy annual grown for all-round use in summer bedding, hanging baskets and containers. Frost hardy to 5°F (zone 7).

Jan	sow 🖐	**Recommended Varieties**
Feb	sow 🖐	*Petunia hybrida:*
Mar	sow/transplant 🖐	**Millifloras**
Apr	pot on/grow on 🖐	"Fantasy Mixed"
May	harden off/plant 🖐	**Multifloras**
Jun	flowering 🌸	"Celebrity Bunting"
July	flowering 🌸	"Summer Morn Mixed"
Aug	flowering 🌸	**Floribundas**
Sept	flowering 🌸	"Mirage Mixed"
Oct	/	"Niagara Mixture"
Nov	/	**Grandifloras**
Dec	/	"Daddy Mixed"
		"Lavender Storm"

CONDITIONS

Aspect Choose a sunny, south-facing situation for petunias in beds and containers.

Site Avoid spots exposed to wind (which damages the flowers). Light, free-draining soil with rotted compost/manure mixed in is best. In containers use multipurpose compost.

PETUNIA "ABLE MABEL" is the first of a revolutionary new type of double-flowered "patio" petunia available only as young plants.

GROWING METHOD

Sowing　Sowing can take place January–March where a temperature of 70°F is possible. Sow onto the level surface of a 3½in pot of multipurpose compost, but do not cover seeds, and keep in the light. Seedlings will appear inside two weeks, and should be transplanted to cell trays of multipurpose compost when large enough. Pot on into 3½in diameter pots, grow-on and harden off before planting out in early June.

Feeding　Give a weekly liquid feed with a high-potash fertiliser to encourage flowers. Mix slow-release fertiliser granules with container compost.

Problems　Slugs eat leaves in wet weather—use pellets or slug traps. Plants with mottled, crinkled leaves affected by virus should be destroyed.

FLOWERING

Season　Flowers appear all summer. Pick off dead flowers regularly.

Cutting　Not suitable.

AFTER FLOWERING

General　Remove when flowers end.

FOR A TOUCH OF the patriotic, "Celebrity Bunting" is a stunning multiflora variety with blend of red, white, and blue flowers.

PHLOX
Annual phlox

"TWINKLE MIXED" is a striking variety of annual phlox growing about 6in tall with star-like flowers in various shades.

THE FLOWERS OF annual phlox open at their peak to make rounded heads of color that can completely fill summer containers.

FEATURES

Annual phlox are versatile plants that can be used for bedding, containers, and as unique cut flowers. They are half-hardy annuals, growing between 4–18in tall depending on the variety —taller are better for cutting. Flower color ranges from the blue of "Bobby Sox" to the varied shades of "Tapestry" which is also scented. Several varieties are now available as young plants by mail order. Flowers are long-lived and plants are easy to care for.

PHLOX AT A GLANCE

A half-hardy annual grown for its heads of colorful flowers, for bedding, containers, and for cutting. Frost hardy to 23°F (zone 9).

		Recommended Varieties
Jan	/	
Feb	sow 🖐	*Phlox drummondii:*
Mar	sow/transplant 🖐	"African Sunset"
Apr	grow on 🖐	"Bobby Sox"
May	harden off/plant 🖐	"Bright Eyes"
Jun	flowering 🌱	"Brilliant"
July	flowering 🌱	"Cecily Old & New Shades"
Aug	flowering 🌱	"Double Chanel"
Sept	flowering 🌱	"Phlox of Sheep"
Oct	/	"Tapestry"
Nov	/	"Tutti-Frutti"
Dec	/	"Twinkle Mixed"

CONDITIONS

Aspect Needs full sun.
Site Needs well-drained soil with manure or compost mixed in to improve moisture holding. Phlox grow well in multipurpose compost used to fill summer containers.

GROWING METHOD

Sowing Sow seed in February/March in 3½in pots of multipurpose compost, keep at 64°F, and expect seedlings in 1–3 weeks. Transplant to cell trays or 3½in pots, pinch out the tips when 3in high, and grow on until late May, then harden off and plant after the last frosts in your area.

Feeding Add slow-release fertiliser granules to compost before planting containers, which should be sufficient. Plants in beds can be given a liquid feed every 2–3 weeks in summer.

Problems Plants will struggle on heavy soils in a cold spring so delay planting until warmer weather.

FLOWERING

Season Flowers appear all summer until frosts.
Cutting Tall varieties are good for cutting and some like "Tapestry" have a strong, sweet scent.

AFTER FLOWERING

General Pull up after flowering and compost them.

PORTULACA
Sun plant

DOUBLE-FLOWERED *mixed varieties of portulaca come in a wide range of colors, but attractive single colors are also available.*

SUN PLANTS *can survive the winter in mild seaside gardens, and thrive in the well-drained soil of rockeries.*

FEATURES

Commonly known as sun plant, portulaca grows 6in high with a spreading habit and succulent leaves. The 2in flowers open in sun, although modern varieties open even on dull days. It thrives in poor, dry soils and is easily ruined by too much coddling. A half-hardy annual, for beds, pots, and rockeries.

CONDITIONS

Aspect   A hot, sunny position gives the best plants.

PORTULACA AT A GLANCE

Portulaca is a half-hardy annual grown for summer flowers, and gives good results even on thin soils. Frost hardy to 32°F (zone 10).

Month	Activity	Recommended Varieties
Jan	/	*Portulaca grandiflora:*
Feb	/	"Cloudbeater Mixed"
Mar	sow	"Double Mixed"
Apr	sow	"Kariba Mixed"
May	harden off/plant	"Patio Gems"
Jun	flowering	"Sundance"
July	flowering	"Sundial Mango"
Aug	flowering	"Sundial Mixed"
Sept	flowering	"Sundial Peppermint"
Oct	/	"Swanlake"
Nov	/	
Dec	/	

Site   Unless soil is very well-drained plants are prone to rotting. Otherwise plants grow and flower well even where the soil is quite poor—particularly in seaside gardens—as they are adapted to live on little water. Grow them on their own in patio containers, using soil-based potting compost mixed fifty-fifty with sharp grit. Do not feed, and water only when plants start to wilt. Place pots in blazing sunshine.

GROWING METHOD

Sowing   Sow seeds in March/April in 3½in pots of soil-based seed compost and germinate at 64°F in good light. Keep the seedlings on the dry side and transplant to cell trays of soil-based compost with grit added. Grow on, harden off in late May, and plant after frosts, watering in well, then only when plants wilt.

Feeding   Feeding portulaca is not necessary.

Problems   Seedlings will "damp off" if the compost is kept too wet. If they do fall over, water the pots lightly with a copper-based fungicide.

FLOWERING

Season   Flowers appear throughout summer and into early fall.

Cutting   Not suitable.

AFTER FLOWERING

General   Pull plants up after the first fall frosts and add their fleshy remains to the compost heap.

PRIMULA
Polyanthus

Not an F1 hybrid strain, but "Giant Superb Mixed" polyanthus are tough, large-flowered, and full of character.

F1 "Crescendo Mixed" exhibit the clearer, more uniform colors of a highly bred strain, but seed is more expensive.

FEATURES

Polyanthus, a hybrid type of primula, is perfect in patio pots or mass-planted in the garden for a stunning spring display. Its very brightly-colored flowers up to 2in across, on stems 6–12in tall, rise from neat clumps of bright green, crinkled leaves. A hardy perennial, it is grown as a hardy biennial for spring bedding and containers. Widely available as young plants.

CONDITIONS

Aspect Grows in full sun or light shade under trees.
Site Needs well-drained soil but with plenty of organic matter mixed in to help retain moisture—plants do not like to be bone dry at any stage while growing. For containers use multipurpose compost with gravel or chunks of styrofoam put in the base.

GROWING METHOD

Sowing Polyanthus seed can be tricky to germinate, and the most important rule is not to keep it too warm. Sow in 3½in pots of peat-based seed compost from March–July, barely cover, then stand outside in a covered, shaded spot out of the sun. Seedlings will appear 2–3 weeks later. Transplant to cell trays or 3½in pots of peat-based potting compost, and pot on into 5in pots when roots are well-developed. Grow during the summer in a shaded spot and do not let them dry out. Plant out in October where flowers are required the following spring, in beds or containers with bulbs and other plants.
Feeding Feed fortnightly with liquid feed in summer.
Problems Slugs can devour leaves so use slug pellets. Never bury the crowns or plants may rot.

FLOWERING

Season Flowers appear earlier in mild winters and carry on throughout spring.
Cutting Charming in spring posies.

AFTER FLOWERING

General Polyanthus taken from spring displays can be planted in borders where they will form large clumps and flower regularly every spring.

PRIMULA AT A GLANCE

A hardy biennial grown for its bright spring flowers for use in bedding and containers. Frost hardy to 5°F (zone 7).

Jan	/	Recommended Varieties
Feb	flowering	**Primula hybrids:**
Mar	flowers/sow	"Crescendo Mixed"
Apr	flowers/sow	"Dobies Superb Mixed"
May	flowers/sow	"Giant Superb Mixed"
Jun	sow/grow	"Gold Lace"
July	sow/grow	"Harlequin Mixed"
Aug	grow	"Heritage Mixed"
Sept	grow	"Large Flowered Mixed"
Oct	plant	"Pacific Giants Mixed"
Nov	/	"Spring Rainbow Mixed"
Dec	/	"Unwins Superb Mixed"

RANUNCULUS
Persian buttercup

DOUBLE FLOWERS are characteristic of Ranunculus asiaticus *varieties, and are all clear and bright as in this yellow-flowered plant.*

YOU CAN PLANT ranunculus in beds in spring when the worst of the winter is over, where they will give a bright show of color.

FEATURES

Hardy varieties of *Ranunculus asiaticus* are sown in late summer and fall for flowers during winter and spring. Seed-raised plants reach about 8–10in tall. Flowers are double. Young plants are sometimes offered in spring catalogs for delivery in late summer/fall ready for potting up. Add them to your spring containers as they come into flower—they will grow happily in a cold greenhouse or porch.

RANUNCULUS AT A GLANCE

A half-hardy annual grown for its large, double, buttercup-like flowers that appear in spring. Frost hardy to 23°F (zone 9).

Jan	grow	
Feb	grow	
Mar	flowering	
Apr	flowering	
May	flowering	
Jun	/	
July	/	
Aug	sow	
Sept	sow/transplant	
Oct	sow/grow	
Nov	grow	
Dec	grow	

Recommended Varieties

Ranunculus hybrids:
"Bloomingdale Mixture"

CONDITIONS

Aspect	Give as much sun as possible, and move containers into shelter during stormy or very frosty weather to stop damage to the flowers.
Site	Use a multipurpose compost for potting up and potting on, and for filling containers if you are creating an "instant" display as the plants come into flower from early spring.

GROWING METHOD

Sowing	Sow seed August–October in 3½in pots of peat-based compost, just covering the seeds. Stand outdoors in shade and keep moist—if they get too hot the seeds will not come up. When seedlings appear, bring them into full light and transplant when large enough into 4in pots. Grow outdoors until frosts start, then move under protection at night and out during the day. A cool porch is useful. In winter keep plants dry under cover.
Feeding	Feeding is not usually required.
Problems	No special problems.

FLOWERING

Season	Late winter and throughout spring.
Cutting	Cut when the buds are just unfurling.

AFTER FLOWERING

General	Plants will survive most winters in a sheltered spot and can be planted out in borders.

RESEDA
Mignonette

MIGNONETTE FLOWERS individually are insignificant, but the strong sweet fragrance is striking and well worth the effort of sowing.

THE FLOWERHEADS of Reseda odorata branch out as they develop. Sow along path edges so the fragrance can be enjoyed.

FEATURES

Mignonette has greenish, pink, red, yellow, or coppery flowers and grows to 12in. It is not particularly striking but is grown mainly for its strong, fruity fragrance—grow it near doors, windows, in patio pots, and near sitting areas to appreciate the qualities of this easily-grown hardy annual. It makes a good addition to cottage-style borders.

RESEDA AT A GLANCE

An easily grown hardy annual grown for its highly fragrant spikes of summer flowers. Frost hardy to 5°F (zone 7).

Jan	/	Recommended Varieties
Feb	/	*Reseda odorata:*
Mar	sow 🌱	"Crown Mixture"
Apr	sow/thin out 🌱	"Fragrant Beauty"
May	thin out 🌱	"Machet"
Jun	flowering 🌸	"Sweet Scented"
July	flowering 🌸	
Aug	flowering 🌸	
Sept	flowers/sow 🌸🌱	
Oct	sow 🌱	
Nov	/	
Dec	/	

CONDITIONS

Aspect	Needs full sun.
Site	Needs well-drained soil—dig in organic matter and add lime to acid soils.

GROWING METHOD

Sowing	Seed is sown directly into the ground in short drills ½in deep, 6in apart. Thin seedlings to 6in apart. Sowing can take place in March/April or September/October. Fall-sown plants need protecting with cloches during cold spells, and should not be thinned until spring. For pots, sow a pinch of seeds in each unit of a cell tray and thin to 2–3 seedlings, grow on and plant up when ready—reseda does not like root disturbance.
Feeding	Extra feeding is not usually necessary
Problems	Free of troubles.

FLOWERING

Season	Flowers appear from late spring on fall-sown plants, later on spring-sown.
Cutting	Cut when just a few flowers are opening. Dried flowers retain their fragrance.

AFTER FLOWERING

General	Pull plants up when they are past their best, but leave a few to produce seeds and self-sow.

RICINUS
Castor oil plant

THE VARIETY "IMPALA" is an excellent choice if you want bold, dark leaves for a dramatic show, growing 4ft tall.

BY MIDSUMMER the leaves of ricinus will have formed a dense canopy when grown in beds and planted 2–3ft apart.

FEATURES

A striking and memorable plant grown for its large, lobed, exotic-looking leaves, which are used for bedding, borders, and large tubs and containers. The often brightly-colored summer flowers are followed by spiny seed clusters. By nature an evergreen shrub, ricinus is fast growing and plants are raised fresh from seed each year—in long hot summers they can reach 6ft by 3ft tall and wide. Annual flowering climbers like thunbergia or ipomoea will climb its stems, their bright orange/blue flowers contrasting with the often deeply colored ricinus foliage. All parts of the plant are poisonous, especially the seeds. Treat as a half-hardy annual and scrap plants at the end of the summer.

RICINUS AT A GLANCE

A half-hardy annual with large, exotic leaves in a range of colors, and prized as bold bedder. Frost hardy to 32°F (zone 10).

Jan	/	**Recommended Varieties**
Feb	/	*Ricinus communis:*
Mar	sow	"Carmencita"
Apr	pot on	"Carmencita Pink"
May	harden/plant	"Impala"
Jun	leaves	"Gibbsonii"
July	leaves	"Red Spire"
Aug	leaves	"Zanzibarensis"
Sept	leaves	
Oct	/	
Nov	/	
Dec	/	

CONDITIONS

Aspect   Must have full sun. In northern areas choose a sheltered, south-facing spot.

Site   Soil should be well-drained with plenty of rotted compost or manure dug in. Use loam-based or multipurpose potting compost in containers. In windy spots, stake plants.

GROWING METHOD

Sowing   Soak the hard seeds overnight in warm water, then sow individually in 3½in diameter pots of soil-based compost, 2in deep in March, and keep at 70°F. Seedlings appear within three weeks. Pot on into 5in diameter pots when 6in tall. In beds plant 3–6ft apart after the last frosts.

Feeding   Apply liquid feed weekly from early summer, or mix slow-release fertiliser with the potting compost before planting.

Problems   Red spider mite attacks leaves. Wetting the leaves thoroughly every day can help, or use a spray containing bifenthrin.

FLOWERING

Season   The large leaves keep coming all summer long and are joined latcr by clusters of flowers that rise up above them.

Cutting   Leaves are useful for flower arranging, but avoid getting the sap on skin.

AFTER FLOWERING

General   Plants are usually killed by the first frosts of fall. Ripe seeds can be saved for sowing again the following spring.

RUDBECKIA
Coneflower

RUDBECKIA "RUSTIC DWARFS" is one of the best seed-raised foms. It produces a range of flower colors, yellow through to red, with dark firey centers or cones. Rudbeckia is also known as black-eyed Susan.

FEATURES

Rudbeckia or coneflower is one of the easiest and most versatile of all annuals. Try tiny "Toto" at just 8in in patio containers, or, where space allows, "Indian Summer" at 3ft. There are intermediate varieties in many shades, and some have an unusual and striking green center or "cone." Half-hardy.

CONDITIONS

Aspect   Rudbeckias need full sun to succeed.
Site   Soil must be well-drained but have rotted

RUDBECKIA AT A GLANCE

Grown for its large, showy flowers, rudbeckia grows well in bedding/containers and is half-hardy. Frost hardy to 5°F (zone 7).

Jan	/	Recommended Varieties
Feb	sow	*Rudbeckia hirta:*
Mar	sow/transplant	**Tall varieties**
Apr	grow on	"Goldilocks"
May	harden off/plant	"Indian Summer"
		"Marmalade"
Jun	flowering	"Rustic Dwarfs"
July	flowering	**Short varieties**
Aug	flowering	"Becky Mixed"
Sept	flowering	"Sonora"
Oct	flowering	"Toto"
Nov	/	**Green cone/centre**
Dec	/	"Irish Eyes"

compost or manure worked in before planting out. For container growing use multipurpose compost with slow-release fertiliser mixed in.

GROWING METHOD

Sowing   Sow February/March in pots of multipurpose compost and keep at 64°F. Seedlings appear in 1–2 weeks and are fast growing, soon ready for transplanting into cell trays or 3½in pots. Pot larger varieties on into 5in pots when roots fill the pots, and grow outdoors from mid-May, covering with garden fleece at night if frosty. Plant 6–24in apart after the last frosts.
Feeding   Rudbeckias are strong growers and need little extra feeding in the soil, but give container plants a fortnightly liquid feed unless fertiliser granules are mixed with the compost first.
Problems   Slugs can attack after planting so protect with slug pellets or a barrier of sharp grit.

FLOWERING

Season   Summer is the peak period for flowering and regular removal of faded heads should ensure some color right up to the first fall frosts.
Cutting   Good for cutting because of its strong stems. "Sonora" is especially good, and "Indian Summer" has flowers up to 8in across.

AFTER FLOWERING

General   Pull plants up and use for compost when they have been knocked down by frosts.

SALPIGLOSSIS
Salpiglossis

PETAL VEINING in salpiglossis is intricate and gives rise to the common name of painted tongue. Many different colors are available.

THE EXOTIC LOOK can be had by growing mixed salpiglossis in large bold drifts. Choose a variety like "Casino" at just 18in.

FEATURES

Salpiglossis blooms are trumpet-shaped and come in a range of colors, all with patterned veins. They must have shelter and warmth to do well, so for guaranteed success use them in containers on sunny patios or in south-facing beds protected from the wind. Choose mixed colors or try dark brown "Chocolate Pot," striking "Kew Blue" or even the blue/yellow mix Chili Blue." Half-hardy, growing up to 2ft. Available as young plants.

CONDITIONS

Aspect   Must be in full sun and protected from wind.

SALPIGLOSSIS AT A GLANCE	
Half-hardy annual grown for its exotic flowers but needing a sheltered spot in the yard to do well. Frost hardy to 32ºF (zone 10).	
Jan /	**Recommended Varieties**
Feb sow	***Salpiglossis sinuata:***
Mar transplant/sow	"Batik"
Apr grow on	"Bolero"
May harden off/plant	"Carnival"
Jun flowering	"Casino"
July flowering	"Chili Blue"
Aug flowering	"Chocolate Pot"/
Sept flowering	"Chocolate Royale"
Oct /	"Festival Mixed"
Nov /	"Flamenco Mixed"
Dec /	"Kew Blue"
	"Triumph Mixed"

Site   Drainage must be good or plants will rot—prepare soil by digging in plenty of rotted manure or compost well before planting. Use multipurpose compost in containers and make sure there is a 2in layer of gravel in the base to guarantee good drainage. Support plants with twigs or short canes as they get taller and begin to flower.

GROWING METHOD

Sowing   Sow in a 3½in pot in February/March and just cover the fine seed. Keep at a temperature of 75ºF in a light place, and when seedlings are large enough transplant to cell trays or 3½in pots. Grow on and then harden off in late May before planting after frosts in early June. Plants are quite brittle so handle carefully.

Feeding   Little additional feeding should be needed for plants in bedding displays, but containers can be liquid-fed every two weeks if slow-release fertiliser is not used; otherwise just water well.

Problems   The flowers are very prone to bruising and damage by wind and heavy rain, so pick off casualties after unsettled spells to avoid an attack by gray mold which can cause rotting.

FLOWERING

Season   Flowers appear throughout the summer.
Cutting   Weak-stemmed as a cut flower.

AFTER FLOWERING

General   Pull up after fall frosts and compost.

SALVIA
Scarlet sage

IF BRIGHT RED hurts your eyes, try one of the newer mixed salvia varieties containing more subtle shades of mauve, pink, and salmon.

TO APPRECIATE SALVIAS to the full, grow them in wide, low pans on the patio and keep fed and watered throughout the summer.

FEATURES

Salvia splendens or scarlet sage is used in bold groups in bedding and is also a useful container plant. Most varieties grow to 1ft with similar spread, but giants like "Rambo" with red flowers reach 2ft. Flowers are long and tubular, in spikes, and colors other than the typical vibrant red include pink, mauve, salmon, pastel shades, and even bicolors such as "Salsa Bicolor Mixed," with white tipped blooms. Choose single colors or mixtures. Grown as a half-hardy annual but is in fact a perennial plant. Several varieties are usually available as young plants by mail order.

SALVIA AT A GLANCE

A half-hardy annual grown for its often bright flowers which are useful for bedding and pots. Frost hardy to 32°F (zone 10).

		Recommended Varieties
Jan	/	
Feb	sow	*Salvia splendens:*
Mar	sow/transplant	"Blaze of Fire"
Apr	grow on	"Firecracker"
May	harden off/plant	"Orange Zest"
Jun	flowering	"Phoenix Mixed"
July	flowering	"Phoenix Purple"
Aug	flowering	"Rambo"
Sept	flowering	"Red Arrow"
Oct	/	"Scarlet King"
Nov	/	"Scarlet O'Hara"
Dec	/	"Sizzler Burgundy"
		"Sizzler Mixed"

CONDITIONS

Aspect   Plant salvias in a warm spot in full sun.
Site   Tolerates a wide range of soils but drainage must be very good or plants may rot. Mix in well-rotted compost or manure before planting and use multipurpose compost for filling patio pots and windowboxes. Make sure plastic containers have drainage holes, and drill some if necessary, then put in 2in of gravel.

GROWING METHOD

Sowing   February/March is the time to sow salvias, using 3½in pots of multipurpose compost. Lightly cover seeds and keep in a bright spot such as a windowsill at 64°F; expect seedlings in 2–3 weeks. Transplant into cell trays or 4in pots, grow on, harden off in late May before planting 6–12in apart.
Feeding   Liquid feed plants in beds monthly. Mix slow-release fertiliser with compost at planting.
Problems   Heavy wet soils can cause root rots, and slugs and snails will eat leaves of young plants in damp and wet spells. Use slug pellets.

FLOWERING

Season   Cut faded spikes right back and plants will often produce a succession of flowers right into the late summer months.
Cutting   Not suitable.

AFTER FLOWERING

General   Dig out when over and compost.

SCABIOSA
Sweet scabious

FOR A COTTAGE GARDEN feel, make sure you include pink scabious heads with other plants such as this white candytuft.

AS A BORDER FILLER sweet scabious is very useful and can be sown in any gaps during March and April for flowers from June.

FEATURES

Also known as pincushion flower, varieties of *Scabiosa atropurpurea* are easily-grown hardy annuals. The rounded flowerheads come in shades of blue, mauve, purple, pink, white, or crimson. Growing to 12–20in with tall, wire-like stems, scabious is best used for growing in big patches and for use as a filler in between other plants in a mixed or cottage-garden style border. A related variety, "Paper Moon," is grown for its spherical heads of dry bracts that follow the flowers.

SCABIOSA AT A GLANCE

An easily-grown hardy annual with rounded flowerheads that are useful in borders and for cutting. Frost hardy to 5°F (zone 7).

Jan	/	**Recommended Varieties**
Feb	/	*Scabiosa atropurpurea:*
Mar	sow	"Ace of Spades"
Apr	sow/thin out	"Border Hybrids"
May	thin out	"Dobies Giant Hybrids"
Jun	flowers/thin out	"Double Mixed"
July	flowering	"Dwarf Double Mixed"
Aug	flowering	"Tall Double"
Sept	flowering	
Oct	/	*Scabiosa stellata:*
Nov	/	"Paper Moon"/"Ping
Dec	/	Pong"/"Drum Stick"

CONDITIONS

Aspect Prefers full sun and protection from wind.
Site Well-drained soil is best—prepare ground by digging in organic matter well in advance.

GROWING METHOD

Sowing Sow outdoors March/April where plants are to flower, in short drills ½in deep. Thin plants to 6–12in apart by early summer, and keep weed-free.
Feeding Extra feeding in summer is not needed.
Problems No particular problems.

FLOWERING

Season Flowers appear from mid- to late summer.
Cutting Excellent and long-lasting cut flower.

AFTER FLOWERING

General Pull plants up when they are over.

SCHIZANTHUS

Poor man's orchid

THE EXOTIC APPEAL of schizanthus earns it the common name of poor man's orchid. Each flower has a network of darker veining.

THE FINELY DIVIDED leaves are the perfect foil for the large heads of flowers. Varieties like "Pierrot" are distinctly dome-shaped.

FEATURES

Also known as butterfly flower, schizanthus is stunning when used in bedding or in large pots and troughs. It has fern-like foliage and brilliantly colored, trumpet-shaped flowers in rich tones of pink, purple, magenta, pastels, or white. The flower throats are intricately patterned. Only the dwarf varieties reaching 8–12in are worth growing outdoors, and they must have shelter from strong winds and the hot midday sun. Schizanthus is a half-hardy annual and very sensitive to even slight frost.

SCHIZANTHUS AT A GLANCE

A half-hardy annual grown in containers on patios or in south-facing borders for summer flowers. Frost hardy to 32°F (zone 10).

Jan	/	**Recommended Varieties**
Feb	/	*Schizanthus pinnatus:*
Mar	sow 🖐	"Angel Wings Mixed"
		"Disco"
Apr	transplant 🖐	"My Lovely"
		"Pierrot"
May	harden off 🖐	"Star Parade"
Jun	plant/flowers 🖐 🌿	
July	flowering 🌿	

CONDITIONS

Aspect	Must be sheltered and have full sun.
Site	Well-drained soil that has been enriched before planting with rotted manure or compost produces strong plants. Peat- or coir-based potting compost guarantees good results when containers are used.

GROWING METHOD

Sowing	Seeds are sown in March at 61°F in small pots of peat- or coir-based seed compost, and seedlings appear after 1–2 weeks. Transplant to cell trays or 3½in pots, grow through spring and plant after hardening off, in early June. Space plants 6–12in apart. Pinch out growing tips when 4in high to make bushy plants.
Feeding	Liquid feed monthly, and water containers regularly—if slow-release fertiliser is added to the compost extra feeding is not necessary.
Problems	No special problems.

FLOWERING

Season	Flowers reach a peak in mid to late summer and keep coming if faded stems are removed.
Cutting	Not usually used as a cut flower.

AFTER FLOWERING

General	The soft leafy plants soon break down when put on the compost heap.

SENECIO
Dusty miller

A WHITE WOOLLY LAYER covering the otherwise green leaves gives Senecio cineraria *its attractive silvery-gray appearance.*

OVERWINTERED PLANTS will keep on growing the following season, get larger, and also produce heads of bright yellow flowers.

FEATURES

Grown for its attractive silver-gray foliage, *Senecio cineraria* is often found listed under "cineraria" in seed catalogs. Use in bedding schemes and as a foliage container plant. Plants grow up to 12in tall and wide in summer, but if left outdoors over winter can be twice that if the yellow flowerheads are allowed to develop. Usually grown as a half-hardy annual, senecio is naturally an evergreen, eventually developing a tough woody base.

SENECIO AT A GLANCE

Prized for its silver-gray leaves and grown as a foliage bedding plant and for using in containers. Frost hardy to 23°F (zone 9).

Jan	/	**Recommended Varieties**
Feb	sow 🖐	
Mar	sow 🖐	*Senecio cineraria:*
		Fine, divided leaves
Apr	transplant 🖐	"Dwarf Silver"
May	harden off/plant 🖐	"Silver Dust"
Jun	leaves 🌿	
July	leaves 🌿	**Rounded leaves**
Aug	leaves 🌿	"Cirrus"
Sept	leaves 🌿	
Oct	leaves 🌿	
Nov	/	
Dec	/	

CONDITIONS

Aspect Must have full sun.
Site Well-drained soil is needed, but plants do well in light, sandy soils, especially in seaside gardens. Use multipurpose compost in pots.

GROWING METHOD

Sowing Start plants in February/March at 68°F, by sowing seed in a small pot of compost and just covering. Expect seedlings after 1–2 weeks and keep in good light. Keep compost slightly on the dry side to avoid "damping off." Transplant to cell trays or 3½in pots, grow on, then harden off at the end of April and plant in May, 12in apart.

Feeding Planted containers need liquid feed every two weeks, and regular watering. Plants stand dry spells outside but water them if they wilt.

Problems If seedlings collapse, give a light watering with a copper-based fungicide.

FLOWERING

Season The silvery leaves are attractive all summer.
Cutting Foliage can be used in arrangements.

AFTER FLOWERING

General Pull up and compost in fall. In many areas plants will survive the winter if left and produce bigger clumps of leaves and flowers.

SOLENOSTEMON
Coleus or flame nettle

"BLACK DRAGON" is a modern variety of coleus with black-edged, pinkish-red leaves, and is useful for specific color themes.

LEAF COLOR is apparent from an early age with solenostemon, making it possible to group the different colors when planting.

FEATURES

Look under "coleus" in seed catalogues for a wide range of varieties of this striking foliage plant. A half-hardy annual, solenostemon is a valuable bedding and container plant with large multicolored leaves that add a certain "tropical" and eccentric element to summer gardens. As well as mixtures, dark-leaved varieties like "Black Dragon" can be put to use in color-themed displays. Size range is 8–18in depending on variety, and it is important to remove all flowerheads as they appear or the plant will stop producing leaves. Varieties are available as young plants.

CONDITIONS

Aspect   Flame nettles need full sun to really thrive and also need shelter from persistent winds.

Site   Well-drained soil that has had plenty of rotted manure or compost mixed in before planting produces strong plants with good color. Where they are grown in patio containers use multipurpose compost with slow-release fertiliser granules added at planting time.

GROWING METHOD

Sowing   March is the time to sow seed, in 3½in pots of multipurpose compost, just scattering the seed on the surface—don't cover. Keep at 75°F where they get bright light. Seedlings grow slowly but when they are large enough, transplant to 3½in pots or large cell trays. Pinch out the growing tip when plants are 3in tall to encourage bushy growth and the maximum number of leaves. Harden off in late May and plant after frosts, 6–12in apart.

Feeding   Liquid feeding every two weeks during summer maintains vigorous leaf growth. If slow-release fertiliser has been used, feed only monthly with half-strength liquid feed.

Problems   Slugs and snails attack young plants, so protect with slug pellets or a barrier of sharp grit around each plant.

FLOWERING

Season   All flowers should be removed as soon as they appear to encourage maximum leaf growth. Plants generally stay colorful until frosts.

Cutting   Not suitable.

AFTER FLOWERING

General   Favorite plants can be lifted and potted up in fall, and kept dry over winter in a frost-free greenhouse or cool room. Take cuttings from these plants in spring.

SOLENOSTEMON AT A GLANCE

A half-hardy annual grown for its brightly-colored leaves which are used in bedding and for patio pots. Frost hardy to 32°F (zone 10).

Month	Activity	Recommended Varieties
Jan	/	**Solenostemon scutellarioides:**
Feb	/	
Mar	sow	"Black Dragon"
Apr	transplant	"Camelot Mixed"
May	harden off/plant	"Dragon Sunset & Volcano, Mixed"
Jun	leaves	"Fairway"
July	leaves	"Flame Dancers"
Aug	leaves	"Magic Lace"
Sept	leaves	"Salmon Lace"
Oct	/	"Top Crown"
Nov	/	"Wizard Mixed"
Dec	/	

TAGETES
Marigold

THESE SINGLE-FLOWERED French marigolds are much daintier than their loud cousins with larger double flowers.

SINGLE FLOWER COLORS are useful in color-themed displays and this double-flowered French marigold would go well with blues.

FEATURES

The marigold "family" is made up of African and French types, and tagetes. All are easily grown half-hardy annuals and their flowers are among some of the loudest available—bright oranges, reds, yellows, and bronzes that set borders and containers alight. Plant size varies from 6in dwarfs to 3ft giants, and there are unusual flower colors such as "Vanilla" and even bright stripey-petalled varieties such as "Mr Majestic." Use them for bold bedding or as reliable patio container plants. Flowers can be single, semi or fully double and up to 3in across. Many varieties are also available as young plants.

TAGETES AT A GLANCE

A half-hardy annual grown for its bright flowers which are ideal for bedding and patio pots/troughs. Frost hardy to 32°F (zone 10).

Jan	/	
Feb	sow 🖐	**Recommended Varieties**
Mar	sow 🖐	**African marigolds**
Apr	sow/transplant 🖐	"Inca Mixed"
May	harden off/plant 🖐	"Shaggy Maggy"
		"Vanilla"
Jun	flowering 🌸	**French marigolds**
July	flowering 🌸	"Boy O'Boy Mixed"
Aug	flowering 🌸	"Mischief Mixed"
Sept	flowering 🌸	"Mr Majestic"
		Tagetes tenuifolia:
Oct	/	"Lemon Gem"
Nov	/	"Red Gem"
Dec	/	

CONDITIONS

Aspect   Must have a sunny position.
Site   Marigolds are not too fussy about soils, but mixing in rotted compost before planting helps keep soil moist. For container growing use multipurpose compost with slow-release fertiliser granules mixed well in. Tall varieties of African marigold need shelter from wind.

GROWING METHOD

Sowing   All marigolds can be sown February–April, but a May sowing on a windowsill will also be successful as they are fast growers and soon catch up. Just cover the large seeds with compost and keep at 70°F. Seedlings will appear in a week and can be transplanted to cell trays. Grow on, harden off in late May and plant after frosts. Nip off any flower buds that appear before and two weeks after planting.
Feeding   Fortnightly liquid feeding keeps plants in beds going strong. Keep containers well watered.
Problems   Slugs and snails can strip plants overnight so protect with slug pellets in wet/warm spells.

FLOWERING

Season   Early sowings produce earlier flowers and vice-versa. Late sowings provide handy color in late summer and if grown in pots, plants can be used to revive flagging summer containers.
Cutting   African marigolds are useful for cutting.

AFTER FLOWERING

General   Pull plants up when finished and compost.

THUNBERGIA
Black-eyed Susan

BLACK-EYED SUSAN is one of the brightest and showiest of all the annual climbers, and readily entwines the stems of other plants. It hates having its roots disturbed so sow seeds straight into small pots, and pot 2–3 plants on together when necessary. Plant out after frosts.

FEATURES

The flowers of thunbergia can be orange, yellow, or white, and sometimes the black eye is missing altogether. Grow as a half-hardy annual for indoors and out. Outdoors, grow up wigwams of 5ft canes, either in borders, or large tubs for a moveable display of color. In hanging baskets thunbergia soon entwines the chains, making an effective camouflage. In patio tubs train plants up through other tall annuals like ricinus and sunflowers, or plant them around the base of outdoor plants in early summer. In colder areas grow plants in the conservatory or porch to guarantee a good show of flowers. Seed pods tend to set very easily which reduces the ability of the plant to keep flowering, so nip these off regularly.

THUNBERGIA AT A GLANCE

A half-hardy annual climber flowering in summer for patio containers, baskets, and bedding. Frost hardy to 32°F (zone 10).

Jan	/	
Feb	/	**Recommended Varieties**
Mar	sow	*Thunbergia alata:*
Apr	pot on/grow on	"Susie Mixed"
May	harden/plant out	
Jun	flowers	
July	flowers	
Aug	flowers	
Sept	flowers	
Oct	/	
Nov	/	
Dec	/	

CONDITIONS

Aspect A south-facing spot in full sun is essential. In conservatories direct hot sun should be avoided or the leaves may be scorched.

Site In containers use multipurpose compost with slow-release fertiliser added. Well-drained, moisture retentive soil, with rotted manure or compost is needed outdoors.

GROWING METHOD

Sowing Soak seeds overnight then sow three to a 3½in diameter pot in March. Germinate at 64°F. Germination is erratic and seedlings may take a month to emerge. A small wigwam of canes will support the shoots. Grow several plants on in large pots during May, then harden off and plant after the last frosts. They dislike root disturbance.

Feeding Liquid feed once a week in summer.

Problems Red spider mite attacks leaves. Wet the leaves daily or use a spray containing pirimiphos-methyl. Indoors use the predator phytoseiulus. Whitefly will feed on the leaves and cause sticky "honeydew." Use a spray containing permethrin or the natural encarsia indoors.

FLOWERING

Season Flowers appear all summer and the flowering period is extended when plants are grown under some form of protection.

Cutting Not suitable.

AFTER FLOWERING

General Nip off faded flowers. Remove outdoor plants after frosts and add to the compost heap.

THUNBERGIA

TITHONIA
Mexican sunflower

THE DAHLIA-LIKE FLOWERS of tithonia have an "exotic" feel to them and each one can be up to 3in across, on strong stems.

THE HEART-SHAPED LEAVES of Mexican sunflower are an added bonus, and each flower also has a distinct swollen "neck."

FEATURES

Tithonia, as its common name suggests, comes from warmer areas, so does well when there is plenty of sun. Grow as a half-hardy annual. "Fiesta del Sol" is just 1ft tall, while "Torch" can reach 4ft. Flowers are large, exotic-looking and dahlia-like, red-orange, and have a distinct swollen "neck."

CONDITIONS

Aspect   Must have full sun or plants will suffer.

TITHONIA AT A GLANCE

A half-hardy annual grown for its large orange flowers on strong stems. Use in bedding and pots. Frost hardy to 32°F (zone 10).

Jan	/	**Recommended Varieties**
Feb	sow	
Mar	sow	*Tithonia rotundifolia:*
Apr	sow/transplant	**Tall varieties**
May	harden off/plant	"Goldfinger"
Jun	flowering	"Torch"
July	flowering	
Aug	flowering	**Short varieties**
Sept	flowering	"Fiesta del Sol"
Oct	/	
Nov	/	
Dec	/	

Site   Not fussy about soil, but needs good drainage. Plant in a fairly sheltered spot away from cold driving winds. Tithonia has a tendency to go pale and yellow when growing conditions are poor. Grow plants in containers if the soil is heavy, using multipurpose compost.

GROWING METHOD

Sowing   Sow seeds February to April in 3½in pots of multipurpose compost, just covering them, and germinate at 64°F in a warm place or heated propagator. Transplant to individual 3½in pots or large cell trays and grow on. Harden off for 2–3 weeks and plant in early summer when the soil warms up. If seedlings or young plants turn yellow they are being kept too cold. Can also be sown outdoors in early June where plants are to flower.

Feeding   Feed container-grown plants twice a month with liquid feed.

Problems   Slugs may attack the leaves after early summer rains so protect with slug pellets.

FLOWERING

Season   Flowers appear from midsummer and later sowings continue to give color into fall.

Cutting   Suitable for use as a cut flower.

AFTER FLOWERING

General   Pull up after flowering. May self-seed.

TORENIA
Wishbone flower

WISHBONE FLOWER gets its common name from the dark markings found on the lower lip of the flowers of some varieties.

SHELTER IS ESSENTIAL for success with torenia, which can also be potted up and grown-on as a flowering plant for indoors.

FEATURES

Wishbone flower needs to be in the "front row" of a summer bedding scheme, or used around the edge of pots and troughs. The variety "Susie Wong" has bright yellow flowers with black throats, and a spreading habit making it ideal for baskets. Half-hardy annuals, torenias grow no more than 1ft in height.

CONDITIONS

Aspect   Choose a sheltered spot with sun.

TORENIA AT A GLANCE

A low growing half-hardy annual grown for its colorful lipped flowers, for edging in beds and pots. Frost hardy to 32°F (zone 10).

Jan	/	**Recommended Varieties**
Feb	/	
Mar	sow 👌	*Torenia fournieri:*
Apr	sow/transplant	"Clown Mixed"
May	grow/harden off	"Susie Wong"
Jun	plant/flowers	
July	flowering	
Aug	flowering	
Sept	flowering	
Oct	/	
Nov	/	
Dec	/	

Site

Dig in rotted manure or compost a few weeks ahead of planting out, or use multipurpose compost for container growing. Soil and compost used must be free-draining. Avoid planting where winds are persistent.

GROWING METHOD

Sowing   Sow the very small seeds in pots or trays in March/April, barely cover and keep at 64°F in a well-lit place. When large enough the seedlings can be transplanted to cell trays and grown on until late May, then hardened off and planted well after the last frosts, 6in apart, or in groups in patio pots. Plant five plants to a 16in diameter hanging basket, four around the sides and one in the center. "Susie Wong" will creep in and out of other plants.

Feeding   Feed regularly every 2–3 weeks with a balanced liquid plant food.

Problems   Trouble free.

FLOWERING

Season   Throughout summer.
Cutting   Not used as a cut flower.

AFTER FLOWERING

General   Pull or dig out the plants when flowering has stopped. They will sometimes self-seed, and they will then produce seedlings in the following year.

TROPAEOLUM
Nasturtium

"MOONLIGHT" is a climbing variety of nasturtium reaching 6ft with soft yellow flowers against light green leaves.

FOR DOUBLE VALUE grow "Alaska Mixed" with light green leaves speckled with creamy-white, plus red and yellow flowers.

FEATURES

With big seeds and quick growth, tropaeolum, better known as nasturtium, is one of the easiest of all hardy annuals to grow. Plants just 9in tall are perfect for bedding and patio planters, while others will scramble up thought a dull hedge. The color range is huge, and single and mixed colors are available. For pretty leaves too, grow "Alaska Mixed," which is speckled with white.

TROPAEOLUM AT A GLANCE

A hardy annual grown for its colorful flowers and often variegated leaves. For beds and containers. Frost hardy to 32°F (zone 10).

		Recommended Varieties
Jan	/	*Tropaeolum majus:*
Feb	sow 🖐	**Tall climbers**
Mar	sow 🖐	"Climbing Mixed"
Apr	transplant 🖐	"Jewel of Africa"
May	transplant 🖐	**Short, mixed colors**
Jun	flowering 🌿	"Alaska Mixed"
July	flowering 🌿	"Gleam Mixed"
Aug	flowering 🌿	"Tip Top Mixed"
Sept	flowering 🌿	**Single colors**
Oct	/	"Empress of India"
Nov	/	"Gleaming Mahogany"
Dec	/	"Moonlight"

CONDITIONS

Aspect	Needs full sun.
Site	Poor, thin soil gives excellent results when grown under hedges or in bedding displays.

GROWING METHOD

Sowing	Simply push the large seeds 1–2in into the soil in April, in groups of 3–5 where plants are to flower. Fleshy seedlings appear 2–3 weeks later and they can all be left to develop and form a large clump. If needed for containers, sow three seeds to a 3½in pot at the same time and keep warm until seedlings appear, then keep outdoors.
Feeding	Feeding encourages leaves at the expense of flowers, although if other plants are growing in a container or basket, some extra feeding is unavoidable. Don't feed plants growing in soil.
Problems	Aphids and caterpillars feed under the leaves, so check regularly and squash if seen.

FLOWERING

Season	Flowering is all summer long.
Cutting	Not used cut, but flowers and the peppery leaves can be used raw in summer salads.

AFTER FLOWERING

General	Pull up and compost. Self-seeds very easily.

VERBENA
Verbena

SOFTER PASTEL SHADES can be found in modern varieties of verbena—these are just a few flowers of the variety "Romance Pastels."

"PEACHES & CREAM" has a unique color that makes it a real winner, at 8in, for patio containers and hanging baskets.

FEATURES

Most verbenas grow 6–12in tall and are prized for their heads of bright flowers. Mixtures or single shades like "Peaches & Cream" are used for planting containers or for bedding. Raise from seed—although this is tricky—or grow them from mail order plants. Most trailing verbenas are not seed raised but bought as ready-grown plants from garden centres and mail order catalogs in spring.

VERBENA AT A GLANCE

A half-hardy annual used in bedding and containers. Masses of bright flowers appear during summer. Frost hardy to 32ºF (zone 10).

Jan	/	
Feb	/	
Mar	sow 🖎	
Apr	transplant 🖎	
May	grow/harden off 🖎	
Jun	flowering 🌼	
July	flowering 🌼	
Aug	flowering 🌼	
Sept	flowering 🌼	
Oct	/	
Nov	/	
Dec	/	

Recommended Varieties

Verbena hybrida:
Mixed colors
  "Crown Jewels"
  "Novalis Mixed"
  "Raspberry Crush"
  "Romance Pastels"
Single colors
  "Adonis Blue"
  "Apple Blossom"
  "Peaches & Cream"
Spreading/trailing
  "Misty"

CONDITIONS

Aspect	Needs full sun for best results.
Site	Use multipurpose compost in containers, and mix rotted compost with soil outdoors.

GROWING METHOD

Sowing	To succeed with verbena seed, sow on the surface of peat-based seed compost in March and cover the seeds with a thin layer of fine vermiculite. Water and keep at 70ºF. Seedlings appear 2–3 weeks later, and should be kept slightly on the dry side. When large enough, transplant seedlings to cell trays or individual 3in pots, and grow on. Plant after hardening off in late spring/early summer.
Feeding	Feed monthly with balanced liquid feed.
Problems	Powdery mildew can attack leaves—use a spray containing sulfur at the first signs.

FLOWERING

Season	Flowers appear all summer.
Cutting	Not used for cutting.

AFTER FLOWERING

General	Pull up when finished and use for compost.

VIOLA CORNUTA
Viola

DIMINUTIVE "Bambini" violas are guaranteed to steal your heart with their inquisitive whiskery faces.

FOR A TOUCH OF DRAMA try combining the moody "Blackjack" with a clear yellow variety in a hanging basket.

FEATURES

Violas are smaller than pansies but they are no less prolific, and what they lack in size they make up for in sheer character. Most are varieties of *Viola cornuta*, and all are quite hardy, being sown in spring or summer. Grow single colors, mixtures like "Bambini," or trailing yellow "Sunbeam" for hanging baskets. Violas grow to about 6in, making bushy little plants for bedding or containers. Try planting them in cottage style wicker baskets. Available as young plants.

VIOLA AT A GLANCE

A hardy annual grown for its pretty little pansy flowers which appear on branching plants. Frost hardy to 5°F (zone 7).

		Recommended Varieties
Jan	/	
Feb	sow 🖐	Viola hybrids:
Mar	sow 🖐	"Bambini Mixed"
Apr	sow/flower 🖐🌼	"Blackjack"
May	sow/flower 🖐🌼	"Blue Moon"
Jun	sow/flower 🖐🌼	"Cuty"
July	sow/flower 🖐🌼	"Juliette Mixed"
Aug	grow on/flowers 🌼	"Midnight Runner"
Sept	grow on/flowers 🌼	"Princess Mixed"
Oct	plant 🖐	"Sorbet Yesterday, Today & Tomorrow"
Nov	/	"Sunbeam"
Dec	/	

CONDITIONS

Aspect Grows well in sun or dappled, light shade.
Site Soil does not need to be over-prepared, but must be well-drained. For container growing use multipurpose compost.

GROWING METHOD

Sowing Sow from February under cover for flowers the same summer, or outside May–July for flowers the following spring. Either way, sow in a 3½in pot of multipurpose compost and barely cover seeds. In early spring keep at 60°F and transplant seedlings when large enough to cell trays, grow, harden off, and plant in late May. When summer sowing, stand the pot outside in shade to germinate then treat seedlings the same, planting out in October where you want the plants to flower.

Feeding Extra feeding is not usually necessary.
Problems Use slug pellets if the leaves are attacked.

FLOWERING

Season Spring-sown plants flower during summer, summer-sown the following spring/summer.
Cutting The delicate cut stems of "Queen Charlotte" are sometimes used for making scented posies.

AFTER FLOWERING

General Plants often carry on as short-lived perennials, and also self-seed freely.

VIOLA TRICOLOR
Wild pansy

EACH FLOWER of wild pansy is like a tiny whiskered "face" and individual plants all vary from each other very slightly.

ONE PLANT left in the ground to mature through the summer will shed hundreds of seeds that will germinate the next spring.

FEATURES

Viola tricolor is the wild pansy, also known commonly as heartsease or Johnny-jump-up. It is usually grown as a hardy annual but can also be treated as a biennial. Much daintier than its relatives the pansies, these plants are at home in cottage-style beds and as pot edging. A few single-colored varieties are available, such as the unusual "Bowles' Black," having black flowers with a small central yellow "eye."

CONDITIONS

VIOLA AT A GLANCE

A hardy annual grown for its pretty little pansy flowers which appear on branching plants. Frost hardy to 5°F (zone 7).

		Recommended Varieties
Jan	/	
Feb	sow	*Viola tricolor*
Mar	sow	Single colors:
Apr	sow/flower	Blue
May	sow/flower	"Prince Henry"
Jun	sow/flower	Yellow
July	sow/flower	"Prince John"
Aug	grow on/flowers	
Sept	grow on/flowers	
Oct	plant	
Nov	/	
Dec	/	

Aspect	Grows well in sun or dappled, light shade.
Site	Soil does not need to be over-prepared, but must be well-drained. Multipurpose compost is best for growing *Viola tricolor* in containers.

GROWING METHOD

Sowing	Sow from February under cover for flowers the same summer, or outside May–July for flowers the following spring. Either way, sow in a 3½in pot of multipurpose compost and barely cover seeds. In early spring keep at 60°F and transplant seedlings when large enough to cell trays, grow, harden off, and plant in late May. When summer sowing, stand the pot outside in shade to germinate, treat seedlings the same, and plant in October.
Feeding	Extra feeding is not usually necessary.
Problems	Use slug pellets if the leaves are attacked.

FLOWERING

Season	Spring-sown plants flower during summer, summer-sown the following spring/summer.
Cutting	Not suitable for cutting.

AFTER FLOWERING

General	Pull plants up and compost, or leave a few to shed seeds. They will sometimes grow as perennials and last for several years.

VIOLA WITTROCKIANA
Pansy

PANSY FLOWERS have "faces" that tend to face the sun, especially in early spring. Use them in patio pots with bulbs like tulips.

"JOLLY JOKER" is a unique and prolific variety of summer-flowering pansy with orange and rich royal purple two-tone flowers.

FEATURES

Pansies are hardy and will flower almost all year around. There are two groups, summer flowering, and fall/winter flowering. None grow more than 8in tall. Flowers are like large flat "faces" up to 3in across. Colors vary enormously from single, pastel shades to striking bicolors, and are available in mixtures or as single colors. Many varieties are available as young plants by mail order. Most are varieties of *Viola wittrockiana*.

VIOLA AT A GLANCE

Hardy and grown either as an annual or a biennial for flowers in summer and fall/winter. Frost hardy to 5°F (zone 7).

Jan	/
Feb	sow
Mar	sow
Apr	sow/flower
May	sow/flower
Jun	sow/flower
July	sow/flower
Aug	grow on/flowers
Sept	grow on/flowers
Oct	plant
Nov	/
Dec	/

Recommended Varieties

Viola wittrockiana:
Summer flowers
 "Antique Shades"
 "Padparadja"
 "Romeo & Juliet"
 "Watercolors"
Fall/winter flowers
 "Homefires"
 "Ultima Pastel Mixed"
 "Universal Mixed"
 "Velour Mixed"

CONDITIONS

Aspect Fall/winter pansies need full sun. Summer flowering varieties like dappled shade.

Site Add plenty of manure to the soil. Winter pansies need excellent drainage. Use multipurpose compost for containers.

GROWING METHOD

Sowing Sow from February under cover for flowers the same summer, or outside May–July for flowers the following spring. Either way, sow in a 3½in pot of multipurpose compost and barely cover seeds. In early spring keep at 60°F and transplant seedlings when large enough to cell trays, grow, harden off, and plant in late May. When summer-sowing, stand the pot outside in shade to germinate then treat seedlings the same, planting out in October where you want the plants to flower.

Feeding Liquid feed summer plants every two weeks.

Problems Spray with permethrin if aphids attack.

FLOWERING

Season Spring-sown plants flower in summer, fall-sown from October onward.

Cutting Pansies last a few days in water.

AFTER FLOWERING

General Pull up and compost when finished.

ZINNIA
Zinnia

ZINNIA FLOWERS tend to come as doubles but plants sometimes appear that are single like this. Zinnias are good bee plants.

IF PINCHED WHEN YOUNG zinnias make bushy, branching plants that fill gaps in mixed borders quickly. Take dead flowers off.

FEATURES

There is a zinnia for every garden. Dwarf varieties at 6in tall are suited to beds and containers, while "Dahlia-Flowered Mixed" has big heads on stems 2ft high, and is useful for mixed borders. Modern varieties have fully double flowers, and some like "Zebra Mixed" are stripey. "Starbright Mixed" is an unusual variety with masses of small orange and gold flowers. Red, yellow, pink, scarlet, orange, lavender, purple, white, and even green are typical flower colors. Half-hardy annual.

ZINNIA AT A GLANCE

A half-hardy annual grown for its bright flowers in a wide range of colors, for bedding and cutting. Frost hardy to 32°F (zone 10).

Jan	/	Recommended Varieties
Feb	/	Zinnia hybrids:
Mar	/	**Tall varieties**
Apr	/	"Allsorts"
May	sow	"Dahlia-Flowered Mixed"
Jun	thin out	"Zebra Mixed"
July	flowering	**Short varieties**
Aug	flowering	"Belvedere"
Sept	flowering	"Fairyland"
Oct	flowering	"Persian Carpet Mixed"
Nov	/	"Starbright Mixed"
Dec	/	"Thumbelina"

CONDITIONS

Aspect Zinnias enjoy heat and need sun and shelter.
Site Must have well-drained soil, previously improved with rotted organic matter. For containers use multipurpose compost.

GROWING METHOD

Sowing Although half-hardy, zinnias grow best when sown direct where they are to flower, in short drills ½in deep. Do this is in May and cover seedlings with a piece of garden fleece on frosty nights. Thin out seedlings so the young plants are eventually 6–24in apart, depending on their final size. To grow dwarf varieties in containers sow 2–3 seeds to a 3in pot at the same time, leave just the strongest, grow on, and plant when ready, not disturbing the roots.
Feeding Extra feeding is usually not necessary.
Problems Powdery mildew can be a problem, so avoid planting too close—sulfur sprays can help. Stem rots cause plants to collapse suddenly.

FLOWERING

Season Flowers appear from midsummer onward.
Cutting Very good cut flower. "Envy Double" is a striking plant with double green flowers.

AFTER FLOWERING

General Pull up in fall and compost.

GROWING CLEMATIS

Swagging walls, fences and pergolas or scrambling over trees and shrubs, clematis is the queen of climbers. It ascends by wrapping leaf stalks around a support and blooms for

FEATURES

Starry or flared bell flowers, in a kaleidoscope of dashing hues, are freely borne on new or year-old shoots. Many, such as Chinese lantern flowered Clematis *tangutica* are followed by spheres of feathery seed heads, dramatic when sparkling with frost.

There are species and hybrids to suit every situation and most are frost hardy. In tiny yards or on patios or terraces, you can grow smaller varieties so that they cascade over the side. Although most shed their leaves, a small group of sculptural evergreens have a special charm.

There are six fascinating groups:
Early-flowering species (Group 1)
Choice spring varieties include blue C. alpina 'Pamela Jackman', C. macropetala 'Markham's Pink' and white C. montana f. grandiflora.

Early-flowering hybrids (Group 2)
Resulting from crossing two or more species and cheering early summer, double-flowered, silver-mauve 'Belle of Woking' and purple-blue 'The President' glorify a west-facing wall or fence.

Late-flowering species (Group 3)
Clouds of tiny, fragrant, starry white blooms billowing from C. flammula and flared tulip-like red blooms peeping from C. texensis 'Princes of Wales', make July to October special

Late-flowering hybrids (Group 3)
It's rich purple 'Jackmanii' and any of the C. viticella clan, such as white and green 'Alba Luxurians' flourish from July to September.

Evergreens (Group 1)
Skeined with scented pink-budded, white-flowered blooms in spring, leathery scimitar-leaved 'Apple Blossom' enjoys a warm, sunny aspect. In winter, reddish-spotted, cream- and fern- leaved *C. cirrhosa* 'Freckles' prefers in a sheltered spot.

Herbaceous (Group 3)
A small non-climbing group of clematis that complements border perennials. An enchanting

LEFT: Many people grow clematis because of their attractive and often scented flowers: they come in a wide variety of different colors, shapes and sizes. They also have long-flowering periods so, if you

combination is the deep blue and hyacinth-flowered C. heracleifolia 'Wyevale, to 3ft, which flowers from August to September, and scented, white and bronzy leaved recta purpurea, 2-4ft. Both flower from late summer to fall.

CONDITIONS

| Aspect | There are species and varieties to suit every spot. |
| Site | Soil should be free-draining and fortified with well-rotted organic matter. Ideally, you should grow plants where the roots are shaded but stems can climb into bright sunlight. |

GROWING METHOD

Planting	Take out a generous hole 18in across and 15in deep and fork old manure or rotted garden compost into the base. Fill in with a mix of fertile top soil and add two well worked-in gloved handfuls of bone meal. Tap the plant from its pot, tease out coiled roots at the base and set the root ball 6in deeper than it was in its pot to encourage a multi-stemmed branching system to form. Water in copiously. Finish by mulching with old manure or pulverized bark to keep roots cool. Fan-train shoots over trellis or plastic-coated wires spaced 1ft apart.
Feeding	Clematis are voracious feeders, so top dress them with 113g per square meter (4oz per square yard) of blood, fish and bone meal in spring, mid and late summer. Water it in.
Pruning	*Group 1 (Early flowering and evergreens):* Don't cut them back unless they outgrow their allotted space. Shorten flowered shoots when blooms fade to just above a joint. *Group 2 (Early flowering hybrids):* Cut out dead shoots in February. Shorten stems when blooms fade to encourage a second flush of blossom in late summer. Dead-head regularly. *Group 3 (late flowering hybrids, species and herbaceous varieties):* Shorten all stems to fat buds 12in from the base in February or March.
Problems	Slugs and snails rasp bark and devour new buds and shoots. Control them with blue slug pellets. Wilt Disease causes shoots to collapse suddenly and die back to ground level. Thankfully, new stems appear from the base. There are no effective fungicides, so instead cut back affected shoots. Plant deeply so that if stems die back to soil level, underground buds are triggered into growth and replace them.

FLOWERING

NELLY MOSER

MONTANA 'TETRAROSE'

'Nelly Moser', which blooms twice (in May and June and again in September), flaunts 7-9in carmine-striped, pale mauve-pink blooms. It colors well if trained against an east-, north- or west-facing wall or fence, but objects to direct sunlight which causes its magnificent flowers to fade. Growing only to around 10ft, it's ideal for clothing an arch, or a trellis around a patio.

It flowers on shoots made the previous year, so remove dead or weak stems in late June and tie in the strongest new growth to flower the following season. Devise a riveting focus by planting it next to it lavender-blue 'Lasurstern' which is similar in height and should be treated in the same way.

Transforming May and June with a foam of large 3-4in lilac-rose flowers amid bronzy-green foliage, Clematis montana 'Tetrarose' grows to 20ft on a large wall, fence or sizable pergola.

Though happy facing north, east, south or west, it is sensible to capitalize on its hardiness by planting it to cloak a cold, shaded wall or fence seared by icy winds. Alternatively, set it to climb and drape a conifer or umbrella over old apple. No pruning is necessary. If it outgrows its allotted space, trim it when flowers fade in early summer.

NELLY MOSER AT A GLANCE

Flowers well when positioned against an east-,west- or north-facing wall or fence. Fully hardy to frost hardy.

JAN	rest	NOV	rest
FEB	rest	DEC	rest
MAR	planting		
APR	feeding, mulching	OTHER EARLY-FLOWERING FORMS:	
MAY	flowering		
JUN	flowering	'Royalty'	
JULY	pruning, propagation	'Proteus'	
AUG	tie in shoots	'Guernsey Cream'	
SEPT	flowering		
OCT	planting		

MONTANA AT A GLANCE

This variety is especially good for covering a north-facing wall. Fully hardy to frost hardy.

JAN	rest	OCT	planting
FEB	rest	NOV	rest
MAR	planting, feeding	DEC	rest
APR	planting, mulching	OTHER MONTANA FORMS:	
MAY	flowering	'Elizabeth'	
JUN	flowering	'Alexander'	
JULY	pruning	'Pink Perfection'	
AUG	propagation, feeding		
SEPT	planting		

SILVER MOON

'Silver Moon' is a large-flowered variety that will enliven a dull north-facing wall or fence, but will be equally happy elsewhere. Cloaked with pearly-pink blooms, which will grow to 5-7in across, on stems to 8-10ft high, it brightens May, June and August. It is suitable, too, for planting in a large patio pot from which blossom-clad shoots will spill appealingly. Create a feature all will admire by combining it with a contrasting-hued climbing rose, such as 'Royal Gold', scarlet 'Sympathie', yellow and red 'Night Light' or rose-pink 'Parade'. No pruning is necessary unless it outgrows its allotted space. Then, in a mild spell in February or early March, shorten all stems to within a pair of fat buds 12-18in from the ground.

SILVER MOON AT A GLANCE

Thrives when grown against a west-facing wall. Fully hardy

JAN	rest	OCT	planting
FEB	pruning	NOV	rest
MAR	planting, feeding	DEC	rest
APR	planting, mulching		
MAY	flowering		
JUN	flowering		
JULY	propagation		
AUG	flowering, feeding		
SEPT	planting		

LIBERATION

Introduced in 1995 to commemorate the Channel Islands' 50th year of freedom from oppression by occupying forces, 'Liberation' is a joy. Flaunting deep pinkish-red blooms with cerise-barred petals, to 6in in diameter, on robust stems to 10ft, it enchants us in late spring and early summer and again in early fall. It needs tempering with white-flowered plants because of its vibrant colors. Ideally, twin it with Solanum jasminoides 'Album', a scrambler whose clusters of starry flowers stud shoots from July to October. It performs on year-old stems, so no regular pruning is required - merely shorten dead or weak growth to stocky buds from February to early March. Prune again, cutting back flowered stems by half their length in midsummer, to trigger new shoots and a dazzling bonus of blossom in the fall.

LIBERATION AT A GLANCE

Flourishes against an east or west-facing wall. Fully hardy to frost hardy.

JAN	rest	NOV	rest
FEB	rest	DEC	rest
MAR	planting, feeding		
APR	planting, mulching		
MAY	flowering		
JUN	flowering		
JULY	propagation		
AUG	feeding		
SEPT	planting		
OCT	planting		

GROWING
PERENNIALS

Many of the most beautiful and best-loved flowering plants are perennials. Like annuals, perennials provide a colorful display, but they have the advantage that they don't need to be changed at least twice a year. Perennials are easy-care plants that have a major place in low-maintenance gardens.

Perennials remain alive for a number of years, unlike annuals, which usually last only one season, and biennials, which grow and flower through a second season or year. Perennials form a variable group in terms of their size and foliage, flower shape, style, and color. In fact, there is a perennial to suit almost every climate, aspect, and soil, and some can even be grown in containers. Perennials can also be planted among shrubs, to form a background for bulbs or annuals, or in their own separate areas. Perennial borders make lively, exciting features.

ABOVE: The white form of the purple coneflower, showing its attractive, recurved petals.

LEFT: A tender, bright pink argyranthemum, and scabious, in the foreground, add perennial interest to this colorful, mixed border featuring soft hues offset by green.

PERENNIALS COMBINE with annuals to form a free-flowing, rich, colorful border, a highlight of mid-summer in this gorgeous cottage yard. A pink shrub rose is flanked by two varieties of aster, while deep blue delphiniums add scale and height at the rear.

EVERGREEN OR HERBACEOUS?

Some perennials are evergreen but many are herbaceous. Most herbaceous perennials grow rapidly during the spring and summer to flower during the summer and fall. After flowering they gradually die back to the crown or fleshy roots, and they remain dormant during cold winters. Since most of the hardy herbaceous perennials originate from climates with very severe, cold winters, they die down naturally in the fall. In warmer areas, where they do not become completely dormant and some growth continues all year around, the plants do not live as long. However, it is simple to renew these perennials, since division is easy and most increase rapidly. In time, a few can even become invasive.

PLANTING PERENNIALS

Soil preparation

Because perennials are long-term plants and close-planted, good soil preparation is essential. Although some perennials, such as astilbes and hostas, enjoy damp soil, many prefer well-drained conditions. If you are planting any of the latter group, check your garden's drainage before planting. Dig some holes in the bed, fill them with water, and see how long it takes to drain away. If there is still water in the holes 12

PERENNIALS FOR SUN AND SHADE

SUNNY BORDERS

- Agapanthus
- Delphinium
- Diascia
- Eryngium
- Gypsophila
- Helenium
- Hemerocallis
- Oenothera
- Papaver
- Sedum
- Stachys

SHADY BORDERS

- *Alchemilla mollis*
- Aquilegia
- Bergenia
- Candelabra primula
- Digitalis
- Epimedium
- *Gunnera manicata*
- Helleborus
- Hosta
- Polygonatum
- Primula
- Pulmonaria

PURE WHITE shasta daisies light up the summer garden, putting on a strong display from early summer to early fall.

A HIGH STONE WALL marks the boundary of this meadow yard filled with golden fern-leaf yarrow, daisies, and purple loosestrife.

hours later, you will need to improve the drainage by installing a system of sub-soil drains.

If the soil is very heavy clay, which remains wet but not waterlogged for a long time, you should dig approximately 10.5oz per sq yd of gypsum. Digging in large quantities of decayed manure or compost a few weeks before planting will also improve clay soils, and it is essential in sandy soils that have poor moisture and nutrient retention.

Thorough weeding of the area is necessary, too, as it is difficult to remove weeds in densely planted beds. Remove the weeds you can see, dig or fork over the area again, water, and wait for the next group of weeds to emerge. You may need to repeat this step if the area has been neglected for any length of time. Hand weeding or spraying with glyphosate should eliminate most weeds, but you will need to be persistent to control oxalis, bindweed, and ground elder. This sounds like a lot of work when you are eager to plant out your garden, but it will be worth the wait and the effort in the long term.

Planting perennials from containers

Garden centers and nurseries will stock some perennials, especially when they are in flower. These can be planted in the yard, like any other container-grown plant. When the plant is removed from its pot, loosen the rootball a little so that the roots can extend into the surrounding soil. It is essential that the planting hole is about twice the width of the container and approximately the same depth. The soil level around the plant should be exactly the same as it was in the container. Give a thorough soaking after planting. Also apply a deep mulch to the soil around the plant.

Planting bare-rooted perennials

There are also nurseries that specialize in perennials. These nurseries often advertise in popular gardening magazines, have detailed catalogs with thorough plant descriptions, and sell by mail-order. Plants are delivered during their dormant season, which for the majority is from late fall through the winter. Plants are mailed bare-rooted or in small pots,

THESE GOLDEN-YELLOW, green-tipped spikes of a red hot poker cultivar provide a strong focus in this pastel border.

THE TALL, VERTICAL CLUMP of pink dahlias and the midnight blue spires of delphinium are a colorful mix. They form a bright, imaginative backdrop for the rich mix of annuals and perennials edging this beautiful garden bed, clearly illustrating the versatility of perennials.

carefully packed and labelled. On arrival, they should be planted immediately. However, if the ground is frozen, or you are not ready to plant them, either unpack and water them (if necessary) and store in a bright, cool, frost-free place, or "heel in" as a temporary measure. To do this, dig a trench large enough to contain the plant roots in a sheltered part of the yard. Finally, lay the plants on their sides, cover the roots with soil, and lightly water them.

When planting bare-rooted plants, again make sure the hole is at least twice the width of the rootball, and deep enough to take the roots without kinking them. If some roots are very long, trim them cleanly with pruning shears. Hold the plant in the hole with one hand and fill the hole, poking soil between the roots. Sometimes you can make a slight mound in the center of the hole so that the roots can be spread out over it, keeping the crown high. Make sure the crown of the plant is not buried: if necessary, lift the plant and push more soil in around the roots.

Water thoroughly immediately after planting, if the soil is dry, but until the plants have developed plenty of shoot growth they will not require too much watering. The area around the plants should be mulched. If the soil has been well prepared, feeding at this time is not necessary, but you may give a very light sprinkling of general fertilizer.

CARE OF PERENNIALS

Perennial plantings in areas that have been well prepared need little maintenance. You must remove deadheads through the flowering season to prolong blooming, and cut back or tidy up after flowering. Established perennials will only need watering in prolonged dry spells, and feeding in the spring when growth commences. When they become too crowded they should be divided some time between the fall and late winter, or early spring. This may be only necessary every three or four years. For details, see plant entries in the A–Z section.

Watering

Never give perennials a light watering—it encourages surface rooting at the expense of a deep root system. The plants need big, strong roots to sustain several years of growth, and benefit most from being given a deep, regular watering. On sandy soils, choose such perennials as sedum, oenothera, and dianthus that tolerate dry conditions. A deep mulch around the plants will help conserve moisture, as will adding quantities of organic matter to the soil as the mulch breaks down.

Feeding

Perennials should not need a lot of feeding. Apply an all-purpose plant food as growth begins; if the soil has been well prepared this should be enough for the whole growing season. If your soil is very poor, you may like to use a slow-release granular fertilizer to feed plants through the growing season, or to apply a second helping of plant food as the flower buds begin to appear. A mulch of decayed manure or compost around the plants serves two functions: it improves the soil condition, and also supplies small amounts of nutrients to the plants.

Keep the entire area free of weeds until the plants cover the ground. This will ensure that any fertilizer you apply will feed your perennials and not any unwanted weeds. Avoid high nitrogen fertilizers, as they tend to promote leaf growth at the expense of flowers. Rose food is ideal.

THE PENSTEMONS AND SALVIAS in the foreground make a gorgeous foil for the stiff, upright growth of Russell lupins.

Cutting flowers and deadheading

A number of perennials make very good cut flowers, and many are grown for the cut flower trade. The various daisies, chrysanthemums, Russell lupins, delphiniums, pinks, and Peruvian lilies are just a few of the perennials that are commercially grown. Regularly picking the flowers will help to ensure a long succession of bloom. If the flowers are not removed they will mature, most setting seed so that the flowering cycle will finish abruptly as the plant decides its reproductive work is over. If you do not want to take cut flowers, remember to remove deadheads regularly.

Exceptions to this rule are plants such as cardoon and globe thistle that have decorative seedheads. Some gardeners prefer to leave them on the plant. Many remain attractive even when dry, and they can add interest to the yard in late fall and winter, especially when covered in frost or snow.

AFTER FLOWERING

After the flowering season is over, perennials can be cut back almost to the ground. If you live in an area prone to heavy frosts, some of the more tender perennials will then need to have the crown of the plant covered. A thick layer of straw, or dead leaves, held in place by a few sticks in windy sites, will protect them from winter damage.

Alternatively, you could leave some stems sticking out of the ground to create extra, interesting shapes over winter. Grasses are especially invaluable. They are at their best when covered with frost or snow, or when helping to cast a web of shadows from the low winter sun. Wild birds also benefit from the seedheads.

THE BRIGHT, HOT COLORS of orange and yellow feature in this very effective planting, which shows up so impressively against the cool green of the lawn. The large clump of red hot pokers and a generous drift of deep apricot-orange geum are especially notable.

INCREASING YOUR STOCK OF PERENNIALS

Division

Clumps of perennials should be divided when they become congested, or when you want to plant sections elsewhere in the yard. In general, most perennials need dividing every three or four years, possibly longer. Division is done after flowering or while the plants are dormant.

If you want some pieces to plant elsewhere, you can sever a section with a knife or put a spade through the clump, and lift away what you want. This might lose some of the peripheral pieces, but the process is quick and simple. Otherwise, dig up the whole clump, shake off the excess soil, and pull the clump apart or cut it into sections. Replant the sections immediately, trimming off very long roots. Remember that the outer growths are the youngest, to be saved, and that the center of the plant may have died, in which case it can be discarded. You may need to divide very large, heavy clumps by pushing two garden forks, back to back, into the center to prise it apart. A sharp spade may also be used, but this needs a lot of force and will, of course, result in the loss of some sections of plant. This may not be of any consequence with vigorous perennials.

If you are unable to replant immediately or have pieces to give away, wrap them in damp newspaper or hessian and keep in a shaded, sheltered spot, giving you time to decide where to plant them. "Heeling in," as described on the previous page, is another way to store plants temporarily, and they are less likely to dry out. They can, of course, be potted up in a good quality potting mix.

Taking cuttings

Many perennial plants can be grown from cuttings, and a number, including geraniums and diascias, are among the easiest plants to strike. Others that grow readily from cuttings include penstemons and sedums.

Make a mix of two or three parts of coarse sand and one of peat or peat substitute compost. Put the prepared mix in clean pots, preferably no larger than 4in across. A pot of this size will take a good number of cuttings that will not be forced to sit in a large amount of soil that remains wet when watered, taking too long to dry out, consequently rotting the roots.

Take tip cuttings of unflowered shoots, no more than 2–4in long. Cut, do not tear, pieces from the parent plant. Take the cuttings early in the morning, placing the pieces in a clean plastic bag, and quickly put in a cool, shady place. Trim the cuttings by removing the lower leaves, allowing just a very few to remain on top. Cleanly cut the base of the cutting below a node (leaf junction). Another aid to rooting is to "wound" the cutting by carefully scraping about $\frac{3}{8}$in of the outer bark or stem cover at the base of the stem. Hormone rooting powders can also be used, but are not usually necessary with most perennials.

Use a clean stick or pencil to make a hole in the compost. Put the cutting in the hole and carefully firm the surrounding mix. Once all of your cuttings are in the pot you can water them thoroughly and put the pot in a warm, sheltered place out of direct sunlight. In warm months geraniums and daisies may be well rooted after three weeks, but many plants can take a considerable time. Check regularly to see if the cuttings need water, but do not keep them wet or, as explained, they will rot.

DIVIDING A CLUMP

Step 1: Use a garden fork to lift the whole perennial clump from the soil.

Step 2: Separate matted clumps by inserting two garden forks, back to back, firmly into the clump.

Step 3: First press the fork handles together, and then force them apart to split the clump in two. Repeat until the clumps are the size you want.

Step 4: Use pruning shears to cut off dead, rotten or damaged roots. The clumps are now ready for replanting.

STRIKING A CUTTING

Step 1: Take a cutting just below a leaf node or joint. Use a sharp knife or pruning shears so that the cutting is not bruised. Trim it if necessary.

Step 2: Make a hole in the compost with your finger and insert the cutting into it. Firm the soil gently around it. If you are placing more than one cutting in the pot, plant them around the edge, giving them plenty of space.

Step 3: Water the cuttings in well, but take care not to dislodge them. Make sure the water is draining away well, since the cuttings will rot if the soil remains wet.

Step 4: To make a humid atmosphere and keep the soil and cuttings moist, make a frame of sticks or wire tall enough to cover the cuttings. Place a polythene bag over the frame, and stand the pot out of direct sunlight.

A ROMANTIC YARD PATH is bordered by old-fashioned favorites, including perennial daisies and scented pinks.

A number of plants, including perennials such as sea lavender, romneya, and perennial phlox, can be grown from root cuttings. As the plant will be disturbed when the cuttings are taken, this task is best done during the winter.

• Remove the soil from around the base of the plant until you reach the roots. Trace them back until they are $\frac{1}{8}$–$\frac{1}{16}$in thick, and cut off some cleanly with a sharp knife or pruning shears. Immediately place them in a plastic bag so they do not dry out.

• Wash the soil from the roots and cut them into 1–2in lengths. If you intend to plant them vertically you will need to know which way is up; cut all the tops straight across and the bottoms at an angle.

• Place the cuttings vertically in a container, or lay them in horizontally and cover with about $\frac{3}{16}$in of John Innes No.1. Water thoroughly and check regularly to see whether further watering is needed.

• Once good shoots have appeared, your new plants can be potted up individually into small pots or planted into the ground. It is important to keep the cuttings moist, but if you saturate the compost the roots will rot.

WHAT CAN GO WRONG?

Perennials can be attacked by a number of insect pests and diseases; problems that occur on specific plants are discussed in the individual plant entries. Slugs and snails are among the worst pests for herbaceous perennials, since they can destroy newly emerging growth as it appears in the spring. If each successive burst of leaves is destroyed, the plant will eventually give up. You must search for and destroy these pests, perhaps picking them off by hand, or using bait or beer traps.

Overwatering or poorly drained heavy soils can also damage or kill perennials, especially if they are too wet during their dormant period, when there is no foliage to transpire moisture from the plant. Waterlogged soils also provide ideal conditions for the growth and spread of various soil-borne, root-rotting fungi. A few plants, such as astilbe and hosta, actually enjoy damp or boggy ground, but most enjoy conditions with good drainage.

Yellow leaves
• Plants may have been overwatered or they may be too dry. You are more likely to overwater a perennial in a pot than in a border. They may also need feeding if this has not been done for some time. Try a light application of fertilizer; in warm weather there should be an improvement within two to three weeks. Toward the end of the growing season you can expect to see some leaves yellowing as they finish their useful life. Do not worry if a few leaves, especially down toward the ground, become brown or yellow during the active spring period.

Curled or distorted leaves
• Keep a regular check against aphids—they can be a terrible problem. They are small, sap-sucking insects that may be black, brown, green, or clear. They cluster thickly on the new growth of plants, sucking out the sap. This may cause curling or distortion of leaves, and flowers may fail to open if the sap has been sucked from the buds or they, too,

A HEALTHY display of violets.

may be distorted. Close inspection usually reveals these tiny insects; they can be squashed and wiped off the stems, hosed off, or sprayed with insecticidal soap or pyrethrum-based sprays. Aphids need to be controlled, since they also transmit virus diseases from plant to plant.

Silvery mottling on foliage
• Silver markings or discoloration of foliage may be the first sign of thrip attack. These tiny insects attack plant tissue and suck the sap. Unlike most sap-sucking insects, they attack the top, not the underside of the leaf. There are several different types that cause plant damage. They are readily recognizable, usually having black bodies and wings edged with hairs. Apart from the physical damage, some thrips are responsible for transmitting diseases from plant to plant. Since many thrips use weeds as hosts, it is important to keep them out of your beds and borders. If thrips are causing damage, make sure that the plants are not stressed through lack of water. When spraying, use an appropriate contact or systemic insecticide.

Curled and browned flowers
• Check plants for thrips because they can attack pale-colored flowers. For their control, see "Silvery mottling on foliage."

TAKING ROOT CUTTINGS

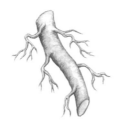

Step 1: To take root cuttings from most perennials, trace the roots back and cut out a section some ⅛–³⁄₁₆in thick.

Step 2: Wash any soil from the roots and cut them into sections 1-2in long. Mark the top of each so you know which way up to plant them.

Step 3: Place the root cuttings vertically in a container, making sure that they are the correct way up. Water them thoroughly.

Alternatively, if plants have thin roots, take cuttings in the same way, but lay them horizontally and cover with a thin layer of compost.

Holes in leaves or on leaf edges
• If your plants have chewed edges or large areas of leaf missing, check for snails. They are the most likely culprits. Pick the snails off and destroy them, or use a bait if you do not have a pet.
• If there is no sign of snails, start looking for caterpillars. Chewing insects such as caterpillars can do a great deal of damage in a short time because they can be such voracious feeders. They can be well camouflaged, lying along leaf margins or hiding under leaves. Try first to find and destroy them, but if the damage continues, dust the plants with derris.

Mottled leaves
• Leaf mottling may be the result of mite damage. Mites are not true insects, having eight legs like other members of the arachnid family. Mites are sap-suckers, and foliage attacked by mites appears mottled and discolored. With the aid of a magnifying glass, the tiny creatures and their clear circular eggs can sometimes be seen on the underside of leaves. If severe mite attacks go unnoticed initially, there may be fine webbing on the underside of foliage, too. With light attacks, hosing under the leaves every two to three days is often sufficient to reduce their population to an acceptable,

non-damaging level. Mites are much worse in warm, dry weather or on plants that may be sheltered by the overhanging eaves of a building. Make sure that plants are well watered and well nourished. If mite numbers reach unacceptable levels, clearly getting out of hand, you may need to spray with an appropriate insecticide. Many general, broad spectrum insecticides are useless against mites.

Gray/white powder on leaves
• This is probably caused by the common fungal disease, powdery mildew. In humid areas this disease is a constant problem. For plants that are very susceptible to powdery mildew, much work is being done to breed plant-resistant varieties. Meanwhile, it may be necessary to spray with a fungicide such as carbendazim or copper oxychloride, or alternatively, you can dust the plants

A VIBRANT show of argyranthemums.

with sulfur. If you have any kind of problem with powdery mildew, avoid watering the plants late in the day, so that you do not increase the humidity around them overnight.

Black or dark spots on leaves
• There are many strains of fungal leaf spots that can attack a wide range of plants. If only a few leaves are affected, remove and destroy them. Avoid watering late in the day and, where possible, avoid splashing the foliage, which will spread the fungal spores. Many fungal leaf spots respond well to simple fungicides such as copper oxychloride, but there are other effective fungicides available to the home gardener.

Yellow spots on top of leaves
• Yellow spots on the upper side of leaves that have blisters, or pustules on the underside, are likely to be some form of rust. There is an enormous number of rust strains, and they can attack a wide range of plants and perennials, including chrysanthemums. It is a good idea to remove the worst affected leaves immediately, and to avoid overhead watering, which quickly splashes the spores around, increasing contamination. Copper oxychloride will control some rusts, though you may find you need to use a more specific fungicide.

PLANNING A PERENNIAL GARDEN

Many perennials have a long flowering period, and well-planned beds of perennials can display a succession of flowers over many months. This does, however, take a good deal of planning and usually some trial and error.

If you are planting a large area, it's best to design it on paper first, so that you can place the tallest plants at the back or in the center of the bed, also giving you time to devise your color scheme. You can experiment by using a variety of plants, all with flowers in one color or shades of one color, or you may opt for a planting of bright contrasts. Whatever scheme you choose, allow for plenty of plants to create a full, rich scene. A well-planted perennial border or garden is close-planted, so that every bit of soil is covered, providing foliage and floral interest throughout the season.

ABOVE: These rich purple spikes belong to the spectacular Salvia *"Ostfriesland," a cultivar of* Salvia nemorosa.

LEFT: True perennials, such as purple Liatris spicata, *and the yellow daisies of* Coreopsis verticillata, *mix well with annual red strawflowers and* Dahlia *"Bishop of Llandaff."*

THE LUSH GREEN SCENE, composed of hostas, candelabra primulas, and other shade-tolerant perennials, in a fern-filled woodland garden on the mild west coast of Scotland. Such a scene can easily be reduced and modified for the borders in a shaded city yard.

USING PERENNIALS

Perennials are among the most versatile of plants, and the vast majority of gardeners use them in conjunction with permanent plantings of shrubs, annuals, and bulbs. They are plants that require far less work and maintenance than annuals, while still giving a great deal of seasonal color and interest. In fact many low-growing perennials, such as penstemon, lamb's ears, pinks, and bergenia, make excellent border plantings, while taller growers, such as phlox and *Acanthus mollis*, can be planted among shrubs. Long-flowering plants, such as achillea and corydalis, can be used to give color between seasonal annual displays. They also give interest to a garden bed where bulbs have finished flowering and are in the process of dying down.

PERENNIAL BORDERS

Traditionally, perennials have often been close planted in a border. To get an idea of how a well-grown perennial border should look, visit the great public gardens. Gardeners have been refining the art of perennial borders for a very long time, and both first-time and experienced gardeners will find plenty of new, imaginative ideas in these schemes. Specialist nurseries often have special exhibit beds where you can also see how well various perennials combine.

FORMAL GARDENS

It is difficult for a perennial garden to look really formal, but many of the best perennial schemes have been informally planted within a formal framework. Some are enclosed within walls, while many are contained within low, formally trimmed hedges. The garden beds are laid out in strict geometric style, resembling an ornate piece of embroidery when viewed from above, their angular shapes defined by tightly pruned hedges, often of box or lavender. Sometimes the garden beds are also defined by close-mown paths of grass.

Probably the closest one can get to a formal perennial scheme is by creating a mirror-planting effect. Each part of the design mirrors the next, and the sections are divided by paths of grass, brick, gravel, or stone. For a mirror planting to be successful, the whole of the area must be in full sunlight, otherwise there is absolutely no chance of growth rates and flowering times being the same, or as near as one can get to that, given that you are dealing with living plant material.

PLANT ARRANGEMENT

Perennials come in many shapes and sizes, which is a great advantage when planning a garden. If your perennial garden is to be sited against a picket or wall you might decide to place the tallest growers at the back. This both forms a backbone and gives you the space to stand back and fully appreciate them. So, for example, the long tall spears of delphiniums generally stand behind their lower-growing neighbors. If you are designing an island bed, the tall plants are traditionally placed in the center for a formal effect, or slightly off-center so it does not look quite so inflexibly schematic. Smaller plants radiate out, down toward the front of the border, giving a graduated, tiered effect. But such arrangements are not strictly necessary. You might prefer, instead, to give a more informal look by gently mixing heights, creating undulations. When doing this, the most important point to remember is that no plant should be hidden by its neighbor, or cast in total shade, and that all should be visible from some vantage point so that you can appreciate their color and shape.

A number of plants, such as mulleins and red hot pokers, give very strong vertical accents that contrast well with lower, more variably shaped plants. And striking foliage plants, such as cardoon and *Melianthus major*, are grown more for their strong structural shape than for their flowers. (Note that the latter is tender for the first two years, but once it has a shrubby base it can be left outside all-year around in milder areas, provided it is given some frost protection.) These big plants must be sited carefully and probably not used to excess. A contrast in leaf color, shape, and texture will also add considerable interest to the perennial garden. If you have the luxury of being able to create a very large or long perennial border, you will need to think about repeating some of the shapes and colors to tie the planting together. The other great advantage of growing perennials is that you can move them around when they are dormant, or semi-dormant, if you are not totally satisfied with their appearance or performance. They allow you to modify the design.

Everyone would love to have a yard that is in full flower for months at a time. Planning to ensure a succession of blooms over many months is the hard part of designing a garden. Even if you consult the best reference books by the best writers, reliable local nurseries, and experienced friends, you will find that plants behave differently in different situations; in the end, what counts is personal experience. Prior research is essential, providing vital guidance, and it is worth walking around your neighborhood to see exactly which plants are being grown successfully.

USING COLOR

Color is, of course, a most important consideration. If you are making a large perennial garden it is a good idea to put your planting suggestions on paper, even using colored pencils or paints to help you see how the colors work together. You do not need to be an artist—rough shapes or blobs of color will do. You would not want or expect to have all the plants in flower at the one time, but you need to think about overlapping flowering times.

If you want a cool-looking yard you could restrict yourself to white, blue, cream, or pale pink flowers, with some silver foliage plants as accents. Red, yellow, and orange flowering plants will give you a hot and vibrant look. Sometimes the addition of an area of very strong color lifts the yard out of the ordinary. Some very famous long perennial borders cover a wide color range, starting with very soft pastel colors, ending with strong, hot colors. Another idea is to position clumps of the same plant at intervals along a border, as the repetition will add to the effect of the design. Even if you have only a small space to work with, you will find the repetition gives more form to the garden.

BLUE LUPINS and white poppies provide a cool contrast with the bright reds and yellows in the extensive borders behind.

PERENNIALS FOR ALL SEASONS

At every season of the year there is some perennial plant in flower. Winter brings the delicate and subtle beauty of the winter or Lenten rose (*Helleborus* spp.), and also bergenia in mild areas. Spring brings a succession of flowers in both mild and cold districts. Columbines, armeria, Solomon's seal, candelabra primula, geum, pinks, and heuchera are just a few of the beautiful spring-flowering perennials. Summer brings bergamot, achillea, platycodon, and rudbeckias, some of which flower well into the fall. Fall perennials include chrysanthemums, favored for their garden display and cut flowers, while red hot pokers, sedum, and asters provide color and interest at a time when annuals are either being pulled out or planted for the next season. These fall-flowering perennials, along with some fall-flowering bulbs such as colchicums and nerines, will carry your yard beautifully into winter.

Perennials also generally combine well with spring bulbs. While the perennials are still dormant, or are just beginning to put on new growth, the bulbs produce flowers, providing a combination of foliage and blooms. Then, when the bulbs have finished performing and the foliage is beginning to look untidy and start dying, the perennials begin to take over, becoming the dominant garden feature.

ACANTHUS MOLLIS
Bear's breeches

LITTLE FLOWERS in purple and white open along tall spikes above the foliage.

THE BEAR'S BREECHES in this Scottish garden are thriving in the open. The masses of handsome foliage suit a large yard where you can stand back and see the plants in perspective.

FEATURES

Also known as bear's breeches, this handsome foliage plant grows from 28 to 39in high, and can make a clump close to 39in wide. The dark, glossy leaves provided the inspiration and model for the decoration on Corinthian columns. This striking feature plant is at its best when mass-planted, although one generous clump can be extremely effective in quite a small area. It enjoys full sunlight, but also tolerates shade. The stiff flower spikes of purple-and-white flowers appear among the foliage from the spring into summer. It can be quite a vigorous grower, although it dies back after flowering. It can multiply quickly once established, but is rarely troublesome.

ACANTHUS AT A GLANCE

A. mollis is a vigorous Mediterranean perennial liking dry, stoney ground. Hardy to 5°F (zone 7), with bold, shapely foliage.

Jan	/	**Recommended Varieties**
Feb	sow 🖐	
Mar	divide 🖐	*Acanthus mollis*
Apr	transplant 🖐	"Fielding Gold"
May	flowering 🍃	*A.m.* "Hollard's Gold"
Jun	flowering 🍃	*A.m.* Latifolius Group
July	/	
Aug	/	**Companion Plants**
Sept	/	*Bergenia* x "Ballawley"
Oct	divide 🖐	Forsythia
Nov	/	Gypsophila
Dec	/	*Syringa vulgaris*

CONDITIONS

Aspect It flowers best in full sun, but also grows in light shade.

Site Needs well-drained soil that contains plenty of organic matter to aid water retention. Give plants a deep layer of mulch with compost in the spring, and then a second application in mid-summer, if necessary.

GROWING METHOD

Propagation Grows from seed sown in spring, or divide clumps in the spring or fall. Plant new divisions 12–16in apart. Young plants must be given ample water in dry weather during the spring and summer. After flowering, cut back on the watering.

Feeding Apply a complete plant food as growth starts during the spring.

Problems Since slugs and snails can cause a lot of damage to young growth, badly disfiguring it, take precautions. No other problems are known.

FLOWERING

Season The tall spikes of purple-and-white flowers appear in late spring and summer.

Cutting It is possible to use this as a cut flower; the dried spikes make good indoor decoration.

AFTER FLOWERING

Requirements Protect young plants with straw over winter. Cut off the flowering stems once faded.

ACHILLEA
Yarrow

LONG-FLOWERING and not as invasive as the species, the new hybrid achilleas will give great pleasure for months.

ACHILLEA IS ALSO KNOWN *as soldier's woundwort, nosebleed, and sanguinary, which reflects its value in herbal medicine.*

FEATURES

Yarrow are vigorous perennials offering heights from 2in to 4ft. The species has flattish heads of white flowers and feathery foliage, but cultivars have flowers in a lovely range of shades, including yellow, pink, apricot, and crimson. Flowers are long-lasting. Yarrow is quick and easy to establish, and may need to be controlled; however, the runners are quite easy to pull out. Some of the cultivars are less invasive than the species.
A. filipendulina has flat heads of bright yellow flowers that last all summer. Selected forms have deep or pale yellow blooms. Best planted in large drifts, yarrow is ideal for the back of borders or among annuals.

ACHILLEA AT A GLANCE

Mainly deciduous perennials grown for their attractive, daisy-like summer and fall flowers. Hardy to 5°F (zone 7).

		Recommended Varieties
Jan	/	*Achillea* "Coronation Gold"
Feb	sow	
Mar	sow	*Achillea filipendulina* "Cloth of Gold"
Apr	transplant	*A. f.* "Gold Plate"
May	divide	*A.* x *lewisii* "King Edward"
Jun	flowering	
July	flowering	*A. millefolium* "Cerise Queen"
Aug	flowering	*A. m.* "Lilac Beauty"
Sept	flowering	*A. m.* "White Queen"
Oct	/	*A.* "Moonshine"
Nov	/	*A. tomentosa*
Dec	/	

CONDITIONS

Aspect   Needs full sunlight for the best results, but will tolerate some shade for part of the day.
Site   Any well-drained soil is suitable.

GROWING METHOD

Propagation   Grows easily if established clumps are lifted and divided in the spring. Plant the vigorous new divisions 8–12in apart, and discard the old ones. New, young plants need regular watering in prolonged dry spells, but once established achillea is remarkably drought-tolerant, and needs only an occasional deep drink.
Feeding   Apply a complete plant food as growth commences in the spring.
Problems   No specific pest or disease problems are known to attack achillea.

FLOWERING

Season   The long flowering period lasts throughout the summer into early fall. Regular removal of the spent, fading flower stems will significantly prolong blooming.
Cutting   The flowers are good for cutting because they have a reasonably long vase life. Take handfuls of cut flowers for the vase as soon as the heads are fully open. Also excellent for drying.

AFTER FLOWERING

Requirements   Cut off any spent flower stalks that remain on the plant in late fall.

AGAPANTHUS
African blue lily

THE BLUE AND WHITE flowering heads of agapanthus are composed of numerous flowers. They make a striking feature.

THIS DENSE PLANTING of agapanthus needs little attention and rewards the gardener with its wonderful summer flowers.

FEATURES

Agapanthus has dark green, strap-shaped leaves that grow to about 20in long. It produces rounded heads of blue or white flowers on top of stems 39in or more tall, but even without the flowers it makes a great foliage accent. It is hardy in moderate areas, but in colder regions needs winter protection. The Headbourne hybrids are particularly hardy. It can be grown in containers, and looks excellent in eye-catching tubs. Several attractive dwarf forms have foliage that rarely exceed 8in.

CONDITIONS

Aspect   Tolerates some shade, but the flowering will be poor. Full sunlight is ideal.

AGAPANTHUS AT A GLANCE

A vigorous perennial, forming bold, eye-catching flowering clumps, from southern Africa. Many hardy to 23°F (zone 9).

		Recommended Varieties
Jan	/	
Feb	sow	*Agapanthus africanus*
Mar	sow	*A. a.* "Albus"
Apr	divide	*A. caulescens*
May	transplant	"Lilliput"
Jun	/	"Loch Hope"
July	flowering	"Peter Pan"
Aug	flowering	*A. praecox* "Variegatus"
Sept	flowering	
Oct	/	
Nov	/	
Dec	/	

Site   Grows in almost any soil, but well-drained ground with organic matter is perfect. In colder yards, grow near a south-facing wall.

GROWING METHOD

Propagation   Divide clumps in the spring, ensuring that each division has a crown and a good batch of healthy roots. The latter can be shortened and some outer leaves removed, if necessary. Plant approximately 10in apart. Also grows from seed sown in the spring. It needs regular watering to establish, but once settled it can cope with long, dry periods. However, for the best growth and flowering, do not let new, young plants dry out.

Feeding   Apply complete plant food in the early spring. Potted plants will perform better with an application of slow-release granules, or a monthly liquid feed, carefully following the manufacturer's recommended rate.

Problems   There are no particular problems, but clumps will harbor groups of snails. Pick off.

FLOWERING

Season   Blooms appear in mid- to late summer, depending on the conditions.

Cutting   Agapanthus can be used as a cut flower if the stems are plunged into boiling water for 15 seconds immediately after cutting.

AFTER FLOWERING

Requirements   No pruning needed, other than cutting off spent flower stems and dead leaves. Protect crowns over winter with a thick mulch of straw or dry leaves.

ALCHEMILLA MOLLIS
Lady's mantle

LONG USED as a folk medicine to help heal wounds and gynecological problems, lady's mantle is today usually grown for its decorative value and ability to self-seed. The pure lime-green flowers brighten the yard, making a marvellous contrast against the wide, lobed leaves.

FEATURES

This is a quick-growing herbaceous perennial mostly used as a border plant to edge paths and beds. An abundant self-seeder, it is good for suppressing weeds, filling any free spaces, often popping up in cracks in paths. Growing anywhere between 8 and 16in high, one plant may spread to 11–16in. The rounded, slightly hairy leaves overlap one another, and the plant produces trusses of bright lime-green flowers through summer. It provides a lovely contrast with other, stronger colors. The leaves tend to trap raindrops or dew, adding to the effect.

ALCHEMILLA AT A GLANCE

A. mollis is a hardy perennial grown for its prolific self-seeding and attractive lime-green foliage. Hardy to 5°F (zone 7).

Month	Activity	Companion Plants
Jan	/	
Feb	sow	Delphinium
Mar	sow	Dicentra
Apr	transplant	Eremurus
May	transplant	Eucomis
Jun	flowering	Euonymus
July	flowering	Geranium
Aug	flowering	Gladiolus
Sept	flowering	Lupin
Oct	divide	Rose
Nov	/	
Dec	/	

CONDITIONS

Aspect   Thrives in full sun, although it tolerates a degree of light shade.

Site   Needs well-drained soil that has a high organic content.

GROWING METHOD

Propagation   Self-sown seedlings can be easily transplanted to other positions. Clumps can be divided in the spring or fall with the divisions spaced 8–10in apart. Newly planted specimens may need watering, but mature plants tolerate dry periods. Justifiably known as a great survivor and spreader.

Feeding   Apply a complete plant food as the new growth begins.

Problems   No specific problems are known.

FLOWERING

Season   Masses of lime-green flowers appear from late spring through the summer.

Cutting   A great favorite with flower arrangements.

AFTER FLOWERING

Requirements   If you do not want plants to self-seed, trim spent flowers as soon as they fade. Once flowering has finished and growth begins to die down, the plants can be cut back hard with shears, or even a trimmer if you want to be ruthless.

ALSTROEMERIA
Peruvian Lily

ALSO KNOWN AS THE LILY of the Incas, the Peruvian lily can be placed in a mixed perennial border as here, or planted between shrubs. Bold groupings are best. Gardeners can choose from a colorful range of species and cultivars, but may be unable to obtain some of the varieties sold by florists.

FEATURES

The Peruvian lily is grown commercially on a large scale, since the flowers are long lasting when cut. In the garden it is a herbaceous perennial with flower spikes growing mostly 12–24in high, although there are dwarf forms and very tall ones. The flowers are beautifully marked with streaks and spots of color, contrasting with a wide range of base colors of cream, yellow, orange, pink, and red. If conditions are suitable, these plants spread by means of fleshy rhizomes (roots) to form large clumps. Also excellent when grown in pots.

ALSTROEMERIA AT A GLANCE

A hardy perennial surviving 14°F (zone 8). Grown for their excellent showy flowers—many make unbeatable cut flowers.

		Recommended Varieties
Jan	/	
Feb	/	*Alstroemeria ligtu*
Mar	/	hybrids
Apr	sow 🖐	"Orange Gem"
May	/	"Orange Glory"
Jun	transplant 🖐	"Princess Mira" (and all
July	flowering 🍃	"Princess" varieties)
Aug	flowering 🍃	"Solent Crest"
Sept	flowering 🍃	"Solent Rose"
Oct	divide 🖐	"Stamoli"
Nov	/	"Strapripur"
Dec	/	"Staroko"
		"Stasilva"

CONDITIONS

Aspect	Needs full sunlight and shelter to thrive, especially in colder areas. Also requires shelter from strong wind. Makes an excellent potted greenhouse plant.
Site	Must have very free-draining soil containing plenty of decayed organic matter.

GROWING METHOD

Propagation	Many grow readily from seed sown in the spring, but division of established clumps is easiest; spring is generally considered the best time. Bare-root plants can be hard to establish; pot-grown plants, available in the summer, are better. Plant the roots 2in deep and about 6in apart. In a prolonged dry period, water the bedded plants regularly in the spring and summer, but restrict watering after flowering.
Feeding	Apply slow-release granular fertilizer in spring.
Problems	No specific problems are known.

FLOWERING

Season	Most species and their cultivars flower from the spring into summer, some into fall.
Cutting	This is a first-class cut flower.

AFTER FLOWERING

Requirements	Cut off spent flower stems at ground level. Protect crowns with straw during cold winters.

ANEMONE X HYBRIDA
Windflower (Anemone x hybrida, syn. A. hupehensis var. japonica)

ELEGANT SIMPLICITY *is the best way to describe the form of the Japanese anemone with its white, yellow, and green color scheme.*

RELIABLE IN BLOOM *year after year, the Japanese anemone is an attractive garden addition that softens stiff, geometric schemes.*

FEATURES

Also known as the Japanese windflower, this herbaceous perennial is one of the great joys of the fall garden. The leaves are three-lobed, somewhat maple-like, and the single or double flowers are carried on stems up to 39in high. Flowers may be single or double-colored white, pale, or deep pink. Once established, they spread into large clumps quite rapidly, traveling by underground stems, and also self-seeding. Some consider them invasive, but plants can be easily dug out and a mass-planting in full bloom is a real delight. Grow where they can remain undisturbed for some years. Site at the back of a shady bed or in dappled sunlight under trees.

ANEMONE AT A GLANCE

A. x hybrida is a free-flowering, quick-spreading herbaceous perennial with lovely, pale pink flowers. Hardy to 5°F (zone 7).

Jan	/	Recommended Varieties
Feb	/	*Anemone x hybrida*
Mar	divide	"Honorine Jobert"
Apr	transplant	*A. x h.* "Konigin Charlotte"
May	/	*A. x h.* "Luise Uhink"
Jun	/	*A. x h.* "Margarete"
July	/	*A. x h.* "Pamina"
Aug	flowering	*A. x h.* "Richard Ahrends"
Sept	flowering	
Oct	sow	
Nov	/	
Dec	/	

CONDITIONS

Aspect	Prefers shade or semi-shade with shelter from strong winds.
Site	Grows best in well-drained soil that contains plenty of organic matter.

GROWING METHOD

Propagation	Increase from root cuttings in the winter, or divide established clumps in early spring, ensuring that each division has a thick set of roots. This vigorous plant can sometimes be tricky to divide and transplant. Replant the new, vigorous younger growths from the outside of the clump, generally about 12in apart. New young plants need ample watering in prolonged dry spells during the growing season.
Feeding	Fertilizing is not essential, but a complete plant food can be applied in the spring.
Problems	No specific problems are known.

FLOWERING

Season	Flowers appear prolifically from late summer through the fall months.
Cutting	Though they seem perfect for cut-flower displays, the flowers do not last that well.

AFTER FLOWERING

Requirements	Cut back spent flower stems to ground level once they begin to fade, and cut the plant right back to the ground in late fall.

AQUILEGIA
Columbine

WIDELY CONTRASTING COLORS successfully combine in the flowers of this modern, long-spurred hybrid columbine.

AN OPEN WOODLAND SETTING is ideal for columbines, letting them freely self-seed to form bold, distinctive groups.

FEATURES

These old-fashioned favorites, also called granny's bonnets, give a fine display in the garden and make decorative cut flowers. The foliage is often blue-green, and the flowers come in single colors—white, pink, crimson, yellow, and blue—and combinations of pastel and brighter shades. There are also excellent black-and-whites ("Magpie"). The older forms have short-spurred flowers that resemble old-fashioned bonnets, especially "Nora Barlow," a good double that is a mix of red, pink, and green. Modern hybrids are long-spurred and are available in many single colors and bicolors. Plants may be 16–28in tall. Columbines are not long-lived but are easily grown from seed. Ideal for the dappled yard, grow them under deciduous trees and in borders.

AQUILEGIA AT A GLANCE

A clump-forming perennial, happy in semi-shade, perfect for the "cottage garden" where it freely self-seeds. Hardy to 5°F (zone 7).

		Recommended Varieties
Jan	/	*Aquilegia bertolonii*
Feb	/	A. canadensis
Mar	sow 🖑	A. flabellata
Apr	transplant 🖑	A. f. var. pumila
May	flowering 🌣	A. `f. var. f. alba
Jun	flowering 🌣	"Henson Harebell"
July	/	"Magpie"
Aug	/	Music series
Scpt	divide 🖑	A. vulgaris "Nora Barlow"
Oct	sow 🖑	
Nov	/	
Dec	/	

CONDITIONS

Aspect Prefers semi-shade and thrives in woodland gardens, but full sunlight is not a problem.
Site Needs well-drained soil that contains plenty of organic matter.

GROWING METHOD

Propagation Clumps are quite hard to divide, but it can be done, fall being the best time. Columbine also grows from seed sown in early spring or in the fall. Self-sown plants are hardy, but note that they may not always be true to type. Set plants approximately 12in apart. New, young plants must not be allowed to dry out in prolonged dry spells in the spring and summer months. Keep a careful watch.
Feeding Apply complete plant food in the spring as the new growth begins to emerge.
Problems No particular pest or disease problems are known for this plant.

FLOWERING

Season There is a long flowering period from mid-spring to mid-summer.
Cutting Flower stems can be cut for the vase, and they make an attractive display, but the garden show lasts considerably longer.

AFTER FLOWERING

Requirements Spent flower stems can either be removed or left on the plants, enabling the seeds to mature. Cut back the old growth to ground level when it dies off.

ARMERIA MARITIMA
Sea thrift

EACH FLOWERHEAD resembles a tiny bouquet, which is why thrift makes a fine cut flower, alone or in a composition with other flowers.

POOR STONY GROUND, which resembles thrift's natural habitat, provides ideal conditions for growing this plant.

FEATURES

Also known as sea thrift, this evergreen perennial grows in little grassy mounds 2–5in high. It occurs naturally in northern Europe and around the Mediterranean, often in very exposed situations, including clifftops. The rounded flowerheads are carried above the foliage on stems 6–12in tall. Flowers vary in color in the species and may be white, pink, or almost red, and there are a number of named cultivars available. Thrift can be used as a groundcover or edging plant, or can be planted in rock gardens, on dry walls, or in poor soil where few other plants will survive. It also makes a good container plant.

CONDITIONS

Aspect Needs full sunlight all day. Thrift tolerates dry, windy conditions and salt spray, and is an excellent choice for coastal yards.

Site Grows in any kind of soil, so long as it is very well drained. Adding sharp sand will improve the drainage.

GROWING METHOD

Propagation Divide established clumps in the spring and replant about 6–8in apart. The species can be grown from seed sown in the spring, or from semi-ripe cuttings taken in the summer

Feeding Give a light dressing of complete fertilizer in early spring.

Problems Thrift has a tendency to rot if soils are in any way too heavy, poorly drained, or overwatered In humid weather and in sheltered positions it may also be susceptible to the fungal disease called rust. Use a fungicide to attack the problem.

FLOWERING

Season Thrift has a long flowering period through the spring and summer, provided the plants' deadheads are regularly removed.

Cutting Makes a good cut flower.

AFTER FLOWERING

Requirements Regularly remove spent flower stems to give a prolonged flowering period.

ARMERIA AT A GLANCE

A. maritima is an attractive evergreen, clump-forming perennial that colonizes inhospitable areas. Hardy to 0°F (zones 6–7).

Jan	/	Recommended Varieties
Feb	/	*Armeria maritima*
Mar	division 🖐	"Alba"
Apr	/	*A. m.* "Corsica"
May	transplant 🖐	*A. m.* "Launcheana"
Jun	flowering 🌿	*A. m.* "Ruby Glow"
July	flowering 🌿	*A. m.* "Splendens"
Aug	flowering 🌿	*A. m.* "Vindictive"
Sept	/	
Oct	/	
Nov	/	
Dec	/	

ASTER
Michaelmas daisy

RICH MAUVE *flowers virtually obscure*
the foliage on a mature plant.

THE ATTRACTIVE Aster ericoides,
which has produced many excellent cultivars.

ONE OF *the best of the reds is the low-*
growing "Winston Churchill."

FEATURES

There is a wide variety of asters, and all of them flower in late summer and the fall. The most commonly grown is *A. novi-belgii*, which has a range of cultivars from dwarf forms 10in high to tall varieties reaching 39in. Flowers are blue, violet, pink, red, or white, and all are good for cutting. *A. ericoides* has very small leaves and produces stems of white flowers up to 39in high. *A.* x *frikartii* grows about 30in tall and has violet-blue flowers. All of these plants are extremely easy to grow and tolerate a wide range of conditions. They multiply readily. Taller varieties need staking.

ASTER AT A GLANCE

Hardy perennials creating large clumps, giving strong fall color in most situations. Hardy to 5°F (zone 7).

Month	Activity		Recommended Varieties
Jan	/		
Feb	sow	🌱	*Aster alpinus*
Mar	sow	🌱	*A. amellus* "Framfieldii"
Apr	divide	🌱	*A. a.* "Jacqueline Genebrier"
May	transplant	🌱	"Coombe Fishacre"
Jun	/		*A. ericoides* "Golden Spray"
July	flowering	🌸	*A.* x *frikartii* "Monch"
Aug	flowering	🌸	*A. novae-angliae*
Sept	flowcring	🌸	*A. novi-belgii* "Audrey"
Oct	divide	🌱	
Nov	/		
Dec	/		

CONDITIONS

Aspect   Grows best in full sun. Tolerates light shade, but blooming may not be so prolific and growth will be less compact.

Site   Add well-rotted organic matter to the soil. Feed and water well to counter disease.

GROWING METHOD

Propagation   Divide clumps in late winter. These plants are prolific growers—one plant will multiply itself tenfold in a season. Replant divisions 8in apart. The best results are from regular watering during the spring and summer, especially in long, dry periods.

Feeding   Apply complete plant food in early spring.

Problems   Powdery mildew can be a major problem, especially with varieties of *A. novi-belgii*. Mildew-resistant varieties include *A.* x *frikartii* and varieties of *A. amellus*.

FLOWERING

Season   The long flowering display lasts from late summer into the fall.

Cutting   Cut flowers last very well if given a frequent change of water.

AFTER FLOWERING

Requirements   Cut off spent flower stems close to ground level after blooming. Plants will gradually die back, but should not need more close attention until new growth appears in the next spring.

ASTILBE HYBRIDS
Astilbe

SOFT AND FEATHERY, *the pale pink plumes on this astilbe will provide a long display of bright flowers and fern-like foliage.*

UPRIGHT SIDE BRANCHES *are an unusual feature of this deep pink astilbe cultivar. They give an eye-catching, stiff appearance.*

FEATURES

These perennial hybrids revel in moist soil and light shade, although they can be grown in an open, sunny position if well watered. The shiny, compound leaves are quite attractive, with astilbe also bearing tall plumes of soft flowers 20in or more tall, in shades of pink, red, mauve, or white. They look best when mass-planted, and are ideal for surrounding ponds, or naturalizing in a wild garden. They can be used as cut flowers, but they are probably best left in the yard where their big, theatrical effect can be enjoyed for much longer. They can quickly flag in a heat wave; water at the first sign of wilting.

ASTILBE AT A GLANCE

A rhizomatous perennial that enjoys damp soil. Striking, tall flowerheads can reach 4ft tall. Hardy to 5°F (zone 7).

Jan	/	Recommended Varieties
Feb	sow	***Astilbe x arendsii***
Mar	divide	"Brautschleier"
Apr	transplant	*A.* x *a.*"Bronce Elegans"
May	flowering	*A.* x *a.*"Fanal"
Jun	flowering	*A.* x *a.* "Irrlicht"
July	flowering	*A.* x *a* "Snowdrift"
Aug	flowering	*A.* x *crispa* "Perkeo"
Sept	flowering	"Rheinland"
Oct	/	***A. simplicifolia***
Nov	divide	"Sprite"
Dec	/	

CONDITIONS

Aspect   These are versatile plants, performing equally well in bright sunlight and dappled shade.

Site   The ideal soil is rich in organic matter and retains plenty of moisture. Regular, heavy applications of mulch are essential.

GROWING METHOD

Propagation   Divide clumps in late fall, ensuring that each division has a crown and a decent set of roots. Plant at 8–10in spacings. New, young plants need plenty of water in prolonged dry spells in the spring and summer months. Do not let them dry out.

Feeding   Apply a general fertilizer as growth starts in the spring, and repeat 6–8 weeks later.

Problems   No specific problems are known.

FLOWERING

Season   Flowers from late spring through the summer. The flower display is longer lasting in a cooler summer.

Cutting   Flowers can be cut for indoor decoration.

AFTER FLOWERING

Requirements   Spent flowerheads will turn a pleasant rich brown color, and are quite attractive through the winter months. They add considerable interest to the yard. Do not cut back spent flower stems to ground level until the following spring.

ASTRANTIA MAJOR
Masterwort

ASTRANTIA MAJOR *"HADSPEN BLOOD" is a striking, vibrant red, more of an eye-catcher than the species, which is much whiter. Both can be used to link and soften more permanent shrubby features, or as part of a free-flowing, flowery display for late spring and early summer.*

FEATURES

Also known as masterwort, ***Astrantia major*** is a "must-have" for the "cottage garden," a clump-forming perennial that produces delightful sprays of green or pink, sometimes reddish flowers, surrounded by green-veined white bracts. A native of central Europe, it grows about 24in tall, forming clumps 18in wide. Flowering in early and mid-summer, it can be left to colonize areas of dappled shade, though it also enjoys full sunlight. There are some excellent cultivars, including the new "Hadspen Blood," a striking blood red, "Shaggy" with long bracts, and "Sunningdale Variegated," with pale pink bracts and yellow/cream leaves. Best in large clumps.

ASTRANTIA AT A GLANCE

A. major is a clump-forming perennial grown for its abundant, attractive flowers. Excellent cultivars. Hardy to 0°F (zones 6–7).

Jan	/		Recommended Varieties
Feb	/		
Mar	divide		*Astrantia major alba*
Apr	divide		*A. m.* "Claret"
May	transplant		*A. m.* "Hadspen Blood"
Jun	flowering		*A. m. involucrata*
July	flowering		"Shaggy"
Aug	sowing		*A. m. rosea*
Sept	/		*A. m. rubra*
Oct	/		*A. m.* "Sunningdale
Nov	/		Variegated"
Dec	/		

CONDITIONS

Aspect	Thrives in either dappled shade or a more open, sunny position.
Soil	Likes compost-rich, moist, fertile soil, though it will tolerate drier conditions. Woodland gardens and streamsides are ideal.

GROWING METHOD

Propagation	Can either be grown from seed sown in late summer, once ripe, or by division in the spring. Plant out at least 18in apart, or closer for an immediate covering. Do not let young plants begin to dry out in a prolonged dry spring or summer spell. The variants do not require such moist conditions, and will tolerate drier soil.
Feeding	Lay a mulch around the plants in the spring. This has two advantages: it enriches the soil and also prevents moisture loss.
Problems	Slugs can be a major problem, attacking the stems and foliage. Pick off when seen. Powdery mildew can also strike; spray against attacks.

FLOWERING

Season	The one flowering spell is in early and mid-summer.
Cutting	Makes good cut flowers, which can be used to soften a stiff, structural arrangement, or as part of a more flowery display.

AFTER FLOWERING

Requirements	Cut down the spent flower stems, and tidy up the foliage.

AURINIA SAXATILIS
Golden dust

A SHARP, ATTRACTIVE CONTRAST, with the bright yellow flowers of golden dust against clusters of green, spoon-shape foliage.

YELLOW AND BLUE always make a lively color combination, as this wonderful planting of golden dust and Italian lavender proves.

FEATURES

This is a little, rounded, evergreen perennial that can grow from 4 to 12in high, forming a mound up to 16–20in across. In the species the flowers are a clear yellow, but the various cultivars produce flowers in white, cream, lemon, or rich gold. Since its natural habitat is rocky, mountainous country, it is ideal for a rock garden, for dry, sloping ground, or for edging garden beds, provided the drainage is excellent. It is also ideally suited to troughs and the edges of large pots, perhaps containing a shrub. Although golden dust is a perennial, some gardeners grow it as part of an annual spring display.

CONDITIONS

Aspect	Needs an open position in full sunlight.
Site	Soil must contain plenty of chalk, sand, or grit, and be free-draining but not rich.

GROWING METHOD

Propagation	Grows readily from seed sown in the fall. Cultivars can be grown from tip cuttings taken in late spring and early summer. Space the plants about 4in apart, giving them plenty of growing room. Aurinia is sold among the alpines at garden centers.
Feeding	Small amounts only of complete plant food may be given in early spring as a boost, but feeding is not essential.
Problems	No specific problems are known besides poor drainage. Overwatering pot-grown specimens can quickly rot and kill the plants.

FLOWERING

Season	Flowers appear from mid- to late spring, the flowers completely covering the plant and hiding the foliage.
Cutting	The flowers are not suitable for picking.

AFTER FLOWERING

Requirements	It is probably easiest to shear radically over the whole plant with clippers, unless you are waiting for the seed to ripen. Shearing the plants also helps to keep a compact, neatly rounded shape.

AURINIA AT A GLANCE

A. saxatilis is an evergreen, hardy perennial that forms thick clumps topped by yellow flowers. Hardy to 0°F (zone 6–7).

Jan	/	**Recommended Varieties**
Feb	/	*Aurinia saxatilis*
Mar	transplant	"Citrina"
Apr	/	*A. s.* "Compacta"
May	flowering	*A. s.* "Dudley Nevill"
Jun	flowering	*A. s.* "Goldkugel"
July	/	*A. s.* "Silver Queen"
Aug	/	
Sept	/	**Companion Plants**
Oct	sow	*Aurinia corymbosa*
Nov	/	Aubrieta
Dec	/	

BERGENIA
Elephant's ears

THE WELL-DEFINED, SOLID SHAPE of bergenias makes them ideal edging plants, as this neat row beside a path demonstrates. Bergenias have other advantages, too, in that they flower in the shade and from late winter onward, both features that are not common among perennials.

FEATURES

An excellent evergreen, groundcover plant, it is also known as elephant's ears, because of the large, rounded leaves approximately 8–12in long. They are often leathery and glossy, generally green, many turning reddish in the fall. The flowers are held on short stems, from mid-spring to early summer, some, such as "Morgenrote," repeat-flowering in cool conditions. The color range is invariably shades of pink, with some white forms. Bergenia is not a fussy plant, and enjoys a wide range of conditions, from bright sun to shade, and from moist to dry ground. Long-living and easy to propagate, it can colonize areas beneath trees, edge paths, or front a border.

BERGENIA AT A GLANCE

A versatile evergreen with large, ornamental foliage that thrives in a range of conditions. Hardy to 0°F (zones 6–7).

		Recommended Varieties
Jan	/	
Feb	flowering 🌸	*Bergenia* "Abendglut"
Mar	flowering 🌸	*B.* "Baby Doll"
Apr	flowering 🌸	*B.* "Bressingham Salmon"
May	flowering 🌸	*B.* "Bressingham White"
Jun	/	*B. cordifolia* "Purpurea"
July	/	*B.* "Morgenrote"
Aug	/	*B. purpurescens*
Sept	/	*B.* "Silberlicht"
Oct	divide ✋	
Nov	divide ✋	
Dec	/	

CONDITIONS

Aspect Grows in either full sunlight or shady areas, but avoid extremes of the latter.

Site Likes well-composted, moist soil with good drainage, but it will also tolerate much poorer conditions that bring out a richer winter leaf color. Provide a late fall mulch.

GROWING METHOD

Propagation Grows from seed sown in spring, producing hybrids, or divide in the spring or fall every five years to rejuvenate a declining plant. Plant up to 24in apart, depending on the variety, or closer for immediate coverage.

Feeding Feed generously in early spring with a complete plant food, especially on poorer ground, and give a generous layer of mulch later in the fall.

Problems Slugs and snails can be a major problem to the new, young foliage, ruining its shapely appearance. Pick off, or treat with chemicals. Spray with a fungicide if leaf spot occurs.

FLOWERING

Season The flowers appear from late winter or early spring, depending on the variety, for a few weeks.

Cutting Though the flowers are useful in cut flower arrangements, the foliage, especially when red in winter, makes a particularly attractive foil.

AFTER FLOWERING

Requirements Remove the spent flower stems and foliage.

CAMPANULA
Bellflower

CAMPANULA PERSICIFOLIA ALBA makes a valuable addition to a white border, flowering prolifically in early and mid-summer.

CAMPANULAS ARE THE MAINSTAY of the cottage or woodland garden, freely spreading, adding plenty of color and charm.

FEATURES

Also known as the bellflower, campanula contains about 300 species of annuals, biennials, and perennials. Generally easy to grow in either full sunlight or dappled shade, on walls, banks, and in borders, it has a wide range of flowers, from the tubular to the saucer-shaped. They also vary considerably in height, from the low, 3in-high spreaders, like *C. betulifolia,* to the 5ft-tall *C. lactiflora.* The former are excellent at the front of a border, the latter need staking at the rear. There are many excellent forms: *C. glomerata* "Superba" is a vigorous grower, reaching 24 x 24in, while *C. burghaltii* produces pale lavender tubular bells around the same time.

CAMPANULA AT A GLANCE

A near 300-strong genus, thriving in a wide variety of conditions, grown for their abundant flowers. Hardy to 5°F (zone 7).

		Recommended Varieties
Jan	/	
Feb	/	*Campanula arvatica*
Mar	sow 🖑	*C. carpatica*
Apr	transplant 🖑	*C. garganica*
May	flowering 🌱	*C. latiloba*
Jun	flowering 🌱	*C. medium*
July	flowering 🌱	*C. persicifolia*
Aug	flowering 🌱	*C. thyrsoides*
Sept	flowering 🌱	*C. trachelium*
Oct	divide 🖑	
Nov	/	
Dec	/	

CONDITIONS

Aspect Campanula thrive in both sunny yards and those with dappled shade.

Site There are three broad types of campanula, each requiring different conditions: well-drained, fertile soil for border plants; moist, fast-draining ground for the rock garden species; and a gritty scree bed for the alpines that dislike being wet over winter.

GROWING METHOD

Propagation Grow the species from seed in spring in a cold frame, or from cuttings, and sow alpines in a frame in the fall. Varieties must be propagated by spring cuttings, or spring or fall division if they are to grow true to the parent.

Feeding Apply a complete plant food in the spring, especially on poorer soils, or plenty of dug-in, organic material.

Problems Slugs and snails are the major problem, and if not kept under control they can ruin a border display. In some areas *C. persicifolia* is prone to rust.

FLOWERING

Season The long-lasting flowers appear from midwinter to the spring.

Cutting Makes an excellent display of cut flowers, especially the taller plants.

AFTER FLOWERING

Requirements Cut back to the ground in late fall.

CENTRANTHUS RUBER
Red valerian

TRUSSES *of rich crimson and softer pink valerian provide months of bright color in the yard, rivalling the display of annuals.*

RED VALERIAN *flourishing in the conditions that suit it best—the fence provides shelter, and the raised bed warmth and good drainage.*

FEATURES

This evergreen perennial is very easy to grow, but it often exceeds its allotted space by self-seeding (seedlings are easy to pull out). It has a long flowering period and can survive in poor, dry soil. It generally reaches 16in tall, but in good soil tops 28in. Flowers are a deep pink to red, and there is a white form, too. Ideal for a low-maintenance yard, it is often planted in mixed borders for its long display. It is also grown in large rock gardens and on dry, fast-draining slopes. Self-sown plants can be found in almost no soil on rocky outcrops, and thrive in chalky ground.

CENTRANTHUS AT A GLANCE

C. ruber is a hardy, herbaceous perennial, a favorite in "cottage gardens" with tall, red summer flowers. Hardy to 10°F (zones

		Companion Plants
Jan	/	
Feb	sow	*Argyranthemum foeniculaceum*
Mar	sow	
Apr	transplant	*A. frutescens*
May	transplant	Cytisus
Jun	flowering	*Geranium robertianum*
July	flowering	*Hedera colchica* "Dentata Variegata"
Aug	flowering	
Sept	flowering	*Helleborus orientalis*
Oct	/	Stipa
Nov	/	Yucca
Dec	/	

CONDITIONS

Aspect Likes full sunlight all day.
Soil Needs very well-drained soil, but it need not be particularly rich.

GROWING METHOD

Propagation Grows readily from tip cuttings taken in late spring and summer, or from seed sown in the spring. Space the plants 8in apart.
Feeding Fertilizer is generally not necessary, but you may give a little complete plant food in the spring, as new growth begins. Needs regular watering to establish, after which plants are extremely drought-tolerant.
Problems No specific problems are known.

FLOWERING

Season The very long flowering period extends from the spring until early fall, especially if plants are cut back after each flowering flush to encourage plenty of new buds.
Cutting Does not make a good cut flower.

AFTER FLOWERING

Requirements No attention is needed, beyond removing the spent flower stems. This has a double advantage: it keeps the plant looking neat, and prevents abundant self-seeding.

CHRYSANTHEMUM HYBRIDS
Dendranthema

CASCADING OVER *the fence onto the massed erigeron below, this wonderful garden chrysanthemum gives a prolific display.*

THE QUILLED PETALS *are characteristic of this open "spider" style of chrysanthemum, as is the shading of color.*

HYBRID CHRYSANTHEMUMS *are justifiably highly popular in the cut flower trade, and are available for most of the year.*

FEATURES

Chrysanthemums probably originated in China, but were introduced into Japan a very long time ago. A big favourite in garden and florists' displays, they are the highlight of the late summer and fall border. They are also widely used as a long-lasting cut flower. Chrysanthemums have been renamed and moved to the genus *Dendranthema*, though the name has yet to find favor. Four kinds to look out for include: the Korean (e.g. "Yellow Starlet"), which gives a long flowering performance but dislikes excessively wet winters (store inside in severe conditions); the thigh-high, dwarf, bushy pompons ("Mei Kyo"), with a sea of rounded flowers; the clump-forming rubellums (named hybrids of *C. rubellum*), which are the hardiest, have a woody base, but again dislike extreme damp; and the sprays ("Pennine"), which are grown both for the border and cutting.

Color
The color range is wide, covering white, cream, yellow, many shades of pink and lilac, burgundy, pale apricot, and deep mahogany.

Types
There are many forms of chrysanthemum, and they have been classified by specialist societies and nurseries according to floral type. Some of the types are decorative, anemone-centered, spider, pompon, single, exhibition, and Korean spray. There is virtually a shape for every taste.

Staking
Many of the taller varieties need staking, which needs to be carefully planned if the display is to avoid looking too structured. One reliable, traditional method is to insert bamboo canes at intervals around and through the planting, and thread twine from cane to cane in a criss-cross fashion, perhaps 20–24in above the ground.

CONDITIONS

Aspect
Grows best in full sunlight, with protection from strong winds.

Site
Needs well-drained soil that has been heavily enriched with organic matter before planting. Plants should also be mulched with decayed compost or manure.

THIS UNUSUAL chrysanthemum has the central petals incurved, like those of the Korean spray, while the outer ones are spread wide.

THE RUSSET COLORS of these flowers seem appropriate to their fall flowering season, when the leaves are turning.

GROWING METHOD

Propagation In the spring, lift and divide the new suckering growth so that each new plant has its own roots and shoots. Cuttings of the new growth can be taken. Set the plants 16in apart.

Feeding Once the plants are well established you can fertilize them every four to six weeks with a soluble liquid fertilizer.

Problems • You can spot chrysanthemum leaf miners by the wavy white or brown lines in the foliage. Hold up the leaf to the light and you might see the pupa or grub. Control by immediately removing the affected leaves and crushing the grubs, or better still by regular spraying with a systemic insecticide.

• Chrysanthemum eelworm is evident by browning, drying leaves. Immediately destroy all infected plants. There is no available remedy.

• A number of fungal diseases can attack these plants, including leaf spot, powdery mildew, rust, and white rust. Avoid overhead watering or watering late in the day, and ensure that residue from previous plantings is cleared away. You may need to spray with a registered fungicide. White rust is a particularly serious disease, and affected plants are probably best removed and destroyed.

• Watch for aphids clustering on new growth. Pick them off by hand, wash them off, or use an insecticidal spray.

FLOWERING

Season Flowering time is mid- to late fall. The exciting new race of Yoder or cushion chrysanthemums from America are dwarf, hardy, free-flowering (starting in late summer), and perfect for the front of the border. Those to look out for include "Lynn," "Robin," and "Radiant Lynn."

Cutting Cut flowers will last two to three weeks, with frequent water changes, so long as the foliage is removed from the parts of the stems that are underwater.

AFTER FLOWERING

Requirements Once flowering has finished, cut off plants 5–6in above the ground.

CHRYSANTHEMUM AT A GLANCE

Chrysanthemums are the colorful mainstay of the the end-of-season border. The hardy forms will tolerate 5°F (zone 7).

		Recommended Varieties
Jan	/	
Feb	sow	"Anna Marie"
Mar	sow	"Bronze Elegance"
Apr	divide	"Cappa"
May	transplant	"Faust"
Jun	/	"Lord Butler"
July	/	"Mrs Jessie Cooper"
Aug	flowering	"Poppet"
Sept	flowering	"Salmon Fairie"
Oct	/	
Nov	/	
Dec	/	

CONVALLARIA
Lily-of-the-valley

LILY-OF-THE-VALLEY makes a vivid display because of the strong contrast between the shapely oval leaves and the small, bright white flowers. It can be left to naturalize in woodland conditions, or allowed to spread through a shady border. Though invasive, it is quite easily controlled.

FEATURES

Lily-of-the-valley is a one-species (sometimes considered three) genus, featuring the bell-shaped, fragrant *Convallaria majalis*. A native of Europe, it grows in woods and meadows, and produces 8in-tall stems of nodding white flowers shortly after the foliage has unfurled. Given the correct conditions—specifically, a cool, moist area—it can spread extremely quickly by means of underground shoots, but it is easily controlled. There are several attractive forms, "Albostriata" having cream striped foliage, and "Fortin's Giant" has flowers up to $\frac{1}{2}$in across. Lily-of-the-valley is essential in a woodland area, or in a damp shady spot where little else of note will grow.

CONVALLARIA AT A GLANCE

Basically a one-species genus with wonderful, waxy, scented spring flowers. Hardy to 5°F (zone 7). Good cultivars available.

Jan	/	Companion Plants
Feb	/	
Mar	/	Bergenia
Apr	transplant 🖐	*Euphorbia robbiae*
May	flowering 🌱	Galanthus
Jun	/	Primula
July	/	Pulmonaria
Aug	sow	Rodgersia
Sept	division 🌱	
Oct	division 🌱	
Nov	/	
Dec	/	

CONDITIONS

Aspect Shade is essential.

Site The soil must be damp, rich, and leafy. For an impressive, vigorous display, apply a thick mulch of leaf mold around the clumps of plants every fall.

GROWING METHOD

Propagation When the seed is ripe, remove the fleshy covering, and raise in a cold frame. Alternatively, divide the rhizomes in the fall. A 6in piece will provide approximately six new plants. The success rate is generally high. Make sure that young plants are not allowed to dry out. Mulch them to guarantee against moisture loss.

Feeding Every other year, apply a scattering of complete fertilizer in the spring.

Problems *Botrytis* can be a problem, but is rarely anything to worry about.

FLOWERING

Season One brief display in late spring.

Cutting Lily-of-the-valley makes excellent cut flowers, providing a striking spring display, while emitting a gentle sweet scent. They can also be lifted and grown indoors in a pot to flower the following spring. When finished, replace in the garden.

AFTER FLOWERING

Requirements Remove the spent flower stems, but leave the foliage intact to provide the energy for next year's display.

COREOPSIS
Coreopsis

COREOPSIS ARE *wonderful plants that can quickly colonize a space, between shrubs, for example, to produce striking, bright yellow flowers.*

THIS DOUBLE-FLOWERED FORM *of golden coreopsis provides many weeks of marvellous color throughout the summer.*

FEATURES

Perennial coreopsis carries a profusion of bright yellow daisy-like flowers over a long period, generally through summer into the fall, though some do flower in spring. Regular deadheading will ensure a long display. *C. lanceolata*, known as calliopsis, has become naturalized in many parts of the world. The strong-growing *C. grandiflora* may grow 24–36in high, with *C.verticillata* about 8in shorter. There are several species worth trying, some with dwarf form or flowers displaying a dark eye. The foliage is variable, too. The plants are easy to grow. Plant in bold clumps in a mixed border.

COREOPSIS AT A GLANCE

A genus with well over 100 species that make a big contribution to the summer and early fall display. Hardy to 5°C (zone 7).

		Recommended Varieties
Jan	/	
Feb	/	*Coreopsis auriculata* "Schnittgold"
Mar	/	
Apr	sow	*C.* "Goldfink"
May	divide	*C. grandiflora* "Early Sunrise"
Jun	flowering	*C. g.* "Mayfield Giant" "Sunray"
July	flowering	
Aug	flowering	*C. verticillata*
Sept	flowering	*C. v.* "Grandiflora"
Oct	/	*C. v.* "Zagreb"
Nov	/	
Dec	/	

CONDITIONS

Aspect Prefers an open, sunny position throughout the day, with little shade.

Site Performs best in well-drained soil enriched with organic matter, but it will grow in poor soils, too. Over-rich soil may produce a profusion of foliage with poor flowering.

GROWING METHOD

Propagation Grows most easily from divisions of existing clumps lifted in the spring. Space new plants at approximately 12in intervals. Species can be grown from seed sown in mid-spring. Since cultivars of *C. grandiflora* can be ephemeral, sow seed for continuity.

Feeding Apply complete plant food when growth begins in the spring. However, no further feeding should be needed.

Problems No pest or disease problems are known.

FLOWERING

Season The long flowering period extends through the summer and fall. *C.* "Early Sunrise," *C.lanceolata*, and "Sunray" all flower in their first year from an early sowing.

Cutting Flowers can be cut for indoor decoration.

AFTER FLOWERING

Requirements Cut off spent flower stems and tidy the foliage as it dies back. In mild, frost-free winters, coreopsis may not totally die back.

CORYDALIS
Corydalis

THE FOLIAGE and flowers of Corydalis ochroleuca *are dainty and highly decorative. It looks good in walls and ornamental pots.*

THE BLUE SPECIES and forms of corydalis are highly prized. This is Corydalis flexuosa, *with long, upcurving spurs on its flowers.*

FEATURES

Pretty, fern-like foliage and tubular, spurred flowers are characteristic of the 300 or so species of corydalis. Only a small number of species are grown in cultivation, and they mainly flower in shades of yellow or blue, but there are some in pink or crimson. Some of the brilliant blues make a distinctive feature, and a recent cultivar with electric blue flowers, known as *C. flexuosa* "China Blue," is now widely available. It mixes well with *C. solida* "George Baker," salmon-pink, and *C. ochroleuca,* white. Heights vary from 6 to 24in. Many corydalis are excellent rock garden plants, while others are suitable for mixed borders or planting under deciduous trees. Many varieties may be available only from specialist nurseries that grow alpine plants.

CORYDALIS AT A GLANCE

A large group of annuals, biennials, and perennials, growing in a wide range of moist and dry conditions. Hardy to 5°F (zone 7).

Jan	/	**Recommended Varieties**
Feb	/	*Corydalis cashmeriana*
Mar	/	*C. cava*
Apr	divide 🖑	*C. cheilanthifolia*
May	transplant 🖑	*C. elata*
Jun	flowering 🌺	*C. lutea*
July	flowering 🌺	*C. sempervirens*
Aug	flowering 🌺	*C. solida*
Sept	divide 🖑	*C. s.* "Beth Evans"
Oct	sow 🖑	*C. s.* f. *transsylvanica*
Nov	/	*C. s.* f. "George Baker"
Dec	/	

CONDITIONS

Aspect   The preferred aspect varies with the species. Some tolerate an open, sunny position, while others need degrees of dappled sunlight. Species grown in "hot spots" should be given plenty of shade.

Site   Needs very well-drained soil that is able to retain some moisture in the summer.

GROWING METHOD

Propagation   Grows from seed sown as soon as it is ripe, in the fall. The seed is ripe when the small elongated capsules, which form after the flowers have fallen, turn brown and dry. Some species can be divided, while others produce tubers from which offsets can be taken. Plant at 4–6in intervals. New young plants need regular watering in prolonged, dry weather during the spring and summer months.

Feeding   Apply a sprinkling of slow-release fertilizer when growth commences in the spring.

Problems   There are no specific pest or disease problems.

FLOWERING

Season   Most species flower in the spring, or from spring into summer. *C. flexuosa* dies down in the summer.

Cutting   The flowers are unsuitable for cutting.

AFTER FLOWERING

Requirements   Remove spent flower stems, unless you are waiting for seed to set. Tidy up the foliage as it dies back.

CYNARA CARDUNCULUS
Cardoon

CARDOON LOOKS similar to a Scotch thistle. Its purple flowers can be left to dry, and then used for a striking indoor arrangement.

THE SILVERY LEAVES of cardoon are distinctive, large, and shapely, and a big clump forms a geometric, sculptural feature.

FEATURES

A close relative of the globe artichoke, the cardoon is generally grown for its arching, 39in-long, silver-gray foliage. Growing up to 78in tall and almost 78in wide, it is a terrific accent plant for the back of a border, or it can be combined with low-growing green plants in an open position. Both the color and form stand out against most other plants. The purple, thistle-like flowers develop in the summer, and the dried heads left on the plant make a decorative fall feature. Cardoon is edible, being grown for the tasty, fleshy base of each leaf. It is difficult to place in a small yard, since you need room to stand back and appreciate its startling form.

CYNARA AT A GLANCE

C. cardunculus is a clump-forming perennial grown for its long, striking foliage and purple flowers. Hardy to 0°F (zones

Jan	/	Companion Plants
Feb	/	
Mar	sow 🖐	Brugmansia
Apr	divide 🖐	Centranthus
May	transplant ✍	Echinops
Jun	flowering 🌿	Geranium
July	flowering 🌿	Miscanthus
Aug	flowering 🌿	Rose
Sept	flowering 🌿	Salvia
Oct	/	Yucca
Nov	/	
Dec	/	

CONDITIONS

Aspect   Needs full sun all day for best results. Also requires shelter from strong, leaf-tearing winds.
Soil   Needs rich, well-drained soil. Before planting, dig in large amounts of manure or compost.

GROWING METHOD

Propagation   Propagate in late spring, or grow from seed. Position plants at least 4ft apart. Seed-grown plants vary in quality, and do not normally reach maturity in their first year. During the growing season, regular, deep watering is essential for new, young plants in prolonged dry spells.
Feeding   Apply a complete plant food as growth commences in the spring, and repeat in mid-summer. When cardoon is grown as a vegetable it is given a weekly liquid feed.
Problems   Beware of the sharp points on the flowerheads.

FLOWERING

Season   The purple, thistle-like flowers appear during summer on stems 6½–10ft high.
Cutting   If the flowers are allowed to dry on the plant, they can be cut and used as part of a big, bold indoor decoration.

AFTER FLOWERING

Requirements   Once the flowers have lost their decorative value, cut off the whole stem low down. As the plant starts to die off and look untidy, cut it back just above the ground.

DELPHINIUM
Delphinium

DOZENS OF *individual flowers make up the striking spires of the delphinium. Blue shades, from pale to purple, predominate.*

THESE STAKED DELPHINIUMS, *growing in the shelter of a house, should remain stately and upright through the flowering season.*

FEATURES

Tall, handsome, and stately, delphiniums make an outstanding feature in perennial borders. Growing 39–78in high, the long-lasting spires of blooms, originally were in a rich blue only, but now offer shades of pink, lavender, white, and red. Delphiniums should be mass-planted at the back of a border for the best effect, but they can also be placed as accent plants at intervals across a border. They mix well with climbers like clematis. Tall-growing varieties may need staking unless they are in a very sheltered spot. Colors can be mixed, but the best effect comes from massing plants of the same color.

DELPHINIUM AT A GLANCE

A hardy annual, biennial, and perennial, it is grown for its striking, vertical spires, thick with flowers. Hardy to 5°F (zone 7).

Jan	/	Recommended Varieties
Feb	sow	*Delphinium* "Bruce"
Mar	sow	"Cassius"
Apr	transplant	"Emily Hawkins"
May	transplant	"Lord Butler"
Jun	flowering	"Our Deb"
July	flowering	"Rosemary Brock"
Aug	flowering	"Sandpiper"
Sept	/	"Sungleam"
Oct	divide	"Walton Gemstone"
Nov	/	
Dec	/	

CONDITIONS

Aspect Needs full sun and shelter from strong winds, and staking if it is not well sheltered.

Soil Needs well-drained soil enriched with copious amounts of decayed manure or compost before planting. Water regularly and mulch.

GROWING METHOD

Propagation Divide established clumps in the fall, ensuring each division has a crown and its own roots. Place them about 12in apart. Grows from seed sown in the spring, but the results are variable. Take 3in basal cuttings in mid-spring.

Feeding Apply complete plant food once growth begins in the spring, and each month until flowering.

Problems Watch for aphids on new growth, and hose off or spray with pyrethrum or insecticidal soap. In humid conditions a bad attack of powdery mildew may need to be tackled by spraying with a fungicide. Beware of slugs.

FLOWERING

Season Blooms for a long season through early and late summer.

Cutting Flowers make a good display, and can be dried.

AFTER FLOWERING

Requirements Remove the flower stems when the main blooms fade and small spikes may flower in late summer and early fall.

DIANTHUS CARYOPHYLLUS
Wild carnation

FRINGED PINK FLOWERS and silver-gray buds and stems make this a classic.

UPWARD-ANGLED CANES are one way of making sure that top-heavy blooms do not tumble onto a path. The other, more discrete method is to employ a series of small twiggy sticks.

FEATURES

Carnations are very popular, both as cut flowers and as a garden subject. Flowers are carried singly or in groups on stems 12–20in high, although florists' carnations may be taller. *Dianthus caryophyllus* from the Mediterranean, a woody perennial with elegant stiff stems, bears richly scented, purple-pink flowers that grow taller than the average, reaching 32in under perfect conditions. It has given rise to several excellent series. The Floristan Series comes in a wide color range, and makes good cut flowers, the Knight Series is shorter and bushier, and includes yellow, white, and orange blooms, and the Lilliput Series, shorter still at 8in, includes a rich scarlet.

DIANTHUS AT A GLANCE

D. caryophyllus is a colorful woody perennial, part of the large dianthus family of over 300 species. Hardy to 5°F (zone 7).

		Companion Plants
Jan	/	
Feb	/	Campanula
Mar	sow	Cistus
Apr	/	Crepis
May	transplant	Eryngium
Jun	flowering	Helianthemum
July	flowering	Portulaca
Aug	flowering	Sedum
Sept	/	Tulip
Oct	/	
Nov	/	
Dec	sow	

CONDITIONS

Aspect　Needs full sunlight all day. Protect from very strong winds.

Soil　Needs very well-drained soil, with plenty of additional, well-decayed organic matter. Unless the soil is alkaline, apply a light dressing of lime before each planting.

GROWING METHOD

Propagation　Grows easily from cuttings taken at almost any time. Use leafy side shoots and strip off all but the top leaves. Roots form in 3–5 weeks. Set newly rooted plants 8in apart. Water regularly to establish, then occasionally in dry weather. Carnations tolerate dry conditions well.

Feeding　Little fertilizer is needed if the soil contains plenty of organic matter, but you may give a complete feed twice, in the spring and again in mid-summer.

Problems　Carnation rust, a fungal disease, is common in warm, humid conditions. Grayish spots appear on leaves or stems, and the foliage may curl and yellow. Take prompt action by immediately spraying with a fungicide. Remove caterpillars when seen.

FLOWERING

Season　The crop of flowers appears in the summer, but it can be forced for other times. Remove any excess buds to produce good-sized, main blooms.

Cutting　An excellent cut flower. Recut stems between nodes (joints) to aid water uptake.

DIANTHUS CULTIVARS
Pinks

DIANTHUS CULTIVARS *make reliable, popular edging plants with bright colors and, in many cases, a rich, pervasive scent.*

ONE OF THE BEST *pinks for the garden, or as a cut flower, "Doris" is vigorous, long-flowering, and sweetly scented. A "must-have."*

FEATURES

Pinks are crosses of **D. caryophyllus** (wild carnation) and **D. plumarius** (cottage pink). Allwood Brothers nursery in West Sussex, England, has bred an enormous range of cultivars that are free-flowering, given the correct conditions. The gray-green foliage grows in a tufted mat and flowering stems are 4–12in tall. Most flowers are heavily scented and may be single or bicolored, some with a clear margin of contrasting color. Most are white, pink, red, deep crimson, or salmon, with cultivars ideally suited for the rock garden.

CONDITIONS

Aspect   Needs full sunlight all day, and protection from strong winds.

Site   Needs very free-draining soil, enriched with additional decayed organic matter, well ahead of planting. Use a soil-testing kit to determine whether your soil is acid—if so, add quantities of lime according to the manufacturer's instructions. Beware of exceeding the recommended rate—it will do more harm than good.

GROWING METHOD

Propagation   Grows easily from cuttings taken in late summer and the fall. Start fresh plants every three or four years to keep vigorous, compact growth. Space the plant approximately 6–12in apart, depending on the variety. Water until the plants are well established.

Feeding   Apply complete plant food in the early spring, when active spring growth begins.

Problems   Aphids and slugs are the two major problems. The former can be tackled by a regular spraying program with, for example, malathion. The latter can be seen late at night or early in the morning. Either treat chemically, or pick off by hand and drown.

FLOWERING

Season   Some pinks only flower during the spring, others have a long flowering period from the spring to early fall.

Cutting   Pinks make excellent cut flowers, providing indoor decoration and scent.

AFTER FLOWERING

Requirements   Cut off any spent flower stems to the ground as they fade. No other pruning action is necessary.

DIANTHUS AT A GLANCE

The cultivars include perennials in a wide color range, many richly scented. Generally hardy to 5°F (zone 7).

Month	Activity	Recommended Varieties
Jan	/	
Feb	/	**Dianthus alpinus**
Mar	sow	"Bovey Belle"
Apr	transplant	"Devon Glow"
May	transplant	**D. deltoides**
Jun	flowering	"La Bourboule"
July	flowering	"Monica Wyatt"
Aug	flowering	"Sam Barlow"
Sept	/	"Whitehill"
Oct	sow	"Widecombe Fair"
Nov	/	
Dec	/	

DIASCIA
Twinspur

ONE OF THE MOST USEFUL garden plants, twinspur produces flowers throughout the growing season, from the spring to fall, and at 12in tall, it makes the perfect front-of-border filler, tolerating a sunny position, and one with a degree of shade. Despite a short lifespan, it is easily propagated.

FEATURES

Twinspur has an extremely long flowering season, lasting from the spring until the first frosts. Though there is a large number of forms available, ranging from "Lilac Mist" to "Salmon Supreme," the color range is quite limited, essentially only including shades of pink. Diascia requires moist, rich soil, but over-feeding results in fewer flowers. The height ranges from 6 to 12in, which means the taller plants can be given free reign to burst through their neighbors, adding to the display. "Salmon Supreme" is an attractive low-spreader, being

6in high. **D. vigilis** is twice as tall, hardier, and even more free-flowering.

CONDITIONS

Aspect	Enjoys full sun; though it tolerates some shade, it will not flower as long or as prolifically.
Soil	Moisture-retentive, well-drained ground.

GROWING METHOD

Propagation	This is essential, since diascias are short-lived, but propagation is easily managed. Success rates are high by all methods, though cuttings are particularly easy. Either sow the seed when ripe or in the following spring, take cuttings during the growing season, or divide in the spring. Since young plants might die in severe winters, keep indoor cuttings as possible replacements.
Feeding	Mulch well in the spring to enrich the soil.
Problems	Slugs and snails are the main enemies. Pick them off or use a chemical treatment.

FLOWERING

Season	An unusually long season from the spring, beyond the end of summer, to the first frosts.
Cutting	Diascias cut well, and although they do not last particularly long in water, replacements are quickly available from the parent plant.

AFTER FLOWERING

Requirements	Cut ruthlessly to the ground after flowering to promote a second flush of flowers.

DIASCIA AT A GLANCE

A near 50-strong genus of annuals and perennials, with a pink color and a long flowering season. Hardy to 23°F (zone 9).

		Recommended Varieties
Jan	/	
Feb	sow 🖜	*Diascia barberae* "Ruby Field"
Mar	divide 🖜	
Apr	transplant 🖜	D. "Dark Eyes"
May	flowering ❀	D. "Hector's Hardy"
Jun	flowering ❀	**D. integerrima**
July	flowering ❀	D. "Lilac Mist"
Aug	flowering ❀	D. "Rupert Lambert"
Sept	flowering ❀	D. vigilis
Oct	/	
Nov	/	
Dec	/	

DICENTRA SPECTABILIS
Bleeding heart

THE ARCHING STEMS of this bleeding heart carry masses of bright pink, heart-shaped flowers resembling tiny lockets.

THE BLEEDING HEART is well worth growing for its foliage alone, since the delicate, fern-like leaves are very decorative.

FEATURES

With fern-like foliage and curving stems bearing pretty pink-and-white, heart-shaped flowers, bleeding heart is an all-time favorite perennial. It appeals to children and adults alike. There is a cultivar, "Alba," which has pure white flowers. Another species less commonly grown is **D. formosa**, which has very ferny foliage, but its flowers are not so completely heart-shaped. Bleeding heart can be grown in a mixed border or in the filtered shade of trees. Plants may reach 16–24in tall in good conditions, and form a clump approximately 20in wide.

DICENTRA AT A GLANCE

D. spectabilis is a clump-forming perennial, with arching stems and decorative deep pink flowers. Hardy to 0°F (zones 6–7).

		Recommended Varieties
Jan	/	
Feb	/	*D.* "Adrian Bloom"
Mar	sow	"Bountiful"
Apr	transplant	*D. cucularia*
May	transplant	*D. f. alba*
Jun	flowering	"Langtrees"
July	flowering	"Ruby Slippers"
Aug	/	*D. macrantha*
Sept	/	*D. spectabilis*
Oct	division	*D. s.* "Alba"
Nov	sow	"Stuart Boothman"
Dec	/	

CONDITIONS

Aspect   Dicentra grows best in filtered sunlight. Strong, hot, drying winds make it shrivel up. A sheltered position protects against late frosts.

Site   Needs well-drained soil rich in organic matter. Dig in copious quantities of decayed manure or compost several weeks before planting.

GROWING METHOD

Propagation   Divide large established clumps in the fall, and plant divisions 10–12in apart. Also grows from seed sown in the spring or fall. Needs regular, deep watering during dry periods in the spring and summer.

Feeding   Apply a sprinkling of a complete plant food whenever growth begins in the spring.

Problems   There are no specific pest or disease problems known for this plant.

FLOWERING

Season   Blooms for several weeks during late spring and early summer.

Cutting   Flowers are not suitable for cutting.

AFTER FLOWERING

Requirements   Cut out spent flower stems. As the foliage yellows and dies off, cut it off just above the ground.

DIGITALIS
Foxglove

A SUPERB DISPLAY of Digitalis grandiflora, *the yellow foxglove, which sends up 39in-high spires. It is an excellent choice for gaps toward the rear of the border, although you may have to weed out some seedlings that spread beyond the main clump.*

FEATURES

Foxgloves are essentials for the "cottage garden," self-seeding in unexpected places, with their tall spires of often richly colored flowers. They grow in most soils and situations, from the shady to the sunny, and dryish to damp, although performance is variable at these extremes. They also make a large group of biennials and perennials ranging in height from 24in to 6½ft. The common foxglove (**D. purpurea**) can be grown as a perennial, but its lifespan is short, and the biennial is generally the preferred option. The color range includes red, yellow, white, and pink with the early summer Fox Hybrids. **D. grandiflora** has the largest flowers.

DIGITALIS AT A GLANCE

Foxgloves are grown for their tall spires of attractive, tubular flowers, usually in soft hues. Hardy to 5°F (zone 7).

			Recommended Varieties
Jan	/		
Feb	/		*Digitalis ferruginea*
Mar	sow		D. grandiflora
Apr	transplant		D. lanata
May	transplant		D. parviflora
Jun	flowering		D. purpurea
July	flowering		D. p. Excelsior Group
Aug	/		
Sept	/		
Oct	/		
Nov	/		
Dec	/		

CONDITIONS

Aspect Dappled shade for part of the day is ideal, but it is not absolutely essential. Foxgloves are undemanding plants, and will grow in a wide range of yards.

Site The soil conditions can vary, but humus-rich ground gives the best results.

GROWING METHOD

Propagation Sow seed of new varieties in containers within a cold frame during the late spring. Space seedlings up to 18in apart. If you already have some plants, seeding is not necessary, since the foxglove is a prolific self-seeder. Dig up a new plant and transplant to where it is required. Water in well, and do not let it dry out.

Feeding Provide a complete feed in the spring. In particularly dry soil, provide a protective spring mulch.

Problems Leaf spot and powdery mildew can strike. Spraying is the best treatment.

FLOWERING

Season Flowers appear in early and mid-summer.

Cutting While they make good cut flowers, handle with extreme caution. The foliage can irritate the skin, and all parts are poisonous.

AFTER FLOWERING

Requirements Leave just a few stems to seed where the foxgloves look good, mixing well with other plants, otherwise deadhead to avoid masses of invasive seedlings.

ECHINACEA PURPUREA
Purple coneflower

BOLDER THAN many perennials, coneflowers are sometimes slow to appear in the spring but they are definitely worth the wait.

THIS FINE STAND of bright purple coneflowers adds a striking touch to this scheme. The flowers fade as they age, but petals don't fall.

FEATURES

Native to the prairie States of America, the coneflower is a hardy, drought-resistant plant. Its dark, cone-shaped center is surrounded by rich pink ray petals, and there are cultivars available in shades of pink-purple and white. They make excellent cut flowers. Coneflowers often grow over 39in tall, and are a great addition to a perennial border because they bloom over a long period, from mid-summer into the fall, when many other plants have finished. Echinacea should be mass-planted to get the best effect. Excellent varieties include *E. purpurea* Bressingham Hybrids, "Magnus," and "White Swan."

ECHINACEA AT A GLANCE

E. purpurea is an attractive, daisy-like perennial with purple flowers, ideal for naturalizing or borders. Hardy to 5°F (zone 7).

		Companion Plants
Jan	/	
Feb	sow	Allium
Mar	sow	Delphinium
Apr	transplant	Geranium
May	transplant	Gladiolus
Jun	/	Iris
July	flowering	Lavandula
Aug	flowering	Rosemary
Sept	flowering	Yucca
Oct	divide	Delphinium
Nov	/	Rose
Dec	/	

CONDITIONS

Aspect Prefers full sunlight all day. Although it is tolerant of windy conditions, the blooms will have a better appearance if the plants are sheltered from strong winds.

Site Needs well-drained, rich soil. Poor or sandy soils can be improved by digging in large quantities of compost or manure before planting.

GROWING METHOD

Propagation Divide existing clumps in the early spring or fall, and replant divisions 8–10in apart. It can be grown from seeds sown in early spring, which may produce color variations. Echinacea needs regular watering to establish itself in prolonged dry spells, but occasional deep soakings in dry weather are enough, as it tolerates dry conditions well.

Feeding Apply complete plant food in early spring and again in mid-summer.

Problems No specific problems are known.

FLOWERING

Season There is a long flowering period from late summer into the fall.

Cutting Cut flowers for the vase when they are fully open, but before the petals separate.

AFTER FLOWERING

Requirements Remove spent flower stems. The whole plant can be cut back to ground level in winter.

ECHINOPS
Globe thistle

THESE METALLIC BLUE *globe thistles form an elegant picture against a stone wall.*

EARLY MORNING LIGHT *accentuates the rounded, slightly spiky heads of these globe thistle flowers, planted here in a bold drift in a countryside yard.*

FEATURES

This plant's very distinctive appearance makes a good accent in a mixed planting. Taller species need to be placed at the rear of a border, but others can be planted in bold groups through the bed. Most have foliage that is stiff, prickly, and finely divided, with silvery stems growing from 12in to $6\frac{1}{2}$ft tall. Some of the species have foliage that has fine white hairs on the underside. The flowerheads are usually white or metallic blue, and are highly prized for their decorative value when cut and dried. The most commonly grown is *E. ritro* and its cultivars, some of which have deep blue flowers. *E. sphaerocephalus* has pale gray-to-silvery flowers.

ECHINOPS AT A GLANCE

A group of annuals, biennials, and perennials grown for their geometric shapes and blue flowers. Hardy to 23–50°F (zones 9-11).

Jan	divide	
Feb	divide	**Recommended Varieties**
Mar	sow	*Echinops bannaticus*
Apr	/	"Blue Globe"
May	transplant	*E. b.* "Taplow Blue"
Jun	/	*E. ritro ruthenicus*
July	flowering	*E. r.* "Veitch's Blue"
Aug	flowering	
Sept	flowering	**Companion Plants**
Oct	divide	Buddleja
Nov	divide	Kniphofia
Dec	divide	Perovskia

CONDITIONS

Aspect   Prefers full sunlight all day.
Site   Soil must be very well drained but need not be rich. The globe thistle can be grown in poor, gravel-like, or sandy soils.

GROWING METHOD

Propagation   It can either be grown from seed, from division of existing clumps, or from root cuttings. All propagation is done from the fall to winter. Plant out about 16in apart and water regularly to establish. Although drought-tolerant, this plant benefits from occasional deep watering during prolonged dry spring and summer periods.
Feeding   Apply a complete plant food or poultry manure in early spring.
Problems   There are no known pest or disease problems, but plants will rot on sticky clay or poorly drained soil.

FLOWERING

Season   Each species or variety will flower for approximately two months.
Cutting   Flowerheads required for drying should be cut before the blooms are fully open.

AFTER FLOWERING

Requirements   Cut off any remaining spent flowerheads, unless you want the seed to ripen. As the plant dies down, clean away dead foliage, wearing gloves to protect yourself against the foliage.

EPIMEDIUM
Barrenwort / Bishop's miter

NEW GROWTH on the bishop's miter bears attractive bronze or pink shadings, but the older foliage is plain green.

A DENSE CARPET of bishop's miter makes wonderful groundcover under a grove of shapely Japanese maples.

FEATURES

This low-growing perennial is grown more for its attractive foliage than its flowers, although the blooms are quite attractive. The shape resembles a bishop's miter, giving rise to its common name. Many species have small, starry flowers in white, cream, or yellow, although there are pale and rose-pink varieties, too. This is a woodland plant that makes a good groundcover or filler for shady parts of the yard. Some die down completely in winter, while others remain evergreen. Plants are rarely more than 12in tall. Combine it with plants such as Solomon's seal, primrose, or lenten rose, which enjoy similar woodland-type conditions.

EPIMEDIUM AT A GLANCE

An evergreen, deciduous perennial making excellent groundcover in shady situations. Small flowers. Hardy to 5°F (zone 7).

Month	Activity	Recommended Varieties
Jan	/	
Feb	sow 🖐	*Epimedium cantab-rigiense*
Mar	/	
Apr	transplant 🖐	*E. grandiflorum*
May	flowering 🌸	*E. g.* "Nanum"
Jun	/	*E. g.* "Rose Queen"
July	/	*E. perralderianum*
Aug	/	*E. pinnatum colchicum*
Sept	sow 🖐	*E.* x *rubrum*
Oct	divide 🖐	*E.* x *versicolor* "Sulphureum"
Nov	/	
Dec	/	

CONDITIONS

Aspect   Epimedium needs dappled shade and protection from strong winds.

Site   Requires well-drained soil, heavily enriched with organic matter. Regular mulching is beneficial to retain moisture.

GROWING METHOD

Propagation   Clumps can be divided in the fall, although with some varieties this is not easy. Pull apart or cut away sections of plant, keeping both roots and a bud or shoot on each piece. Plant 6–8in apart. Some species seed readily. Keep young plants well watered until they are well established.

Feeding   Apply a slow-release fertilizer in the spring.

Problems   Snails may attack soft new growth when it appears, so take precautions.

FLOWERING

Season   The small flowers appear in spring, along with the leaves. But shear off the foliage of all varieties in winter, even when green (except *E. perralderianum*), to prevent the flowers being obscured. Fresh leaves will quickly follow.

Cutting   Flowers can be cut for the vase and last quite well in water.

AFTER FLOWERING

Requirements Spent flower stems can be clipped off. Old, dead foliage should be tidied up and removed

ERYNGIUM
Sea holly

AN OUTSTANDING PLANT for the Mediterranean-style garden is Eryngium maritimum. *It has strong architectural features with a stiff, branching habit, and mid- to late summer flowers. It can be grown in the border, or better still, in a gravel bed to highlight the shape.*

FEATURES

Sea holly is a 230-species strong genus, with annuals, biennials, and perennials. Although they are related to cow parsley, they bear no resemblance, being grown for their marvellous, attractive, spiky appearance, blue flowers (though some are white or green), and ability to thrive in poor, rocky, sunny ground. Heights can vary considerably, from E. **alpinum**, 28in tall, which as its name suggests grows in the Alps, to E. **eburneum** from South America, which can reach 5ft, and E. **pandanifolium**, which is much taller at 10ft. One of the most attractive is the Moroccan E. **variifolium**, which has rounded, white-veined foliage setting off the pale blue

flowers. It is also more manageable at 14in high—good for the front of a border.

CONDITIONS

Aspect	Grow in full sunlight, well out of the shade.
Site	There are two types of sea holly, with different growing needs. Most prefer fast-draining, fertile ground (e.g. E. **alpinum** and E. **bourgatii**), and some (e.g. E. **eburneum**) poor stony ground, out of the winter wet.

GROWING METHOD

Propagation	Sow the seed when ripe; alternatively, take root cuttings in late winter, or divide in the spring.
Feeding	Only for the first kind of sea holly, which benefits from a spring feed and some well-rotted manure. Good drainage is important.
Problems	Slugs and snails are the main problem when sea holly is grown in the border, damaging the new, young leaves. Promptly remove when seen, or use a chemical treatment.

FLOWERING

Season	The earliest sea hollies begin flowering in early summer, while others last from mid- to early or mid-fall in dry weather.
Cutting	Sea holly makes an invaluable cut flower. They also make exceptional dried arrangements, combining with other architectural plants and softer, flowery ones.

AFTER FLOWERING

Requirements	Cut back the spent flowering stems to the ground.

ERYNGIUM AT A GLANCE

Annuals, and deciduous/evergreen perennials grown for their shape. Hardiness varies from 13°F (zone 8) to 0°F (zones 6–7).

		Recommended Varieties
Jan	/	
Feb	sow	Eryngium alpinum
Mar	division	E. a. "Blue Star"
Apr	transplant	E. bourgatii
May	transplant	E. b. "Oxford Blue"
Jun	flowering	E. giganteum
July	flowering	E. x oliverianum
Aug	flowering	E. x tripartitum
Scpt	flowcring	
Oct	sow	
Nov	/	
Dec	/	

EUPHORBIA
Spurge

THE HIGHLY VERSATILE spurge tolerates a wide range of conditions. One of its chief attractions is its striking bracts.

A MIXED BORDER showing the value of propagating your own euphorbia. Strong shapes, flowing clumps, it even thrives in the shade.

FEATURES

A large group of important shrubs, annuals, biennials, perennials, and subshrubs, ranging from tree-like succulents to structural clumps for the border. The latter spurges, evergreen and deciduous, grow in a wide range of conditions, from shade to sun, and tend to be quite sturdy, many leaning at 45° if not standing upright. Many of the evergreens benefit from being cut back to produce vigorous new spring growth. For example E. **characias** yields stems covered in small, stiff, outward-pointing leaves and yellow-green flowers. A big clump makes a bold, striking feature. E. **griffithii** "Fireglow," deciduous, is about half as high and produces early summer orange-red terminal bracts. It spreads to form a large colony. And E. **schillingii**, a recent find in Nepal by plant hunter Tony Schilling, flowers in late summer and has yellow bracts.

CONDITIONS

Aspect	Depending on your choice of plant, spurges like full sunlight or light shade.
Soil	This can vary from light, fast-draining soil to damp, moist ground, rich with leaf mold.

GROWING METHOD

Propagation	Sow the seed when ripe, or the following spring. Alternatively, divide perennials in the spring, or take spring cuttings.
Feeding	Spurges that require rich soil can be given a scattering of complete plant food and mulched in the spring. Those that require fast-draining ground need only be fed.
Problems	Aphids can be a problem in a bad year; spray at the first sign of an attack.

FLOWERING

Season	Flowers appear in the spring or summer.
Cutting	While the stem structure of most spurges makes them theoretically good as cut flowers, note that the milky sap can badly irritate the skin; if any part of the plant is ingested, severe discomfort results. Wear gloves and goggles.

AFTER FLOWERING

Requirements	Cut back the brownish or lackluster stems in the fall to promote fresh new growth.

EUPHORBIA AT A GLANCE

A genus of some 2,000 species. The border kind tend to be grown for their structure. Frost-tender to hardy 0°F (zones 6–7).

		Recommended Varieties
Jan	/	
Feb	/	Euphorbia amygdaloides
Mar	divide 🖐	var.
Apr	transplant 🖐	robbiae
May	flowering 🌱	E. characias
Jun	flowering 🌱	E. characias wulfenii
July	flowering 🌱	E. griffithii "Dixter"
Aug	flowering 🌱	E. myrsinites
Sept	flowering 🌱	E. palustris
Oct	sow 🖐	E. polychroma
Nov	/	
Dec	/	

GERANIUM
Cranesbill

THE FOLIAGE *on this clump-forming, North American* Geranium macrorrhizum *is as attractive as its pink-white or pink flowers. The leaves are scented and quickly form a dense carpet.*

GERANIUM PRATENSE, *with its deep violet flowers that bloom over a long period.*

FEATURES

There are a great many perennial species of the true, hardy geranium, and many are reliable, long-flowering plants. Most cranesbill geraniums (not to be confused with tender, pot-plant pelargoniums) are easy to grow and are ideal in perennial borders, as edging plants, or as an infill between shrubs. Some species self-sow freely, but unwanted seedlings are easily removed. Cranesbills range from about 6 to 39in tall. Most have attractive, deeply divided leaves, and the flowers cover a range of shades, mostly in violet, blue, pink, rose, and cerise. Species worth seeking out include *G. endressii* and its cultivars, especially "Wargrave Pink," *G. pratense*, *G. psilostemon*, *G. himalayense*, and *G. sanguineum*. A variety of *G. sanguineum*, "Lancastriense," is a dwarf-growing type that can be used as groundcover.

GERANIUM AT A GLANCE

A genus of some 300 annuals, biennials, and perennials grown for their big flowering clumps. Most are hardy to 5°F (zone 7).

Jan	/	**Recommended Varieties**
Feb	sow	
Mar	sow	***Geranium himalayense***
		"Gravetye"
Apr	divide	"Johnson's Blue"
May	transplant	***G.* x *oxonianum***
Jun	flowering	"Wargrave Pink"
July	flowering	***G. palmatum***
Aug	flowering	***G. pratense*** "Mrs Kendall
Sept	flowering	Clark"
Oct	sow	***G. psilostemon***
Nov	/	
Dec	/	

CONDITIONS

Aspect   Most like sunlight; others prefer shade.

Site   Needs open, well-drained soil, but it need not be rich. Very acid ground should be limed before planting; use a soil-testing kit to ascertain the quantity required.

GROWING METHOD

Propagation   Most cranesbills are easily grown from seed sown in the fall, but note that the results will be variable. They can also be grown from cuttings taken in the growing season. Established clumps can be lifted and divided in the spring. The exact spacing depends on the variety, but it is usually within the range of 8–16in. Established plants tolerate dry conditions and rarely need watering, except in prolonged droughts.

Feeding   Apply a little complete plant food when growth starts in the spring.

Problems   No specific pest or disease problems are known for these plants.

FLOWERING

Season   Cranesbills flower through the spring, into late summer.

Cutting   Flowers do not cut well.

AFTER FLOWERING

Requirements   Remove spent flower stems, unless you want the plants to seed. Some pruning may be needed through the growing season if growth becomes too rampant. Prune to maintain

GEUM CHILOENSE
Avens

THE BRIGHT RED *double geum "Mrs J Bradshaw," a justifiably popular perennial.*

LIKE MOST PERENNIALS, *geums look best when planted together in large numbers. Here a mass of deep red flowers looks wonderful against a background of green foliage.*

FEATURES

Although there are many species of geum, the two most commonly grown are cultivars. "Lady Stratheden" has double yellow flowers, and "Mrs J Bradshaw" bright scarlet double flowers. Flowers appear on stems 12–20in tall high that emerge from large rosettes of slightly hairy, lobed compound leaves. Foliage is generally evergreen, but may be herbaceous in some areas. Geums can be planted as accent plants, preferably in groups, in the wild garden or near the front of a mixed border. While flowers are not very suitable for cutting, they give a long, vibrant display in the yard if they are regularly deadheaded.

GEUM AT A GLANCE

A brightly colored perennial, essential for the spring border, with plenty of attractive cultivars. All hardy to 0°F (zones 6–7).

Jan	/	**Recommended Varieties**
Feb	sow 🖐	"Borisii"
Mar	divide 🖐	"Fire Opal"
Apr	transplant 🖐	"Lady Stratheden"
May	flowering 🌸	*G. montanum*
Jun	flowering 🌸	"Mrs J Bradshaw"
July	/	*G. rivale*
Aug	/	*G. urbanum*
Sept	/	
Oct	divide 🖐	
Nov	/	
Dec	/	

CONDITIONS

Aspect Prefers full sunlight, but it can also be grown successfully in dappled shade.

Site Needs well-drained soil. Plants will benefit from the addition of plenty of decayed manure or compost before planting.

GROWING METHOD

Propagation Clumps can be divided in the spring or fall. Cut back foliage to reduce moisture loss while divisions re-establish. It also grows from seed sown in spring, but plants may not be true to type. Plant about 10–12in apart. Since most popular varieties tend to be short-lived, propagate often for a regular supply.

Feeding Apply complete plant food in early spring and again in mid-summer.

Problems No particular problems are known.

FLOWERING

Season There is a long flowering display, through late spring and mid-summer. Young vigorous plants will keep going to the fall.

Cutting Regular cutting (or deadheading) is essential to prolong the display.

AFTER FLOWERING

Requirements None, apart from the removal of spent flower stems and any dead foliage that may accumulate under the rosette.

GUNNERA MANICATA
Gunnera

THE HUGE, theatrical, eye-catching leaves of Gunnera manicata.

*DAMP GROUND at the bottom of this steep bank allows the clump of gunnera to thrive in its favorite conditions. The attractive pink-flowering shrub beside it is a hawthorn (*Crataegus *species).*

FEATURES

This is not a plant for small yards. Growing to 8½ft high, clumps grow 10–13ft wide. The huge rhubarb-like leaves can be well over 42in in diameter, and are supported by long, stout, hairy stems. This is a magnificent feature plant from Africa, Australasia, and South America. It needs a damp or wet yard area, beside a pond or stream, or to the edge of a lawn. In summer it produces a dramatic tall spike of greenish flowers, often completely concealed by the foliage, but this plant is grown for the impact of its giant, architectural foliage. It is herbaceous, dying right back to the ground in winter. This is not a difficult plant to grow in the correct conditions, but it must be carefully sited. It needs space to grow, and gardeners need space to stand back and admire it.

GUNNERA AT A GLANCE

One of the largest, most spectacular perennials, it produces huge, often lobed, leaves. Spectacular flower spike. Hardy to 5°F (zone 7).

Jan	/	**Recommended Varieties**
Feb	/	
Mar	/	*Gunnera arenaria*
Apr	transplant ✍	*G. flavida* (groundcover)
May	transplant ✍	*G. hamiltonii*
Jun	/	*G. magellanica*
July	flowering ✾	(groundcover)
Aug	/	*G. manicata*
Sept	sow ✍	*G. prorepens*
Oct	/	*G. tinctoria*
Nov	/	
Dec	/	

CONDITIONS

Aspect Grows both in semi-shade and sunlight in cool, damp areas.

Site Likes a rich, moist soil. Dig plenty of organic matter into the ground before planting, and mulch crowns heavily with decayed compost or manure for protection.

GROWING METHOD

Propagation Divide small clumps in the spring, replanting them no less than 6½ft apart. Cuttings can be taken from new growth, too. Pot them up and nurture them until they are well rooted. Plants can be raised from seed, but this is slow and difficult. Keep moist throughout the spring and summer.

Feeding Apply pelleted poultry manure as new growth commences in the early spring to give the plant a boost. Add a fresh mulch of rotted manure at the same time.

Problems No specific pest or disease problems are known for gunnera.

FLOWERING

Season Heavy spikes of greenish flowers are produced in early summer.

Fruits The inflorescence is followed by fleshy red-green fruits, which can be ornamental.

AFTER FLOWERING

Requirements As the weather becomes cold in the fall and leaves begin to brown, cut off the foliage and cover the crown of the plant with a thick layer of straw. Use a large leaf as a hat to keep it dry.

GYPSOPHILA PANICULATA
Baby's breath

THE WONDERFUL, MASSED DISPLAY OF Gypsophila paniculata *"Pink Star" in full bloom. The rippling, airy mound of flowers justifiably led to its common name, baby's breath. It makes a stunning sight in its native habitats, spreading across the sandy steppes of the Far East and eastern Europe.*

FEATURES

Baby's breath is an eye-catching border perennial that grows to 4ft high, and produces a summer flower display that looks like a puffy aerial cloud. The flowers appear in mid- and late summer, and are white on the species, though there are gently colored cultivars. "Compacta Plena" is soft pink, "Flamingo" is lilac-pink, and "Rosenschleier" pale pink. The latter is also quite short, at 1ft tall, and is worth repeat-planting in a long border. "Bristol Fairy" has the advantage of large, white flowers, ½in across, but it is not as vigorous as the rest and is relatively short-lived, needing to be propagated every few years. *G. paniculata* mixes well with contrasting, vertical plants.

CONDITIONS

Aspect	Full sunlight is required for it to thrive.
Site	Free-draining soil is essential, since the plant's native habitat is sandy steppes and stony sites in eastern Europe, Central Asia, and China.

GROWING METHOD

Propagation	Sow seed in a cold frame in spring, or in pots in a gently heated greenhouse in winter. Species can be propagated by root cuttings, again in late winter. Though adult plants tolerate some dryness, the young plants must not be allowed to dry out. Water regularly in the growing season. Plant out in its final position, since it dislikes disturbance.
Feeding	A scattering of complete plant food in the spring.
Problems	Generally problem-free.

FLOWERING

Season	The one flowering period is mid- and late summer; an unmissable sight.
Cutting	Makes excellent cut flowers—the light sprays of white-to-pink flowers add considerably to any arrangement, formal or flowery.

AFTER FLOWERING

Requirements	Cut back to ground level in the fall.

GYPSOPHILA AT A GLANCE

A striking, tallish herbaceous perennial that gives an impactful, flowery mid-summer display. Hardy to 0°F (zones 6–7).

		Companion Plants
Jan	/	
Feb	/	*Agapanthus africanus*
Mar	sow	*Geranium himalayense*
Apr	transplant	*Iris* "Magic Man"
May	/	*Osteospermum*
Jun	/	"Whirligig"
July	flowering	*Salvia cacaliifolia*
Aug	flowering	*Silene coeli-rosa*
Sept	/	*Solanum crispum*
Oct	/	
Nov	/	
Dec	/	

HELENIUM AUTUMNALE
Sneezeweed

STILL ONE OF THE BEST and most popular cultivars of sneeze-weed, "Moerheim Beauty" has been a favorite since the 1930s.

ORANGE AND TAWNY COLORS are a feature of sneezeweed, a reliable perennial that brightens the fall yard.

FEATURES

As its Latin name suggests, this herbaceous perennial flowers from late summer to mid-fall. The basic species has bright golden, daisy-like flowers with dark centers, but many of the most popular cultivars have flowers in rich tones of orange-red or copper-red. "Butterpat," "Moerheim Beauty," and "Waldtraut" are among the most popular varieties. Sneezeweed can grow 39–60in or more high, eventually forming large clumps over 20in across. Its flowers cut well, but the plant is probably more valuable for its contribution to the fall garden. Place at the back of a perennial border or among shrubs. Easy to grow.

HELENIUM AT A GLANCE

A group of annuals, biennials, and perennials, grown for their prolific, bright flowering display. Hardy to 5°F (zone 7).

		Recommended Varieties
Jan	/	
Feb	sow	
Mar	sow	"Butterpat"
Apr	transplant	"Chipperfield Orange"
May	transplant	"Crimson Beauty"
Jun	/	"Moerheim Beauty"
July	flowering	"Rotgold"
Aug	flowering	"The Bishop"
Sept	flowering	
Oct	/	
Nov	/	
Dec	/	

CONDITIONS

Aspect   Needs to be grown in full sunlight throughout the day. Avoid shade.

Site   Needs a moisture-retentive soil heavily enriched with organic matter. Helenium will not thrive in dry soil. Mulch around clumps to help keep soil moist.

GROWING METHOD

Propagation   Established clumps can be lifted and divided about every three years. Discard the oldest central sections and replant the divisions about 12in apart in the spring or fall. Give new young plants a regular watering throughout the growing season.

Feeding   Apply complete plant food as new growth commences in the spring.

Problems   Sneezeweed is generally free from problems, although slugs and snails can damage newly emerging growth in damp weather.

FLOWERING

Season   The flowering season starts in mid-summer and continues into the fall.

Cutting   Flowers cut well for indoor decoration.

AFTER FLOWERING

Requirements   Spent flower stems should be removed. As the plant dies down, cut off and remove dead foliage. It can be chopped and left on the ground as a mulch. With flowers blooming into the fall, the foliage remains in good condition until attacked by frost.

HELLEBORUS
Lenten rose

PRETTY SHADINGS of color are shown on the Lenten rose. Seedlings often produce unexpected colors, which can be maintained if the plants are then propagated by division.

NATIVE to Corsica and Sardinia, this is the green-flowered Helleborus argutifolius.

FEATURES

Various species of hellebores are known as the Christmas or Lenten rose because of their flowering times—mid-winter or early spring. *H. niger*, which has pure white flowers with green centers, can be difficult to grow to perfection; *H. argutifolius* (syn. *H. corsicus*) and H. *orientalis* are more resilient. *H. argutifolius* has lovely lime-green flowers and spiny-toothed leaf margins, while *H. orientalis* is more variable and may have white, green, pink, or mottled flowers. Cultivars include a deep crimson variety. These perennials are mostly evergreen and are best planted under deciduous trees, where they can remain undisturbed. Some are fairly short-lived, but they tend to self-seed freely so that numbers readily increase, creating an impressive sight.

HELLEBORUS AT A GLANCE

A free-spreading, attractively flowering perennial in a wide range of colors. Excellent in woodland. Hardy to 23–59°F (zones 9–11).

Jan	flowering ✿	**Recommended Varieties**
Feb	flowering ✿	
Mar	flowering ✿	*Helleborus argutifolius*
Apr	divide ✎	(syn. *H. corsicus*)
May	transplant ✎	*H. foetidus*
Jun	/	*H. lividus*
July	/	*H. niger*
Aug	/	*H.* x *nigercors*
Sept	/	*H. orientalis* Cultivars
Oct	/	*H.* x *sternii* Blackthorn
Nov	/	Group
Dec	/	*H. viridis*

CONDITIONS

Aspect	Prefers dappled sunlight under trees, or in other partially shaded spots.
Site	Soil must be well enriched with organic matter, and able to retain moisture. Excellent in winter containers.

GROWING METHOD

Propagation	Divide clumps in the spring or summer, directly after flowering, replanting the divisions about 8–12in apart. Seed can be sown when ripe, but seedlings will take about three years to flower. Seedlings often produce interesting shades. Recently planted hellebores need plenty of water in prolonged, dry spells in the spring and summer.
Feeding	Apply a little complete plant food in the spring. Mulch each spring with manure or compost to aid moisture retention.
Problems	Leaf blotch can disfigure and weaken plants. Spray with a fungicide. Beware aphids, particularly after flowering. Slugs attack the flowers and foliage.

FLOWERING

Season	From mid-winter to early spring.
Cutting	Lenten roses provide attractive cut flowers at the time of year when supply is short.

AFTER FLOWERING

Requirements	Prune off the dead flower stems and any dead leaves. Do not disturb.

HEMEROCALLIS
Daylily

MAHOGANY RED is one of the many strong colors available in the huge range of daylily cultivars now produced by specialist growers.

THE MASS-PLANTING of this creamy yellow daylily increases its impact. Blooms will appear one after the other for many weeks.

FEATURES

Easily grown in a wide range of conditions, the daylily is a trouble-free plant with single or double flowers. As its name suggests, individual flowers last only one day, but they are produced over a long period. They come in a wide range of colors, the main ones being shades of yellow, orange, red, magenta, and purple. There is an enormous number of exciting, attractive hybrids available from specialist growers. The clumps of grassy foliage may be 10 to 39in high; some are evergreen, while others die down in winter. While straight species are not as readily available as the hybrids, they are important in hybridizing new varieties and several species are worth seeking out. They include *H. altissima* from China, which has pale yellow fragrant flowers on stems approximately 5ft high, and *H. lilio-asphodelus*, which has pale yellow fragrant flowers above leaves 22in high.

| Categories | Daylilies have been divided into five categories that list them according to flower type. The divisions are circular, double, spider-shaped, star-shaped, and triangular. Most are single; hot weather can produce extra petals and stamens. |

Categories Daylilies have been divided into five categories that list them according to flower type. The divisions are circular, double, spider-shaped, star-shaped, and triangular. Most are single; hot weather can produce extra petals and stamens.

Dwarf forms The number of dwarf forms available is steadily increasing and they may be better suited to today's smaller yards. Those with a reliable reflowering habit can also be successfully grown in pots. Use a good quality potting mix and crowd three plants into an 8in pot for good effect. "Little Grapette," "Little Gypsy Vagabond," "Penny's Worth," and "Stella d'Oro" are good ones to try, all growing about 12 x 18in.

Uses Mass-plantings of dwarf or tall forms create the best effect. Daylilies are not plants that should be spread around the yard. Use large numbers of a single variety or use varieties of similar color; it is clearly preferable to planting a mixture of types or colors. In a mixed border they give a very pleasing effect,

"BURNING DAYLIGHT," one of the top daylilies, blooms prolifically in sunlight or semi-shade.

MANY OF the finest daylily cultivars are in creamy yellow or orange tones, not surprisingly, as these are the colors of many of the species.

CONDITIONS

Aspect   Grows best in full sun but tolerates semi-shade. Can be mass-planted on banks or sloping ground as the roots are very efficient soil binders.

Site   Grows in any type of soil, wet or dry, but to get maximum growth from the newer hybrids the soil should be enriched with manure or compost before planting.

HEMEROCALLIS AT A GLANCE

A genus of semi-, evergreen, and herbaceous perennials; 30,000 cultivars that give a long summer show. Hardy to 5°F (zone 7).

		Recommended Varieties
Jan	/	
Feb	sow	"Burning Daylight"
Mar	sow	"Cartwheels"
Apr	transplant	"Golden Chimes"
May	transplant	"Neyron Rose"
Jun	flowering	"Pink Damask"
July	flowering	"Red Precious"
Aug	flowering	"Stafford"
Sept	flowering	"Whichford"
Oct	divide	"Zara"
Nov	/	
Dec	/	

GROWING METHOD

Propagation   Divide established clumps in the spring or fall. Cut back foliage before or directly after division. Spacing may be from 6 to 12in, depending on the variety. New plants need regular watering to establish. Once established, plants are very drought-tolerant, but better-sized blooms can be expected if deep waterings are given every week or two.

Feeding   Grows without supplementary fertilizer, but an application of complete plant food in early spring encourages stronger, more vigorous growth.

Problems   Daylilies growing in very soggy ground tend to survive quite well but produce few flowers. Otherwise, no problems.

FLOWERING

Season   Depending on the variety, plants may be in bloom any time from late spring until the fall. Most flowers only last one day.

Cutting   Single flowers can be cut for the vase. Attractive and well worth using.

AFTER FLOWERING

Requirements Cut off any spent flower stems.

HEUCHERA SANGUINEA
Coral flower

DAINTY LITTLE PINK FLOWERS are massed above the attractive foliage, making the North American coral flower an excellent choice for the front of a border or a garden bed. Here they are planted to provide an excellent foil for the abundant blooms of white roses behind.

FEATURES

This perennial forms a low rosette of lobed leaves that make a neat plant for edging, or for mass-planting at the front of the border. The foliage is evergreen. Established plantings produce a striking display of blooms. The flower stems, which stand above the foliage, are from 12 to 18in tall. The species has red flowers; cultivars are available with pink, white, or deeper crimson blooms. Note the superb foliage varieties ("Palace Purple"— chocolate-colored; "Pewter Moon"—gray; and "Snow Storm"—white flecked). New American varieties include "Pewter Veil."

HEUCHERA AT A GLANCE

H. sanguinea is a red-flowering, summer perennial forming low, wide clumps, 6 x 12in. Hardy to 5°F (zone 7).

		Recommended Plants
Jan	/	
Feb	sow 🖉	*Heuchera americana*
Mar	sow 🖉	"Chocolate Ruffles"
Apr	divide 🖉	*H. cylindrica*
May	transplant 🖉	"Green Ivory"
Jun	flowering 🌸	"Helen Dillon"
July	flowering 🌸	"Persian Carpet"
Aug	flowering 🌸	"Pewter Moon"
Sept	/	"Rachel"
Oct	divide 🖉	"Red Spangles"
Nov	/	"Scintillation"
Dec	/	

CONDITIONS

Aspect	Prefers full sun but tolerates light shade.
Site	Needs very well-drained, open-textured soil. Permanently wet soil will kill this plant.

GROWING METHOD

Propagation	Clumps can be divided in the spring or in the fall, but ensure that each division has its own set of healthy roots. It can also be grown from seed sown in the spring; cuttings will also root quite freely. Plant at approximately 8–10in intervals for a good effect.
Feeding	Apply a complete plant food when growth commences in the spring.
Problems	Vine weevil grubs may devour roots and stems. Destroy the infected clump, and use severed shoots as cuttings.

FLOWERING

Season	It flowers well through most of the summer, with a few spikes hanging on until the early fall.
Cutting	Flowers do not last well as cut blooms.

AFTER FLOWERING

Requirements	Promptly remove any spent flower stems once they begin to look untidy. Apart from the removal of any dead leaves, this is all that is necessary.

HOSTA
Plantain lily

LEAVES PATTERNED VARIOUSLY in lime-green and blue make this Hosta "Frances Williams" an outstanding garden feature. Here it lights up a dull area under a tree, the little available light being reflected outward by the lime-green. In shady areas where few flowers bloom, it is a real bonus.

FEATURES

Also known as the plantain lily, this herbaceous perennial is grown for its attractive, decorative foliage. It is long-lived, and foliage may be tiny or up to 18in wide and 36in high. There are hundreds of cultivars with leaves that may be light or dark green, chartreuse or yellow, gray-green or blue. Many are variegated. Leaf texture also varies: it can be smooth or shiny, matt or powdery, puckered or corrugated. Hostas are excellent at forming big, bold clumps that keep down the weeds, but until they emerge in late spring some weeding will be necessary; they also benefit from heavy mulching. Hostas look best mass-planted near water features, or when allowed to multiply in shady areas under trees.

Variegations Cultivars with cream, white, or yellow variegations will brighten a shady part of the yard, and so long as the tree or shrub canopy is high enough to let sufficient light reach the hostas, they will maintain their variegation. Likewise, plants with sharp chartreuse or acid-lime-colored foliage can be used to give a lift to shady areas. Types can be mixed to create a wealth of different effects.

Flowers The bell-shape flowers, mostly in mauve shades, appear in the summer and are held high above the foliage. Some species, such as *H. plantaginea* and its cultivar "Grandiflora," produce pure white, lightly fragrant flowers. However, few gardeners plant hostas just for the flowers; the leaves alone are

HOSTA AT A GLANCE

A mainly clump-forming perennial from the Far East. Grow in pots or the garden for the foliage. Hardy to 0°F (zones 6–7).

Month	Activity	Recommended Varieties
Jan	/	
Feb	/	"Aureomarginata"
Mar	sow	"Blue Angel"
Apr	divide	"Francee"
May	transplant	"Frances Williams"
Jun	flowering	"Golden Tiara"
July	flowering	"Love Pat"
Aug	divide	*H. lancifolia*
Sept	flowering	"Shade Fanfare"
Oct	/	"Wide Brim"
Nov	/	
Dec	/	

PURE WHITE FLOWERS *appear on some species of hosta, such as* Hosta plantaginea *and some of its cultivars.*

STRONGLY PUCKERED LEAVES *in a bluish color and white flowers are characteristic of* Hosta sieboldiana *"Elegans."*

HOSTAS, RODGERSIAS, *and ferns revel in the light shade and constant damp soil prevalent in woodlands.*

good enough.

Companions Since hostas do not come into leaf early in the spring, the early-flowering bulbs, such as snowdrops and snowflakes, or early perennials, such as corydalis, can be planted among them. They make a bright, successful show.

CONDITIONS

Aspect Most hostas grow in full sunlight if well watered. They thrive in shade or dappled light. Blue-leaved forms can be the hardest of all to place because they turn green with either too much sun or too heavy shade. Yellow or gold forms are best with direct sunlight in the early morning or late in the afternoon.

Site Needs rich, moisture-retentive soil. Large amounts of decayed manure or compost should be dug into the ground before planting. Mulch plants after planting. Superb in tubs, getting bigger and better each year.

GROWING METHOD

Propagation Divide the fleshy underground rhizomes in early spring. Most hostas are best divided every

four to five years. Plant the dwarf cultivars 6in apart, the larger ones at intervals of 36in. Several species can be raised from seed, though they may not be true to type.

Feeding Apply pelleted poultry manure in the spring.

Problems Slugs and snails can be a major problem. Pick off snails, and avoid watering in the evening. Place slug pellets or sharp sand around the leaves.

FLOWERING

Season Flowers are produced in the summer. The color range varies from white to purple.

Cutting Hosta provides cut flowers; the foliage is also attractive.

AFTER FLOWERING

Requirements Cut off any spent flower stems in the spring. Continue watering the plants until the foliage begins to die down, and then tidy up the clumps, which can look unsightly. Mulch the area with supplies of compost or manure. Some hostas (*sieboldiana*) produce good fall tints. The seedheads can be left on for winter

KNIPHOFIA
Red hot poker

FLAME-COLORED pokers and soft purple perovskia both tolerate dry conditions.

THE COLORS in this generous planting of red hot pokers reflect both the yellow achillea behind and the red plants in the foreground. The abundant grassy foliage provides a valuable contrast.

FEATURES

These evergreen perennials, also known as torch lilies, make great feature plants, with their bright flower spikes in cream, orange, red, yellow, and many shadings of these colors. Flower stems stand high above the grassy foliage, which may be anywhere from 24in to 6½ft tall. Even out of flower, the distinctive foliage makes red hot poker a good accent plant. Since clumps should remain undisturbed for many years, plant red hot pokers in their final position.

CONDITIONS

Aspect   Needs full sunlight all day. A valuable plant because it tolerates a wide range of exposed windy or coastal areas.

KNIPHOFIA AT A GLANCE

A genus of some 70 species of evergreen and deciduous perennials, grown for their flowering spires. Hardy to 5°F (zone 7).

		Recommended Varieties
Jan	/	
Feb	/	"Bees Sunset"
Mar	sow	"Brimstone"
Apr	divide	"Buttercup"
May	transplant	*K. caulescens*
Jun	flowering	"Little Maid"
July	flowering	"Royal Standard"
Aug	flowering	"Samuel's Sensation"
Sept	flowering	"Sunningdale Yellow"
Oct	flowering	*K. triangularis*
Nov	/	
Dec	/	

Site   Needs well-drained soil. Although it tolerates poorer soils, especially sandy ones, you will get better results if the soil is enriched with manure or compost.

GROWING METHOD

Propagation   Well-established clumps can be divided in late spring. Foliage on new divisions must be reduced by half to allow successful root regrowth to take place. The smaller-growing forms can be planted at 20in spacings, but the large growers may need up to 30in or more. Needs regular watering to establish in prolonged dry spells, after which it is very drought-tolerant.

Feeding   Grows without supplementary fertilizer, but complete plant food applied in the spring should noticeably increase the quantity and quality of the flowers.

Problems   No specific problems are known.

FLOWERING

Season   Flowering times can vary slightly with species and cultivar. Generally, red hot pokers flower in late summer and early fall.

Cutting   The flowers last well when cut if the stems are scalded for approximately 10 seconds. They make an invaluable tall, stiff background for a display of smaller, flowery cuttings.

AFTER FLOWERING

Requirements   Spent flower stalks should be promptly cut off. Any dead leaves should be pulled away to give the clump a clean look. Protect the crown with straw or leaves in cold areas.

LEUCANTHEMUM
Shasta daisy

LONG-STEMMED shasta daisies are an ideal component of flower arrangements.

A CONTINUOUS PLANTING of shasta daisies fills this awkward narrow space between a path and a low brick wall. The cheerful white flowers appear throughout the summer.

FEATURES

Leucanthemum x *superbum* (Shasta daisy) looks wonderful when planted in a mixed border, where the large white flowers mix with more brightly colored flowers. Despite being easy to grow and multiplying rapidly, the daisies do not become a menace. Flower stalks can grow 24–36in tall, while the dark green leaves are only 4–6in high. Shasta daisies make striking cut flowers, livening up any arrangement. There are a number of named cultivars, some, such as "Esther Read," "Wirral Supreme," and "Cobham Gold," with double flowers. (Despite its name, the flowers on "Cobham Gold" are cream, not gold.) "Everest" is probably the largest of the single cultivars, though it is rarely available.

LEUCANTHEMUM AT A GLANCE

L. x *superbum* is a vigorous, clump-forming perennial with many attractive cultivars, mainly in white. Hardy to 23°F (zone 9).

Jan	/	Recommended Varieties
Feb	/	
Mar	divide 🖑	*Leucanthemum* x *super-*
Apr	transplant 🖑	*bum*
May	transplant 🖑	"Aglaia"
Jun	flowering 🌼	"Alaska"
July	flowering 🌼	"Bishopstone"
Aug	flowering 🌼	"Cobham Gold"
Sept	flowering 🌼	"Horace Read"
Oct	divide 🖑	"Phyllis Smith"
Nov	/	"Snowcap"
Dec	/	

CONDITIONS

Aspect	Prefers full sunlight all day and wind protection.
Site	The soil should be well drained, and improved by the addition of decayed compost or manure.

GROWING METHOD

Propagation	Divide the clumps in early spring or late summer, replanting only the younger, vigorous, outer growths, each with its own set of roots and shoots. Plant the divisions approximately 10in apart. Cuttings of young, short shoots can also be taken in early spring.
Feeding	Apply complete plant food as growth begins in the spring. Liquid fertilizer applied in late spring should help produce better blooms.
Problems	The main problems are aphids, slugs, earwigs, and chrysanthemum eelworm. The first can be tackled with a proprietary spray, and the second and third by traps (saucers filled with beer, and inverted flower pots filled with straw placed on bamboo canes). In the case of eelworm, evident from browning/blackening, drying foliage from the base upward, the whole plant must be destroyed.

FLOWERING

Season	Flowering is all summer long.
Cutting	Cut flowers regularly for indoor decoration, which will also prolong the garden display.

AFTER FLOWERING

Requirements Cut back spent flower stems to the ground.

LIGULARIA
Ligularia

A MARVELLOUS ligularia display—spikes of bright yellow, eye-catching flowers. No matter what size your border, there is a suitable ligularia. They vary from the medium to tall, at 6ft high. Big groupings invariably succeed much better than a few individual flowers.

FEATURES

Ligularia, with its bright yellow daisies, has four key advantages. It mainly flowers in mid- and late summer, and tolerates dappled shade, making it invaluable for the border. It often has interesting, well-displayed foliage; it can be shaped like a kidney, a five-pointed star, or be oval, held on tallish stems. The fourth advantage is that these are tall plants, adding height to schemes, being from 36in to 6ft tall. They can be used in small groups to punctuate arrangements of smaller plants, or form an impressive massed display. The flowers are yellow or orange. *L. dentata* "Othello" has purple-tinged leaves with a red underside, and "Desdemona" has brownish-green leaves, similarly colored beneath. With room for only one ligularia, "The Rocket" offers height, yellow flowers, black stems, and interesting, big-toothed foliage.

CONDITIONS

Aspect   Tolerates full sun and some light shade. Also requires shelter from cutting winds.

Site   The soil must be moist—ligularias grow well beside ponds and streams—for a big performance. If the soil begins to dry out to any degree, the plants quickly show signs of distress by wilting.

GROWING METHOD

Propagation   Increase the species by sowing seed or division in the spring or fall. Cultivars can only be raised by division. Make sure that the emerging new growth is well-watered, and never allowed to dry out. Set out from 24in to 4ft apart.

Feeding   Border plants need plenty of well-rotted manure or compost, and a deep mulch to guard against moisture loss.

Problems   Slugs and snails can be a major problem, especially as the leaves emerge. Pick off or treat chemically.

FLOWERING

Season   Generally from late summer into the fall, but some flower in mid-summer, and *L. stenocephala* in early summer.

Cutting   It is not advisable to strip the plants of their impressive flowering stems, especially when you only have room for a few plants.

AFTER FLOWERING

Requirements   Cut back to the ground.

LIGULARIA AT A GLANCE

A genus of 150 species of perennials grown for their tall flower spikes and large, architectural foliage. Hardy to 0°F (zones 6–7).

Jan	/	Recommended Varieties
Feb	sow	*Ligularia dentata*
Mar	sow	*L. d.* "Desdemona"
Apr	transplant	*L. d.* "Othello"
May	transplant	"Gregynog Gold"
Jun	/	*L. przewalskii*
July	flowering	"The Rocket"
Aug	flowering	*L.wilsoniana*
Sept	/	
Oct	divide	
Nov	/	
Dec	/	

LOBELIA CARDINALIS
Cardinal flower

THIS LOBELIA is also known as cardinal flower, an apt description, since the tall spikes of flowers are the same scarlet as a cardinal's robes.

IN ITS NATURAL HABITAT in North America this lobelia grows on wet meadows and river banks. It thrives on plenty of moisture.

FEATURES

To most people, lobelia is a small edging plant with bright blue flowers. There are, however, about 400 species of lobelia, many of them perennials. This herbaceous species with bright scarlet flowers is also known as the cardinal flower and grows to about 36in tall. With its dark green leaves and bright flowers, it really stands out—it is sometimes used as a feature plant. It can also be used in a mixed border or mass-planted among shrubs, so long as the ground retains plenty of moisture.

LOBELIA AT A GLANCE

L. cardinalis is a clump-forming, short-lived perennial, grown for its striking, vivid red flowers. Hardy to 5°F (zone 7).

Jan	/	
Feb	/	**Recommended Varieties**
Mar	sow	*Lobelia* "Cherry Ripe"
Apr	divide	"Dark Crusader"
May	transplant	"Kompliment Scharlach"
Jun	/	"Queen Victoria"
July	flowering	*L. siphilitica*
Aug	flowering	*L. tupa*
Sept	flowering	
Oct	/	
Nov	/	
Dec	/	

CONDITIONS

Aspect   Grows in full sunlight or semi-shade.
Site   Needs rich and moisture-retentive soil, as these plants are not tolerant of drought. A streamside setting is ideal.

GROWING METHOD

Propagation   Plants are usually divided every two or three years, in the spring. Plant the divisions about 12in apart. Lobelia must be kept moist and well watered while it is in active growth, especially during prolonged dry spells in the spring and summer.
Feeding   Apply a complete plant food, and a mulch of compost or manure in the spring.
Problems   Slugs and snails will attack the flower spikes. Put down slug pellets or beer traps.

FLOWERING

Season   There is a long flowering period through the summer and fall period when the brilliant scarlet blooms appear.
Cutting   Flowers are not suitable for cutting.

AFTER FLOWERING

Requirements   Cut off spent flower stems. The dark-leaved hybrids ("Cherry Ripe") are not fully hardy and need a thick, protective winter mulch.

LUPINUS POLYPHYLLUS
Lupins

RUSSELL LUPINS are noteworthy for their rich colors, including this pinky-red.

LUPINS ARE traditional favorites for perennial borders, where they provide vertical interest. Here they are growing among oriental poppies, campion, and gray-leaved germander.

FEATURES

This herbaceous perennial lupin is generally known as the Russell lupin, named after the hybridizer who began developing many fine strains of this plant early this century. It produces tall, densely packed spires of blooms in myriad colors. Growing well over 42in tall, these are plants for a massed display. They flower in early to mid-summer and can look unsightly after flowering; placed at the rear of a border the problem is solved. Although they can be cut for indoor use they give much more value in the yard, with several spikes per plant. The only irritation is that plants can be short-lived, and should therefore be divided regularly.

LUPINUS AT A GLANCE

L. polyphyllus is an attractive, summer-flowering perennial with striking vertical spires of purple flowers. Hardy to 5°F (zone

Jan	/
Feb	/
Mar	sow
Apr	transplant
May	transplant
Jun	flowering
July	flowering
Aug	/
Sept	/
Oct	sow
Nov	/
Dec	/

Recommended Varieties

Band of Noble Series
"Esmerelder"
"Helen Sharman"
"Kayleigh Ann Savage"
"Olive Tolley"
"Pope John Paul"
"The Page"
"The Chatelaine"

CONDITIONS

Aspect Grows in full sunlight or semi-shade, but it does need wind protection.

Site Soil need not be rich—moderate fertility will suffice—but it must be well drained. Light, slightly sandy, acidic soil is ideal.

GROWING METHOD

Propagation Division of these plants may be difficult. Many strains come true from seed, which should be soaked in warm water before planting in the spring or fall. Cuttings can be taken from new shoots emerging from the crown in early spring. Set plants approximately 12–16in apart. Give ample water to young plants to help them establish.

Feeding Needs little fertilizer, as lupins fix nitrogen in nodules on their roots. High potash fertilizer may be applied as buds begin to form.

Problems Powdery mildew may be a problem in humid conditions; if necessary, spray with a fungicide. Control lupin aphids with an appropriate spray. Virus may cause stunting and discoloration. Destroy affected plants.

FLOWERING

Season Early and mid-summer.

Cutting Flowers may be cut for the vase.

AFTER FLOWERING

Requirements Cut off the spent flower stems before they manage to set seed. This will encourage smaller spikes to follow.

LYCHNIS CORONARIA
Rose campion

THE DISTINCTIVE ARRANGEMENT of petals on Lychnis chalcedonica *has given rise to its common name, Maltese cross. The bright red flowers show up well against white or blue flowers.*

TRUE CAMPION, Lychnis coronaria, *has abundant, bright cerise flowers.*

FEATURES

Rosettes of soft, silver-gray foliage make *Lychnis coronaria* a very useful plant in the garden, and they contrast with the deep cerise or magenta flowers that appear on stems 12–16in high. There is also a white-flowered form. Easily grown in a sunny, well-drained position, rose campion tends to be short-lived, but it self-seeds prolifically to provide a fresh supply. It can be grown as a border plant or as part of a mixed perennial display. *L. flos-jovis* is another species where silvery foliage effectively combines with purple-red blooms. Another popular species of lychnis is the Maltese cross, *L. chalcedonica*, which has mid-green leaves and produces a rounded head of bright scarlet flowers. Pink and white forms, and a double, "Flore Plena," are also available.

LYCHNIS AT A GLANCE

L. coronaria is a flowery, short-lived purple-red perennial that gives a prolific late summer display. Hardy to 5°F (zone 7).

		Recommended Varieties
Jan	/	*Lychnis alpina*
Feb	/	L. *chalcedonica*
Mar	sow	L. *coronaria* Alba Group
Apr	division	L. *c.* Atrosanguinea Group
May	transplant	L. *flos-cuculi*
Jun	/	L. *viscaria* subsp.
July	flowering	"Splendens Plena"
Aug	flowering	L. *yunnanensis*
Sept	flowering	
Oct	sow	
Nov	/	
Dec	/	

CONDITIONS

Aspect   Grows best in full sunlight, but it tolerates shade for part of the day.
Site   Needs very well-drained soil, but the soil need not be especially rich.

GROWING METHOD

Propagation   Tends to self-seed. These plants may show variation from the parent plant. Divide clumps in spring, discard the oldest, lackluster sections, and space the new vigorous ones about 8in apart. There are some beautiful strains to be raised from seed, with mixtures of white, deep violet, carmine, and rose-pink flowers, and a pastel eye.
Feeding   Needs little fertilizer. A little complete plant food may be given in early spring.
Problems   No pest or disease problems are known, but overwatering or prolonged summer rain in heavy ground may cause rotting.

FLOWERING

Season   Flowers in mid- to late summer, but it is well worth the wait, with a big showy display that maintains interest in the border at a time when many other plants are flagging.
Cutting   Flowers are unsuitable for cutting.

AFTER FLOWERING

Requirements   If you do not want plants to self-seed, deadhead with vigilance as the flowers fade. This should also prolong blooming. Completely spent stems should be cut off as low to the ground as possible.

LYSIMACHIA PUNCTATA
Loosestrife

A STRONG, MASSED DISPLAY of loosestrife. Individually unremarkable, a clump makes a splendid feature beside a pond or stream.

FEATURES

Loosestrife, which is widely naturalized in Europe and northeast North America, has stalks of bright yellow flowers in summer. It thrives in damp, boggy ground and can easily become invasive. The flowering stems reach 3ft high, bearing slightly coarse foliage. Other species offer white flowers on stiff, blue-green stems (*L. ephemerum*), while *L. nummularia* "Aurea" is a complete contrast. It grows 2in high, but spreads indefinitely, with evergreen, bright yellow leaves and summer flowers in a matching color. With room for only one, try *L. clethroides*, which has attractive white flowers (36 x 24in). The new variegated form, *L. p.* "Alexander" is a great success.

CONDITIONS

LYSIMACHIA AT A GLANCE

L. punctata is an erect, herbaceous perennial grown for its yellow flowers and ability to colonize damp areas. Hardy to 0°F (zones 6–7).

Jan	/	
Feb	/	**Recommended Varieties**
Mar	/	*Lysimachia atropur-*
Apr	divide 👈	*purea*
May	/	*L. ciliata*
Jun	flowering ✿	*L. clethroides*
July	flowering ✿	*L. minoricensis*
Aug	flowering ✿	*L. nummularia* "Aurea"
Sept	/	*L. thyrsiflora*
Oct	divide 👈	*L. vulgaris*
Nov	/	
Dec	/	

Aspect   Loosestrife tolerates both full sun and light, dappled shade, but growing in the former gives by far the best results.

Site   Moist ground is essential. Add plenty of organic matter to border plants, and mulch well to guard against moisture loss.

GROWING METHOD

Propagation   Seed can be difficult. The most reliable method is by spring or fall division.

Feeding   Humus-rich ground produces the best display. Fork plenty of well-rotted manure and compost around the plants in the spring.

Problems   Colonies of slugs and snails can be a major problem, attacking and disfiguring the new, emerging foliage. Either pick off by hand or treat chemically. Plants grown in areas cut by strong winds may need to be staked.

FLOWERING

Season   Flowers appear in the summer, their timing depending on your chosen variety.

Cutting   They make unremarkable cut flowers, given the enormous competition in summer, but are nonetheless very useful when bulking out large displays with their flowering spires.

AFTER FLOWERING

Requirements   Cut back the old, spent flowering stems down to the ground.

MACLEAYA CORDATA
Plume poppy

THE PLUME POPPY starts inauspiciously, but quickly puts out tall, white summer flowers, making it an indispensable feature plant. It is a key ingredient for the rear of the border, where its lobed, olive-green foliage makes a lovely background for smaller plants. The plume poppy does not need staking.

FEATURES

The plume poppy is an essential plant for the rear of the border, tall, graceful, and showy. Growing 8ft tall, it sports long, thin stems with mid- and late summer panicles of pale white flowers. "Flamingo" has pinkish flowers. The large, lobed foliage is equally attractive. With more room in the border, *M. microcarpa* can be grown. It is slightly invasive and has pink flowers, while "Kelway's Coral Plume" produces coral-pink flowers opening from pure pink buds. The plume poppy's natural habitat is Chinese and Japanese meadows, where it makes large impressive colonies, spreading quickly through the damp soil by underground rhizomes and flowering all summer long.

MACLEAYA AT A GLANCE

M. cordata is a rhizomatous perennial with gray-green foliage, grown for its tall flower spikes. Hardy to 0°F (zones 6–7).

		Companion Plants
Jan	/	
Feb	/	Clematis Gypsophila
Mar	/	Hibiscus
Apr	division 👌	Miscanthus
May	/	Lobelia
Jun	/	Osteospermum
July	flowering 🌸	Rose
Aug	flowering 🌸	Salvia
Sept	/	
Oct	division 👌	
Nov	/	
Dec	/	

CONDITIONS

Aspect   Macleaya likes full sun and light shade, although the former produces a longer, better display. Avoid dark areas and open, windy sites; shelter is required.

Site   Light, well-drained soil is ideal.

GROWING METHOD

Propagation   The quickest, easiest results are either by making spring or fall divisions, or by separating lengths of rhizome when the plant is dormant. Make sure each has its own root system. Water new plants well, and space out at 3ft intervals.

Feeding   Provide moderate applications of compost and well-rotted manure in the spring as a mulch.

Problems   Colonies of slugs can be a severe problem, badly attacking the new, vigorous growth. Either pick off by hand or treat accordingly with chemicals.

FLOWERING

Season   Flowers appear in mid- and late summer, on long, thin stems, producing an airy display.

Cutting   Macleaya make very attractive cut flowers, requiring a regular change of water, their airy panicles adding considerably to both formal and flowery arrangements.

AFTER FLOWERING

Requirements   Cut back old growth to the ground.

MECONOPSIS
Himalayan blue poppy

NO OTHER blue flower has quite the same startlingly clear color as the amazing blue poppy, a true delight whenever it can be grown.

WOODLAND CONDITIONS where the soil never dries out are essential for the Himalayan or Tibetan blue poppy.

FEATURES

Meconopsis betonicifolia is the beautiful blue poppy everyone loves. There is probably no other plant that produces such an intense sky-blue flower. Its natural habitat is very high altitude alpine meadows in China. Plants do not flower the first year, and they die down in winter, growing and blooming in the second year. If meconopsis is prevented from blooming the first time it sets buds, it is more likely to become perennial. Growing to almost 6½ft in its native habitat, in cultivation it is more likely to be 20–28in tall. Looks best when grown as part of a massed display, or threaded through a border.

MECONOPSIS AT A GLANCE

M. betonicifolia is a deciduous perennial, making a strong show, with blue or white early summer flowers. Hardy to 0°F (zones 6–7).

Jan	/
Feb	/
Mar	sow
Apr	transplant
May	transplant
Jun	flowering
July	flowering
Aug	flowering
Sept	flowering
Oct	sow
Nov	/
Dec	/

Recommended Varieties

Meconopsis cambrica
M. betonicifolia
M. grandis
M. napaulensis
M. quintuplinervia
M. x *sheldonii*
M. x *s.* "Slieve Donard"
M. superba

CONDITIONS

Aspect Needs partial, dappled shade; also provide some protection from strong, cutting, drying winds.

Site Needs well-drained soil that is rich in organic matter. In colder regions it grows best in acid soil.

GROWING METHOD

Propagation Grows from fresh ripe seed sown in the fall, or in spring. Give winter seedlings frost protection in a greenhouse, but beware of damping off, and plant out in late spring or early summer. Initially, water well. Do not waterlog or the crowns will rot.

Feeding Apply a little general fertilizer in the spring.

Problems Overwet soil, especially during winter, will rot the crown. Downy mildew may be a problem in some seasons. Spray plants with a fungicide at the first sign of an attack.

FLOWERING

Season Abundant flowers begin appearing at the start of summer.

Cutting While they make extremely good cut flowers, they do not last long.

AFTER FLOWERING

Requirements Remove spent flower stems, unless you are waiting for seed to ripen. Once growth dies down, cut it off at ground level.

MELIANTHUS MAJOR
Honey bush

NECTAR-RICH, *these dark red flowers are very attractive to insects. The foliage too is unusual, with its distinctive color and form.*

THE BLUE-GREEN FOLIAGE *of honey flower is a feature in itself. Only in a large yard will you appreciate the full effect.*

FEATURES

This very striking evergreen plant, with its unusual blue-green foliage, really stands out. It is grown as a feature in a mixed border or as a focal point in an annual or perennial display. In a large yard it could be repeat-planted to tie together various arrangements. Honey bush can grow to 6ft in height, and it spreads by suckers, forming a large clump if left undivided. The dark mahogany-red flowers contain copious quantities of nectar, attractive to bees. Although native to South Africa, and initially tender here, after two years the base becomes woody and it can survive outside if given good frost protection in mild areas. It can also be grown in a large pot.

MELIANTHUS AT A GLANCE

M. major is a tender, southern African plant with wonderful, architectural foliage. It is damaged below 41°F (zone 11).

		Companion Plants
Jan	/	
Feb	/	Canna
Mar	sow	Choisya
Apr	divide	*Hosta* "Krossa Regal"
May	transplant	Philadelphus
Jun	flowering	Pinus
July	flowering	Pseudopanax
Aug	flowering	Salvia
Sept	/	
Oct	/	
Nov	/	
Dec	/	

CONDITIONS

Aspect   Needs full sun all day (i.e. a south-facing wall).

Site   Soil must be well drained but it need not be specially rich—in fact over-rich soils will produce good foliage effects but poor flowering. However, the outstanding architectural foliage is the main reason for growing this striking plant.

GROWING METHOD

Propagation   Grows from seed sown in the spring or from division of suckers from an existing plant, also in spring. Plant at least 39in apart. For best growth, give deep watering every week or two in hot, dry spells during the growing season. It will, however, tolerate drought well.

Feeding   Apply a complete plant food in the spring.

Problems   Red spider mites may strike. Use an appropriate insecticide.

FLOWERING

Season   Dark crimson flowers may appear in late summer or earlier on long stems that survive the winter.

Cutting   Flowers are probably best left on the plant, as they do not smell particularly pleasant.

AFTER FLOWERING

Requirements   Cut off the spent flower stems, unless you are waiting for seed to set and ripen. Protect the base and roots with straw or bracken against frost. The older and woodier the plant, the better its chance of survival.

MONARDA DIDYMA
Bergamot

THE HOT-PINK FLOWERS on this bergamot are easy to place in the yard. They combine well with blue or white schemes.

FOR COLOR over a long period, this brilliant red variety of bergamot, "Cambridge Scarlet," is hard to beat. It requires little care.

FEATURES

This aromatic herbaceous perennial is also known as bee balm and Oswego tea. The name "bee balm" refers to its nectar-rich flowers, which are very attractive to bees, and "Oswego tea" to its use by the Oswego Indians and early colonists of North America as a tea substitute. Growing approximately 36in tall, bergamot flowers from mid- to late summer. The heads of tubular flowers are red, pink, white, or purple, with some outstandingly named cultivars, including "Cambridge Scarlet" and "Croftway Pink." It is easy to grow—being a member of the mint family, its roots spread vigorously. It makes a lively addition to a mixed planting for its bright scarlet or pink flowers.

MONARDA AT A GLANCE

M. didyma is a clump-forming perennial with lance-shape leaves, and bright, late summer flowers. Hardy to 0°F (zones

Jan	/	
Feb	sow	
Mar	sow	
Apr	transplant	
May	transplant	
Jun	/	
July	flowering	
Aug	flowering	
Sept	/	
Oct	sow	
Nov	/	
Dec	/	

Recommended Varieties

"Aquarius"
"Beauty of Cobham"
"Cambridge Scarlet"
"Croftway Pink"
"Fishes"
"Mahogany"
"Prarienacht"
"Sagittarius"
"Scorpion"

CONDITIONS

Aspect Grows in either full sunlight or semi-shade, but flowering will be best in the open.
Site Needs well-drained soil that is made moisture-retentive by the addition of large amounts of decayed organic matter.

GROWING METHOD

Propagation Lift and divide clumps in the spring before new growth begins. Replant the young, vigorous outer growths 8–12in apart. Plants usually need dividing every two or three years. Bergamot may be also be grown from seed sown in the early spring or fall, but this does not develop true to type. It needs regular, deep watering through prolonged dry spells in the heat of summer.
Feeds If the soil is well supplied with humus, but a little fertilizer is needed. Apply some complete plant food in the spring.
Problems Since snails love to eat the new growth as it appears, take precautions. Mildew can be a problem at times. You may need a fungicide spray or it might become severe. Remove all dead and diseased leaves.

FLOWERING

Season Flowers in mid- and late summer.
Cutting Makes a decent cut flower. Use the scented leaves in a potpourri.

AFTER FLOWERING

Requirements Prune off spent flower stems. Cut plants back to ground level once growth begins to die

OENOTHERA
Evening primrose

THOUGH EVENING PRIMROSE is thought of as yellow, the flowers of Oenothera speciosa *"Rosea" are pink-and-white, with yellow.*

O. SPECIOSA "ROSEA" *is doubly attractive because it grows 12in high, mixes well with argyranthemum, and forms large clumps.*

FEATURES

Evening primrose is an essential plant for formal and cottage-style yards. While each flower (white, yellow, or pink, depending on the variety) opens and fades fast, barely lasting 24 hours, there is an abundance of new buds developing through the summer and early fall. The plant has two extra advantages. Often fragrant, and often tall, it can make an eye-catching addition to the border. *O. biennis*, the traditional favorite, is actually an annual or biennial. *O. fruticosa*, a biennial or perennial, has two fine forms, "Fyrverkeri" ("Fireworks"), which has red buds opening to yellow flowers and purple-tinged leaves, and subsp. *glauca*, with yellow flowers and purple leaves.

CONDITIONS

Aspect   Grow in an open, sunny position.
Site   Moderately rich soil will suffice, although evening primrose can self-seed and appear in even the stoniest ground.

GROWING METHOD

Propagation   Sow seed or divide in early spring, or take cuttings of non-flowering shoots. Keep in a frost-free place in winter, plant out in spring.
Feeding   Not necessary, although moderate quantities of manure will suffice in especially poor soil.
Problems   Slugs tend to be the main problem, attacking tender new growth. Pick off or treat with chemicals. The sturdy kinds of evening primrose are free-standing, but others (*O. macrocarpa*) may require support.

FLOWERING

Season   Lasts from late spring to late summer, with flowers tending to open in early evening.
Cutting   Short-lived but attractive flowers.

AFTER FLOWERING

Requirements Collect seed when ripe, if required, and then cut spent stems to the ground.

OENOTHERA AT A GLANCE

A genus of mainly annuals and biennials, with excellent perennials. Scented and yellow flowering, they are hardy to 5°F (zone 7).

Jan	/	Recommended Varieties
Feb	sow	*Oenothera biennis*
Mar	divide	*O. fruticosa*
Apr	transplant	*O. f.* "Fyrverkeri"
May	flowering	*O. f.* subsp. *glauca*
Jun	flowering	*O. macrocarpa*
July	flowering	*O. speciosa* "Rosea"
Aug	flowering	*O. stricta* "Sulphurea"
Sept	/	
Oct	/	
Nov	/	
Dec	/	

PAEONIA
Paeony species and cultivars

THIS HALF-OPENED peony flower gives a hint of delights to come, with a touch of white against the bright pink.

GLORIOUS COLOR and perfume combine in this extensive planting of peony cultivars to produce a spectacular result.

FLUTED PETALS give extra interest to this single white peony. The large mass of central stamens adds a touch of color.

FEATURES

Beautiful to look at and fragrant, too, peonies are among the aristocrats of the plant world, and although there are only 33 wild species, there are many hundreds of cultivars. Peonies were prized by the Chinese for many hundreds of years, and by the early 18th century they had developed the garden peonies from which the forms of *P. lactiflora* (often referred to as Chinese peonies) are generally descended. Peonies were first introduced into Europe at the end of the 18th century. Peonies are divided into two groups: the tree peonies, which are shrubby and derived from *P. suffruticosa*, and the herbaceous peonies, of which the cultivars of *P. lactiflora* are most commonly grown. Although the name "tree peony" is used, this is an exaggeration— they rarely grow more than 6½ft tall. Herbaceous peonies grow about 39in high and wide. Plants are long-lived.

Flowers   Flowers may be single or double and come in every shade of pink, red, purple, white, and cream, many with a delicious light perfume. Some flowers have a large central boss of golden stamens, and some have fringed or crimped edges on the petals. Among the categories of flowers recognised are: small, 2–4in across; medium, 4–6in across; large, 6–8in across; and very large, over 8in across. Tree peonies are generally 2–12in. Other categories have been developed in the United States where a great deal of hybridizing is practiced.

CONDITIONS

Aspect   Needs full sunlight or semi-shade, with protection from strong winds.

Site   Soil must be well drained, but heavily enriched with manure or compost. Dig it over deeply to allow the free spread of roots.

THE ATTRACTIVE FOLIAGE greatly adds to the value of peonies and often emerges with lovely rich red and bronze tints.

THE VERY POPULAR double cultivar "Rubra Plena" is a rich crimson anemone-centered peony that looks very like a camellia.

GROWING METHOD

Propagation Divide plants in the spring or fall, taking care not to break the brittle roots. Each division must have roots and dormant growth buds. Crowns should be replanted 1in below the surface, and spaced about 20in apart. Plants can be raised from seed but they will take four to five years to reach flowering size, and only the species will be true to type. Peony seeds generally need two periods of chilling with a warm period between, and care should be taken not to disturb the seeds during this time. Most seeds germinate during the second spring after sowing.

Feeding Apply a general fertilizer in early spring. At the same time, mulch but avoid the crown.

PAEONIA AT A GLANCE

A genus of over 30 species of clump-forming perennials and sub-shrubs, often with highly scented flowers. Hardy to 5°F (zone 7).

Jan	/	**Recommended Varieties**
Feb	/	
Mar	/	*P. cambessedesii*
Apr	divide 🖑	"Defender"
May	transplant 🖑	*P. lactiflora* "Bowl of Beauty"
Jun	flowering 🖑	*P. l.* "Festiva Maxima"
July	/	*P. l.* "Sarah Bernhardt"
Aug	/	*P. mlokosewitschii*
Sept	/	*P. obovata*
Oct	sow 🖑	
Nov	sow 🖑	
Dec	sow 🖑	

Problems Botrytis or gray mold is the main problem with peonies. It can cause rotting of stems and leaf bases. Destroy affected foliage, improve drainage and air circulation, and spray with a fungicide. Replace the top layer of soil carefully around the plants.

FLOWERING

Season The flowering period is invariably in early summer. Some peonies bloom for only a short time, but the flowers on other types are much longer lasting.

Cutting Cut flowers for indoor use when the blooms are opening. Peonies are excellent cut flowers, which will last longer if kept in a cool part of the home and given frequent water changes.

AFTER FLOWERING

Requirements Remove spent flower stems, but allow the foliage to die down naturally before trimming it back. Some varieties produce lovely fall color. Do not cut down the flowering stems of varieties such as *P. mlokosewitschii* that produce handsome berries.

HINT

Disturbance Peonies may flower poorly, if at all, in the first year after planting, but this should improve year by year. Generally speaking, peonies are best left undisturbed; even 50-year old clumps can be seen flowering profusely. It may be wiser to increase your stock by buying young container-grown plants than split a precious specimen.

PAPAVER ORIENTALE
Oriental poppy

THIS FRINGED red flower indicates the wide range of colors within P. orientale. *No border should be without one.*

THE STRIKING SHAPE of Papaver orientale. *Note the straight, slightly furry stem with, here, pink flowers and a black basal mark.*

FEATURES

The oriental poppy is a clump-forming perennial with a variety of different forms, and colors ranging from soft hues to sharp red. They all bear the hallmarks of the species *P. orientalis* from northeast Turkey and Iran, which has a large cupped bowl of a flower with paper-thin petals. Growing up to 36in tall, with a similar spread, they self-seed freely, creating attractive colonies. They look the part in both wild or natural gardens, and large mixed borders. "Black and White" is a striking contrast of white petals and a black mark at its base. "Cedric Morris" is soft pink with a black base. "Indian Chief" is reddish-brown.

PAPAVER AT A GLANCE

P. orientalis is a perennial with 12in-long leaves, and big, cupped flowers in a range of colors. Hardy to 0°F (zones 6–7).

Jan	/	**Recommended Varieties**
Feb	/	
Mar	/	*Papaver orientale*
		"Allegro"
Apr	division	*P. o.* "Beauty of Livermere"
May	flowering	*P. o.* "Black and White"
Jun	flowering	*P. o.* Goliath Group
July	flowering	*P. o.* "Mrs Perry"
		P. o. "Patty's Plum"
Aug	/	*P. o.* "Perry's White"
Sept	/	*P. o.* "Picotee"
Oct	sow	*P. o.* "Turkish Delight"
Nov	/	
Dec	/	

CONDITIONS

Aspect	Provide full sunlight, the conditions it receives in its natural habitat.
Site	Rich soil and good drainage bring out the best in these plants.

GROWING METHOD

Propagation	Since they self-seed freely, propagation may not be necessary. Slicing off sections of root in late fall or early winter will provide abundant new plants. The success rate is invariably high. Alternatively, divide clumps in the spring, or sow seed in pots in the fall in a cold frame. Plant out the following spring, 9in apart.
Feeding	Add plenty of rich, friable compost in spring to add fertility to poor soils. This also improves the drainage, which needs to be quite good.
Problems	Fungal wilt and downy mildew can be problems; spray at the first sign.

FLOWERING

Season	The flowers appear from late spring to mid-summer.
Cutting	Poppies do not make good cut flowers.

AFTER FLOWERING

Requirements	When the flowers have died down, severely cut back the foliage to the ground. This will produce a second showing of attractive summer leaves.

PENSTEMON
Beard tongue

MANY MONTHS of fine bloom can be expected from this fine red cultivar—well into the fall, if it is regularly deadheaded.

A GENEROUS PLANTING of these attractive white cultivars makes a perfect surround for this small ornamental fountain.

FEATURES

This very large group of perennials consists of 250 species and countless cultivars, all originating in a wide variety of habitats in the southern and western United States. Their tubular or funnel-shaped flowers come in a range of shades of pink, red, purple, lavender, blue, and white, some with a contrasting throat. There is a large range of cultivars in many of these shades. Collections of young rooted cuttings can also be bought. Penstemons have a long flowering period, through the summer to mid-fall, especially if the spent blooms are regularly cut, but many plants can be short-lived. Take cuttings regularly. The various species and hybrids grow anything from 4 to 24in tall.

PENSTEMON AT A GLANCE

A large genus of perennials grown for their late-season flower display. Hardiness varies from the frost-tender to 5°F (zones 10–7).

		Recommended Varieties
Jan	/	
Feb	sow 🖐	"Alice Hindley"
Mar	sow 🖐	"Beech Park"
Apr	transplant 🖐	"Chester Scarlet"
May	transplant 🖐	"Evelyn"
Jun	flowering 🌼	"Garnet"
July	flowering 🌼	"Margery Fish"
Aug	flowering 🌼	"Osprey"
Sept	flowering 🌼	"Pennington Gem"
Oct	flowering 🌼	"Rubicundus"
Nov	/	
Dec	/	

CONDITIONS

Aspect Grows best in full sunlight with some protection from strong, cutting winds. Since most varieties are not fully hardy, warmth and shelter are essential.

Site Needs very open and well-drained soil.

GROWING METHOD

Propagation They grow well from cuttings taken in mid-summer, then overwintered in a greenhouse frame. A wide range of penstemons can be grown from seed, which is widely available. They need a cold period before germination; sow in the fall or refrigerate the seed for three weeks before sowing in the spring.

Feeding Apply a general fertilizer as new growth commences in the spring.

Problems No specific pest or disease problems, but root rot may occur on sticky clay soil.

FLOWERING

Season Most have a fairly long flowering period, from the summer to mid-fall. However, many can only be seen as true perennials in milder parts of the country, being killed by winter frosts; raise new stock to replace any losses. "Garnet" is the hardiest.

Cutting This is not a satisfactory cut flower.

AFTER FLOWERING

Requirements Either cut entirely to the ground, or leave some stems as frost protection. Protect clumps with a mulch of straw or bracken.

PHLOX PANICULATA
Perennial phlox

THE ATTRACTIVE, individual flowers on the heads of perennial phlox last right through the season, making it essential in any border.

A GREAT STANDBY for the summer yard, perennial phlox fills the whole of the back of this border with two shades of pink.

FEATURES

Easy to grow and producing a summer-long display of flowers, perennial phlox has a place in any perennial collection. Plants may grow from 16 to 36in tall, and the clumps spread rapidly; position new plantings 12in apart. The large heads of flowers, some with a contrasting eye, come in shades of red, pink, orange, mauve, purple, and white. This plant looks best mass-planted, either in solid blocks of one color or in mixed colors. Also note the highly popular, new variegated cultivars. With mixed plantings, ensure that the taller forms do not obscure the shorter ones.

PHLOX AT A GLANCE

P. paniculata is an erect, herbaceous perennial with scented flowers, and many excellent cultivars. Hardy to 5°F (zone 7).

Jan	/	Recommended Varieties
Feb	sow	Phlox paniculata "Alba
Mar	sow	Grandiflora"
Apr	transplant	P. p. "Blue Ice"
May	transplant	P. p. "Bumble's Delight"
Jun		P. p. "Eventide"
July	flowering	P. p. "Le Mahdi"
Aug	flowering	P. p. "Prince of Orange"
Sept	flowering	P. p. "Prospero"
Oct	divide	P. p. "White Admiral"
Nov	/	
Dec	/	

CONDITIONS

Aspect   Prefers full sunlight with some protection from strong wind.

Site   Needs a well-drained soil enriched with organic matter.

GROWING METHOD

Propagation   Divide clumps in the fall every three or four years, making sure that each division has a crown and a good set of roots. Replant only the younger, vigorous outer growths, discarding the rest. Plants propagated from root cuttings will be free of eelworm.

Feeding   Apply a complete plant food the in spring and mulch well with rotted manure or compost, but do not cover the crowns.

Problems   Powdery mildew can be a problem. Spray with a fungicide. Phlox eelworm causes leaves to shrivel, and shrubs distort. Plants must be destroyed.

FLOWERING

Season   From the summer into early fall.

Cutting   It makes a good cut flower.

AFTER FLOWERING

Requirements   Remove spent flower stems as they fade. In late fall, cut off any remaining growth. Give the plants a thorough tidy-up for the winter.

PHYSOSTEGIA VIRGINIANA
Obedient plant

THE SHORT SPIKES of flowers are attached to the obedient plant by a joint, so they can be rearranged as you please.

OBEDIENT PLANT looks best in large plantings. It is well worth devoting yard space to it, since the flowers last for several months.

FEATURES

This is an easy-care, fast-growing perennial. Since it spreads by stolons (runners) and seed, large clumps can develop in one season. Excess plants are quite easily removed. The dark green leaves are only 4–6in long, but flowering stems bring the height up to 4ft. The flowers in the species are pinky-mauve, but there are cultivars with flowers in various shades of pink, red, and white. It looks best when planted in large drifts in a border, or among shrubs. The common name refers to the fact that flowers remain fixed the way they are turned. It is also sometimes known as "false dragon's head."

PHYSOSTEGIA AT A GLANCE

P. virginiana is a spreading, tall perennial with purple or lilac-tinged flowers lasting into the fall. Hardy to 32°F (zone 10).

Jan	/	
Feb	/	
Mar	divide 🐾	
Apr	transplant 🐾	
May	transplant 🐾	
Jun	/	
July	flowering 🌸	
Aug	flowering 🌸	
Sept	flowering 🌸	
Oct	sow 🐾	
Nov	/	
Dec	/	

Recommended Varieties

Physostegia virginiana
  "Alba"

P. v. "Crown of Snow"

P. v. "Red Beauty"

P. v. "Summer Snow"

P. v. "Vivid"

P. v. subsp. **speciosa**
  "Bouquet Rose"

CONDITIONS

Aspect   Grows well in both full sunlight and semi-shade. However, some form of protection from strong winds is desirable. The taller varieties may need staking.

Site   Tolerates a wide range of soils, but the best results occur when it's grown in well-drained soil, rich in organic matter.

GROWING METHOD

Propagation   Divide old clumps in the spring, planting new divisions in groups for the best effect. The oldest sections can be discarded. Because of its vigorous habit, you need to divide it every couple of years. Physostegia tolerates dry periods well, but you must water young plants regularly until they are established.

Feeding   Apply a complete plant food in spring. Mulch with decayed organic matter at the same time.

Problems   No specific problems are known.

FLOWERING

Season   Flowers appear from mid- to late summer into the fall.

Cutting   Frequent cutting of blooms should produce a second flush of flowers. Scald-cut the stems to prolong their vase life.

AFTER FLOWERING

Requirements   Remove spent flower stems and tidy up growth as it dies down.

PLATYCODON
Balloon flower

THE BUDS *of platycodon swell into a balloon shape, hence the common name, then pop open to reveal these beautiful flowers.*

THIS WELL-ESTABLISHED CLUMP *of balloon flower is supported by stakes guaranteeing height, as well as color.*

FEATURES

Also known as Chinese bellflower, this herbaceous perennial grows approximately 20in high, slightly taller in perfect conditions. It has a shortish flowering period in late summer, and the open, bell-shape flowers come in a range of blue shades, but also in white and pale pink. Flowers last well when cut. There are several named cultivars available, including double and semi-double examples. Since clumps are compact and spread slowly, they are best planted where they can remain undisturbed for some years. The new growth appears in late spring; mark its position to avoid hauling it out as a weed.

PLATYCODON AT A GLANCE

P. grandiflorus *is* a one-specie genus grown for its beautiful purple-blue flowers. Several fine cultivars. Hardy to 5°F (zone 7).

Jan	/	Companion Plants
Feb	/	Aster
Mar	sow	Clematis
Apr	divide	Dahlia
May	transplant	Fuchsia
Jun	/	Osteospermum
July	/	Phygelius
Aug	flowering	**Rhodochiton atrosan-**
Sept	flowering	**guineus** Rose
Oct	/	
Nov	/	
Dec	/	

CONDITIONS

Aspect   Grows in sun or dappled sunlight.
Site   Grows best in a well-drained soil enriched with plenty of organic matter.

GROWING METHOD

Propagation   Seed is the best means of propagation; sow in the spring. Young shoots can be taken as cuttings, and the double forms must be grown from cuttings. Also, clumps can be lifted and divided in the spring; replant the divisions approximately 8–10in apart. Give newly bedded plants a regular watering during prolonged dry spells in the spring and summer.
Feeding   Apply a complete plant food when new growth begins to appear in the spring.
Problems   Slugs can be a major problem devouring new growth. Either pick off by hand or treat chemically.

FLOWERING

Season   A relatively short display, which is more than compensated for by the nature of the exquisite flowers.
Cutting   Flowers can be cut for the vase.

AFTER FLOWERING

Requirements   Cut all spent flower stems right back to the ground, and then the whole plant as the growth dies off.

POLYGONATUM
Solomon's seal

A HORIZONTAL STEM of pretty white Solomon's seal flowers is suspended above a groundcover of lungwort and dead nettle.

SOLOMON'S SEAL grows tall in the dappled shade of this yard, where it is teamed with hostas, lady's mantle, and foxgloves.

FEATURES

This lovely herbaceous perennial is ideal for naturalizing in the dappled shade of a yard. The plant has a graceful, arching habit with stems 24–36in long. The finely veined foliage tends to stand up on the stem, while the tubular white bell flowers hang down. It grows from a creeping rhizome and will spread to form a colony of plants, given the correct conditions. If space is no problem, plant several to start your display, letting them form large colonies. A number of other species are grown, some, such as **P. odoratum**, with scented flowers; "Flore Pleno" has double flowers. There are two variegated, eye-catching forms.

POLYGONATUM AT A GLANCE

P. x hybridum (multiflorum) is a rhizomatous perennial with green-tipped white flowers and black fruit. Hardy to 0°F (zones

Jan	/	Recommended Varieties
Feb	/	
Mar	divide	P. biflorum
Apr	transplant	P. falcatum
May	flowering	P. f. "Variegatum"
Jun	/	P. hookeri
July	/	P. odoratum "Flore Pleno"
Aug	/	P. verticillatum
Sept	/	
Oct	sow	
Nov	/	
Dec	/	

CONDITIONS

Aspect Needs a sheltered spot in part or full shade.
Site The soil should drain well but be heavily enriched with organic matter to retain some moisture at all times. The plants benefit from an early spring mulch.

GROWING METHOD

Propagation Established clumps can be divided in early spring; new divisions should be positioned 8–10in apart. This plant is best left undisturbed for several years, if possible. Young plants need to be watered regularly during the growing season; do not let them dry out.
Feeding Apply complete plant food as new growth commences in the spring.
Problems Plants can be severely devastated by attacks of sawfly larvae, which reduce them to skeletons. Either treat with a spray, or pick off the caterpillars.

FLOWERING

Season Flowers appear in late spring.
Cutting Flowers can be cut for indoor decoration. They last fairly well and make a good display.

AFTER FLOWERING

Requirements Do not cut down the flower stems or you will end up weakening the plant, and consequently losing the attractive, yellow fall tints.

POTENTILLA
Cinquefoil

A SMART RED AND WHITE MIX of cinquefoil with annual heartsease, or Viola tricolor, *growing through it.*

DESPITE THE SMALL FLOWERS, these bright little plants are difficult to overlook in any perennial yard.

FEATURES

There are over 500 species of cinquefoil, including annuals, perennials, and small shrubs. All have the characteristic five-lobed leaf, and the single or double flowers may be white or in shades of yellow, red, or pink. Cinquefoil belongs to the rose family, and the foliage can be attractive, even when plants are not in flower. They may be from 2–20in or more high. The short types make good edging plants, while the taller ones can be used successfully in a mixed planting. Since flower stems tend to flop over, they may need light support. Many red cinquefoils are hybrids of **P. atrosanguinea**, while some yellows derive from **P. argyrophylla** and **P. recta**. Some cinquefoils tend to self-seed.

POTENTILLA AT A GLANCE

A 500-species genus, mainly of herbaceous perennials and shrubs. An excellent color range. Hardy to 0°F (zones 6–7).

Month		Recommended Varieties
Jan	/	
Feb	/	**Recommended Varieties**
Mar	sow	
Apr	transplant	Potentilla cuneata
May	transplant	"Gibson's Scarlet"
Jun	flowering	P. megalantha
July	flowering	P. nepalensis "Miss
Aug	flowering	Willmott"
Sept	flowering	"William Rollison"
Oct	sow	
Nov	/	
Dec	/	

CONDITIONS

Aspect While it needs full sunshine, cinquefoil will also tolerate some dappled shade.

Site Needs well-drained soil enriched with some organic matter.

GROWING METHOD

Propagation Species and single-flowered varieties grow from both seed and cuttings. Sow the seed in early to mid-spring. The hybrid doubles must be grown from divisions taken during the spring or fall, or you can use spring cuttings. The plant spacing depends on ultimate size, and may be anywhere from 6 to 16in.

Feeding Apply a complete plant food as new growth commences in the spring.

Problems Since these plants can easily flower themselves to death, propagate regularly to ensure you always have a good supply.

FLOWERING

Season Flowers may begin in late spring in warm spells, but the main flowering period is during the summer months. Give the plant a light trim in early spring to force plenty of new growth and buds.

Cutting Flowers do not last well when cut.

AFTER FLOWERING

Requirements Cut off spent flower stems at ground level, and tidy up the plants as the growth dies off. In milder areas the foliage may hang on.

PRIMULA VULGARIS
Primrose

A CARPET OF PALE YELLOW PRIMROSES is one of the finest ways to announce the arrival of spring in the yard. Given a cool, sheltered spot, they will thrive and multiply year by year, even if they receive little attention.

FEATURES

This is the true primrose of European woodlands. The species generally has soft, pale yellow flowers tucked in among the leaves on very short stalks, although white or pale pink forms are occasionally found. Cultivars come in a huge range of colors, with single or double flowers, some on short stalks, others on quite tall ones. Primroses look their best when mass-planted under deciduous trees, or in drifts at the front of a lightly shaded bed or border. They can also be grown well in pots. Plants grow from about 4 to 6in high, with flowering stems about the same height.

PRIMULA AT A GLANCE

P. vulgaris is an evergreen or semi-evergreen with scented, spring, generally pale yellow flowers. Hardy to 5°F (zone 7).

Jan	/	
Feb	sow 🌱	**Recommended Varieties**
Mar	flowering 🌸	
Apr	flowering 🌸	"Ken Dearman"
May	flowering 🌸	"Miss Indigo"
Jun	/	**Primula vulgaris** "Lilacina Plena"
July	/	
Aug	/	P. v. subsp. **sibthorpii**
Sept	sow 🌱	"Wanda"
Oct	divide 🌱	
Nov	/	
Dec	/	

CONDITIONS

Aspect Prefers to grow in semi-shade, and must have protection from the summer sun.

Site Grows best in a medium-to-heavy moisture-retentive soil, heavily enriched with organic matter. Mulch around the plants in spring.

GROWING METHOD

Propagation Lift and divide the crowns after flowering, in late fall, and replant about 4–6in apart. Sow your plant's own seed when ripe (from late spring to early fall); sow bought seed in early spring. Do not let young plants dry out.

Feeding Little fertilizer is needed if the soil is well enriched with plenty of humus, but a little general fertilizer in early spring gives an extra boost.

Problems Generally trouble-free.

FLOWERING

Season Flowering usually lasts for several weeks during the spring. Deadheading prolongs the blooming. Massed displays look best.

Cutting Makes a fine small bouquet, mixed with a range of other early spring miniatures.

AFTER FLOWERING

Requirements In suitable conditions, plants may self-seed. Remove dead leaves around the plant base.

PRIMULA SPECIES
Candelabra primulas

PRIMULA PULVERULENTA *happily combine here with hostas, both enjoying the damp conditions of a bog garden.*

THE CHARACTERISTIC TIERS *of flowers are well displayed in this healthy clump of white perennial primulas.*

FEATURES

Candelabra primulas, which produce their flowers in distinct whorls or tiers up the stems, form one group among the several hundred species of primula. Most are herbaceous, but **P. helodoxa**, which has clear yellow flowers, is evergreen. Other species in this group include **P. aurantiaca**, **P. bulleyana**, **P. japonica**, and **P. pulverulenta**. Flowers may be white, or in shades of yellow, orange, pink, red, or purple. Plant heights vary from 24 to 39in. These are plants that need to be placed in large groups for maximum impact. They need damp soil, often being planted around ponds and water features. Given the right conditions, these plants give a great show every year.

PRIMULA AT A GLANCE

Candelabra primulas are deciduous or semi-evergreen, flower on tall stems, and brighten up damp areas. Hardy to 5°F (zone 7).

Jan	/	Recommended Varieties
Feb	sow	Primula beesiana
Mar	sow	P. bulleyana
Apr	flowering	"Inverewe"
May	flowering	P. japonica
Jun	/	Pagoda Hybrids
July	/	P. japonica
Aug	/	P. pulverulenta
Sept	sow	
Oct	divide	
Nov	/	
Dec	/	

CONDITIONS

Aspect   Candelabra primulas thrive in dappled shade.
Site   Needs deep, moisture-retentive soil that is heavily enriched with organic matter, but it clearly dislikes being waterlogged over the winter months.

GROWING METHOD

Propagation   Lift and divide the crowns after flowering, in late fall, and replant about 4–6in apart. Sow your plant's own seed when ripe (from late spring to early fall); sow bought seed in early spring. Do not let young plants dry out.
Feeding   Little fertilizer is needed if the soil is well enriched with plenty of humus, but a scattering of general fertilizer in early spring gives an extra boost.
Problems   Generally trouble-free.

FLOWERING

Season   This charming, essential primula flowers during the spring.
Cutting   Flowers probably last a few days in the vase, and they add considerable charm to any arrangement, but the massed garden display is more rewarding.

AFTER FLOWERING

Requirements   Spent flower stems can be cut off, unless you are waiting for seed to set. In good conditions many of the species will self-seed.

PULMONARIA
Lungwort

FLOWERING PULMONARIA *are an essential feature of the spring yard.*

THE SPOTTED FOLIAGE *of lungwort makes dense and attractive groundcover under trees. It is a reliable grower, so long as it gets regular water in the spring and summer.*

FEATURES

Lungwort is well suited to planting under trees, between shrubs, or at the front of a shady border. The abundant flowers appear before the leaves have fully developed, and are mostly in shades of blue, pink, and white. The foliage is very handsome, often silver-spotted, and if sheared over after flowering, produces a second, fresh mound of leaves. The whole plant is rarely more than 10–12in high, and when established is very decorative, even out of flower. The plant gets its common name from the similarity between a spotted leaf and a diseased lung.

PULMONARIA AT A GLANCE

A genus of 14 species of deciduous and evergreen perennials. A flowering spreader for damp shade. Hardy to 0°F (zones 6–7).

		Recommended Varieties
Jan	/	
Feb	/	Pulmonaria angustifolia
Mar	flowering	P. a. "Munstead Blue"
Apr	flowering	P. longifolia "Bertram
May	flowering	Anderson"
Jun	divide	P. officinalis Cambridge
July	/	Blue Group
Aug	/	P. o. "Sissinghurst White"
Sept	/	P. rubra
Oct	divide	P. saccharata Argentea
Nov	/	Group
Dec	/	

CONDITIONS

Aspect   Grows best in light shade, or in borders that are shady during the hottest part of the day. The leaves quickly wilt under a hot sun.

Site   The soil should be heavily enriched with decayed organic matter, but it also needs to drain quite well.

GROWING METHOD

Propagation   Grows from ripe seed, or by division of clumps, either after flowering or in the fall. Replant divisions approximately 6in apart. Better still, let plants freely hybridize. Young and established plants need moist soil during the growing season.

Feeding   Apply a little complete fertilizer in early spring and mulch well.

Problems   No specific problems are known.

FLOWERING

Season   Lungworts flower in the spring.

Cutting   Flowers last quite well in a vase.

AFTER FLOWERING

Requirements   Spent flowers can be cut off if you do not want seeding to occur. After the flowers have finished, the foliage can be cut back to produce new fresh growth for the summer. Otherwise, little attention is required until the fall, when the foliage can be tidied as it fades.

PULSATILLA VULGARIS
Pasque flower

FOLK MEDICINE makes use of the pasque flower, but it should be treated with caution, since it can be fatal if used incorrectly.

LIGHT FROST here coats buds of the pasque flower, showing up its silky hairs. They will be more obvious on the seedheads.

FEATURES

The soft purple flowers appear before the leaves on this small, spring-flowering perennial. The whole plant is covered with silky hairs, giving it a delicate appearance that belies its hardy nature. After the petals have fallen, a decorative seedhead forms. The finely divided leaves grow from 4 to 6in long, while the flowers may be on stems 4–12in tall. Pasque flower should be planted in groups or drifts to get the best effect. There are now pink, white, and red forms available. Since the leaves and flowers may cause skin irritation, wear gloves when handling if you have sensitive skin.

PULSATILLA AT A GLANCE

P. vulgaris is an attractive, clump-forming perennial, with bell-like, silky flowers in shades of purple. Hardy to 0°F (zones 6–7).

Month	Activity	Recommended Varieties
Jan	/	
Feb	/	Pulsatilla alpina subsp. apiifolia
Mar	/	
Apr	flowering	P.halleri
May	flowering	P. halleri subsp. slavica
Jun	flowering	P. vernalis
July	sow	P. vulgaris
Aug	sow	P. v. "Eva Constance"
Sept	/	P. v. var. rubra
Oct	divide	
Nov	/	
Dec	/	

CONDITIONS

Aspect — Prefers full sun but tolerates semi-shade.

Site — Needs very well-drained, gritty soil, rich in organic matter. They thrive on lime.

GROWING METHOD

Propagation — Divide existing clumps after the foliage has died down, and then replant the divisions approximately 6–8in apart. Named varieties must be divided, but the species can also be grown from seed sown as soon as it is ripe in July. Overwinter the seedlings in a greenhouse or frame. Pot up when the new leaves begin to show in the spring.

Feeding — Apply a little general fertilizer when growth commences in the spring.

Problems — No specific pest or disease problems are known for this plant.

FLOWERING

Season — Flowers appear in the spring and early summer, generally before the leaves. They last well and the display is prolonged by the pretty, silky seedheads.

Cutting — The flowers are unsuitable for cutting, but the seedheads add to an attractive display.

AFTER FLOWERING

Requirements — Plants should be left alone until the seedheads have faded or fallen. Cut off spent stems, and trim off the foliage as the plant dies.

ROMNEYA COULTERI
Californian tree poppy

CRIMPED WHITE PETALS *around a mass of golden stamens make the matilija poppy as effective in close-up as in a group.*

THE BLUE-GREEN FOLIAGE *and splendid white flowers of the matilija poppy make an eye-catching display in the garden.*

FEATURES

Also known as the matilija poppy, this lovely perennial is not always easy to accommodate. It is native to the canyons and dry riverbeds in parts of California where there is generally rain only in winter, and where summers are hot and dry. When conditions are suitable, this plant can spread via underground roots. The large, white, summer flowers have beautiful crinkled petals that look like silk. Plants grow from 3 to 6½ft tall, and the blue-green foliage is deeply cut and attractive. Place these perennials in groups among shrubs or mixed perennials. Most plants available are likely to be hybrids of the standard species and *R. coulteri* var. *trichocalyx.*

ROMNEYA AT A GLANCE

R. coulteri is a deciduous sub-shrub with gray-green leaves and highly attractive white summer flowers. Hardy to 0°F (zones 6–7).

Jan	/	Companion Plants
Feb	/	
Mar	sow 🖑	Ceanothus
Apr	division	Clematis
May	transplant 🖑	Delphinium
Jun	flowering 🌼	Helenium
July	flowering 🌼	Hemerocallis
Aug	flowering 🌼	Pelargonium
Sept	/	Pennisetum
Oct	/	Philadelphus
Nov	/	
Dec	/	

CONDITIONS

Aspect   Romneya needs bright, full sunlight all day.
Site   Needs well-drained, preferably sandy or gravelly loam; avoid thick, heavy, wet clay. They can be tricky and slow to establish, but thereafter thrive, given the correct conditions.

GROWING METHOD

Propagation   Grows from seed sown in the spring, but it is easiest propagated from root cuttings or suckers growing away from the main plant in spring. Wait until plants are very well established before attempting to disturb the roots—something they do not react well to. Position plants approximately 16in apart. Water regularly in the spring, when the foliage is growing and buds are appearing; thereafter, water occasionally in prolonged, dry spells.
Feeding   Give a little complete plant food in early spring.
Problems   Poor drainage can kill Californian tree poppies. Can become invasive.

FLOWERING

Season   Right through the summer.
Cutting   Like all poppies they make lovely cut flowers. Scald or burn the stems before arranging.

AFTER FLOWERING

Requirements   Cut off spent flowers. As the plant flowers on new growth, it is best to cut it down to the ground in winter. Protect the crown with straw or bracken in cold areas.

RUDBECKIA
Coneflower

THE DAISY-LIKE flower shape of the coneflower, a bright color, and a central dark marking. It looks best in a bold group display.

A VALUABLE, forceful, late summer display from a mass planting of coneflowers, especially useful when many borders are starting to fade.

FEATURES

The coneflower rewards a bright, sunny position with a bold display of daisy-like flowers. The genus consists of annuals, biennials, and perennials, with some traditional garden favorites. *R. fulgida*, Black-eyed Susan, grows 36 x 18in, producing yellow-orange flowers at the end of summer, into the fall. "Goldsturm" has bigger flowers but only grows two-thirds as tall. For a powerful, vigorous display at the back of the border, try *R. lacinata*. It has thin, wiry stems, lemon-yellow flowers, and puts on a mid-summer to mid-fall display that can reach 8ft high, while its spread is relatively contained at just 3ft.

RUDBECKIA AT A GLANCE

A near 20-species genus with annuals, biennials, and perennials, often with striking, yellowish flowers. Hardy to 0°F (zones 6–7).

Month	Activity	Recommended Varieties
Jan	/	
Feb	/	"Goldquelle"
Mar	sow	"Herbstonne"
Apr	divide	*Rudbeckia fulgida* var. *deamii*
May	transplant	
Jun	/	*R. f.* var. *sullivantii* "Goldsturm"
July	flowering	
Aug	flowering	*R. laciniata*
Sept	flowering	*R. maxima*
Oct	flowering	
Nov	divide	
Dec	/	

CONDITIONS

Aspect A bright, open sunny position is essential. Avoid shady areas. The plant's natural habitat is North American meadows and big, open woods.

Site Do not plant in over-dry, Mediterranean-style yards. The soil must remain heavy and lightly damp. In the wild *R. fulgida* grows in marshy valleys.

GROWING METHOD

Propagation Either divide in the spring or fall, or sow seeds in the spring in a cold frame. Do not let the new, young plants dry out.

Feeding Fertility must be quite high. Dig large quantities of well-rotted manure and compost into poor soil.

Problems Slugs can be a major problem. Keep watch, and pick them off by hand or treat chemically. A potentially good flowering display can be quickly ruined if they take control.

FLOWERING

Season A long flowering season from the summer to late fall.

Cutting Rudbeckia make good cut flowers, adding height and color to any arrangement. They are especially useful, having a dark-colored central disk (black, brown, or green) in the center of the flower.

AFTER FLOWERING

Requirements Cut back to the ground, although some stems can be left to provide interesting shapes over winter, especially when frosted.

SALVIA
Sage

SALVIA X SYLVESTRIS "MAINACHT" ("MAY NIGHT") is a wonderful, clumpy perennial that sends up spires of rich blue flowers. It can be guaranteed to soften even the most rigid landscaped yard, flowering in early and mid-summer. "Blauhugel" ("Blue Mound") is very similar.

FEATURES

Salvias are a huge plant group of over 700 species, comprising shrubs, herbaceous perennials, and annuals. Most people associate salvias with red or purple flowers, but there are also species with cream, yellow, white, blue, and pink flowers. Many have highly aromatic foliage, with scents ranging from the delicious to the outright unpleasant: the foliage of pineapple sage, *S. elegans* (syn. *S. rutilans*) has a delicious perfume, while the bog sage (*S. uliginosa*) smells rather unpleasant. Most salvias are extremely easy to grow and once established need little attention, beyond occasional deep watering in hot weather and some cutting back after flowering. The tall salvias are ideal for the rear of the border or as fillers between shrubs. There are many others of varying heights that are suitable as edging plants or for planting among annuals, bulbs, and other perennials. *Salvia* x *sylvestris* "Mainacht" ("May Night"), shown above, is an exceptionally good border perennial, but if it is unavailable there are plenty of fine alternatives, including "Rose Queen." Common sage, *S. officinalis*, is a highly popular salvia. It has gray, wrinkly foliage and flowers that are usually pale violet. The one problem is that, in certain conditions, it spreads like a weed. Coming from the Mediterranean, it demands sharp drainage and dislikes a soaking wet summer.

Others
For spring–summer flowers in a range of colors, from cream to lilac and blue, try *S. sclarea*. It is perfectly hardy, and grows up to 3ft high. S. *bulleyana* is equally easy, and grows approximately 16in–3ft high. It has yellow flowers with a brownish lower lip appearing from the middle to the end of summer, and is also fully hardy, coming from western China. For an early summer–autumn flower show, use *S. forsskaolii* from the Black Sea coast. It grows 3ft tall high, and bears white flowers with lips in violet and faint yellow. Alternatively, try *S.* x *superba*. It has violet flowers from mid-summer to the fall, and reaches the same height. For mild areas where you can grow half-hardy plants, there are plenty more salvias, including *S. microphylla*, and the bog sage, *S. uliginosa*. The former has rich green leaves and magenta flowers at the end of summer to early fall. Bog sage has bright blue flowers with a touch of white, and blooms from late summer to the fall. Both reach 3ft high.

CONDITIONS

Aspect   Provide full sunlight, perhaps in a scree bed, and, in the case of half-hardy plants, a position against a south-facing wall.

Site   Any well-drained soil is suitable. Mulching with decayed manure in the early spring improves the soil condition.

SALVIA SCLAREA *VAR.* TURKESTANICA *can be grown as a perennial or biennial. It produces wonderful pink stems of pinky-white flowers, and is perfectly hardy.*

THE ELECTRIC BLUE *Salvia transsylvanica contrasting with a "Star Gazer" lily.*

GROWING METHOD

Propagation Salvias grow from seed that has been sown in the spring, or from cuttings that have been taken in late summer through to the fall. Many species can also be propagated from rooted divisions of an established clump. Simply lift such a clump and you will find numerous pieces with both roots and shoots. The divisions are best taken in the spring months. Set each division approximately 10in apart. Salvias need regular watering to establish. Once established, plants can be drought-tolerant.

Feeding A complete plant food or pelleted poultry manure can be applied in the spring, in poor soil, as the new growth commences. However, note that too much fertilizer will be counter-

productive, merely resulting in all foliage and very few flowers.

Problems The worst problems tend to occur when you provide a certain species with the wrong conditions. Carefully check the notes invariably supplied with plants when buying from a garden center or specialist nursery. As a general rule, avoid damp ground and any shady areas.

FLOWERING

Season Many salvias have a very long flowering period, extending into the fall before being cut down by frost.

Cutting None of the salvias mentioned makes a particularly good cut flower, but their long, dependable flowering season makes them a great asset in any part of the yard.

AFTER FLOWERING

Requirements Borderline, half-hardy species will need plenty of protection in cold areas over winter. Provide a thick, protective layer of straw or bracken, held in place with sticks. As a precaution against any losses, keep a stock of new, young plants. The tender salvias must be kept indoors in winter, in a frost-free place. Plants can be tip-pruned after each flowering flush to promote further blooming. In late fall plants can be cut back to just above ground level. If you do not want to lift and divide a clump you can wait until new growth starts in the spring, and simply divide any growth that is becoming too crowded. A number of perennial salvias are extremely vigorous, but they can be kept in control by pulling out the new plants or the running roots when they are getting invasive.

SALVIA AT A GLANCE		
A large genus with fine perennials. The color range is mainly blue. Hardy plants to 0°F (zones 6–7); half-hardy 23°F (zone 9).		

Jan	/	Recommended Varieties
Feb	/	*Salvia argentea*
Mar	sow	*S. bulleyana*
Apr	divide	*S. forsskaolii*
May	transplant	*S. involucrata* (half-hardy)
Jun	flowering	*S. microphylla* (half-hardy)
July	flowering	*S. patens* (half-hardy)
Aug	flowering	*S. sclarea*
Sept	flowering	*S.* x *superba*
Oct	flowering	*S. uliginosa* (half-hardy)
Nov	/	
Dec	/	

SCABIOSA
Scabious

SCABIOSA CAUCASICA "CLIVE GREAVES" is a wonderful laven-der blue and looks especially impressive when planted in thick clusters.

SCABIOUS ARE VERSATILE PLANTS. They make a wonderful addition to most yards, whether schematic or cottage-style.

FEATURES

Scabious is a vital ingredient of cottage-style, flowery gardens, rock gardens, and mixed borders. From hot, dry, stoney sites, mainly in the Mediterranean, it provides pale hues in blue, pink, yellow, or white. The flowers are held above long, thin stems, many attracting bees and butterflies. Heights generally range from 12 to 36in. There are plenty of interesting choices, and top of the list are the dwarf forms "Butterfly Blue" and "Pink Mist," both relatively new and proving extremely popular. On the plus side, they flower for six months; the down side is they are short-lived. Take cuttings to maintain the display.

SCABIOSA AT A GLANCE

A genus of annuals, biennials, and perennials, providing abundant soft colors. Good for romantic displays. Hardy to 0°F (zones 6–7).

		Recommended Varieties
Jan	/	
Feb	/	***Scabiosa caucasica***
Mar	sow	"Clive Greaves"
Apr	divide	*S. c.* "Miss Willmott"
May	transplant	"Chile Black"
Jun	flowering	*S. columbaria* var.
July	flowering	***ochroleuca***
Aug	flowering	*S. lucida*
Sept	flowering	"Pink Mist"
Oct	sow	
Nov	/	
Dec	/	

CONDITIONS

Aspect	Full sunlight is essential.
Site	Dryish, free-draining soil is important, so that the roots are not plunged in soaking wet ground over the winter months. The soil must also veer from the neutral toward the slightly alkaline.

GROWING METHOD

Propagation	Scabious is not long-lived, and begins to lose its vigor and impact after three years. It is therefore vital to replenish the garden with spring divisions, or to sow fresh, ripe seed in pots in a cold frame to maintain a good supply.
Feeding	Do not over-feed the soil, which will be counter-productive, producing leaf growth at the expense of flowers. Very poor soils, however, may need some additions of compost in the early spring.
Problems	Spray at the first sign of powdery mildew.

FLOWERING

Season	The flowers appear right through the summer, in some cases not until mid-summer, often into early fall.
Cutting	Scabious make excellent sprays of cut flowers, and are indispensable for indoor arrangements, either adding to flowery schemes or softening more rigid, structured ones.

AFTER FLOWERING

Requirements	Cut all spent stems down to the ground.

SEDUM SPECTABILE
Ice plant

DENSE FLOWERHEADS of Sedum spectabile "Brilliant" provide a rich source of nectar, attracting butterflies and other insects.

BILLOWING HEADS of sedum add color to the fall yard. Here they edge a mixed border, with white beard tongue behind.

FEATURES

One of over 600 species of succulent sedums, spectabile is unusual because it is frequently used in perennial plantings where many succulents look out of place. It has fleshy, soft green leaves on stems that can reach 24in tall. Similar varieties are available with purple and variegated leaves. Since the new growth appears at the base of older stems, dividing plants is easy. The large heads of flowers are a soft mauve-pink in the species, but there are cultivars with colors ranging from bright hot pinks to rosy red, and the brick red of "Herbstfreude" ("Autumn Joy"). The plants flower from late summer into the fall. This is an easy-care plant that accepts a wide range of conditions.

SEDUM AT A GLANCE

S. spectabile is a clump-forming, late season perennial with pink flowers. Many excellent forms. Hardy to 5°F (zone 7).

Jan	/	Recommended Varieties
Feb	/	
Mar	/	Sedum alboroseum
Apr	divide 🖐	"Mediovariegatum"
May	/	S. cauticola
Jun	/	"Herbstfreude" ("Autumn Joy")
July	/	"Ruby Glow"
Aug	flowering 🌸	S. spectabile "Brilliant"
Sept	flowering 🌸	S. telephium maximum
Oct	divide 🖐	"Atropurpureum"
Nov	sow 🖐	
Dec	/	

CONDITIONS

Aspect   Prefers full sun, but tolerates some light shade for part of the day.

Site   While it can grow in a sandy, well-drained soil, it will tolerate a heavier soil, which gives it an advantage over other sedums.

GROWING METHOD

Propagation   Clumps of plants are easily pulled apart or sliced apart with a spade in the spring or late fall. The divisions are best replanted at approximately 6–8in intervals. Division gives very high success rates. It is also possible to propagate sedum by striking from stem cuttings. Water regularly to establish new young plants.

Feeding   Slow-release fertilizer can be applied in the spring, as new growth commences. Avoid overfeeding, because this may result in plenty of sappy leaf growth at the expense of a display of flowers.

Problems   Plants in containers may rot at the base if overwatered. Vine weevil grubs may devour both bases and roots with devastating effect.

FLOWERING

Season   The late, highly rewarding display occurs at the end of summer, running through the fall.

Cutting   A long-lasting cut flower.

AFTER FLOWERING

Requirements   Leave the skeletal flowerheads over winter to provide attractive, burnished tints.

SISYRINCHIUM
Sisyrinchrium

SISYRINCHIUM IDAHOENSE "ALBUM" *is a clump-forming white flower that at 5in tall is ideal for edging borders.*

SISYRINCHIUM MACROCARPON *is 30in tall, has eye-catching vertical foliage, and gentle yellow flowers in early summer.*

FEATURES

This is a star plant for the border, with spires of pale yellow flowers over summer, 36in high, and iris-like, strap-shaped foliage. The only problem is that it can self-seed too much for the liking of some, although with vigilance the seedlings are easily removed. The genus also offers blue, mauve, and white flowers. *S. idahoense* is a lovely violet-blue, with a yellow throat, growing 12in high, while *S. graminoides* is slightly taller at 20in, with a deeper blue flower, although it self-seeds more prolifically. For a dwarfish, low-growing white, try "Pole Star," good for the rock garden, where it can best be seen and appreciated. It grows to just 1 x 2½in, and is perfectly hardy.

SISYRINCHIUM AT A GLANCE

S. striatum is an evergreen perennial with spires of pale yellow flowers and long, stiff, pointed leaves. Hardy to 5°F (zone 7).

Jan	/	**Recommended Varieties**
Feb	/	
Mar	sow 🖐	*Sisyrinchium angusti-folium*
Apr	transplant 🖐	"Biscutella"
May	/	"Californian Skies"
Jun	flowering 🌱	*S. californicum*
July	flowering 🌱	"E. K. Balls"
Aug	/	*S. idahoense*
Sept	divide 🖐	*S. macrocarpon*
Oct	/	"Quaint and Queer"
Nov	/	*S. striatum* "Aunt May"
Dec	/	

CONDITIONS

Aspect	Full sun is required, well away from the shade.
Site	Relatively poor soil is adequate, but free-draining ground is essential. Do not let the plants stand out in damp, wet soil over the winter months.

GROWING METHOD

Propagation	Divide in late summer to guarantee a supply of vigorous plants, since mature ones become quite lackluster after three years. Alternatively, sow seed in the spring. To prevent any established plants from self-seeding, cut off the flowers the moment they begin to fade.
Feeding	Some enriching with well-rotted manure or compost will provide a boost to poor areas of ground. High levels of fertility, however, are not necessary.
Problems	Generally trouble-free.

FLOWERING

Season	Flowers in early and mid-summer.
Cutting	They make unusual, striking cut flowers, adding smart verticals to any arrangement, forming a basic structure. Use both flowering stems and foliage.

AFTER FLOWERING

Requirements	Cut back the flowering stems to the ground, either promptly to prevent large-scale self-seeding, or later to increase numbers,

SOLIDAGO
Golden rod

THE HIGHLY DISTINCTIVE sight of golden rod: a bright spray of yellow flowers, and long, thin, dark green leaves.

A PERFECT EXAMPLE OF HOW an invasive plant, such as golden rod, can be reigned in and controlled by hard landscaping.

FEATURES

Golden rod forms large colonies of sometimes quite tall yellow plants, reaching 6ft high. The small flowers in themselves are nothing special, but they appear in such profusion that they make quite an impact. There are plenty of varieties to choose from. The key differences are more to do with height than color. "Crown of Rays" grows to 24in high, and as its name suggests has bright yellow flowers. "Goldenmosa" is almost as bright and grows slightly taller, and has yellow-green foliage. But if you need a golden rod for the rear of the border, especially one where the soil is quite poor, the best choice is "Golden Wings." It can reach 6ft tall, topping smaller plants with its late summer and early fall show. The best choice of golden rod for growing at the front of the border is the 8in-high "Queenie" or *S. virgaurea minuta*.

CONDITIONS

Aspect   Grow in full sunlight in the border. Avoid borders that are in the shade.

Site   Free-draining soil, preferably quite sandy or gritty, is ideal.

GROWING METHOD

Propagation   Golden rod self-seeds, but to be sure of getting new plants that are true to type, spring or fall division invariably give successful results.

Feeding   High soil fertility is not in any way essential. Very poor ground can be improved in the spring, however, by digging in some quantities of well-rotted manure.

Problems   Powdery mildew can strike quite severely; treat with a fungicide at the first sight of an attack. Repeat sprayings are necessary to control major outbreaks.

FLOWERING

Season   Generally mid- to late summer, though sometimes slightly before and after.

Cutting   Not the best cut flowers—there are better alternatives—but they effectively bulk up any arrangement.

AFTER FLOWERING

Requirements   Cut back spent flower stems.

SOLIDAGO AT A GLANCE

Varieties of golden rod create mainly big, bold, clumps of bright yellow flowers. Can be invasive. Hardy to 0°F (zones 6–7).

Month		Recommended Varieties
Jan	/	***Solidago cutleri***
Feb	/	*S. flexicaulis* "Variegata"
Mar	/	"Golden Baby"
Apr	divide	"Goldenmosa"
May	transplant	"Queenie"
Jun	/	*S. virgaurea minuta*
July	flowering	
Aug	flowering	
Sept	/	
Oct	/	
Nov	/	
Dec	/	

STACHYS BYZANTINA
Lamb's ears

SINCE LAMB'S EARS, or lamb's tails, needs good drainage, grow it in an attractive container if your soil is relentlessly heavy and damp.

MORE TRADITIONAL is this planting, where lamb's ears edge a garden bed. The plants will multiply rapidly, given the right situation.

FEATURES

Lamb's ears is a low-growing, evergreen perennial most often used as an edging plant. It could also be used to edge rose beds, but wherever it is planted it must have excellent drainage and full exposure to the sun. The leaves are densely covered with hairs, giving them a white, or pale gray, woolly appearance, hence its common name. It produces pink-purple flowers on spikes that stand above the foliage, but they are not especially attractive; it is grown for its foliage, not the flowers (*S. macrantha* "Robusta" and *S. officinalis* are the exceptions). "Cotton Boll" has woolly flowers good for dried flower arrangements if they are cut when fully open. Plants grow 6–8in tall, but spread a good distance.

STACHYS AT A GLANCE

S. byzantina is a valuable garden plant, noted for its front-of-the border color and soft, silky foliage. Hardy to 0°F (zones 6–7).

		Recommended Varieties
Jan	/	
Feb	/	*S. coccinea*
Mar	sow	*Stachys byzantina* "Big Ears"
Apr	divide	
May	transplant	*S. b.* "Cotton Boll"
Jun	flowering	*S. b.* "Primrose Heron"
July	flowering	*S. macrantha*
Aug	flowering	*S. m.* "Robusta"
Sept	flowering	*S. officinalis*
Oct	divide	
Nov	/	
Dec	/	

CONDITIONS

Aspect   Full sunlight is essential all day for the plants to thrive and perform well.

Site   Needs very fast-draining soil. It grows well in poor, sandy, or gravelly soil. Avoid thick, wet, heavy clay at all costs.

GROWING METHOD

Propagation   Grows readily from cuttings that are taken in the spring or fall. The new divisions must be planted out approximately 8in apart. Water new plants regularly. Once they are established, they need only be watered very occasionally.

Feeding   Grows without supplementary fertilizer, but a little complete plant food can be applied in the early spring.

Problems   There are no specific problems, but container plants will quickly fail if they are overwatered, and border plants rot if waterlogged.

FLOWERING

Season   Flowers are produced in the summer, sometimes into the fall, but the tactile gray foliage is by far the chief attraction.

Cutting   Use the foliage in an arrangement; the flower spikes can be cut and dried for later use.

AFTER FLOWERING

Requirements   Cut spent flower stems at the base. Trailing growth can be shortened at any time, but plants may need to be cut back hard in the early spring.

STOKESIA LAEVIS
Stokes' aster

THE FLOWERING HEADS of Stokes' aster are quite complex, made up from many "petals" (more properly bracts or ray florets).

IT IS HARD to understand why the pretty Stokes' aster should go out of fashion, but it is certainly grown less often than before.

FEATURES

Stokes' aster is an easily grown plant that provides great decorative value throughout its long flowering period from mid-summer to early fall. It makes excellent cut flowers, too. Flower stems 12–20in tall rise from a cluster of dark green basal leaves. Although this plant is completely herbaceous in cold areas, the basal growth remains evergreen in mild winters. Its flowers are reminiscent of large cornflowers or asters, and come in shades of blue, white, and mauve. This plant can look outstanding in mass plantings, but is equally at home in a mixed border, or when grown in wooden tubs or pots.

STOKESIA AT A GLANCE

S. laevis is an evergreen, perennial, sprawling plant with large, purple, flat, late summer flowers. Hardy to 5°F (zone 7).

Month	Activity	Companion Plants
Jan	/	
Feb	sow 🖐	Aster
Mar	divide 🖐	Box
Apr	transplant 🖐	Dahlia
May	transplant 🖐	Fuchsia
Jun	/	Miscanthus
July	/	Penstemon
Aug	flowering 🌼	Potentilla
Sept	flowering 🌼	Stipa
Oct	flowering 🌼	
Nov	divide 🖐	
Dec	/	

CONDITIONS

Aspect While Stokes' aster prefers full sunlight, it barely tolerates dappled shade. Provide a shelter to protect from strong winds.

Site Needs well-drained soil enriched with compost or manure.

GROWING METHOD

Propagation Divide established clumps in the spring or fall, replanting divisions approximately 10in apart. The plant can also be grown from root cuttings taken in the early spring, and from fall seed. It tolerates dry periods, but looks best if given an occasional deep watering during prolonged, dry spells. Provide young plants with twiggy support.

Feeding Apply some complete plant food in the spring.

Problems Poorly drained, heavy soils induce root or crown rot, which kills plants.

FLOWERING

Season The long flowering period is from late summer into the fall.

Cutting Cut flowers regularly for the vase. This both gives a good ornamental display and prolongs the garden show, inducing plenty of new flower buds.

AFTER FLOWERING

Requirements Prune all spent flower stems. As the growth dies back, promptly clear away all of the dead foliage.

THALICTRUM
Meadow rue

THE FLUFFY PINK FLOWERS of meadow rue do not last long, but the pretty foliage persists well until the fall.

FINER FOLIAGE, *smaller starry flowers and very full growth are features of the related* Thalictrum delavayi *and its cultivars.*

FEATURES

Thalictrum aquilegiifolium is easy and quick to grow, a herbaceous perennial reaching about 42in tall. The rather fern-like, blue-green foliage is attractively lobed, and the flowers are mauve-pink in dense, fluffy heads. While the floral display does not last long, the foliage adds months of charm. Meadow rue can be planted in mixed borders or in light shade under trees. There are a number of cultivars, including a white form and one with violet blooms. Also try *T. delavayi* (syn. *T. dipterocarpum*) and its cultivars "Album" and "Hewitt's Double." This has finer foliage and the pink-mauve flowers are star shaped.

THALICTRUM AT A GLANCE

T. aquilegiifolium is a clump-forming, rhizomatous perennial with gorgeous sprays of purple flowers. Hardy to 5°F (zone 7).

		Recommended Varieties
Jan	/	
Feb	/	*Thalictrum aquilegiifoli-*
Mar	divide	*um* var. *album*
Apr	transplant	*T. a.* "Thundercloud"
May	/	*T. delavayi*
Jun	flowering	*T. flavum* subsp. *glau-cum*
July	flowering	*T. kiusianum*
Aug	/	*T. minus*
Sept	/	*T. rochebruneanum*
Oct	sow	
Nov	/	
Dec	/	

CONDITIONS

Aspect	Grow in either light shade, or in a border with morning sun followed by plenty of afternoon shade.
Soil	Likes well-drained soil that has been enriched with organic matter.

GROWING METHOD

Propagation	Grows from seed sown in the spring or fall, or by divisions of a clump made in spring. Plant the new divisions approximately 10–12in apart. Do not let the young plants dry out— give regular, deep waterings through dry springs and summers.
Feeding	As growth begins in the spring, apply complete plant food and mulch around the plants with well-decayed manure or compost.
Problems	No specific pest or disease problems are known to attack this plant. Generally trouble-free. Note that growth begins late in spring, so avoid damaging new growth while weeding.

FLOWERING

Season	Flowers appear during early summer, depending on temperatures.
Cutting	Both the foliage and flowers can be cut for the vase.

AFTER FLOWERING

Requirements	Cut off any spent flower stems, unless you want to save seed. When the plants die down in the fall, cut off the foliage at ground level.

TIARELLA
Foam flower

THE FOAM FLOWER produces both a fine early summer bloom display, and often burnt-red-colored fall foliage.

GIVEN A FREE RUN, Tiarella polyphylla *produces a large, spreading clump with wonderful spires of white flowers.*

FEATURES

Tiarella trifoliata is a North American clump-forming rhizomatous perennial, making excellent groundcover in light shade. From late spring to mid-summer it produces light airy sprays of white flowers, on 12in-long panicles, held above the foliage. A more invasive plant is *T. cordifolia*, foam flower, from east North America, where it grows in mountainside woods, forming extensive colonies, remorselessly spreading by underground stolons. *T. wherryi*, also from North America, is more compact and less invasive—the better choice for a smaller, shady area. Its natural habitat is shady ravines and rocky woods. The white flowers are tinged pink. "Bronze Beauty" is a popular choice, benefiting from contrasting white flowers and bronze-red foliage.

CONDITIONS

Aspect	Thrives in both dappled and darkish shade, which is its natural habitat.
Site	It tolerates a wide range of soils, but naturally prefers rich, fertile ground, damp but definitely not boggy.

GROWING METHOD

Propagation	Division is the simplest method, although ripe seed can also be sown. Sow in pots in the fall in a cold frame, and keep young plants well watered. Do not let them dry out.
Feeding	The ground needs to be quite rich. Fork in leaf mold and compost in the early spring, and again in the fall, between plants.
Problems	Slugs can strike, but given the situation, out of the way in the shade, and the plant's vigor, it is rarely a major problem. Treat with slug pellets if matters get out of hand.

HARVESTING

Season	A profusion of white flowers appear from late spring to mid-summer.
Cutting	There are better choices for airy white sprays in the summer, but nonetheless they make good cut flowers.

AFTER FLOWERING

Requirements	Cut back to the ground.

TIARELLA AT A GLANCE

T. trifoliata is a North American white perennial, ideal for spreading quickly through shady sites. Hardy to 5°F (zone 7).

Jan	/	
Feb	/	
Mar	sow	**Recommended Varieties**
Apr	divide	*Tiarella cordifolia*
May	flowering	"Elizabeth Oliver"
Jun	flowering	*T. polyphylla*
July	flowering	*T. p.* pink
Aug	/	*T. wherryi*
Sept	sow	*T. w.* "Bronze Beauty"
Oct	/	
Nov	/	
Dec	/	

TRADESCANTIA
Tradescantia / spiderwort

SPIDERWORT FLOWERS *look like small purple irises but each lasts only a day. The surrounding buds are waiting their turn to open.*

DENSE PLANTINGS *of spiderwort produce plenty of flowers that thrive in filtered sunlight, ideal for a mixed or herbaceous border.*

FEATURES

This North American herbaceous perennial is a spreading plant with tapering, strap-like leaves and showy, triangular flowers in rich purple, rose-pink, or white. The flowers generally last only one day but they appear in succession over a long period. There are several named cultivars available. Spiderwort grows from 12 to 24in high, and is multi-stemmed. It is easy to grow in the correct conditions and can make a tall groundcover in filtered sunlight under trees. In a mild winter it may not die down completely.

TRADESCANTIA AT A GLANCE

T. virginiana is a purple, repeat-flowerer in a genus of largely tender indoor plants. Ideal for the border. Hardy to 5°F (zone 7).

		Recommended Varieties
Jan	/	
Feb	/	*Tradescantia* x *andersoniana* "Bilberry Ice"
Mar	divide	
Apr	/	*T.* x *a.* "Isis"
May	/	*T.* x *a.* "Osprey"
Jun	flowering	*T.* x *a.* "Purple Dome"
July	flowering	*T.* x *a.* "Red Cloud"
Aug	flowering	*T.* x *a.* "Zwanenburg Blue"
Sept	flowering	
Oct	divide	
Nov	divide	
Dec	/	

CONDITIONS

Aspect	It requires full sunlight or partial shade.
Site	It grows best in soil that is well drained, but is also heavily enriched with plenty of decayed, organic matter.

GROWING METHOD

Propagation	Clumps can be lifted and divided in the spring and fall. The species can be grown from seed sown in the fall. It is occasionally self-sown. New plantings should be approximately 12–18in apart, depending on how rapidly you need cover. Needs regular watering during a prolonged, dry growing period.
Feeding	Apply a complete plant food when growth starts in the spring.
Problems	No specific problems are known.

FLOWERING

Season	The long succession of flowers starts in early summer and continues through to mid-fall.
Cutting	The buds continue to open when cut.

AFTER FLOWERING

Requirements	Growth starts to yellow and die back after flowering. Clean away dead foliage, and tidy up for the winter.

TRILLIUM
Wake robin

THE WAKE ROBIN is the perfect plant for a moist shady area, whether it be light or deep shade. The plants are quickly identified by their three leaves, three calyces, and three petals.

FEATURES

Trilliums are deciduous perennials that make excellent groundcover in partial or full shade, with spring and early summer flowers. The color range includes white, maroon, pink, yellow, bronze-green, and red-purple. *T. grandiflorum*, the North American wake robin, has 3in-long white flowers and veined petals. It is long-lived and easy to grow, requiring little attention. *T. sessile* "Rubrum" has claret petals and attractively mottled foliage. Several clones bear this name and there is little to choose between them. At the front of a shady, slightly acidic border, try *T. rivale*. It grows 6in tall and wide, has pointed ovate petals, white or pale pink, with purple speckling toward the base. *T. luteum* has scented yellowish flowers and mottled, pale and dark leaves. It grows 16in tall, spreading by almost the same amount.

CONDITIONS

Aspect Mottled or deep shade is required. Avoid open areas with full sunlight.
Site The soil should be the acid side of neutral, although some trilliums will tolerate low levels of alkalinity.

GROWING METHOD

Propagation Preferably divide the rhizomes when dormant, ensuring each section has one strong growing point. Note that they are slow to establish. It is quite possible to sow ripe, late summer seed in a cold frame, but the 5–7 years to flower is prohibitively long.
Feeding The soil needs to be rich, with plenty of well-rotted leaf mold and compost, being damp and free-draining. Where necessary, provide a thick mulch every spring and fall.
Problems Both slugs and snails feed on the tender new foliage. Pick off by hand when this becomes a problem, or use a chemical treatment.

FLOWERING

Season The flowers appear in spring and summer.
Cutting They make attractive cut flowers, especially *T. grandiflorum*, with its near diamond-shaped white flowers.

AFTER FLOWERING

Requirements Cut spent stems to the ground.

TRILLIUM AT A GLANCE

A 30-species strong genus with rhizomatous perennials, excellent for flowering ground cover in shade. Hardy to 5°F (zone 7).

Month	Activity	Recommended Varieties
Jan	/	*Trillium cernuum*
Feb	/	*T. chloropetalum*
Mar	/	*T. cuneatum*
Apr	transplant	*T. erectum*
May	flowering	*T. grandiflorum*
Jun	flowering	*T. g. flore-pleno*
July	/	*T. luteum*
Aug	/	*T. rivale*
Sept	sow	*T. viride*
Oct	divide	
Nov	/	
Dec	/	

VERBASCUM
Mullein

MULLEINS ARE FAMED *for their striking shape and bright flowers, but as seen here they can blend with the gentlest design.*

MULLEINS HAVE *few equals as accent plants, since they are tough and adaptable, capable of tolerating many climates and conditions.*

FEATURES

Not all mulleins are reliably perennial—some are best treated as biennials and replaced after two years. However, most are easy to raise. They are grown for their large rosettes of foliage, often silver or gray, from which emerges a tall, striking spike of flowers up to 6ft high. They make eye-catching accent plants in any sunny part of the yard. The various species and their cultivars have flowers in a range of colors, including white and gentler shades of yellow, pink, and purple. The common mullein, *V. thapsus*, also known as Aaron's rod, freely self-seeds. Mullein has a long folk history, first as a candle, then as a medical treatment.

VERBASCUM AT A GLANCE

A 360-species genus, famed for its dramatic, colored spires in summer. Heights 12in–6ft. Hardy to 5°F (zone 7).

Jan	/	
Feb	/	**Recommended Varieties**
Mar	/	*Verbascum bombyciferum*
Apr	sow	*V. chaixii* "Album"
May	transplant	*V. c.* "Cotswold Beauty"
Jun	flowering	*V. c.* "Gainsborough"
July	flowering	*V. dumulosum*
Aug	flowering	"Golden Wings"
Sept	sow	"Helen Johnson"
Oct	/	"Letitia"
Nov	/	*V. phoeniceum*
Dec	/	

CONDITIONS

Aspect   Grows best in full sunlight all day.
Site   Grows in any kind of well-drained soil, even poor and alkaline ones.

GROWING METHOD

Propagation   Grows from seed sown as soon as it is ripe, or from root cuttings taken in late fall or winter. The seed forms on the spike after the flowers have fallen, and is ripe when it has changed color, becoming brown or black. Sow in pots in a cold frame in either the spring or fall. Plants of the larger mullein species need to be planted out approximately 39in apart.

Feeding   Apply a complete plant food in early spring, when new growth commences.

Problems   No specific problems are known.

FLOWERING

Season   Mullein produces flowers right through the summer, but its amazing spire of a stem remains a big architectural feature long after the flowers have finished.

Cutting   A nipped-off section of the flowering spire considerably adds to a formal, architectural display.

AFTER FLOWERING

Requirements   Cut off the spent flower spike, unless you want seed to set.

VIOLA ODORATA
English violet

DESPITE the range of cultivars available, the violet species is still a big favorite.

VIOLETS PROVIDE great groundcover under deciduous trees or in other shaded, sheltered spots. They do, however, need high levels of sunlight to put on a good flowering display.

FEATURES

Violets have been in cultivation since ancient times, and were highly valued by the ancient Greeks. In Victorian period an enormous number of varieties was grown, including a wide range of the double Parma violets. The violet's sweet fragrance and elegant flowers make them big favorites with gardeners and florists alike. The plants have a creeping habit, spreading up to 12in, and are rarely more than 6–8in tall. There are cultivars with single or double flowers in purple, pink, white, or bicolors, but the deep purple is probably the best loved. There are other violet species to grow in the garden, from the summer-flowering V. *cornuta*, fine under hybrid tea roses, to the spring/summer *V. sororia* and its form, "Freckles."

VIOLA AT A GLANCE

V. odorata is a rhizomatous, semi-evergreen perennial with blue or white flowers. A good self-seeder. Hardy to 0°F (zone

Month		Recommended Varieties
Jan	/	
Feb	/	*Viola cornuta*
Mar	flowering	*V. c.* Alba Group
Apr	flowering	*V. c.* Lilacina Group
May	flowering	*V. c.* "Minor"
Jun	/	*V. odorata* "Alba"
July	/	*V. o.* "Rosea"
Aug	/	*V. sororia* "Freckles"
Sept	divide	*V. s.* "Priceana"
Oct	/	
Nov	/	
Dec	/	

CONDITIONS

Aspect It needs either shade, or light dappled sunshine.

Site For the best results it needs well-drained, moisture-retentive soil, heavily enriched with organic matter.

GROWING METHOD

Propagation Clumps can be lifted and divided, or runners can be dug up and replanted every couple of years, in the spring or fall. Set out at 8in spacings, with the plant crowns kept just above soil level. Violets self-seed, too. Keep young plants well watered during the first growing season.

Feeding Apply complete plant food in spring after flowering ceases.

Problems Slugs and snails can be a major nuisance, devouring tasty new growth. Pick off by hand, or treat chemically.

FLOWERING

Season Violets flower from late winter into early spring.

Cutting Scalding the stems of cut violets before arranging them will certainly increase their vase life.

AFTER FLOWERING

Requirements No special treatment is needed, but excess runners can be removed during the growing season if they are invasive. This has the added benefit of channelling vigor back to the main crown.

GROWING ROSES

A favorite of many, roses, with their single, semi-double or fully double flowers, and their bicolored, multi-colored, striped or 'hand-painted' blooms, are often richly scented and

FEATURES

Plant roses to color beds, borders, patio pots, hanging baskets and rocky yards. Position them so that they form a canopy over pergolas, obelisks, arches, trees, walls and fences.

There are seven distinct groups of roses:

Large-flowered roses (hybrid tea):
These form shapely double blooms on long stems and are good for cutting. They are usually grown as bushes to 3ft high. Choice varieties are soft peachy-pink 'Scent-Sation', golden-yellow 'Lions International' and white 'Polar Star'.

Cluster-Flowered (floribunda)
Sumptuous heads adorn stems from 2-3ft. Plant tangerine-orange 'Razzle Dazzle', sparkling yellow 'Charter 700' and scarlet 'Invincible' to fringe a path or driveway.

English roses
They combine the scent and cupped- or rosette-shaped flower of an old-fashioned rose with the color range and repeat-flowering qualities of a cluster flowered variety. Forming plants from 3-6ft, newcomers include warm-pink 'Anne Boleyn', yellow and spray-flowered 'Blythe Spirit' and scarlet 'Falstaff'.

Miniature and patio
Small cluster-flowered roses that reach 15-24in - they flower all summer and spill from patio pots. Look out for peachy-apricot 'Sweet Dream' and vermilion 'Top Marks'.

Shrub roses
Some varieties treat us to a succession of flowers, others to a billowing surge of bloom in mid-summer. Outstanding varieties included repeat-flowering, creamy white 'Sally Holmes', and single pink and white 'Ballerina'.

Carpeters
Also known as ground-cover roses - they spread and suppress weeds - the famed County Series yields a spectacular display of flush upon flush of blossom. Riveting are single, scarlet and golden-centred 'Hampshire' and semi-double, bright yellow 'Gwent'.

LEFT: The shape of rose flowers vary considerably, from high and split-centered, globular, open cup-shaped and quatered to

Climbers and ramblers
Thrusting skywards to cloak walls, fences, arches, pergolas and trees with a welter of blossom, climbers, such as honey-colored 'Penny Lane', delight us with a succession of perfumed blooms.
Ramblers (including cream 'Bobbie James') usually flower once in a midsummer.

CONDITIONS

Aspect	Roses need bright sunlight to excel. Some, such as 'Canary Bird' and 'Flower Carpet' also flower magnificently in light shade.
Site	Though a few kinds thrive i light sandy or stony soils, most benefit from humus-rich loam. Drainage must be good.

GROWING METHOD

Planting	Garden-center bushes can be planted throughout the year, provided the soil is 'open'. Mail-order plants are delivered bare rooted and dispatched from November to March.
Feeding	Sprinkle a high-potash and magnesium rich granular fertilizer over the root area in April and prick it into the surface. Follow with a 3in mulch. Repeat feeding in June.
Dead heading	Nip off faded blooms at the 'knuckle' to channel energy into new flowering shoots.
Propagation	Take 9in cuttings of ramblers, climbers, miniatures and vigorous cluster-flowered varieties from the fully mature middle part of a pencil-thick side shoot in September. Remove all but two leaves at the top. Make a horizontal cut below the bottom bud and a sloping cut above the top bud. Nip off thorns. Insert cuttings 6in deep in a straight-backed trench lined with sharp sand. Firm soil around them. Roots will form within eight weeks.
Pruning	Prune with secateurs from March to early April. *Large Flowered and Cluster Flowered bushes and standards:* Shorten main stems by half their height, cutting to a bud. Reduce side shoots to two buds. to two buds. *Miniature and shrub roses:* Shorten dead and broken stems to live wood. *Climbers:* Cut back flowered shoots to within 3in of the main stem. *Ramblers:* Prune in September. Remove flowered shoots at ground level and replace with current-year stems.
Problems	Control black spot, mildew and rust disease, together with greenfly and other sap-sucking insects, by spraying with a pesticide containing pirimicarb, bupirimate and triforine. Wearing gloves, remove the suckers, which are more thorny, with paler green leaves than varietal shoots. Twist them from the stock.

SCEPTERED ISLE

GRAHAM THOMAS

Raised by David Austin Roses, 'Sceptred Isle' is an English Rose whose cupped and perfumed soft pink blooms grow freely above the foliage on stems to 3ft. Blooming continuously from early summer to mid-fall, it needs full sun to form a stocky bush. Dead-head regularly.
Create an arresting feature by inter-planting it with silver- and fern-leaved Artemisia 'Powis Castle'. Grown as a standard, it rewards you with a large head of blossom which makes a stunning focal point in a bed or border.

A glorious English Rose, 'Graham Thomas', (named after the famed rosarian and writer), sports unusually rich golden yellow flowers. This color is missing from old-fashioned roses from which the variety was born. Forming a rounded bush to 4ft high and across, its branches elegantly arch. Interestingly, it can also be trained as a climber to 6-8ft. If you plant it to cover a wall, set the root system at least 15in from the brickwork to avoid moisture being sucked from the root area. Fan-train shoots as low as possible to trigger an abundance of blossom.

SCEPTERED ISLE AT A GLANCE

Must have full sunlight in order to thrive and bloom freely.

JAN	rest		deadheading
FEB	rest	OCT	light pruning
MAR	planting, pruning	NOV	planting
		DEC	rest
APR	feeding		
MAY	mulching		OTHER ENGLISH ROSES:
JUN	flowering		'The Countryman'
JULY	flowering, deadheading		'Port Meirion'
AUG	flowering, deadheading		'Barbara Austin'
SEPT	flowering,		'Dr Herbert Gray'

GRAHAM THOMAS AT A GLANCE

Flowers best when grown in full sunlight. Fully hardy to frost hardy.

JAN	rest	SEPT	flowering, deadheading
FEB	rest		
MAR	planting, pruning	OCT	light pruning
APR	feeding	NOV	planting
MAY	mulching	DEC	rest
JUN	flowering, deadheading		
JULY	flowering, feeding		
AUG	flowering, deadheading		

FELICIA

FLOWER CARPET

A prized Hybrid Musk - the family bears large trusses of bloom in early summer and intermittently later - 'Felicia' is a joy. Yielding aromatically fragrant silver-pink blooms amid dark green leaves on sturdy shoots to 5ft long, it's very healthy and seldom suffers from pests and diseases. If there's room, encourage it to flower bounteously by pegging down shoots so they radiate from the center of the bush. Alternatively, set 'Felicia' to cover a trellis-clad sunny wall or fence.

Spreading enthusiastically to 4ft 'Flower Carpet', which grows to 2ft high, treats us to an almost non-stop parade of huge trusses of semi-double bright pink flowers from June to November. Unlike many varieties, it romps in light shade and flowers as well there as in full sun. Its shining, glossy leaves appear to be fully resistant to black spot, mildew and rust.

It is even more alluring when trained as a standard. It's such a profuse performer that flower-bowed branches are liable to snap, so support them with strings tied to a cane fastened to the main stem. It's cousins, 'White Flower Carpet' and 'Sunshine', a new yellow form, are equally healthy and spirited.

FELICIA MOON AT A GLANCE

Performs best when grown in full sunlight. Fully hardy to frost hardy.

JAN	rest	SEPT	flowering, deadheading
FEB	rest	OCT	light pruning
MAR	planting, pruning	NOV	planting
APR	feeding	DEC	rest
MAY	mulching		
JUN	flowering, deadheading		OTHER HYBRID MUSKS:
JULY	flowering, feeding		'Pax'
			'Penelope'
AUG	flowering, deadheading		'Camelia'
			'Francesca'

FLOWER CARPET AT A GLANCE

Flowers freely in full sunlight or light shade. Fully hardy to frost hardy.

JAN	rest	SEPT	flowering, deadheading
FEB	rest	OCT	light pruning
MAR	planting, light pruning	NOV	planting
APR	feeding	DEC	rest
MAY	mulching		
JUN	flowering, deadheading		OTHER FLOWER CARPET FORMS:
JULY	flowering, feeding		'White Flower Carpet'
AUG	flowering, deadheading		'Sunshine'

GROWING BULBS

Bulbs are the easiest of plants to grow—probably no other plant group gives as much variety and pleasure to the gardener with so little effort. Even people without gardens can enjoy bulbs as there are so many that make excellent container plants.

Most people think of bulbs as an essential part of spring, but spring is by no means their only season—there are bulbs that flower through the summer, fall, and even through the depths of the winter. They are usually very easy to look after, and many types will go on giving pleasure for years with minimal attention.

ABOVE: These parrot tulips just breaking from their buds already show the typical ruffled petals and color streaking.

LEFT: Deepest blue hyacinths make a wonderful foil for the bright yellow tulips in this landscape planting.

BULBS, CORMS, TUBERS, AND RHIZOMES

What most people know as bulbs covers a whole range of plants with some kind of underground storage organ that allows their survival over their dormant season, which may be winter or summer. They include true bulbs and plants with corms, tubers, and rhizomes.

• True bulbs are made up of a bud enclosed by modified leaves or fleshy scales from which roots and shoots emerge. The shoots grow out of the pointed top and the roots from the other end. Most, such as onions, daffodils, and hyacinths, have an outer papery cover or tunic; lilies, which are bulbs, too, have a bulb of swollen leaf bases but lack the protective tunic.

• Corms are bulb-like structures formed by the enlargement of an underground stem base. They do not have the "rings" of true bulbs, but stems grow out of the top and roots from the base in the same way. Freesias, gladioli, and crocuses all grow from corms.

• Tubers are swollen underground parts of roots or stems. Dahlias grow from buds at the ends of tubers.

• Rhizomes may grow underground or along the soil surface. They are fleshy, tuberous roots with new growth emerging from the end. Some irises grow from rhizomes (other irises are bulbs). Some bulbous plants described as having rhizomes or tubers appear to have little more than a small crown from which the roots emerge.

For convenience, all the above groups are discussed throughout this book as bulbs.

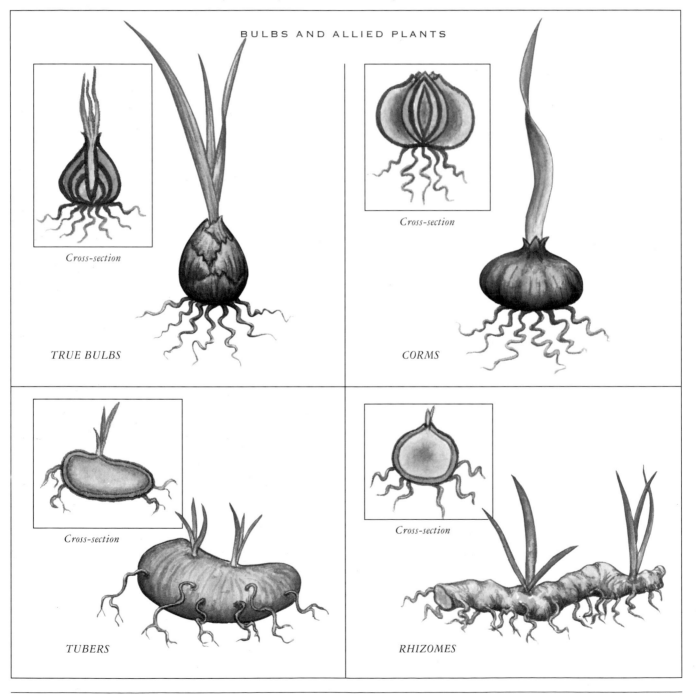

BULBS AND ALLIED PLANTS

Cross-section

TRUE BULBS

Cross-section

CORMS

Cross-section

TUBERS

Cross-section

RHIZOMES

TENDER BULBS

Indoors or out?

Some bulbs are not suitable for growing outdoors in a cold climate, and must be grown in a greenhouse or conservatory, or in the home, to produce good results. In many cases, bulbs can be started into growth under protection and brought outside later in the season when the weather has warmed up: when grown in containers, these look good on patios or even positioned among other flowering plants in borders so that the container is hidden. Other bulbs, however, need to be grown under protection throughout their lives, as their flowers would be spoiled outdoors.

Which bulbs must be considered tender enough for indoor cultivation often depends on the region in which you live, and the situation of your own yard. Species that can be grown successfully outside in the temperate parts of the country would often fail in cold, exposed northern gardens, but even in mild regions a yard may be exposed to chilly, windy weather that makes it unsuitable for the more tender plants.

Experience is often the only way to gain an accurate picture of which plants are hardy enough for your conditions, but when growing dubiously hardy bulbs, always play safe and overwinter one or two specimens under cover in case an unexpectedly cold winter destroys your outdoor stock. Protect slightly tender bulbs by heaping straw, dry leaves, or bracken over the planting site when the foliage has died down in fall: this helps to prevent frost penetrating to the bulbs below ground. Deep planting is also recommended for extra protection.

The table below gives a guide to the plants that need indoor conditions, and those that are risky outdoors in all but the most favored areas of the country. It is often adequate to bring tender bulbs under cover for the winter only: the information under each bulb entry gives further details.

TENDER BULBS

BULBS FOR THE HOUSE, GREENHOUSE, OR CONSERVATORY ONLY

- Clivia
- Gloriosa
- Hippeastrum
- Lachenalia
- Sinningia

BULBS NEEDING PROTECTION OR OVERWINTERING UNDER COVER IN COLD REGIONS

- Amaryllis
- Crinum
- Cyrtanthus
- Dierama
- Eremurus
- Eucomis
- Gladiolus callianthus
- Hedychium
- Hymenocallis
- Ixia
- Nerine
- Polianthes
- Schizostylis
- Sparaxis
- Sprekelia
- Zantedeschia
- Zephyranthes

THE TUBEROUS ROOTS of dahlias can be left in the ground in some areas, but are better lifted and stored in a frost-free place.

AGAPANTHUS PLANTS are suitable for leaving outdoors over winter in warmer areas of the country only.

STRONGLY CONTRASTING white and rich crimson tulips are mass-planted under a silver birch tree in this beautiful garden. The tulip planting is brilliantly set off by the wide, sweeping border of purple Virginian stock.

CHOOSING BULBS

What do you want from your plants?

There are so many bulbs, in such a range of colors, sizes, and forms, that it is all too easy to get carried away when buying them. Their appeal is instantaneous: here they are, ready-packaged, just needing to be popped into the soil—and within a short time, with no further effort, you can expect to be enjoying the brilliant flowers pictured on the display units at garden centers.

Perhaps one of their greatest virtues is that the bulk of bulbs appear for sale at just the time when summer is finally drawing to a close. The summer flowers are nearly over, trees will soon be shedding their leaves, and the days are growing shorter and more gloomy; the cold, wet, miserable weeks of fall stretch out ahead. No wonder we are so pleased to see the arrival of bulbs, with their promise of the spring to come!

But in order to achieve the best possible results from your bulbs, you should plan for them more carefully. Consider the type of garden in which they are to be grown; whether it is mild and sheltered or cold and exposed. Where in the garden are the bulbs to grow? Is there space on a rock garden or in a border? Do you have an area of lawn where bulbs could be naturalized, and if so, are you prepared for the grass to be

untidy while the bulb foliage is dying down? Do you want all your bulbs to flower in spring, or would a longer flowering season be more appropriate? Do you want bulbs in pots for growing on the patio, or varieties that will flower out of season to brighten up the home in the middle of winter? If you have a good idea of what you want from your bulbs *before* you go out to buy them, it could save you making some expensive mistakes.

Choose for color

Consider the color schemes of your bulb planting as you would any other item, either inside your home or outside it. Do you want strong contrasts in color, gradations of a single color, or colors that complement each other? Do you want to create a bright, warm, active look or do you want to give a cooler, calmer impression? Warm, active colors are red, yellow, orange, and bright pink, while blue, lavender, white, cream, pale pink, and pale yellow are cooler colors.

Blue and white spring-flowering bulbs include spring star flower, grape hyacinth, bluebell, and hyacinth, all of which would team well with white or cream daffodils. Some of the brightest bulbs in the "hot" color range are ranunculus and harlequin flowers (sparaxis). Both these are more commonly available in mixed colors but sometimes you can find a supplier who is able to sell them as single colors. Anemones also come in strong colors and these too can be purchased in single colors. Greater impact is generally achieved by planting blocks of single colors rather than mixtures. Try bulbs in blocks of red, orange, and yellow for a tremendous impact, or if you want a quieter look, plant groups of two shades of pink and white.

Many bulbous plants, such as daffodils, come in a wide range of varieties but a quite limited color range: they also look their best if planted in groups of one variety. Corn lily is another good example. Although there is a wide color range available and corn lilies can be purchased in mixtures, these flowers look best if planted in blocks of one color. They can, of course, be planted as mixtures, especially in an informal garden setting, but in nature they would be more likely to grow in blocks of one color.

Consider flowering time

Some gardeners prefer one huge display over three or four weeks in spring while others may find more interest in spreading the season over several months of the year. For instance, with crocus alone, different varieties provide blooms from late fall right through to mid-spring. There is some form of bulbous plant to give a display in every month of the year if that is what you require.

It can be difficult to give precise information on exactly when different species will be in bloom, as the time can vary from one district to another and even from one yard to another because of variation in microclimates. However, if you spend some time noting the times when bulbs flower in your garden, in future seasons you will be able to plan to have a succession of bulbs in flower during many months of the year.

BUYING BULBS

There are several different ways in which you can buy bulbs. Most garden centers, and several other stores, sell bulbs in perforated plastic bags backed by a card giving planting details, along with a picture of the bulb in flower. Bulbs are also available in small netting sacks with attached pictures and growing instructions. Most garden centers and nurseries sell bulbs in bulk in the main planting season, and you can make your own selection from large bins. Another option is to send away for catalogs from bulb-growing nurseries and order bulbs by mail—these growers advertise in popular gardening magazines. The range of bulbs available from specialist nurseries is generally very much more extensive than what is on offer at your local garden center. Mail order is a good option if you want some of the more unusual varieties, and if you want to order a lot of bulbs as it can be a good deal cheaper, though you need to take postal charges into account. When planning to buy by mail order, remember that you need to order well in advance of the planting date; if you leave it until bulbs are starting to appear in the shops, the specialist suppliers are likely to have sold out of many of the less common varieties. When you are on the mailing list of mail order suppliers, they will send you their catalogs in plenty of time in future years.

When buying bulbs at a garden center, try to buy them as soon as possible after they have been delivered, as they tend to deteriorate in the warm conditions, and will soon become bruised as other buyers sort through them to make their choice. Select plump, firm, well-rounded bulbs and make sure there are no soft spots or patches of mold. Especially avoid

HYACINTH BULBS will be on sale from early fall. Select yours early to be sure of getting the best available.

GOLDEN DAFFODILS planted in sweeping drifts beneath a fine magnolia tree show to advantage against an old stone wall.

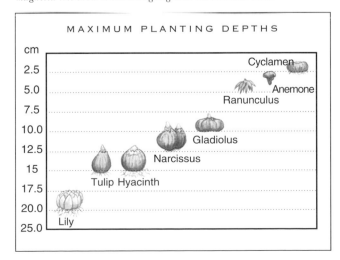

MAXIMUM PLANTING DEPTHS

cm	
2.5	Cyclamen
5.0	Anemone
	Ranunculus
7.5	
10.0	Gladiolus
12.5	Narcissus
15	
17.5	Tulip Hyacinth
20.0	
25.0	Lily

GROUPS OF BRIGHT PINK, fall-flowering nerines provide showy splashes of color as summer flowers fade.

BLUEBELLS, TULIPS, and daffodils are here planted informally in a woodland setting beside a tiny stream.

buying any bulbs that are starting to shoot and showing signs of growth. Unless there is just the tiniest shoot appearing and you know you can plant the bulbs at once, these bulbs will be a bad buy as they will not thrive. Some chain stores and supermarkets sell bulbs and continue to display them long after they should have been planted out or discarded. If you see long pale shoots emerging from bulbs definitely don't buy them. These bulbs have been stored for too long in poor conditions. They are badly stressed and have used up a great deal of their stored reserves of energy and growing capacity so that they may fail completely or do very poorly. Try to make your selection early in the season so that you have a choice of the best on offer.

Bulbs are best planted as soon as possible when you get them home, but if you are forced to delay planting for a short while, store the bulbs in paper bags or nets—not plastic bags—and keep them in a cool, dry, airy place. If the weather is very warm, the crisper drawer of a refrigerator can be a good place to keep bulbs in good condition, but do not put them in the main part of the refrigerator as this will dry them out.

PLANTING BULBS

Choosing a site

For the majority of bulbs, choose an open planting site where they will receive sun for at least half a day. There are a few bulbs that will grow well in shade but most like at least some sun. Even woodland species such as bluebell and wood anemone grow as understorey plants in deciduous woodlands and so receive some sun during their early growing and flowering period, before the trees are fully in leaf.

The vast majority of bulbs need well-drained soil or they will rot. If there is any doubt about the drainage, plant bulbs in raised beds or mix sharp sand or grit with the soil in the planting area. Bulbs like a quite rich, fertile soil. At least a month before planting, incorporate a generous amount of well-rotted manure or garden compost into the planting area.

Positioning the bulbs

Your bulbs will look more natural if you plant them in clumps or groups, not in straight lines. The depth depends on the size of the bulb but it is usually two or three times its diameter (see diagram on page 9). Details of planting depths are given in the individual entries for each bulb, and refer to the depth of soil above the tip of the bulb. Spacing between bulbs is also dependent on size. Larger bulbs are usually set out about 3in apart and smaller ones 1–2in apart, but they can be crowded together for effect.

Be sure to plant the bulbs the right way up. Usually the pointed part points upward, but there are exceptions to this rule: ranunculus and anemone have the claws or points facing down into the soil and some lilies and crown imperials are sometimes planted on their sides to avoid moisture collecting between the scales, which can lead to rotting.

In dry conditions, bulbs may need to be watered in after planting, but it is usually not necessary to water again at least until leaf shoots have appeared.

Planting under trees

Mass-planting of bulbs that flower through winter and early spring under deciduous trees can turn what may otherwise be a somewhat dull area of the garden into a beautiful feature. Although it is sometimes difficult to dig and plant in these areas as the soil is hard and full of matted roots, the result can be well worth the effort. The leaves that fall from the trees in

MAJESTIC WHITE LILIES grown in a large ceramic container make a stunning decoration for a patio.

fall break down into leafmold which provides ideal growing conditions for the bulbs.

INCREASING YOUR STOCK OF BULBS

Left to themselves, many bulbs will multiply of their own accord, but there are a number of ways in which you can help the process along.

Separation
Many bulbs produce offsets or bulblets that can be gently broken away from the mother bulb when the bulbs are lifted, and planted separately. Most first-year bulblets will reach flowering size in two or three years if they are planted

PROPAGATING DAHLIAS

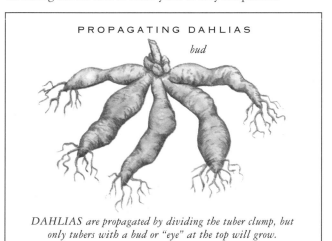

DAHLIAS are propagated by dividing the tuber clump, but only tubers with a bud or "eye" at the top will grow.

THREE WAYS TO PROPAGATE LILIES

1. DETACHING SCALES

THE LILY BULB consists of lots of scales. Remove the outer scales.

PUSH the individual scales, right way up, into a box of moist peat.

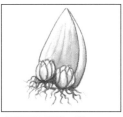

BULBLETS will appear at the base of each scale.

POT UP the scales when the new bulblets appear.

2. DETACHING AERIAL BULBILS

BULBILS grow in the leaf axis of some species. Collect them and pot them up.

3. DETACHING BULBLETS

OFFSETS on the base of some lilies can be detached and planted out.

LIFTING BULBS

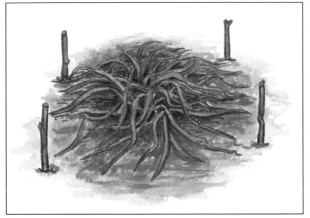

1. PUT A FEW STAKES around the edge of the clump so that you know where to dig when the leaves have died down.

2. AFTER THE LEAVES have died down, use a spade to outline the area of the clump.

3. LIFT THE CLUMP UP with a fork and shake off as much soil as possible.

4. SEPARATE THE BULBS from the clump, clean them, and then store them in a dry, airy place, or replant them.

separately, but some are slower to flower. When separating clumps of dahlia tubers, make sure each tuber has an "eye" attached or it will not sprout and flower.

Scoring and scooping
Cut a V-shape into the base plate of a mature bulb at planting time, taking care not to damage the growth bud of the bulb. This should result in many small offsets being produced by the end of the growing season. Or score through the basal plate of the bulb at right angles with a sharp knife to produce the same result. Depending on species these small offsets should produce bulbs of flowering size in two to four years.

With a sharp-sided teaspoon or curved knife, you can scoop out the entire basal plate and bulblets will form around the rim of the scooped out area. Wear gloves if you are treating hyacinths as the sap can sometimes irritate the skin.

Lilies
These techniques are not suitable for lilies, which are propagated by other methods.
• A mature lily bulb is composed of numerous individual

scales. The individual scales can be carefully removed and planted upright in a coarse, free-draining mixture such as three parts coarse washed sand and one part peatmoss or peat substitute. The scales should produce bulblets at their bases.

• Some lilies produce aerial bulbils in the axis of the leaf and these can be collected as they are about to fall. Potted into pots or trays they should produce leaves by the following spring and reach flowering size in two or three years.
• Other lilies produce bulblets just below the soil surface, around the base of the stem. If these are carefully dug out from among the roots they can be potted up and will form flowering plants in two or three years.

CARING FOR GROWING BULBS

After planting, bulbs need little maintenance. When the plants are actively growing, the soil should be kept moist, but never soggy. Bulbs do not usually need feeding before they flower. They are fed after blooming, when they are storing food for the following season's growth. Special instructions for feeding and watering are included in the entries for individual plants where appropriate.

AFTER FLOWERING

• After flowers have finished, cut off the spent flower stems but do not cut back the foliage. If you cut off the leaves before they have died down naturally, the bulb will not have the reserves to grow and flower the following season.

• After flowering, feed the plants with a liquid or granular balanced fertiliser and continue to water in dry conditions until the leaves begin to die off naturally. This may take about two or three months.

• If bulbs have been planted in clumps, you may be able to plant annuals between the clumps, using either seed or seedlings. Quick growers such as Virginian stock will provide a pretty distraction from the dying bulb foliage. You could also put in summer-flowering annuals or perennials that will be ready to take over the display when the bulbs have truly died down. Or you can, of course, purchase some "potted color"—annuals that are already in bloom.

• Bulbs do not usually need to be lifted every season. Most are left in the ground and lifted only every two or three years, or in a number of cases only every four or five years. Many bulbs

TALL WHITE RANUNCULUS dominate this white border, formed of plants with contrasting shapes, textures, and sizes.

A CARPET OF COLOR has been created in this garden bed by combining white tulips with violas and anemones in a range of colors. To achieve such a pleasing effect, careful planning before planting is necessary.

THE COMPLETE BOOK OF GARDEN FLOWERS 215

TALL BEARDED IRIS make an elegant border for this attractive garden path. Irises come in a rich array of colors.

ZEPHYR LILY, with its starry white flowers and deep green glossy foliage, makes an ideal edging plant. Here it grows with portulacas.

flower well when they are crowded and then it is only necessary to lift and divide clumps when the flower numbers or quality drop off.

• Take care when you lift bulbs that you do not cut or damage them—it is easy to slice into them with a spade or spear them with a fork. Discard damaged, soft, or rotted bulbs immediately. Place the sound bulbs to dry in a cool, airy spot, brush off excess soil, and then store them in nets, old stockings, or in single layers in cardboard boxes. Ideally, bulbs should be stored so that they do not touch each other: they can be kept separate with shredded paper or something similar.

• Because lilies have no protective outer sheath on their bulbs, they must be lifted, the clumps divided if necessary, and the bulbs replanted at once. They can be stored for short periods in damp sphagnum moss but take care that they don't dry out.

• Some bulbous plants, such as freesias, produce quite a lot of seed if the spent flower stems are not cut off. You can collect these seeds when they are ripe or allow them to self-sow. Seedlings may take two to five years to reach flowering size, depending on the type of bulb, and they will probably not be true to type. The results can, however, be interesting as you never know quite what to expect. Particularly good seedlings should be marked at flowering time so that the bulbs can be propagated at the end of the season.

MAKING THE MOST OF BULBS IN THE GARDEN

You may wish to plant groups of bulbs under deciduous trees or in other permanent places in the garden but there are many other options. Bulbs mix well with many herbaceous perennials as the new growth of the perennials tends to camouflage the not-so-attractive foliage of the bulbs as it yellows and dies off. Bulbs in this situation can usually be left in the ground for several years before they need to be lifted and divided.

Many bulbs can be treated like annuals for a seasonal display, then lifted and stored for use the following season. This, of course, creates more work but the results can be well worth the effort, allowing you to create different displays each year. You can have a delightful show of bulbs on their own but consider the possibility of planting bulbs and spring bedding plants together for a really stunning spring display. As well as forming an attractive association, the bedding plants help to mask the dying foliage of the bulbs, which must be left to die down naturally if the bulbs are to flower well next season. Fall-sown hardy annuals will also serve the same purpose. Plant your bulbs and bedding plants at the same time, placing a bulb between each of the plants. For best effect, planting should be quite dense. You can experiment with color combinations or opt for tried and tested associations such as yellow lily-flowered tulips and blue forget-me-nots.

• An early-flowering bedding plant such as white primula could be interplanted with cream or yellow narcissi, or deep blue anemones for a vivid contrast.

• White, yellow-centered primulas would team well with blue *Anemone blanda* and the dwarf narcissus "Tête-à-Tête."

• Other spring-flowering plants to combine with bulbs include polyanthus, wallflowers, and forget-me-nots.

Dwarf bulbs are ideal for growing on a rockery, usually

IF YOU WANT show-quality tuberous begonias, grow them under cover. Here they grow in a conservatory, where they can also be placed on raised benches so the flowers are more easily admired.

providing color and interest before the other alpine plants come into their own. Suitable bulbs include alliums, chionodoxa, crocus, cyclamen, iris, muscari, narcissus, oxalis and rhodohypoxis, among others.

NATURALIZING BULBS IN GRASS

Bulbs naturalized in grass make a very attractive feature in gardens. However, you need to remember that the bulb foliage must be allowed to die down naturally if the bulbs are to perform well in future years, and that means that the grass cannot be mown for several weeks after the bulbs have finished flowering. This can look rather untidy, so a position for naturalized bulbs needs to be chosen with some care. Popular sites are the perimeters of lawns or under deciduous trees. In a small garden with a limited area of lawn used for many purposes, naturalizing in turf may not be a practical idea.

Choose bulbs that will flower at an appropriate period; early spring is convenient because the grass can then be mown from late spring onward. Some summer-flowering bulbs are good in a wildflower meadow, and fall-flowering bulbs such as colchicum also grow well in grass. You can either lift a square of turf, plant a group of bulbs and replace the cut turf, or you can plant larger bulbs individually, using a trowel or bulb-planting tool to cut a hole in the turf. Place the bulb in the bottom of the hole and replace the plug of soil and turf. Give a good watering after planting, both to settle the bulbs and to help the turf re-establish.

After the bulbs have bloomed, give the plants an

MINIATURE PINK NERINES and other small bulbous plants grow between paving stones where they benefit from the sharp drainage.

application of balanced fertiliser and water the area regularly if conditions are dry. When the bulb foliage has yellowed and died off mowing can be resumed—this usually takes some six weeks after flowering.

GROWING BULBS IN CONTAINERS

Many bulbs make beautiful container plants. Pots full of bulbs are ideal for balcony gardens and patios, and for instant color, pots of bulbs in bud or in flower can be plunged into garden beds throughout the growing season.

Use a good quality potting compost, and make sure the base of the container is crocked for good drainage. Plant the bulbs at the same depth as you would in the soil, crowding them into the container for a good flowering display. Keep the compost moist at all times; regular watering will be needed.

Growing bulbs indoors

"Prepared" bulbs are specially treated to flower early—often in time for Christmas. Plant them in a shallow pot or bowl of moist potting compost and put them in a cold place such as a garden shed, keeping them dark by placing them in a black plastic bag. Leave them for 8–12 weeks; when shoots begin to appear, move them into a bright, cool room. When flower buds

A POT OF JACOBEAN LILIES can be brought to the fore when they flower.

POTTING NARCISSI FOR INDOOR USE

1. CHOOSE A POT at least twice as tall as the bulbs.

2. HALF FILL the pot with a good soiless potting compost.

3. POSITION THE BULBS with their tops level with the top of the pot and a small gap between each and around the edge of the pot.

4. COVER THE BULBS with the compost and gently firm it down. Water, drain, and place in a cold (40°F) position in total darkness. A cold, dark period of 8–12 weeks is necessary.

5. WHEN SHOOTS appear, move the pot into a bright, cool position at about 50°F.

6. WHEN BUDS appear, move the pot into its flowering position, still in bright light.

WHAT CAN GO WRONG?

There are relatively few pest and disease problems that regularly beset the home gardener growing bulbs. Bulbs that fail to come up at all have usually been planted too deep or have rotted through disease or waterlogging, especially in clay-based soils. Yellowing foliage early in the growing season may also be caused by waterlogging. More serious pests of bulbs are often associated with storage conditions and it is wise to examine bulbs for damage, decay, or insect pests such as aphids before planting. Diseases specific to certain bulbs are mentioned in the text under individual entries.

Failure to flower

This may be due to a number of reasons, including:
• natural offsets are not sufficiently mature to flower.
• foliage has been cut off prematurely the previous season.
• insufficient sunlight or lack of water while the foliage is still green.
• congestion of bulbs.
• "blindness"—a condition that occurs especially with daffodils and tulips. The flower bud forms but gives up trying to continue on to bloom. It may be due to incorrect storage temperature, lack of chilling, or fluctuating temperatures as the flower bud emerges from the bulb.

Leaf scorch

• This fungal disease affects bulbs of daffodils and narcissi, and others including hippeastrum, crinum, and belladonna lilies. It is worse in wet seasons, and occurs at the top of the bulb scales so that emerging leaves are infected. The leaf tips are reddish and scorched, and later on brown spots appear further down the leaf. Eventually the tissue around these damaged areas goes yellow. Remove and destroy the worst affected leaves and spray with a suitable fungicide if symptoms persist.

Bulb rots

• These may be caused by a number of bacteria or fungi, and lead to rotting and decay of the bulbs either in store or in the ground. They are made worse by poor drainage and overwet soil conditions. Damaged bulbs are particularly prone to infection, so take care when handling or lifting bulbs, and discard damaged ones.

Gray mold (botrytis species)

• Gray mold attacks an enormous range of plants. It may manifest itself initially by spotting on leaves or stems, followed by breakdown of the tissue and the typical furry gray growth. Poor air circulation, overcrowding, overwatering, and cool, humid weather conditions are favorable to its spread. Improve growing conditions and spray if necessary with a suitable fungicide.

Bulb flies

• Bulb flies lay their eggs in the soil near the bulb neck; the maggots tunnel into the bulb to feed. Affected plants produce sparse, yellow foliage and fail to flower. If you are not lifting the bulbs in fall, pull soil up around their necks to fill the holes left by the leaves dying down.

Thrips

• Gladioli are very susceptible to attack by thrips, or thunderflies. These tiny winged insects cause silver streaking and flecking of both foliage and flowers; in a bad attack, the display can be ruined. The pest is worse in hot, dry conditions. Affected plants can be sprayed with a contact insecticide. Thrips overwinter on the corms, so after an attack, dust the corms with HCH dust after lifting and again before planting out in spring.

Lily beetle

• These small, scarlet beetles can be a serious pest of lilies and other plants such as fritillaries. Both larvae and adults feed on the leaves and stems of plants, often causing considerable damage. They are quite conspicuous and should be picked off by hand and destroyed whenever they are noticed; bad infestations can be sprayed with a contact insecticide. Beetles overwinter on weeds and plant debris, so clean up around the planting area in fall.

Aphids

• These may attack a range of bulbous plants and should be sprayed or hosed off as they can carry virus diseases. A bad infestation disfigures flowers and foliage.

MULTI-COLORED RANUNCULUS and anemone are crowded together to produce this bright springtime scene.

begin to show color, move the bulbs to their flowering position in the home.

The bunch-flowered narcissus "Paperwhite" is unusual in that it doesn't need a cold, dark period after planting; bulbs can be left on a cool, light windowsill directly after planting and flowers will appear in about six weeks. Plant mid-November for Christmas blooms.

Usually, non-prepared bulbs will flower at their normal period. They should be planted and left out in a sheltered position in the garden in their containers until flower buds are showing, when they can be brought into the house.

After flowering

If after flowering the whole plant and bulb are planted out into the garden, there is some chance of the bulb flowering the following year. Bulbs that stay in their pots until they have died down will in most cases not reflower the following year. When the foliage on these bulbs has died down, lift the bulbs, store them, and replant them in the garden at the right time the following season. They may not flower that year but should do so the next. They are not suitable for growing as indoor-flowering plants again.

FRAGRANT FREESIAS come in a glorious range of colors to epitomise the joy of the spring garden.

BULBS AS CUT FLOWERS

THIS RUSTIC BASKET of choice hyacinth blooms could not fail to lift the spirits, appearing as they do just when winter draws to a close.

TULIPS MAKE ideal cut flowers and several colorful bunches are here shown to perfection against the terracotta of the containers.

ALLIUM
Ornamental onion

LARGE ROUNDED HEADS are typical of alliums and the starburst effect of this one looks stunning in the yard.

THE PURPLE-PINK FLOWERS of Allium oreophilum (*also known as* A. ostrowskianum) *brighten up the early summer garden.*

FEATURES

There are a large number of *Allium* species, including edible onions, garlic, and chives as well as many ornamental plants. Typically, they produce rounded heads of flowers, often in rosy purple shades, but there are also yellow- and white-flowered species. Some are small-growing and suitable for the rock garden, while others make excellent plants for the middle or back of borders. *A. giganteum* produces its eye-catching heads of mauve-pink, starry flowers on stems 3ft or more high, while *A. moly* grows to only 8in and has loose clusters of golden yellow blooms. Many alliums make excellent cut flowers. They are usually long lasting in water, and the dried inflorescence that remains after the blooms have fallen can be used successfully in dried arrangements, too.

ALLIUM AT A GLANCE

Versatile and varied bulbs with usually rounded heads of starry flowers in spring and early summer.

Jan	/	Recommended species
Feb	/	
Mar	/	*Allium albopilosum*
Apr	flowering	*A. beesianum*
May	flowering	*A. caeruleum*
Jun	flowering	*A. giganteum*
July	flowering	*A. karataviense*
Aug	/	*A. moly* "Jeannine"
Sept	plant	*A. neopolitanum*
Oct	plant	*A. oreophilum*
Nov	/	*A. schubertii*
Dec	/	*A. siculum*

CONDITIONS

Aspect
Site
Best in full sun but will tolerate light shade. Alliums in borders should be positioned where other plants will help to hide their often untidy foliage. Smaller species are suitable for rock gardens. The soil must be well-drained and should contain plenty of well-decayed manure or compost. Add a dressing of lime to acid soils before planting.

GROWING METHOD

Planting
Plant in fall. Planting depth varies according to the size of the bulb: cover bulbs with soil to three times their height.

Feeding
Apply a high potash liquid fertiliser as buds form. Water during dry spells, but never allow the soil to become sodden. After flowering, stop watering altogether.

Problems
Plants may suffer from the fungal disease rust, causing orange pustules on the foliage: destroy affected specimens. Feeding with high potash fertiliser may increase resistance to attacks.

FLOWERING

Season
Flowers in late spring and summer.

Cutting
Cut alliums when about half the flowers are fully open.

AFTER FLOWERING

Requirements Foliage starts to die down before blooming is complete. Cut off the spent flower stems if required. Overcrowded clumps can be divided in fall, replanting immediately.

ALSTROEMERIA
Peruvian lily

THE FLOWERS of alstroemeria are very delicately marked when viewed close-up, and have an almost orchid-like appearance.

SUMMER BORDERS are brightened by these colorful, long-lasting flowers that are also excellent for cutting for the home.

FEATURES

These exotic-looking plants are prolific flowerers and can be spectacular in borders. The open-faced flowers are carried in clusters at the top of 3ft stems; the sword-like foliage is dark green. The plants may take a year to become established and produce flowers, but when they have settled in, flowering is profuse. Container-grown plants become established more quickly. The color range includes yellow, cream, orange, red, salmon, and pink. The Princess series contains dwarf varieties that represent a major breeding breakthrough. Alstroemerias are from South America and are not always reliably hardy; Ligtu hybrids are among the hardiest types.

ALSTROEMERIA AT A GLANCE

When established, these plants produce a profusion of colorful, attractively marked summer flowers on tall stems.

Jan	/	Recommended Varieties
Feb	/	
Mar	plant	Ligtu hybrids
Apr	plant	Princess series
May	/	
Jun	flowering	
July	flowering	
Aug	flowering	
Sept	/	
Oct	/	
Nov	/	
Dec	/	

CONDITIONS

Aspect   Full sun or partial shade.

Site   Alstroemerias do well in a sheltered border and are very effective mixed with herbaceous perennials. They require free-draining soil.

GROWING METHOD

Planting   Plant the fleshy tubers 6in deep in spring, as soon as you obtain them. Handle them carefully, as they are usually brittle and break easily. Do not let them dry out before planting. You can also obtain alstroemerias as container-grown plants in summer.

Feeding   Add a balanced granular fertiliser to the soil before planting. Water plants in very dry conditions, but never allow the soil to become waterlogged.

Problems   Plants may fail to flower in their first season after planting. When established, however, they can be very invasive, and should be planted where their spread can be kept in check. Slugs find them attractive, and should be controlled with slug pellets where necessary.

FLOWERING

Season   Flowers in midsummer.

Cutting   Alstroemerias last very well in water, and should be cut as the buds start to open.

AFTER FLOWERING

Requirements Remove dead heads. When the foliage has died down, protect the crowns with a mulch of dry straw or leaves through the winter. Crowded clumps can be split in spring.

AMARYLLIS BELLADONNA
Belladonna lily

THESE TALL FLOWER STEMS appear before the leaves, which is why belladonna lilies are also known as "naked ladies."

BRIGHT PINK BELLADONNA LILIES brighten the late summer and fall garden. The foliage here is from a clump of daylilies.

FEATURES

This beautiful South African bulb produces its multiple and sweetly perfumed blooms on sturdy purple-green stems 24in or more high. The funnel-shaped flowers may be various shades of pink or white and the flowering stem appears before the leaves, giving the plant its alternative common name of naked lady. This bulb is a great asset in the garden as the flowering period is fall, while the glossy strap-like leaves look good throughout winter and early spring. It makes an excellent cut flower. Best flowering comes from clumps that are left undisturbed for several years.

AMARYLLIS AT A GLANCE

A tall plant producing its stems of fragrant, funnel-shaped flow-ers in fall. Needs a warm, sheltered, sunny position.

		Recommended Varieties
Jan	/	
Feb	/	"Johannesburg"
Mar	/	"Kimberley"
Apr	/	"Major"
May	/	
Jun	plant 🖐	
July	plant 🖐	
Aug	/	
Sept	flowering 🌺	
Oct	flowering 🌺	
Nov	/	
Dec	/	

CONDITIONS

Aspect Prefers a warm, sheltered spot in full sun—the bulbs need a good summer baking to produce the best flowers.

Site A good plant for a flower bed under a south-facing wall. *Amaryllis belladonna* can also be grown in containers, planting the large bulbs singly in 8in pots. Well-drained soil is required: poor soil is tolerated but best results are achieved by digging in decayed organic matter a month or more before planting.

GROWING METHOD

Planting Plant bulbs with their necks just at ground level and 8–12in apart in early to mid-summer.

Feeding Apply a balanced fertiliser after flowering, as the leaves appear. Water in dry periods while the plant is in growth.

Problems It is rarely troubled by any problems.

FLOWERING

Season Flowers in very late summer and fall.

Cutting A good cut flower for large arrangements.

AFTER FLOWERING

Requirements Remove spent flower stems. Protect the crowns with a mulch of peat over winter. Leave bulbs undisturbed for several years. If lifting and dividing, do so in early summer.

ANEMONE
Windflower

THE DARK CENTERS, deep blue or black, of Anemone coronaria *make a stunning contrast to the rich colors of the petals.*

THIS MIXED PLANTING of Anemone coronaria *shows some of the range of color and form available from this lovely plant.*

FEATURES

Anemones, also known as windflowers, form a large and versatile group of plants, the most commonly grown species being *A. coronaria*, *A. blanda* and *A. nemorosa*. *Anemone coronaria* grows from a hard little tuber, *A. blanda* from hard tuberous roots, and *A. nemorosa* from very brittle, creeping rhizomes. The flowers are often very colorful, and can be daisy-like with lots of petals, or cup-shaped, rather like poppies. Anemones flower in spring; *A. coronaria* will also flower in summer, depending on the planting time. They are excellent for cutting.

ANEMONE AT A GLANCE

Low-growing, hardy plants which form a colorful carpet of spring or summer flowers.

		Recommended Varieties
Jan	/	
Feb	flowering 🌿	*Anemone blanda:*
Mar	flower 🌿/plant 👐 *	"Atrocaerulea"
Apr	flower 🌿/plant 👐 *	"White Splendor"
May	/	"Radar"
Jun	flowering 🌿	*Anemone coronaria:*
July	flowering 🌿	"Mona Lisa"
Aug	flowering 🌿	"Mister Fokker"
Sept	plant 👐 **	*Anemone nemorosa:*
Oct	plant 👐 **	"Alba Plena"
Nov	/	"Purity"
Dec	/	"Robinsoniana"
		"Vestal"

* summer flowering   **spring flowering

TYPES

A. coronaria Reaching 6–8in high, *A. coronaria* is available in a lovely range of clear colors including red, white, blue, violet, cerise, and pink, all with a black to deep navy blue center. The most popular strains are "de Caen," with single poppy-like flowers, and "St Brigid," with semi-double to double flowers. There are many named cultivars in both these strains. They can be planted in single blocks of color or mixed at random, and they can be grown in containers as well as making an excellent garden display.

A. blanda This native of Greece and Turkey bears daisy-like flowers, usually in shades of blue, although white and pink forms are available. One of spring's early bloomers, its flowers are carried on stems some 6–10in high above ferny, divided leaves. A variety of cultivars is available now and some of these are grown as potted plants. This species seeds readily and can be naturalized under trees.

A. nemorosa The wood anemone, *A. nemorosa*, likes a cool, moist climate and is often grown massed under deciduous trees, imitating its natural habitat. Here, its starry, white (sometimes lavender blue), single flowers, with their central boss of golden stamens, make a glorious showing in late spring and into early summer. The wood anemone's mid-green foliage is deeply cut. Growth may be from 4–8in high. This species increases rapidly where it finds the growing conditions suitable, and plants will eventually increase to carpet the ground.

THE BRIGHT, DAISY-LIKE flowers of Anemone blanda *brighten up the garden in late winter or very early spring.*

*WOODLAND ANEMONE (*Anemone nemorosa*) makes a pretty groundcover in a cool, moist climate, where it naturalizes readily.*

CONDITIONS

Aspect
All anemones prefer some protection from strong wind. *A. coronaria* is best in full sun, while *A. nemorosa* prefers to be grown in dappled sunlight or with morning sun and afternoon shade. *A. blanda* comes from exposed sites in mountainous districts and so will tolerate full sun or part shade.

Site
A. blanda and *A. nemorosa* grow well under deciduous trees, or on a rock garden, while *A. coronaria* provides bright color toward the front of beds and borders. Soil must be well drained or tubers and roots will rot. All anemone species prefer a soil rich in organic matter although *A. blanda* is happy to grow in quite poor soils as long as drainage is good. Plenty of well-decayed compost or manure should be dug into the ground about a month before planting the bulbs.

GROWING METHOD

Planting
Plant tubers of *A. coronaria* 2in deep and 4–6in apart in September and October for spring flowers, or in March and April to bloom in summer. *A. blanda* and *A. nemorosa* should be planted 2–3in deep and 4in apart in early fall. Take care not to damage brittle roots; soaking the tubers or rhizomes overnight before planting will help them to get established quickly. After planting, mulch soil with bark chips or leafmold.

Feeding
A balanced fertiliser can be applied after flowering, but feeding is not usually necessary in reasonably fertile soils.

Water in after planting if the soil is dry, and ensure the soil is kept moist but not waterlogged when the flower buds start to form.

Problems
Mosaic virus can cause distortion and mottling of the leaves and eventual death of plants. Control aphids, which spread the virus.

FLOWERING

Season
A. coronaria will bloom from late winter until mid-spring, or in mid-summer, depending on planting time. *A. blanda* flowers in early spring while *A. nemorosa* flowers later in spring and into early summer.

Cutting
A. coronaria makes an excellent cut flower. Cut rather than pull flowers from the plant. The flowers of *A. blanda* and *A. nemorosa* may last a few days in the vase but these anemones make a much better showing in the ground. Leaving the flowers on the plants allows seed to form to increase your stock.

AFTER FLOWERING

Requirements If dry, continue to water plants until the foliage dies down. Cut off spent flowerheads unless you require seeds to form. Tubers of *A. coronaria* can be lifted, cleaned, and stored in a dry, airy place until the following fall, or left in the ground as long as drainage is good. The other species are best left in the ground to form large colonies. Lift, divide, and replant in fall if required.

BEGONIA
Begonia

EXQUISITE FORM *and beautiful color shadings make this tuberous begonia a show stopper. It's worth the effort to produce blooms like this.*

THE LARGE, *many-petalled flowers of some begonia hybrids are reminiscent of camellias. This variety is "Roy Hartley."*

FEATURES

Tuberous begonias result from the breeding and selection of several South American species and many are grown by specialists for exhibition. *Begonia tuberhybrida* is the most commonly grown type; the hybrid "Non-Stop" strain is particularly popular for its prolonged flowering. Begonias make excellent house plants, but can also be grown in containers on patios or in beds outdoors; pendulous varieties are especially suitable for hanging baskets. Flowers can take many forms, including single or double, camellia-flowered, or carnation-flowered—some are very simple while others are heavily ruffled. Flowers appear in threes, with the large, central male flower being the showpiece; the small female flowers are usually removed as they develop. The color range includes many shades of red, pink, yellow, cream, and white, with some bicolors. Plants grow some 10–18in high.

BEGONIA AT A GLANCE

Very large, showy flowers are carried throughout the summer. Plants are frost-tender.

Jan	/	
Feb	/	
Mar	plant ✎ (under cover)	
Apr	plant ✎ (under cover)	
May	plant ✎ (under cover)	
Jun	plant ✎ (outside)	
July	flowering ✿	
Aug	flowering ✿	
Sept	flowering ✿	
Oct	/	
Nov	/	
Dec	/	

Recommended Varieties

"Billie Langdon"
"Can-Can"
"Fairylight"
"Orange Cascade"
"Roy Hartley"
"Sugar Candy"

CONDITIONS

Aspect   Begonias prefer dappled sun or light shade, and need shelter from wind.

Site   Grow the plants in the house or conservatory, or in pots or flowerbeds outdoors when all risk of frost has passed. Soil should be rich and moisture-retentive, with plenty of organic matter such as well-rotted garden compost.

GROWING METHOD

Planting   Dormant tubers can be started off in pots of moist peat or compost under cover in spring, pressing the tuber into the soil with the dished side up. Spray the top of the tuber once only with a fine mist of water, and keep the compost just moist. Pot-grown plants can also be bought in leaf later in the spring. Plant out when all risk of frost is over, 9–12in apart.

Feeding   Apply high potash liquid fertiliser every 14 days throughout the growing period. Keep the plants moist at all times, but do not allow the soil to become waterlogged.

Problems   Powdery mildew may be a problem, especially in hot, dry weather. If this occurs, try to improve air circulation around the plants and use a suitable fungicide if necessary.

FLOWERING

Season   From early summer right through to fall.

Cutting   Flowers are unsuitable for cutting.

AFTER FLOWERING

Requirements   Lift tubers as the stems die down in fall. Store them in dry peat in a cool, frost-free place until the following spring.

CAMASSIA
Quamash

The intense blue flower spikes of Camassia leichtlinii *make a striking group among other border plants. A moisture-retentive soil is needed for best results—regular watering is likely to be necessary if the weather is dry. Camassias can cope with heavier soil conditions than many other bulbs.*

FEATURES

The botanical name of this plant is derived from that given to it by Native Americans, who grew the bulbs for food. It is relatively unusual among bulbous plants in preferring moist, heavy soils. The tall, graceful flower stems carry dense spires of starry blue flowers. *Camassia leichtlinii* is very reliable, with 3ft flowering stems: *C. quamash (C. esculenta)* is a little shorter and has flowers varying from white, through pale blue to deep purple. *C. cusickii* produces its 4ft pale lavender flower spikes in late spring.

CAMASSIA AT A GLANCE

Tall, stately spikes of blue, starry flowers provide valuable color in the perennial border in early summer.

		Recommended Varieties
Jan	/	
Feb	/	*Camassia cusickii*
Mar	/	
Apr	/	*Camassia leichtlinii:*
May	flowering	"Electra"
Jun	flowering	"Blue Danube"
July	flowering	"Semiplena"
Aug	flowering	
Sept	plant	*Camassia quamash*
Oct	plant	
Nov	/	
Dec	/	

CONDITIONS

Aspect Full sun or light, dappled shade will suit these bulbs.

Site Camassias make excellent border plants, valuable for early summer color. A moisture-retentive, fertile soil is preferred, though they will also grow adequately in free-draining conditions.

GROWING METHOD

Planting Plant the bulbs in early to mid-fall, 3–4in deep. Space them about 6in apart.

Feeding Feeding is not usually necessary, but an application of a balanced, granular fertiliser can be made in spring, especially on poor soils. Water thoroughly in dry conditions and on free-draining soil.

Problems Camassias are usually trouble free.

FLOWERING

Season Flowers from late spring through early summer.

Cutting Stems can be cut as the lowest buds on the spike begin to open.

AFTER FLOWERING

Requirements Cut down the flowering spikes when the flowers have faded. Do not disturb the bulbs until they become overcrowded, when they can be lifted and divided in fall.

CHIONODOXA
Glory of the snow

"PINK GIANT," a variety of Chionodoxa siehei, *has relatively large blooms in a pale, purplish-pink shade.*

THE BRIGHT BLUE flowers of chionodoxa, with their prominent central white eye, make a cheerful sight in the early spring months.

FEATURES

This dainty little bulb is ideal for rock gardens or raised beds, with its mass of open, star-shaped blue flowers with white centers. They are carried on short spikes of up to a dozen or so flowers per spike. The strap-shaped leaves form loose, rather untidy rosettes. ***Chionodoxa luciliae (C. gigantea)*** grows to 4in tall with clear blue, white-eyed flowers some 1½in or more across. *Chionodoxa siehei*, which used to be known as *C. luciliae,* and is sometimes listed as *C. forbesii*, reaches 4–10in, with slightly smaller flowers that are available in pale blue, white, or purplish-pink forms. The flowers have a distinct white eye and a central boss of stamens, tipped with gold. *C. sardensis* has flowers of a striking gentian blue

with a tiny white center that is almost unnoticeable.

CONDITIONS

Aspect	Full sun or dappled shade is suitable, though they grow best in an open, sunny position.
Site	Chionodoxa is suitable for window boxes, rock gardens, raised beds, the front of borders, or naturalized in grass. Soil should be free-draining, but otherwise these bulbs are not fussy about their growing conditions.

GROWING METHOD

Planting	Plant the bulbs in groups about 3in deep and 3in apart in early fall.
Feeding	A balanced granular fertiliser can be sprinkled over the soil surface in spring, but plants usually grow well without supplementary feeding, except in very poor, thin soils. Watering is necessary only in very dry conditions.
Problems	Apart from occasional slug damage, plants are generally trouble-free.

FLOWERING

Season	Chionodoxa flowers in early spring, sometimes appearing as the snow is thawing to live up to its common name.
Cutting	Flowers can be cut when they begin to open. They are valuable for cutting when few other flowers are available in the garden.

AFTER FLOWERING

Requirements	Lift and divide overcrowded plants when the foliage dies down in early summer after flowering, otherwise little attention is needed.

CHIONODOXA AT A GLANCE

A low-growing bulb producing plenty of bright blue flowers in early spring.

		Recommended Varieties
Jan	/	
Feb	flowering 🌸	*Chionodoxa siehei*:
Mar	flowering 🌸	"Alba"
Apr	flowering 🌸	"Pink Giant"
May	/	"Rosea"
Jun	/	
July	/	
Aug	/	
Sept	plant 👆	
Oct	/	
Nov	/	
Dec	/	

CLIVIA MINIATA
Kaffir lily

CLIVIAS MAKE SHOWY *and colorful house plants, and will bloom for many years if they are given a winter rest.*

THE PALE *creamy yellow flowers of* Clivia miniata citrina *make this unusual plant worth seeking out.*

FEATURES

This evergreen forms a striking house or conservatory plant, with long, deep green, strap-shaped leaves that overlap at the base rather like a leek. In spring or summer, a stout stem pushes between the leaf bases and grows to about 18in, carrying a head of 20 or so bright orange, bell-shaped flowers. These are marked with yellow in the throat and have prominent golden anthers.

Selected hybrids have larger flowers in various rich orange shades: a beautiful yellow-flowered variety, *C. miniata citrina*, has been developed but to date these plants are scarce and expensive, as are cultivars with cream-striped foliage.

CLIVIA AT A GLANCE

A striking house plant with large heads of orange, bell-shaped flowers on stout stems. Minimum temperature 50°F (zone 11).

Jan	/	
Feb	flowering 🌼	**Recommended Varieties**
Mar	flowering 🌼	*Clivia miniata citrina*
Apr	flowering 🌼	"Striata"
May	transplant ✍	
Jun	/	
July	/	
Aug	/	
Sept	/	
Oct	/	
Nov	/	
Dec	/	

CONDITIONS

Aspect Clivia prefers a reasonably bright position in the home, but not one in direct sun, which will scorch the foliage. Provide shading in a greenhouse or conservatory.

Site Grow as a room plant while it is flowering; during the summer the container can be placed in a sheltered position outdoors. Use a loam-based or soiless potting compost.

GROWING METHOD

Planting Clivias are usually bought as house plants in growth.

Feeding Give a high potash liquid feed every two or three weeks from early spring through the summer. Keep the compost thoroughly moist from spring to fall, then keep the plant cool and water it very sparingly in winter.

Problems Mealy bugs can appear as fluffy white blobs between the leaf bases; use a systemic insecticide to control them.

FLOWERING

Season Flowers may be carried any time between late winter and early summer.

Cutting Not suitable for cutting.

AFTER FLOWERING

Requirements Remove spent flower stalks. Repot only when essential; crowded plants tend to flower more reliably.

COLCHICUM AUTUMNALE

Fall crocus, meadow saffron

THE DELICATE COLOR and form of meadow saffron flowers are particularly prominent, as they appear long before the leaves. They are very welcome as they appear in fall when the yard is often looking rather untidy and faded after its summer exuberance.

FEATURES

This is another beautiful plant to brighten and lift the garden in fall. It is unusual in that the 6–9in-high flowers emerge directly from the neck of the corm, the leaves not appearing until months later, in spring. Although the flowers look similar to crocuses, the plants are not related. Up to a dozen rose pink to pale lilac, goblet-shaped flowers emerge from each corm. There is a pure white form, "Alba," and a glorious double form known as "Waterlily," that has a profusion of rose-lilac petals. Always plant in quite large groups for the best effect.

This easy-care bulb gives great rewards. It has a long history of use in herbal medicine but all parts of the plant are poisonous.

COLCHICUM AT A GLANCE

A crocus-like plant valuable for its fall flowers held on delicate stems.

		Recommended Varieties
Jan	/	
Feb	/	
Mar	/	"Alboplenum"
Apr	/	"Album"
May	/	"Pleniflorum"
Jun	/	"The Giant"
July	plant	"Waterlily"
Aug	plant	
Sept	flowering	
Oct	flowering	
Nov	flowering	
Dec	/	

CONDITIONS

Aspect Colchicum grows in full sun or very light shade.

Site Suitable for rock gardens, borders, or for naturalizing in grassed areas or in light shade under trees. For best results grow this plant in well-drained soil to which organic matter has been added.

GROWING METHOD

Planting Corms should be planted in late summer, 3in deep and 4–6in apart, in groups. Established clumps are best divided at this time, too.

Feeding Apply a generous mulch of decayed organic matter in winter. Further feeding is not usually necessary. Water in dry spells when the leaves appear in spring, and throughout their growing period.

Problems No specific pest or disease problems are common for this plant.

FLOWERING

Season Flowers spring out of the ground in fall.

Cutting Cut flowers for the vase when the goblet shape is fully formed but before it opens out. Flowers last about a week in the vase.

AFTER FLOWERING

Requirements Spent flowers may be cut off or left on the ground. Dead foliage may need tidying up at the end of the season.

CONVALLARIA MAJALIS
Lily-of-the-valley

LONG A FAVORITE with spring brides, fragrant lily-of-the-valley is an easy and rewarding bulb to grow.

IDEAL FOR EDGING a shady garden, these beautiful plants are also completely reliable, increasing, and flowering every year.

FEATURES

This is a tough little plant with a dainty appearance that belies its ease of growth. It is ideal for naturalizing in shady spots in the yard and also under trees where it can grow undisturbed. The dainty little white bell flowers are borne in spring; they are delightfully scented and last well in the vase. Flower stems may be 8–10in high, just topping the broadish, furled leaves that clasp the flower stems in pairs. There are several named cultivars but the straight species is by far the most popular. Previously used in folk medicine, the plant is now known to contain several poisonous substances although research continues on its potential medical use. The fleshy rhizomes with their growth shoots are known as "pips."

CONVALLARIA AT A GLANCE

A low-growing plant with very fragrant, dainty white bells on arching stems in late spring. Ideal for light shade.

		Recommended Varieties
Jan	/	
Feb	/	
Mar	/	"Albostriata"
Apr	flowering	"Fortin's Giant"
May	flowering	"Flore Pleno"
Jun	/	"Prolificans"
July	/	*Convallaria majalis rosea*
Aug	/	
Sept	/	
Oct	plant	
Nov	plant	
Dec	plant	

CONDITIONS

Aspect	Prefers to grow in partial shade; ideal under deciduous trees.
Site	A good ground cover plant; also suitable for mixed beds and borders. Soil should be free-draining but moisture-retentive, containing large amounts of decayed organic matter.

GROWING METHOD

Planting	The pips are planted in late fall about 1in deep and 4in apart. Congested clumps can be divided in fall or winter.
Feeding	In early winter apply a generous mulch of decayed manure or compost, or pile on the decaying leaves of deciduous trees. Keep soil moist throughout the growing season, giving a thorough soaking when necessary.
Problems	Few problems are encountered but poor drainage may rot the root system.

FLOWERING

Season	Flowers appear from mid-spring.
Cutting	This lovely cut flower perfumes a whole room. Pull the stems from the plant. It is traditional to use the foliage to wrap around the bunch.

AFTER FLOWERING

Requirements	If possible, leave the plants undisturbed for several years. If clumps are extremely dense and flowering poor, lift and divide sections during fall or early winter.

CRINUM
Swamp lily

LIGHT PERFUME is an added reason to grow these pretty pink crinums. They are a good choice for a sheltered border.

VERY TALL STEMS carry the white flowers of Crinum x powellii *well-clear of the leaves so that the blooms are always well-displayed.*

FEATURES

There are more than 100 species of crinum, but *C.* x *powellii* and the more tender *C. moorei* are the two most commonly grown. Both bear large, scented, lily-like flowers in pale pink or white on stems up to 3ft high; plants have long, strap-shaped, light-green leaves. The flowers appear from middle to late summer and sometimes into fall.

The bulbs can grow very large indeed, up to 6in or more across, and can be very weighty. In time very large clumps are formed and they require considerable physical effort to lift and divide. Crinums need a sheltered position to do well. In cool areas they can also be grown quite successfully in containers that can be moved under cover in fall.

CRINUM AT A GLANCE

Large, scented, lily-like flowers in late summer and fall. This plant needs a sheltered, sunny position to thrive.

Jan	/	Recommended Varieties
Feb	/	*Crinum* x *powellii*:
Mar	/	"Album"
Apr	plant	"Roseum"
May	plant	
Jun	/	*Crinum moorei*
July	/	
Aug	flowering	*Crinum bulbispermum*:
Sept	flowering	"Album"
Oct	/	
Nov	/	
Dec	/	

CONDITIONS

Aspect	Grow crinum in a sunny, south-facing, sheltered position. *C. moorei* is best grown in a pot in a conservatory.
Site	Suitable for borders or as a specimen plant in a container on a patio or similar. Soil must be free-draining but moisture-retentive.

GROWING METHOD

Planting	Plant in spring, which is also the best time to divide existing clumps. *C.* x *powellii* should have the neck of the bulb above soil level, while *C. moorei* should be planted with the nose of the bulb at the level of the soil.
Feeding	Balanced fertiliser may be applied as new growth starts in spring. Keep the soil moist while the plants are in growth. Water plants in containers regularly.
Problems	Not generally susceptible to disease or pests but snails love to eat the foliage and flowers.

FLOWERING

Season	Flowers appear during summer and into the fall months.
Cutting	It is possible to cut blooms for the house but they last longer on the plant.

AFTER FLOWERING

Requirements	Cut off the flowering stalk when the flowers are over. Protect the crowns with a mulch of peat over winter, or move plants under cover. Disturb established plants as little as possible.

CROCOSMIA
Montbretia

THE VIBRANT COLOR of crocosmia flowers gives great decorative value but is matched by vigorous growth that may need to be controlled.

THE CLEAR, GOLDEN YELLOW flowers of "Citronella" make a pleasant change from the intense orange-reds of other varieties.

FEATURES

Also known as montbretia, some types of crocosmia are extremely vigorous and can become invasive in warm areas. It will often survive in old, neglected yards where virtually everything else has disappeared. The foliage is slender, sword-shaped, and upright or slightly arching. The flowers are carried on double-sided spikes that also arch gracefully, reaching some 2–3ft tall. Most types have eye-catching bright reddish-orange flowers that open progressively from the base of the spike. In cold areas, plants should be protected with a mulch of dry leaves over winter, and should be planted in a reasonably sheltered position.

CONDITIONS

Aspect	Grows best in a fully open, sunny position.
Site	Good in beds or borders in well-drained soil.

GROWING METHOD

Planting	Plant corms in spring, 3in deep and about 6in apart. Pot-grown specimens can be planted throughout the spring and summer, even when in flower. It usually becomes necessary to thin out clumps every few years.
Feeding	A balanced fertiliser can be applied in early summer, but feeding is not generally necessary.
Problems	There are no pests or diseases that commonly attack crocosmia.

FLOWERING

Season	There is a long flowering period all through summer. Congested clumps often seem to produce more blooms.
Cutting	Flowers are not suitable for cutting and are better appreciated in the garden.

AFTER FLOWERING

Requirements	Cut off spent flower stems as soon as the blooms have faded to avoid seed setting and plants spreading. When the leaves have died down, protect the corms with a mulch of straw or dry leaves in all but very warm, sheltered yards.

CROCOSMIA AT A GLANCE

A vigorous plant with sword-shaped leaves and brightly colored spikes of flowers through the summer.

		Recommended Varieties
Jan	/	
Feb	/	"Bressingham Blaze"
Mar	plant	"Canary Bird"
Apr	plant	"Citronella"
May	/	"Emily McKenzie"
Jun	/	"Jackanapes"
July	flowering	"Lucifer"
Aug	flowering	"Solfaterre"
Sept	flowering	
Oct	/	
Nov	/	
Dec	/	

CROCUS
Crocus

SAFFRON CROCUS (Crocus sativus) *displays branched bright orange stigmas, the source of saffron, the costly spice used in cooking.*

CROCUS CHRYSANTHUS "ARD SCHENK"—*one of the most popular species—pushes up white goblet-shaped flowers in spring.*

FEATURES

Corm

There are more than 80 species of crocus, mainly late winter and spring flowering, but there are some fall bloomers, too. Crocus are among the earliest flowers to appear in spring, often pushing their flowers up through the snow. In some species flowers appear some weeks before the leaves. Crocus are mostly native to the countries around the Mediterranean Sea where they usually grow at high altitudes. They do, however, extend as far east as Afghanistan.

Appearance
Crocus foliage is short, rather sparse, and looks like a broad-leaf grass. The gorgeous little goblet-shaped flowers are borne on short stems 2–5in high. Most are blue, violet, white, yellow, or cream but some species have pink flowers. Many have deeper colored stripes or feathering on the petals.

Uses
Although unsuitable for cutting, these little bulbous plants are one of the greatest delights of the yard. They are often mass-planted in garden beds, especially at the front of borders. They can be naturalized in lawns or grouped together under deciduous trees. Crocuses are excellent plants for rock gardens and they make good container plants, being especially suitable for winter and early spring window-boxes. The floral display of some individual species in the yard can be short, but by growing a selection of species you can enjoy these charming flowers over an extended period, from early fall right through to late spring.

POPULAR SPECIES

Spring
Some of the most popular spring-flowering species are *C. biflorus*, *C. chrysanthus*, *C. flavus*, *C. minimus*, *C. tommasinianus* and *C. vernus*. Cultivars of a number of these species are available, with the many and varied cultivars of *C. chrysanthus* being especially popular, although each of these species have their admirers. *C. ancyrensis* is particularly early flowering, appearing in January and February.

Autumn
Fall-flowering species include *C. kotschyanus*, *C. niveus*, *C. laevigatus*, *C. longiflorus*, *C. nudiflorus*, *C. sativus* (the saffron crocus), *C. serotinus* (also known as *C. salzmannii*) and *C. speciosus*. *Crocus sativus* is well known as the source of the costliest of all herbs and spices. Native to temperate Eurasia and widely grown in Mediterranean regions, saffron crocus needs a very specific climate to flourish and is an extremely labor-intensive crop to harvest. Saffron comes only from the stigmas of the flowers and 75,000 flowers are needed to make up a pound of pure saffron.

CONDITIONS

Aspect
Prefers an open, sunny position but may be grown in light shade.

Site
Good for rock gardens, raised beds, the fronts of borders or naturalized in grass. Soil must be well-drained, preferably containing plenty of well-rotted organic matter.

FALL-BLOOMING Crocus serotinus here displays its beautiful pale lilac flowers and stiff, grass-like foliage. All crocus look best when planted like this, in a random fashion that mimics their natural growth.

GROWING METHOD

Planting Plant new corms about 2in deep and 2–4in apart. Spring-flowering varieties should be planted in fall, from September to November, while fall-flowering species should be planted in July and August. The corms of some species become quite large over time; lift and plant them further apart as it becomes necessary.

Feeding Apply a light dressing of balanced fertiliser after flowering, particularly in poor soil conditions. Watering is necessary only if conditions are very dry: however, fall-flowering types are likely to need watering after planting in summer.

CROCUS AT A GLANCE	

Low-growing bulbs valuable for their early spring flowers in a range of colors. Good for containers.

Jan	flowering* 🌱	**Recommended Varieties**
Feb	flowering* 🌱	
Mar	flowering* 🌱	*Crocus chrysanthus:*
Apr	flowering* 🌱	"Cream Beauty"
May	/	"Ladykiller"
Jun	/	"Snow Bunting"
July	plant** ✋	*Crocus tommasinianus:*
Aug	plant** ✋	"Ruby Giant"
Sept	🌱**/ ✋ *	*Crocus vernus:*
Oct	🌱**/ ✋ *	"Little Dorrit"
Nov	🌱**/ ✋ *	"Queen of the Blues"
Dec	flowering 🌱**	"Vanguard"

* spring flowering species   ** fall flowering species

Problems Few problems are encountered when crocuses are grown in the right aspect and soil. However, birds can sometimes damage flowers. Some birds, particularly sparrows, seem to be attracted by the shape or color of flowers and can peck them to pieces. If this occurs you will have to place a frame covered in wire netting over the plants.

FLOWERING

Season Flowering depends on the species; some varieties begin flowering in late winter to very early spring, others slightly later in spring. Fall-flowering species flower between September and early December, and may overlap with the earliest of the winter-flowering species growing against a warm wall.

Cutting Crocuses are not good cut flowers although they may last a few days in the vase.

AFTER FLOWERING

Requirements It is essential not to remove crocus leaves before they have yellowed as they are important in building up the corms and, therefore, next season's flowering potential. Plantings may need lifting and dividing every 3–4 years, but they can be left until corms start to push their way to the surface.

CYCLAMEN
Cyclamen

GORGEOUS UPSWEPT PETALS and a range of glorious colors ensure the lasting popularity of florist's cyclamen as house plants.

NEAPOLITAN CYCLAMEN (Cyclamen hederifolium) provides weeks of flowers and many months of decorative foliage.

FEATURES

Cyclamen form an enchanting group of plants admired for their attractive, mostly marbled foliage and distinctive flowers with swept back, slightly twisted petals. Some, such as the florists' cyclamen, have large showy flowers, while many of the species have small flowers growing only 3–4in high. Some cyclamen flower in fall or winter, while others flower in late winter and spring. Native to parts of Europe and countries around the Mediterranean, all share a similar need to be kept rather dry during their dormant period. Plants growing in good conditions can remain undisturbed for many years. The original tubers will increase greatly in size and many new plants will come from self-sown seed.

Uses
The smaller varieties make a great show when planted in masses or drifts. The floral display is quite long-lasting and even out of flower the marbled leaves make a good groundcover for many months of the year. Cyclamen can be grown in light shade under trees, in rock gardens, and in containers.
Potted plants of *C. persicum* hybrids in bloom make excellent house plants and are available from late summer right through the winter. The flowers may be delicately scented. In warm rooms in the home it can be difficult to keep these plants in good condition, and they are sometimes best considered as short-term floral decoration.

TYPES

Florists'
Florists' cyclamen (*C. persicum*) is usually seen as a flowering potted plant for indoor use, and many hybrids are available, including very fragrant miniature types. The beautifully marbled foliage and spectacular flowers make this a very showy plant. The flowers with their swept back petals come in every shade of pink and red, purple, cerise, white, and bicolors, and there are some fancy frilled or ruffled kinds. This species came originally from the eastern Mediterranean but many of the modern hybrids grown bear little resemblance to the original species.

Garden
The most easily-grown garden cyclamen is the Neapolitan cyclamen (*C. hederifolium*) which flowers during fall. It can be grown more successfully in warmer areas than most of the other species. *C. hederifolium* has beautifully marbled foliage about 3–4in high, with the small, clear pink flowers held above the leaves. There is also a pure white form of this species. *C. coum* flowers from late winter into spring and has larger, very deep pink flowers on short stems. Again, there is a white form of this species available. *C. repandum*, another spring bloomer, has probably the largest flowers of all the species cyclamens but none of these have flowers that are the size of the florists' cyclamen. The foliage on *C. repandum* is noted for its reddish undersides.

THESE CYCLAMEN COUM are thriving in an alpine-type sink garden: when they are allowed to self-seed, they soon form dense colonies. The marbled leaves are attractive, as well as the dainty, pale pink and purple flowers with their upswept petals.

CONDITIONS

Aspect   The ideal situation for hardy cyclamen is beneath deciduous trees where there is some winter sun but dappled sunlight for the rest of the year. In the home, florists' cyclamen need a cool, bright position.

Site   Hardy cyclamen can be grown on rock gardens, under trees and shrubs, and in borders. The soil must be well-drained with a high organic content. Indoors, choose a bright, cool windowsill or a conservatory.

GROWING METHOD

Planting   The flattened tubers (often wrongly referred to as corms) should be planted with their tops just below the soil surface. Plant in late summer and early fall at about 6in intervals. Pot-grown seedlings are easier to establish than dry tubers, and can be obtained from garden centers and specialist nurseries.

Feeding   If soil is poor, a sprinkling of balanced fertiliser can be given when growth begins and again after flowering. Florists' cyclamen should be given high potash liquid fertiliser every 14 days from when the flower buds appear until flowering is over. Water carefully from the base to avoid splashing the top of the tuber; never leave the pots standing in water.

Problems   Florists' cyclamen grown indoors often succumb to overwatering, drying out, and a dry, overwarm atmosphere. Vine weevils are attracted to the tubers and may cause the sudden collapse of the plant: use a soil insecticide if they are caught in time.

CYCLAMEN AT A GLANCE

Characteristic, upswept petals on a mound-forming plant with attractive marbled foliage. Suitable for outdoors or as pot plants.

Jan	flowering ☼	**Recommended Varieties**
Feb	flowering ☼	
Mar	flowering ☼	*Cyclamen cilicium album*
Apr	flowering ☼	*Cyclamen coum album*
May	/	*Cyclamen hederifolium*
Jun	/	"Bowles' Apollo"
July	plant ✎	"Silver Cloud"
Aug	plant ✎	*Cyclamen libanoticum*
Sept	flowering ☼	*Cyclamen pseudiber-icum*
Oct	flowering ☼	*Cyclamen purpurascens*
Nov	flowering ☼	*Cyclamen repandum*
Dec	flowering ☼	*Cyclamen persicum:* many

FLOWERING

Season   *C. persicum* flowers through winter into spring. *C. hederifolium* has a long flowering period in fall, while *C. coum* and *C. repandum* flower betwen late winter and spring.

Cutting   Pull flowers from the plant with a rolling motion and cut off the thin base of the stalk.

AFTER FLOWERING

Requirements   Outdoors, leave spent flowering stems to set seed and do not disturb tubers. After flowering, allow pot plants to die down and keep dry over summer. Start into growth again in August.

CYRTANTHUS ELATUS
Vallota, Scarborough lily

SCARLET FLOWERS *with a flared, trumpet-like shape make Scarborough lily a most striking plant.*

IN WARM AREAS *Scarborough lily can be grown outdoors, but it is more reliable as a pot plant for the conservatory or greenhouse.*

FEATURES

Still more commonly known under its earlier botanical name of *Vallota*, this old favorite should be more widely grown. Four or more brilliant scarlet, open trumpet-shaped blooms are held on a sturdy stem some 18in tall among dark green, strappy leaves. The plant originates from South Africa, and unfortunately, is not hardy enough to try outdoors except in the most favored, warmest areas of the country. However, it makes a good pot plant for a cool greenhouse or conservatory, or it can be grown indoors on a sunny windowsill. During the summer, the pots can be taken outside to decorate the patio. The Scarborough lily is not difficult to cultivate, and deserves to be more popular.

CYRTANTHUS AT A GLANCE

A tender bulb with large, trumpet-shaped flowers in summer— an excellent house or greenhouse plant. Min 45°F (zone 11).

Jan	/	
Feb	/	Recommended Varieties
Mar	/	"Pink Diamond"
Apr	/	
May	/	
Jun	plant 🖉	
July	flowering 🌼	
Aug	flowering 🌼	
Sept	flowering 🌼	
Oct	/	
Nov	/	
Dec	/	

CONDITIONS

Aspect   Grows best in a bright, sunny position.
Site   Must be grown as a house or greenhouse plant in all but the very warmest areas of the country.

GROWING METHOD

Planting   Plant bulbs in summer with the tip of the bulb just at or above soil level. Set one bulb in a 5in pot.
Feeding   Apply liquid fertiliser every 14 days as soon as growth appears. Keep the plant well-watered throughout the spring and summer, but reduce watering after flowering.
Problems   No specific pest or disease problems are known for this plant.

FLOWERING

Season   Flowers usually appear in midsummer.
Cutting   Flowers will last well when cut but probably give better decorative value if they are left on the plant.

AFTER FLOWERING

Requirements   Cut off the spent flower stems. Reduce watering and allow the compost to dry out completely between late winter and mid-spring. Do not repot for several years as the plants flower best when the pot is crowded. Offsets are produced freely, and some of these may be removed to pot up and grow on to flowering size in two or three years.

DAHLIA
Dahlia

THE RICH PINK of this freshly opened dahlia will gradually lighten to a delicate pale pink as the flower ages.

BICOLORED DAHLIAS have always had a strong following, whether in small, neat forms or dinner-plate sized blooms.

FEATURES

Dahlias come in many different flower forms and in a huge range of colors. Flower sizes range from tiny pompoms less than 2in across to huge blooms 12in or more wide, and they may be single, double, or semi-double. Most home gardeners are content to have a beautiful garden display but there are many enthusiasts who grow dahlias for showing.

Dahlias are grouped into different classes according to the shape and form of their flowers, and classes include single, anemone-flowered, collerette, waterlily, decorative, ball, pompon, cactus, and semi-cactus. There is also a miscellaneous group for any other type not covered by these classes. Plants can be anywhere from 12in to nearly 5ft high. They have a long flowering season from mid to late summer right through the fall. An ever-increasing range of bedding dahlias can be grown from seed; they form tubers which can be lifted and stored in the normal way in fall. Bedding varieties can also be bought as growing plants in spring.

CONDITIONS

Aspect Dahlias prefer full sun all day with protection from strong wind. The taller varieties need staking.

Site Dahlias are especially suitable for the herbaceous or mixed border, where they provide very welcome late summer color, but they can also be grown as bedding plants or the smaller varieties can be grown in containers. Soil must be well-drained and heavily enriched with manure or compost. Dahlias give best results in rich soil and are heavy feeders.

GROWING METHOD

Planting The tuberous roots should be planted 4–6in deep with the neck containing the sprouting eyes pointing up, in middle to late spring. Spacing between plants depends on variety—set small growers about 12in apart, very large growers 30–40in apart. The stakes and labels should be put in at planting time to avoid damaging tubers later.

Dahlia tubers can also be potted up in moist compost in a warm greenhouse in early spring, and cuttings taken of the shoots that arise from the tubers. These can be potted up individually and planted out in the yard when the risk of frost has passed. This is a good way to increase your stock of a particularly prized variety.

Feeding When flowering has begun, feed dahlias monthly with balanced fertiliser, or apply a high potash liquid feed every 14 days from when the flower buds begin to form. Applying a mulch of well-rotted garden compost will also help to retain soil moisture. Water well after planting tubers if the soil is dry, but further watering is usually unnecessary until after growth begins. During the growing and flowering season, it is important to make sure the plants never go short of water.

Problems Dahlias are affected by a number of viruses, notably dahlia mosaic virus, which causes

THIS SHRUB-LIKE DAHLIA with its clear, scarlet flowers will give many months of color in the garden if dead blooms are regularly removed. Dahlias prefer a sunny corner of the yard where they are protected from the wind.

yellowing foliage and sometimes stunted plants. It is transmitted by aphids. Spotted wilt virus causes spots and rings on leaves; it is carried by thrips and affects a range of plants. Watch for thrips and aphids early in the season and spray if necessary. Snails love dahlia foliage and flowers so take care to control them. They will climb up into the plant and stay there: if plants are being damaged, search for snails on and under the leaves and destroy them, or use slug bait, making sure it is positioned out of the reach of pets and wildlife. Earwigs can also damage blooms, feeding mainly at night and causing ragged holes in petals or distorted blooms. During the day they can be trapped in upturned pots stuffed with straw positioned on stakes among the plants.

FLOWERING

Season   The long flowering period lasts from midsummer to the first frosts. Deadhead the plants regularly to prolong blooming.

Cutting   Cut flowers early in the day, remove lower leaves, and scald stems for 10–15 seconds before arranging them. They are very long lasting in a vase.

AFTER FLOWERING

Requirements Tubers may survive in the ground for several years if the soil is well-drained, but in heavy soils and in cold areas, they are better lifted in late fall. Cut off the stem 6–8in above ground, dig up the clump carefully, and shake off excess soil. Stand upside-down to drain moisture from the stem, then store in a cool, airy place such as a garden shed, lightly covered with sand, soil, or peat, for replanting next spring. Tubers can be divided, but make sure that each section has a portion of stem with a visible bud or "eye"—the tuberous root portion on its own cannot grow.

DAHLIAS AT A GLANCE

Spectacular flowering plants giving four months of bloom. Perfect for cutting, showing, or garden decoration.

Month		Recommended Varieties
Jan	/	"Bishop of Llandaff"
Feb	/	"Daleko Jupiter"
Mar	/	"Firebird"
Apr	plant	"Glorie van Heemstede"
May	plant	"Grenidor Pastelle"
Jun	/	"Hamari Gold"
July	flowering	"Jescot Julie"
Aug	flowering	"Kenora Fireball"
Sept	flowering	"Wootton Cupid"
Oct	flowering	
Nov	/	
Dec	/	

DIERAMA PULCHERRIMUM
Fairy fishing rods, wandflower

SILKY FLOWERS in two shades of pink are suspended from the fine stems of this lovely South African plant.

AN ESTABLISHED CLUMP of fairy fishing rods produces many flowering stems. It is easy to see how the plant gained its common name.

FEATURES

The slender, arching stems of this highly desirable South African plant carry numerous bell-shaped, pendulous flowers and rise out of stiff, evergreen, sword-shaped leaves. Flowers are a rich silvery-pink in the species but there are a number of named cultivars in shades of pink, lilac, and even white.

Dense clumps of established plants produce many flowering stems, which sway in the slightest breeze to give a delightful effect. A mass planting creates a striking feature in the garden and it is often placed near water where the reflections increase its impact. Foliage grows 20in or so high but the flowering stems may be almost 6ft long in the right conditions.

DIERAMA AT A GLANCE

A perennial with graceful, slender, arching stems carrying dainty pink blooms in summer. Needs moist soil to thrive.

		Recommended Varieties
Jan	/	
Feb	/	"Blackbird"
Mar	/	"Peregrine"
Apr	/	"Slieve Donard Hybrids"
May	/	
Jun	/	
July	flowering	
Aug	flowering	
Sept	flowering	
Oct	plant	
Nov	plant	
Dec	/	

CONDITIONS

Aspect Needs full sun all day.
Site Dierama fits well in the herbaceous border. This plant needs well-drained but moisture-retentive, fertile soil containing plenty of well-rotted organic matter such as garden compost or animal manure.

GROWING METHOD

Planting Plant in mid to late fall, 3in deep and 12in apart.
Feeding A balanced fertiliser can be applied annually in early spring or after flowering. Water during late spring and summer if conditions are dry; the soil should remain moist throughout the growing season.
Problems There are no specific pest or disease problems normally experienced with this plant.

FLOWERING

Season Dierama bears its flowers from mid to late summer.
Cutting Not suitable for cutting.

AFTER FLOWERING

Requirements When spent, flower stems can be cut off at ground level, although they can be left to set seed if required. Dierama resents root disturbance, so corms should not be lifted unless it is essential. Self-sown seedlings can often be transplanted successfully to increase your stock of this plant.

ERANTHIS
Winter aconite

THE GLOSSY, golden buttercups of winter aconites, backed by their green leafy ruffs, give a welcome show of color in early spring.

"GUINEA GOLD," a variety of Eranthis x tubergenii, *has particularly large, showy flowers.*

FEATURES

The glossy yellow flowers of this tuber are a welcome sight in early spring. They are backed by a bract that forms a green leafy ruff, giving the flowers a Jack-in-the-green appearance. The true winter aconite is **Eranthis hyemalis**, with divided, pale green leaves and buttercup-yellow blooms: it seeds itself freely and soon spreads to form a carpet. **Eranthis** x **tubergenii** is a more vigorous hybrid, with larger, slightly later flowers. Both types grow to about 4in. Another type is sometimes sold as the Cilicica form of *E. hyemalis*, sometimes as a separate species, **E. cilicica**. It has deep yellow flowers, carried in March, backed by bronzy green, very finely cut foliage, and it grows to 2–3in tall.

ERANTHIS AT A GLANCE

A low-growing plant, welcome for its bright golden-yellow flowers in late winter and early spring.

		Recommended Varieties
Jan	/	
Feb	flowering 🌼	"Guinea Gold"
Mar	flowering 🌼	
Apr	plant 🌱 flowering 🌼	
May	/	
Jun	/	
July	/	
Aug	/	
Sept	plant 🌱 (tubers)	
Oct	/	
Nov	/	
Dec	/	

CONDITIONS

Aspect   Full sun or light shade are acceptable.

Site   Winter aconites are perfect for rock gardens, the fronts of borders, or beneath deciduous trees, which allow sufficient light to the plants during their spring growing period. They prefer a free-draining but moisture-retentive soil.

GROWING METHOD

Planting   Plant the tubers in September, as soon as they are obtained—if they dry out before planting they are difficult to establish. They should be planted 1–2in deep and 3–4in apart. Eranthis are also available freshly lifted, like snowdrops, in spring, when they establish more readily.

Feeding   Ensure the soil is kept moist during the spring, especially where the plants are growing under trees or shrubs. Supplementary feeding is not normally necessary.

Problems   Plants can become invasive where conditions suit them as they seed freely; otherwise no specific problems are generally experienced.

FLOWERING

Season   Flowers from early February to mid-March or into April.

Cutting   Flowers can be cut just as the buds are opening.

AFTER FLOWERING

Requirements   Divide crowded clumps after flowering, replanting the tubers immediately.

EREMURUS
Foxtail lily

THE STATELY yellow spikes of bloom of Eremurus stenophyllus *make this border plant certain to attract attention.*

THE TALLEST member of the group is Eremurus robustus, *its salmon-pink flower spikes towering up to 10ft.*

FEATURES

These stately plants produce tall spires of numerous, star-shaped flowers, giving a very impressive display and making good focal points in the garden. Their foliage is pale green and strap shaped; the flowering spikes tower above the leaves, reaching as much as 10ft or more in some species.

Eremurus robustus is among the tallest, with 8–10ft spikes of salmon-pink blooms: *E. stenophyllus (E. bungei)* grows to about 4ft with orange-yellow flowers. Probably most popular are some of the hybrid varieties at about 6ft, which bear flowers in a range of yellow, orange, and pink shades. Because of their height, plants need a position sheltered from wind.

EREMURUS AT A GLANCE

Tall, stately plants with large, showy flower spikes made up of masses of individual starry flowers.

		Recommended Varieties
Jan	/	
Feb	/	"Shelford Hybrids"
Mar	/	"Ruiter Hybrids"
Apr	/	"Moneymaker"
May	/	
Jun	flowering	
July	flowering	
Aug	/	
Sept	plant	
Oct	plant	
Nov	/	
Dec	/	

CONDITIONS

Aspect　Eremurus are reasonably hardy but demand a sheltered position in full sun.

Site　These are excellent plants for a place at the back of a border, or plant a foxtail lily at the end of a path for a dramatic focal point. Taller varieties usually need staking. Soil must be rich and fertile but free-draining; dig some sharp sand into the site at planting time to improve drainage if necessary.

GROWING METHOD

Planting　In early to mid-fall, set the roots 4–6in deep and 2–3ft apart.

Feeding　Keep the soil moist at all times. A dressing of balanced granular fertiliser can be made over the site in early spring, or high potash liquid feed can be given occasionally during the growing season.

Problems　Usually, no problems are experienced. The young foliage is vulnerable to frost damage and may need protection in early spring when shoots first appear through the soil.

FLOWERING

Season　Flowers in early to mid summer.

Cutting　Flower spikes may be cut as the first flowers are opening. They last well in water.

AFTER FLOWERING

Requirements　Cut down flower stems when the flowers fade. Protect the crowns from frost with a mulch of sand or dry leaves over winter. When overcrowded, divide the clumps in fall.

ERYTHRONIUM
Dog's tooth violet

"PAGODA" IS DESERVEDLY one of the most popular erythronium hybrids, with its tall stems of graceful, nodding, yellow flowers.

THE DOG'S TOOTH VIOLET, E. dens-canis, has beautifully mottled foliage as well as attractive little rose pink flowers.

FEATURES

Plants of the dappled shade of woodlands, erythroniums have attractive spring flowers, star-shaped and generally nodding, with swept-back petals.

The dog's tooth violet (named after the shape of its tuber) is *E. dens-canis*, with pinkish-purple flowers carried about 6in above the attractively mottled leaves. Slightly taller is *Erythronium californicum*, with lush, mid-green, lightly mottled leaves and creamy flowers with bronze backs to the petals. *Erythronium revolutum* grows to 12in, with white, pink, or purple mottled flowers, and has given rise to the popular hybrid "Pagoda," with 6–10 pendent, graceful yellow flowers on a slender, 16in flower stalk.

ERYTHRONIUM AT A GLANCE

Spring-flowering tubers with appealing, pendulous flowers in a range of heights and colors. Many also have attractive foliage.

		Recommended Varieties
Jan	/	
Feb	/	"Pagoda"
Mar	/	"Citronella"
Apr	flowering	
May	flowering	*Erythronium californicum:*
Jun	/	"White Beauty"
July	/	
Aug	plant	*Erythronium dens-canis*
Sept	plant	"Lilac Wonder"
Oct	/	"Rose Queen"
Nov	/	
Dec	/	

CONDITIONS

Aspect As a woodland plant, erythronium thrives in cool conditions and light shade.

Site Excellent under trees or among shrubs in beds and borders or on rock gardens. Fertile, moisture-retentive soil with plenty of organic matter will ensure good growth.

GROWING METHOD

Planting Plant the tubers in groups, 3–6in deep and 4–6in apart in late summer or early fall. Do not let the tubers dry out before planting or you will find it difficult to get the plants established: plant them as soon as possible after purchase.

Feeding Feeding is not usually necessary. Moist soil is essential during the growing season, but the tubers must never become waterlogged. Water carefully during dry spells.

Problems No specific pest or disease problems are usually experienced with this plant. Plants resent disturbance and may be difficult to re-establish if lifted and replanted.

FLOWERING

Season Flowers in mid-spring.

Cutting The taller species can be cut successfully when the buds have opened.

AFTER FLOWERING

Requirements Disturb the roots as little as possible. If clumps become so overcrowded that flowering is adversely affected, they can be lifted and divided in late summer, replanting the tubers immediately.

EUCOMIS COMOSA
Pineapple lily

THE TUFT on top of the flower spike does resemble a pineapple, but the pretty individual flowers below give a softer impression.

THE ROBUST GROWTH of this clump of pineapple lilies shows that the growing conditions in this spot are ideal.

FEATURES

This South African plant gets its common name from the pineapple-like flower spike with its topknot of tufted leaves. The greenish-white or white flowers, sometimes tinged with pink, are scented and packed tightly onto the spike; their weight can sometimes cause the stem to flop over. The broad, sword-shaped leaves are light green and attractively spotted with purple on the underside. This flower is always of interest, whether in the yard or as a potted plant: blooms are extremely long-lasting when cut. Another species in cultivation is *E. bicolor,* with attractive green and purple flowers. Both species grow to about 24in. Pineapple lily grows from a fleshy bulbous rootstock and is dormant in winter.

EUCOMIS AT A GLANCE

A tall, striking bulb with a pineapple-like flower stem. A sunny, sheltered spot is required.

		Recommended Varieties
Jan	/	
Feb	/	
Mar	plant 🖐	*Eucomis bicolor*
Apr	plant 🖐	*E. b.* "Alba"
May	/	*E. comosa*
Jun	/	*E. pole-evansii*
July	flowering 🌿	*E. zambesiaca*
Aug	flowering 🌿	
Sept	/	
Oct	/	
Nov	/	
Dec	/	

CONDITIONS

Aspect Prefers full sun but tolerates light shade. Grows best in warm, sheltered areas, but can also be grown in colder gardens if the rootstock is protected or lifted for winter.

Site Eucomis is good for the middle or back of the flower border. Needs well-drained soil enriched with decayed organic matter before planting time.

GROWING METHOD

Planting Plant in spring, 2–4in deep and 8–12in apart.

Feeding Apply complete plant food as new growth begins. Mulch around plants in summer with well-decayed compost or manure. Keep the soil moist while the plant is actively growing.

Problems No specific problems are known.

FLOWERING

Season Flowers during midsummer.

Cutting The pineapple lily is usually enjoyed as a specimen garden plant, but if there are enough blooms, or if the stems are broken by wind, the cut flowers may last for several weeks if the vase water is changed regularly.

AFTER FLOWERING

Requirements Cut down the flowering stem when the flowers have passed their best. Either dig up the bulb and overwinter in a frost-free place, or in mild districts, mulch the planting area with peat or dry leaves to protect the bulb over winter.

FREESIA
Freesia species and hybrids

THE SPECIES *Freesia alba (also known as* F. refracta) *is the most heavily scented of all freesias, but can be difficult to find.*

THERE ARE MANY *hybrid varieties of freesia, some with strikingly bicolored flowers like these. Most, but not all, are sweetly scented.*

FEATURES

Freesias are loved for their strong perfume as well as their appearance. The wild species have yellow or white flowers and may grow about 12in high: modern hybrids grow 18in or more high and are available in a wide range of colors which includes blue, mauve, pink, red, and purple. However, some of these large-flowered hybrids have no scent. The white-flowered *F. alba* (*F. refracta*) is generally considered to have the best perfume.

For growing outdoors, buy specially prepared freesias and plant them in a sheltered position; they will flower in summer. Other freesias should be planted in containers that are brought into the house and greenhouse in fall for winter flowering.

FREESIA AT A GLANCE

Fragrant, tubular flowers in a wide range of colors are held on delicate spikes. Grow indoors or outside in a sheltered position.

		Recommended Varieties
Jan	flowering** ✿	
Feb	flowering** ✿	"Diana"
Mar	flowering** ✿	"Fantasy"
Apr	plant ✋ *	"Oberon"
May	/	"Romany"
Jun	/	"White Swan"
July	plant ✋ **	"Yellow River"
Aug	plant ✋ **/flowering ✿ *	
Sept	flowering* ✿	
Oct	flowering* ✿	
Nov	/	
Dec	/	

** indoors   *outdoors

CONDITIONS

Aspect Freesias prefer full sun but tolerate very light shade for part of the day.
Site Grow outdoors in a sheltered border. For winter flowers, plant in pots in summer, standing the pots in a sheltered position outside until fall, then bring them into a cool greenhouse or conservatory to flower. Use free-draining, John Innes, or soiless potting compost.

GROWING METHOD

Planting Outdoors, plant 2in deep and the same distance apart in mid-spring. For pot culture, plant 2in deep, six to a 5in pot in July.
Feeding Apply a high potash liquid fertiliser every 14 days through the growing season. Keep the compost just moist at all times.
Problems Aphids may attack the flower stems. Control with a contact insecticide when necessary.

FLOWERING

Season From middle to late winter through to mid-spring indoors, late summer outside.
Cutting Cut when the lowest flower on the spike is fully open and other buds are well-developed.

AFTER FLOWERING

Requirements Remove spent flower stems. When the foliage dies down, lift corms and store them in dry peat until it is time for replanting.

FRITILLARIA
Crown imperial, snake's head fritillary

THE FLOWERS of snake's head fritillary bear a distinctive, intricately checkered pattern that looks a bit like a game board.

SNAKE'S HEAD FRITILLARY is probably the easiest fritillary to grow and is ideal for damp meadows or woodlands.

FEATURES

The name fritillary comes from the Latin word *fritillus*, meaning "dice-box," as the checkered patterns on the flowers of some of the species resemble the checkerboards associated with many games played with dice. There are about 100 species of this striking bulbous plant, which is related to the lilies, but only a relatively small number are in general cultivation. The form and color of the flowers varies considerably from one species to another, and some are fascinating rather than beautiful. The flowers are generally pendent and bell-shaped, carried on leafy stems; their height varies considerably, from low-growing rock garden plants such as the 4–6in *Fritillaria michailovskyi*, to the stately and imposing crown imperials (*F. imperialis*), which can reach well over 3ft tall. Many fritillaries, especially crown imperial, have a strong "foxy" scent to them which some people find unpleasant. All parts of the plant, including the bulbs, possess this scent, which can be quite penetrating.

Uses These plants, especially crown imperial, deserve a prominent place in the spring garden. They are sometimes seen taking pride of place in a bulb garden but are more often included in a mixed border planting with other bulbs and perennials. To show them to their best advantage, plant several of the same type together as individual plants will not have the same impact. Those that multiply readily, such as the snake's head fritillary, can be naturalized in dappled shade. All species can be grown in containers but most are easier to grow in the open ground.

Availability Crown imperials and snake's head fritillaries are readily available from garden centers, but some of the other species may have to be obtained from mail order bulb specialists.

TYPES

F. imperialis The best known fritillary is the majestic crown imperial, *F. imperialis*, which has a cluster of orange, yellow, or red bell-shaped flowers hanging below a crown of green leaves on a stem 20–39in high.

F. meleagris The snake's head fritillary or checkered lily, *F. meleagris*, occurs in the wild in meadows throughout Europe and is one of the easiest to cultivate. The checkered flowers occur in shades of green, purple, magenta, or white.

Others Among the many other species worth growing are *F. acmopetala*, with bell-shaped green and brown flowers; *F. biflora* "Martha Roderick," with brown-streaked cream flowers, *F. camschatcensis*, with very deep purple, almost black flowers; *F. michailovskyi*, with yellow-tipped purple bells, *F. pallidiflora*, with soft yellow flowers veined lime-green or burgundy; *F. persica* with deep purple flowers; *F. pontica* with greenish bells; and *F. pyrenaica*, a deep burgundy purple, spotted green outside while the inside is purple-checked green.

*CROWN IMPERIAL (*Fritillaria imperialis*) is an exciting fritillary that takes pride of place in many keen bulb growers' yards. The "crown" referred to in the common name is the topknot of leaves from which the bell-shaped flowers are suspended.*

CONDITIONS

Aspect   Fritillary grows best in light shade or with morning sun and afternoon shade. Some species take full sun. All are best with protection from strong wind.

Site   Fritillaries can be grown in beds and borders, on rockeries, or in containers, according to species. *F. meleagris* can be naturalized in grass. Soil for fritillaries must be well-drained but should contain plenty of well-rotted compost or manure. The area around the plants should be well-mulched, too. *F. meleagris* prefers a more moisture-retentive soil than some of the other species.

FRITILLARIA AT A GLANCE

Unusual bulbs in a wide range of sizes and flower forms, with striking, pendent, bell-shaped blooms.

Month		Recommended Varieties
Jan	/	
Feb	/	*Fritillaria biflora:*
Mar	/	"Martha Roderick"
Apr	flowering 🌼	
May	flowering 🌼	*Fritillaria imperialis:*
Jun	/	"Lutea"
July	/	"Rubra Maxima"
Aug	/	"Prolifera"
Sept	plant ✍	"The Premier"
Oct	plant ✍	
Nov	plant ✍	*Fritillaria persica:*
Dec	/	"Adiyaman"

GROWING METHOD

Planting   The lily-like bulbs can dry out quickly and should be planted as soon as they are available. Planting depth varies between 2–8in depending on species. Plant the large bulbs of crown imperials on their sides on a layer of sand so that water does not collect in the hollow center.

Feeding   Apply a general fertiliser after flowering or a high potash fertiliser in early spring as growth starts. Water in dry spells during the growing season, especially before flowering.

Problems   Bulbs may rot in badly drained soil.

FLOWERING

Season   Flowers appear from mid-spring to early summer.

Cutting   Despite being quite long-lasting as a cut flower, blooms are rarely used this way because of the unpleasant smell of some flowers. Unfortunately crown imperial is one of these. However, they are so striking in the garden that they are best enjoyed there.

AFTER FLOWERING

Requirements   When flowers have faded, flowering stems can be cut down, but leave the flowerheads on snake's head fritillaries to set seed. Bulbs are best left undisturbed, but if necessary clumps can be divided in summer and replanted immediately.

GALANTHUS
Snowdrop

TRUE HARBINGERS of spring, snowdrops are among the first bulbs to appear in late winter, often pushing up through the snow.

THE DOUBLE SNOWDROP, Galanthus nivalis *"Flore Pleno," is an easily grown, vigorous, and reliable variety.*

FEATURES

The snowdrop (*G. nivalis*) is well-loved for flowering in late winter while conditions are still very bleak. Most of the dozen or so species flower in late winter to early spring although there is one fall-flowering species (*G. reginae-olgae*). *G. elwesii* and *G. caucasicus* are also very early bloomers. There are named varieties of several species available. *G. nivalis* grows only 4–5in high, but taller varieties such as *G. elwesii* can grow up to 10in. The nodding flowers have three long, pure white petals and three shorter ones marked with a bright green horseshoe shape. The dark green foliage may be matt or glossy but is usually shorter than the flowers.

GALANTHUS AT A GLANCE

A small, dainty bulb popular for its late winter and early spring flowers. Very hardy.

Jan	flowering	**Recommended Varieties**
Feb	flowering	"Atkinsii"
Mar	flowering / plant "in the green"	"Cordelia"
		"Sam Arnott"
Apr	/	*Galanthus lutescens:*
May	/	"Magnet"
Jun	/	*Galanthus nivalis:*
July	/	"Flore Pleno"
Aug	/	"Lady Elphinstone"
Sept	plant	"Lutescens"
Oct	plant	"Pusey Green Tip"
Nov	/	"Scharlockii"
Dec	flowering	"Viridapicis"

CONDITIONS

Aspect Grows best in shade or dappled sunlight.
Site Ideal for rockeries, the fronts of beds, and borders or naturalizing under deciduous trees. Soil must contain plenty of decayed organic matter to prevent excessive drying out in summer. Mulching in fall with old manure, compost, or leafmold is beneficial.

GROWING METHOD

Planting Plant bulbs in fall 3–4in deep (deeper in light soils) and about the same apart. Do not allow the bulbs to dry out before planting. Snowdrops are much more reliable when transplanted while in growth, after flowering—known as planting "in the green." Plants are available from specialist suppliers in late winter or early spring.
Feeding Mulch during fall with decayed organic matter. Watering is not usually necessary.
Problems No specific problems are known.

FLOWERING

Season Flowering is from winter through to spring, depending on species.
Cutting Flowers can be cut for indoor decoration.

AFTER FLOWERING

Requirements Existing clumps can be lifted, divided, and replanted as soon as the flowers have faded. Do not leave the plants out of the soil any longer than necessary.

GLADIOLUS CALLIANTHUS
Acidanthera

EACH BLOOM carries an attractive central, deep purple blotch, and has a slightly uneven, star-like shape.

THE SWEETLY-SCENTED white blooms of acidanthera appear late in the summer, when many other bulbs are over.

FEATURES

Although this plant is now classified as a species of gladiolus, many gardeners still know it better under its previous botanical name of *Acidanthera murielae*. The pure white, slightly drooping blooms have a dark purple central blotch, and are sweetly scented; their similarity to a gladiolus flower is obvious, but they are more delicate and graceful. The leaves are erect and sword shaped, growing to about 2ft. The flowers—up to a dozen per corm—are held on slender stems above the tips of the leaves, and appear in late summer.

This is not a plant for cold, exposed yards, requiring a warm, sunny position to do well. In cold regions it can be grown successfully as a conservatory or cool greenhouse plant.

G. CALLIANTHUS AT A GLANCE

A late summer flowering plant with attractive, white, scented blooms. Suitable for growing outdoors in mild areas only.

		Recommended Varieties
Jan	/	"Murieliae"
Feb	/	
Mar	plant (indoors) 👈	
Apr	plant (outdoors) 👈	
May	/	
Jun	/	
July	/	
Aug	flowering 🌸	
Sept	flowering 🌸	
Oct	/	
Nov	/	
Dec	/	

CONDITIONS

Aspect   These plants require full sun.
Site   Acidantheras can be grown in a sheltered, sunny spot outside in mild areas: otherwise grow the corms in pots in a greenhouse or conservatory, moving the pots onto a sheltered patio or similar position in midsummer. Light, free-draining soil is required. In pots, use soiless or John Innes potting compost.

GROWING METHOD

Planting   Plant in late spring, 4in deep and 8–10in apart.
Feeding   Give an occasional application of high potash liquid fertiliser (such as rose or tomato feed) during the growing season. Pot-grown plants should be fed every 10–14 days. Watering is not necessary for plants in the open ground except in very dry conditions; water pot-grown plants sufficiently to keep the compost just moist.
Problems   Plants may fail to flower in cold, exposed yards. Corms may rot in heavy, clay soils.

FLOWERING

Season   Flowers in late summer; mid-August through September.
Cutting   Pick the stems when the buds are showing white at their tips.

AFTER FLOWERING

Requirements Allow the foliage to die down, then lift the corms before the first frosts. Allow them to dry, brush off soil and store in dry, cool, frost-free conditions until the following spring.

GLADIOLUS HYBRIDS
Gladiolus, sword lily

THE STRIKING *red and yellow flowers of* Gladiolus dalenii *ensure this species will always stand out in a crowd.*

A POPULAR *hybrid gladiolus, "Green Woodpecker" is much sought after by flower arrangers because of its unusual coloring.*

FEATURES

The gladiolus with which we are most familiar comes from South Africa as do many other species, but other species originated in the Mediterranean regions and western Asia. There are about 300 species of gladiolus, many of them well worth seeking out for your garden, but the modern garden gladiolus is a hybrid. The stiff, sword-shaped leaves surround a flower spike that appears in spring and may be 39in or more high, but there are dwarf forms less than half this height. Flower spikes carry numerous individual blooms, usually densely packed on the stem and of a characteristic, irregular trumpet shape. The color range is extensive, including various shades of pink, red, yellow, orange, mauve, maroon, white, and green: flowers are often bicolored.

Special types A great range of species and cultivars is now available to add to the familiar hybrids. Baby gladiolus or painted ladies, *G.* x *colvillei*, (sometimes wrongly known as *G. nanus*) grows 12–16in high and comes in a range of colors, including many with contrasting markings. Green and white "The Bride" is perhaps the best known. Other species worth seeking out include *G. tristis*, with pale creamy yellow flowers; *G. dalenii* (syn. *G. natalensis*) with red to yellow flowers; *G. carneus*, with pink flowers; *G. cardinalis*, with rich red flowers marked in white; and *G. communis byzantinus*,

hardy in warmer parts of the country and producing spikes of purple-pink flowers in early summer.

Uses Gladiolus makes a great garden display and cut flower. Dwarf forms make good pot plants.

CONDITIONS

Aspect Grows best in full sun with some shelter from strong wind.

Site Gladiolus can be difficult to place, as their stiff, upright form, which usually requires staking, is very formal. They are often grown in the vegetable garden and used as cut flowers, but with care they can be grown in beds and borders. Soil should be well-drained with a high organic content. Dig in well-rotted manure or compost a month or more before planting.

GROWING METHOD

Planting Corms should be planted 3–4in deep and about 6in apart. Plant hybrid varieties in spring; stagger planting between March and May to give a succession of blooms. Spring-flowering species should be planted in fall; in colder areas of the country they are best overwintered in a cool greenhouse.

Feeding In soils enriched with organic matter

THE GLOWING red blooms of "Victor Borge" make a brilliant splash of color in any garden setting.

THE PURE WHITE of these gladiolus appears even whiter against the blue forget-me-nots. The blooms will last longer in cool areas.

Problems

supplementary feeding should not be necessary. In poor soils apply a balanced fertiliser to the soil before planting. In dry weather, water regularly throughout the growing season. Thrips, which rasp and suck sap from foliage and flowers, are a perennial problem in some areas. Deep colored flowers, such as reds and maroons, show their damage more readily than paler ones, with light-colored flecks spoiling their appearance. The summer months are the worst time for attacks, but the pest may overwinter on corms in store. Dust the corms with a suitable insecticide before storing and again before planting. At planting time, discard corms with dark or soft spots, which may be infected with various fungal rots.

FLOWERING

Season   Hybrids planted in spring will produce flowers through summer into early fall. Fall-planted species will flower in early summer.

Cutting   Cut spikes for indoor decoration when the second flower on the spike is opening. Cut the flower stem without removing the leaves if that is possible. Change the water in the vase daily and remove lower blooms from the spike as they fade.

AFTER FLOWERING

Requirements Lift corms carefully as soon as foliage begins to yellow. Cut off old leaves close to the corm. Dry corms in a warm, airy place for 2–3 weeks and clean them by removing old roots and the outer sheath of corm. To increase your stock of gladiolus, remove the small cormlets from the parent bulb and store them separately. These cormlets should produce full flowering size corms in the second year. If you have had problems with thrips in previous seasons, treat corms with insecticide dust before storing.

GLADIOLUS AT A GLANCE

Popular hybrid varieties have tall, stiff spikes, packed with large, colorful flowers; more delicate species flower in spring.

Jan	/	
Feb	/	
Mar	plant	
Apr	plant	
May	flowering */plant	
Jun	flowering *	
July	flowering	
Aug	flowering	
Sept	flowering plant *	
Oct	/	
Nov	/	
Dec	/	

Recommended Varieties

Hybrids:
  "Amsterdam"
  "Christabel"
  "Esta Bonita"
  "Green Woodpecker"
  "Hunting Song"
  "Lady Godiva"
  "Victor Borge"

G. x *colvillei:*
  "Amanda Mahy"
  "The Bride"

*fall planted species

GLORIOSA
Glory lily

FLUTED RECURVED PETALS *give these flowers an airy, floating effect. Plants grow rapidly in warm, humid conditions.*

THESE GLORIOSA LILIES *at various stages of development display a fascinating range of colors and shapes.*

FEATURES

This climber is always sure to attract attention. It grows from elongated, finger-like tubers, and needs greenhouse or conservatory conditions. A plant will grow up to 8ft in the right conditions, its long, slender stems twining their way through netting or wooden trellis supports by means of tendrils at the tips of the lance-shaped leaves. The unusual lily-like flowers are crimson and yellow, with their wavy-edged petals strongly recurved to show the prominent, curving stamens.
Gloriosa has a long flowering period through summer and fall and usually gives a spectacular display. It is worth growing in a prominent position where it can be admired, but it is not hardy enough to grow outdoors.

GLORIOSA AT A GLANCE

A greenhouse climber with spectacular summer flowers.
Minimum temperature 50°F (zone 11).

		Recommended Varieties
Jan	plant	*Gloriosa superba:*
Feb	plant	"Rothschildiana"
Mar	plant	"Lutea"
Apr	/	
May	/	
Jun	/	
July	flowering	
Aug	flowering	
Sept	flowering	
Oct	/	
Nov	/	
Dec	/	

CONDITIONS

Aspect   Grow in a greenhouse or conservatory, in bright light but shaded from direct summer sun.
Site   Use either soiless or John Innes potting compost.

GROWING METHOD

Planting   The tubers are planted out in late winter or early spring about 2in deep, placing one tuber in a 6in pot of moist compost. Take care not to injure the tips of the tubers.
Feeding   Apply high potash liquid fertiliser every 14 days during the growing season. Water sparingly until growth commences, more freely during active growth but never allow the soil to become waterlogged.
Problems   Slugs may attack the tubers, and poor drainage or overwatering will rot them.

FLOWERING

Season   Flowers throughout the summer.
Cutting   Flowers last well when picked.

AFTER FLOWERING

Requirements   Snap off flowers as they fade. Reduce watering when flowering has finished and allow the tubers to dry out for the winter. Store them dry in their pots or in dry peat in a minimum temperature of 50°F and replant in spring.

HEDYCHIUM
Ginger lily

LONG RED STAMENS contrast nicely with the clear yellow flowers on this kahili ginger. The flowers have a strong perfume.

THIS GINGER LILY needs room to spread out and show off its strong lines. It is a useful landscaping plant.

FEATURES

There are over 40 species of ginger lily although not many species are in cultivation. These plants are strong growers, mostly to about 6ft, their growth originating from sturdy rhizomes. They can be bedded out in borders for the summer, or grown in tubs as a patio or greenhouse and conservatory plant. Mid-green leaves are lance shaped.

The tall, showy heads of flowers are carried in late summer. White ginger or garland flower, *H. coronarium*, has white and yellow, very fragrant flowers while scarlet or red ginger lily, *H. coccineum*, has faintly scented but most attractive blooms in various shades of red, pink, or salmon. Also heavily scented is kahili ginger, *H. gardnerianum*, with large, clear yellow flowers and prominent red stamens.

HEDYCHIUM AT A GLANCE

Large, showy leaves are topped by striking heads of many flowers, often scented. Needs a minimum temperature of 45°F (zone 11).

Jan	/	**Recommended Varieties**
Feb	/	
Mar	plant 🖐	*Hedychium coccineum*
Apr	plant 🖐	*aurantiacum*
May	/	*Hedychium coccineum:*
Jun	/	"Tara"
July	flowering 🌼	*H. coronarium*
Aug	flowering 🌼	*H. densiflorum:*
Sept	flowering 🌼	"Assam Orange"
Oct	/	*H. gardnerianum*
Nov	/	
Dec	/	

CONDITIONS

Aspect   Needs a bright, sunny spot.

Site   In cold areas, grow in a greenhouse or conservatory; otherwise grow in a sheltered border outside. Rich, moisture-retentive soil is necessary; add well-rotted organic matter before planting time.

GROWING METHOD

Planting   Plant in spring, with the tip of the rhizome just buried below the soil surface. Space rhizomes about 24in apart.

Feeding   A balanced fertiliser can be applied as growth begins in spring. Keep the soil moist throughout the growing season.

Problems   There are generally no particular problems experienced.

FLOWERING

Season   Flowers in mid to late summer and early fall.

Cutting   Flowers can be cut for indoor decoration but they will last very much longer on the plant.

AFTER FLOWERING

Requirements Cut flower stems down to the ground when the flowers have faded. Lift the rhizomes when the foliage has died down and overwinter in dry peat in a frost-free place, replanting the following spring. Pot plants can be left in their pots over winter. Rhizomes may be divided in spring to increase your stock.

HIPPEASTRUM
Hippeastrum, amaryllis

"APPLE BLOSSOM" is a cultivar with unusual soft, pastel flowers. Most hippeastrums have very strongly colored flowers in the red range.

BIG, SHOWY TRUMPET FLOWERS on stout stems are a feature of hippeastrums.

FEATURES

There are many species of hippeastrum but the most familiar plants, with their very large, trumpet-shaped flowers, are cultivars or hybrids of a number of species. They are popular winter-flowering house plants; between two and six large flowers are carried on thick stems that are generally over 20in high. Blooms appear all the more spectacular because they appear ahead of the leaves or just as the leaves are emerging. There are many cultivars available but most flowers are in various shades of red, pink, or white, separately or in combination. Because of the very large size of the bulb it is normal to use only one bulb per 7in pot. The bulbs should be allowed to rest during summer if they are to be brought into bloom again.

HIPPEASTRUM AT A GLANCE

A windowsill plant with very showy, large, trumpet-shaped flowers on tall stems in winter and spring. Minimum 56°F (zone 11).

Jan	flowering 🌸	Recommended Varieties
Feb	flowering 🌸	
Mar	flowering 🌸	"Apple Blossom"
Apr	flowering 🌸	"Bouquet"
May	/	"Lady Jane"
Jun	/	"Lucky Strike"
July	/	"Mont Blanc"
Aug	/	"Flower Record"
Sept	/	"Oscar"
Oct	plant 🌱	"Picotee"
Nov	plant 🌱	"Star of Holland"
Dec	plant 🌱	

CONDITIONS

Aspect Needs full sun and bright conditions.
Site Grow as a pot plant in the home or greenhouse. Use soilless potting compost.

GROWING METHOD

Planting Plant with about half to one-third of the bulb above soil level in a pot just large enough to hold the bulb comfortably. Bulbs can be planted any time between October and March. Use "prepared" bulbs for Christmas and early winter flowers.

Feeding Apply a high potash liquid feed every 10–14 days when the bulb starts into growth. Water sparingly until the bud appears, then more freely until the foliage begins to die down.

Problems No problems usually, but overwatering can cause the bulb to rot.

FLOWERING

Season Showy flowers appear in about eight weeks after planting, between late December and late spring.

Cutting With frequent water changes flowers can last well, but are usually best left on the plant.

AFTER FLOWERING

Requirements Remove spent flower stems, continue to water and feed until foliage starts to yellow and die down. Allow the bulbs to dry off in a cool place, repot in fresh compost and resume watering in fall to start them into growth.

HYACINTHOIDES
Bluebell

AN ALL-TIME FAVORITE, *clear sky-blue bluebells don't need a lot of attention to produce a beautiful display year after year.*

NATURALIZED UNDER TREES, *these Spanish bluebells revel in the moist soil formed from the decaying leaf litter.*

FEATURES

This is the ideal bulb for naturalizing under deciduous trees or for planting in large drifts in the yard. The delicately scented blue flowers are a great foil for many spring-flowering shrubs which have pink or white flowers: there is a white and a pink form but the blue is undoubtedly the most popular. The botanical names of these plants have undergone several changes in recent years, and they are sometimes listed under endymion and scilla as well as hyacinthoides. The Spanish bluebell (*H. hispanica*) is a little larger, up to 12in high, and more upright in growth than the English bluebell (*H. non-scripta*). Bluebells multiply rapidly and can be very invasive. They can also be grown in containers.

HYACINTHOIDES AT A GLANCE

Well-known and loved blue flowers in mid to late spring, ideal for naturalizing under deciduous trees.

		Recommended Varieties
Jan	/	
Feb	/	*Hyacinthoides hispanica:*
Mar	/	
Apr	flowering	"Danube"
May	flowering	"Queen of the Pinks"
Jun	/	"White City"
July	/	
Aug	plant	*Hyacinthoides non-scripta:*
Sept	plant	"Pink Form"
Oct	plant	"White Form"
Nov	/	
Dec	/	

CONDITIONS

Aspect   These woodland plants prefer dappled sunlight or places where they receive some morning sun with shade later in the day.

Site   Perfect when naturalized under deciduous trees; bluebells also grow well in borders but don't let them smother delicate plants. A moisture-retentive soil with plenty of organic matter suits them best.

GROWING METHOD

Planting   Plant bulbs 2in deep and about 3–4in apart in late summer or early fall. The white bulbs are fleshy and brittle; take care not to damage them when planting.

Feeding   Not usually required.

Problems   No specific problems are usually experienced.

FLOWERING

Season   Flowers from middle to late spring, with a long display in cool seasons. Flowers do not last as well if sudden high spring temperatures are experienced.

Cutting   Not suitable for cutting.

AFTER FLOWERING

Requirements   Remove spent flower stems unless you require plants to seed themselves. Keep the soil moist until the foliage dies down. The bulbs are best left undisturbed, but overcrowded clumps can be lifted and divided in late summer and replanted immediately.

HYACINTHUS ORIENTALIS
Hyacinth

WELL-ROUNDED FLOWER SPIKES are characteristic of the fine hyacinth cultivars available today. They make excellent pot plants.

HYACINTHS, with cool white flowers and dark green foliage, combine with a silvery groundcover to make a pretty garden picture.

FEATURES

Sweet-scented hyacinths are favorites in the garden or as potted plants. In the garden they look their best mass-planted in blocks of one color. They are widely grown commercially both for cut flowers and as potted flowering plants. Flower stems may be from 6–12in high and the color range includes various shades of blue, pink, and rose, and white, cream and yellow. Individual flowers are densely crowded onto the stem, making a solid-looking flowerhead. Bulbs usually flower best in their first year, the second and subsequent years producing fewer, looser blooms. Some people with sensitive skin can get a reaction from handling hyacinth bulbs, so wear gloves if you think you may be affected.

Types
The most popular hyacinths are the so-called Dutch hybrids; many varieties are available from garden centers and mail order bulb suppliers. Blues range from deep violet to pale china blue: the rose range includes deep rosy red, salmon, and light pink. As well as white varieties, there are those with cream and clear yellow flowers. Some varieties have flowers with a lighter eye or a deeper colored stripe on the petals, giving a two-tone effect.
Roman hyacinths—*H. orientalis albulus*—have smaller flowers loosely arranged on the stems: Multiflora varieties have been treated so that they produce several loosely packed flower spikes from each bulb, and have a delicate appearance that makes them ideal for growing in pots.
Cynthella hyacinths are miniatures growing to about 6in, usually sold in color mixtures.

CONDITIONS

Aspect
Does well in sun or partial shade but does not like heavy shade.

Site
Grow hyacinths in pots and bowls indoors; pots and tubs outside and in flower borders. Soil must be well-drained.

GROWING METHOD

Planting
Plant bulbs 6in deep and 8in apart in early to mid-fall. Apply compost or rotted manure as a mulch after planting.

Feeding
Apply a balanced general fertiliser after flowering. Watering is not usually necessary in beds and borders, but bulbs in containers must be kept just moist during the growing season.

Problems
Hyacinths are not generally susceptible to pest and disease problems, though bulbs will rot if soil conditions are too wet. Forced bulbs indoors often fail to flower if they have not had the correct cold, dark period after planting.

FLOWERING

Season
Flowers appear from late winter to mid-spring. "Prepared" bulbs should be used for Christmas flowering, and must be planted in September.

Cutting
Blooms may be cut for the vase where they will last about a week if the water is changed daily.

AFTER FLOWERING

Requirements Remove spent flower stems and continue to water and feed the plants until the foliage starts to yellow and die down.

BLUE AND WHITE are always an effective combination, a proposition amply demonstrated by this formal garden in which deep violet-blue hyacinths stud a bed of white pansies. Although they are often grown in pots, hyacinths are at their most beautiful in a setting such as this.

POTTED HYACINTHS

Features
Potted hyacinths in bloom make a lovely cut flower substitute and are ideal as gifts. They can be grown to flower in midwinter when their color and fragrance are most welcome.

Outdoors
If growing hyacinths outdoors choose a container at least 6in deep so that you can place a layer of potting compost in the base of the pot before planting. Bury the bulbs 4in below the surface of the compost. Water to moisten the compost thoroughly after planting and place the pot where it will receive sun for at least half a day. Don't water again until the compost is feeling dry or until the shoots appear. When the flower buds are showing color, move the pots indoors. When blooms have faded, cut off spent stems and water as needed until the foliage dies down.

Indoors
If growing hyacinths indoors, choose a container 4–6in deep but plant the bulbs just below the surface of the compost. (In pots without drainage holes, bulb fiber can be used intead of compost.) Water after planting, allow to drain and then transfer the pot to a cool, dark position. The pots can be placed inside a black plastic bag and put into a shed, cold frame or similar place with a temperature of about 40°F. Check from time to time to see if shoots have emerged. When shoots emerge (this usually takes about 10–12 weeks) and reach 1–2in in height, bring the pot into the light, gradually increasing the amount of light as the shoots green up. As buds appear, give them as much sunlight as possible.

In glass
Hyacinths can also be grown in a glass or ceramic container that has a narrow neck. Sometimes you can buy a purpose-built container, usually plastic, that has the top cut into segments so that the bulb sits neatly on it. Fill the container with water to just below the rim. Choose a good-sized bulb, then rest it on top of the rim of the container so that the base of the bulb is in water. Place the container in a cool, dark place and leave it there until large numbers of roots have formed and the flower bud is starting to emerge, when they can be brought into the light. These bulbs are unlikely to regrow and may be discarded after flowering.

HYACINTIIUS AT A GLANCE

Sweetly scented, densely packed flower spikes, ideal for growing indoors or outside. Frost hardy.

		Recommended Varieties
Jan	flowering	
Feb	flowering	"Amsterdam"
Mar	flowering	"Anna Marie"
Apr	flowering	"Blue Giant"
May	/	"City of Haarlem"
Jun	/	"Delft Blue"
July	/	"Gipsy Queen"
Aug	/	"Jan Bos"
Sept	plant	"L'Innocence"
Oct	plant	"Lord Balfour"
Nov	/	"Mont Blanc"
Dec	flowering	"Queen of the Pinks"

HYACINTHUS ORIENTALIS

1.

2.

4.

5.

HYACINTH
(HYACINTHUS ORIENTALIS)

The dense clusters of flowers on hyacinth spikes come in a wonderful range of clear colors.

1. "L'Innocence" is a pure white hyacinth first raised in 1863 and still very popular today.

2. Pale rose-pink "Lady Derby" blooms reliably in the garden or in containers.

3. The subtle stripes on the petals of the violet-blue "Ostara" make this a very attractive hyacinth.

4. "Amsterdam" is an unusually deep pink color. For a real crimson hyacinth select "Jan Bos."

5. Clear primrose yellow "City of Haarlem" breaks away from the traditional pink or blue.

6. This soft mauve-blue hyacinth is still pretty as the flower fades.

3.

6.

HYMENOCALLIS
Spider lily, Peruvian daffodil

THE WHITE or cream flowers of spider lilies are something like an exotic daffodil, with an attractive fragrance.

HYMENOCALLIS CAN be grown outside in reasonably sheltered yards, but the bulbs should be lifted in fall to ensure survival.

FEATURES

Spider lilies are native to various parts of North and South America. They produce broad, strap-shaped, deep green leaves and fascinating, lightly fragrant flowers that are carried on a stout stem. The flower has a trumpet-shaped central cup with long, narrow, petal-like segments surrounding it; flowers are usually white but can be yellow or cream. Hymenocallis can be grown in a sheltered, sunny position outside, but is often treated as a greenhouse or conservatory plant. All spider lilies can be container grown. *H.* x *festalis, H. narcissiflora* and the cultivar "Sulfur Queen" are the deciduous varieties most often grown, while the more difficult to find *H. littoralis* and *H. speciosa* are the most popular of the evergreen species. Hymenocallis is sometimes also listed as ismene.

HYMENOCALLIS AT A GLANCE

A rather tender bulb bearing unusual fragrant blooms like exotic daffodils. Can also be grown as a conservatory plant.

Jan	/	
Feb	/	**Recommended Varieties**
Mar	plant (indoors) 🖉	"Advance"
Apr	/	"Sulfur Queen"
May	🖉(outdoors)/flowering 🌿	
Jun	flowering 🌿	*Hymenocallis* x *festalis:*
July	/	"Zwanenburg"
Aug	flowering 🌿	
Sept	/	
Oct	/	
Nov	/	
Dec	/	

CONDITIONS

Aspect	Grows in full sun or light shade with shelter from strong wind.
Site	In sheltered yards hymenocallis can be grown outside in beds and borders or containers. In cold areas, it is best grown as a greenhouse or conservatory plant. Soil must be free-draining. Use soiless potting compost for pots.

GROWING METHOD

Planting	For growing in containers, plant bulbs in spring with the neck of the bulb just below the soil surface, using one of the large bulbs per 6in pot. Outdoors, plant in May, burying the bulbs 5in deep.
Feeding	High potash liquid fertiliser can be applied as buds form. Mulching around plants with well-rotted organic matter also supplies nutrients. Water sparingly until the shoots show, then water regularly through the growing season.
Problems	No specific problems are usually experienced.

FLOWERING

Season	The fragrant spider lilies are produced in early summer indoors, mid to late summer outside.
Cutting	Makes a delightful and unusual cut flower.

AFTER FLOWERING

Requirements	Allow the foliage to die down after flowering; lift outdoor bulbs and store in dry peat in a frost-free place over winter. Leave potted plants dry in their containers over winter and repot the following spring.

IPHEION UNIFLORUM
Spring star flower

SPRING STAR FLOWER is an ideal edging plant for a sunny yard and it can be left undisturbed for several years.

THE SOFT LILAC of the flowers makes spring star flower very versatile as it blends into most garden color schemes.

FEATURES

This low-growing plant makes an ideal edging but should be planted in large drifts wherever it is grown to produce its best effect. Tolerant of rather tough growing conditions, it is most suitable for filling pockets in a rockery or growing toward the front of a herbaceous border. It also makes a good container plant. It has grey-green, narrow, strappy leaves that smell strongly of onions when crushed; the pale blue, starry, lightly scented flowers are carried on stems 6in or so high.

There are several varieties available with flowers ranging in color from white to deep violet-blue.

IPHEION AT A GLANCE

A low-growing bulb with a profusion of starry blue or white flowers in spring.

Jan	/	Recommended Varieties
Feb	/	"Album"
Mar	flowering 🌱	"Alberto Castello"
Apr	flowering 🌱	"Froyle Mill"
May	flowering 🌱	"Rolf Fiedler"
Jun	/	"Wisley Blue"
July	/	
Aug	/	
Sept	plant ✍	
Oct	plant ✍	
Nov	/	
Dec	/	

CONDITIONS

Aspect   Grows best in full sun but tolerates light shade for part of the day.

Site   Good for a rockery, border, or container. Ipheion needs well-drained soil. It will grow on quite poor soils but growth will be better on soils enriched with organic matter.

GROWING METHOD

Planting   Plant bulbs 2in deep and the same distance apart in fall.

Feeding   Apply some balanced fertiliser after flowers have finished. Water regularly during dry spells while plants are in leaf and bloom.

Problems   No specific problems are usually experienced with this bulb.

FLOWERING

Season   The starry flowers appear from early spring to mid-spring.

Cutting   Flowers are too short to cut for all but a miniature vase but they may last a few days in water.

AFTER FLOWERING

Requirements   Shear off spent flower stems and remove the old foliage when it has died down. If clumps become overcrowded and fail to flower well, they can be lifted in fall, divided, and replanted immediately.

IRIS—BULBOUS TYPES
Irises

THE LOW-GROWING *flowers of* Iris danfordiae *appear very early in the year—usually February or March.*

SEVERAL DIFFERENT *cultivars of* Iris reticulata *are available, in varying shades of blue with yellow markings.*

FEATURES

There are many species of these irises, which have true bulbs as storage organs, unlike the creeping rhizomes of their larger cousins. The leaves are not arranged in the typical fan of sword shapes like rhizomatous irises, but are usually narrow and lance shaped, or rolled. The flowers have the typical iris form with six petals, three inner ones (standards), and three outer ones (falls). The falls are often brightly marked or veined. Many species and varieties are blue with yellow markings on the falls; some types are yellow with brown or green speckling on the falls and others are white with yellow markings. The blue varieties come in many shades, from deep violet and purple through to pale China blue.

Many bulbous irises are early-flowering dwarf forms suitable for growing on rockeries or at the front of beds: they are also excellent for shallow pots ("pans") in the greenhouse or alpine house. Other types are taller and flower in summer; they are valuable for herbaceous and mixed borders, and are particularly good for cutting for flower arrangements. There are also some spring-flowering irises that are far less commonly grown than the other groups.

POPULAR SPECIES

Bulbous irises can be split into three main groups: Reticulata irises, Xiphium irises and Juno irises.

Reticulata   These irises have bulbs with a netted tunic around them which gives them their group name. They are dwarf, growing to about 6in high, and the flowers appear early in the year, usually in February and March. *I. danfordiae* has lightly fragrant flowers whose yellow petals are speckled with greenish brown. *I. reticulata* also has fragrant flowers: the petals are thinner than those of *I. danfordiae* and are blue or purple with yellow markings. Several different cultivars are available. The flowers of *I. histriodes* and its cultivars are larger and have short stems; they are deep to light blue, with dark blue, white, and yellow markings. The flowers open before the leaves reach their full height.

Xiphium   This group of summer-flowering irises is popular and easily grown. It consists of Dutch irises, flowering in early summer, in white, yellow, or blue with contrasting markings; English irises, flowering in early to mid-summer in shades of white, blue, or purple; and Spanish irises, flowering in midsummer in various shades of white, blue, purple, and yellow.

Juno   The Juno irises are not as well-known as the other bulbous types, probably because they are more difficult to grow well. The group includes *I. bucharica*, bearing yellow or white flowers with yellow falls, and *I. graeberiana*, which has lavender flowers with a white crest on the falls. These two are among the easiest Juno irises to grow: others include *I. fosteriana*, *I. magnifica,* and *I. rosenbachiana*, which do best in an alpine house.

WHEN EXAMINED closely, the lightly fragrant flowers of Iris dantordiae *can be seen to have attractive freckling in the throat.*

"KATHERINE HODGKIN," a cultivar of Iris histrioides, *is perhaps the most sought-after of all the dwarf irises.*

CONDITIONS

Aspect
Site All bulbous irises like open, sunny, positions. Reticulatas are good for rock gardens, raised beds, or containers: Xiphiums and Junos for sunny, sheltered borders. Soil needs to be well-drained; Juno irises require a soil containing plenty of well-rotted organic matter.

GROWING METHOD

Planting Plant Reticulatas 3in deep and 4in apart. Xiphiums are planted 4-6in deep and 6in apart, and Juno irises are planted 2in deep and 8in apart, taking care not to damage the brittle, fleshy roots. They are all planted in fall, in September or October.

Feeding Supplementary feeding is not usually necessary.

Problems Bulbs may rot in overwet soil. Bulbous irises in warmer areas of the country may be affected by iris ink disease, causing black streaks on the bulb and yellow blotches on the leaves. Destroy affected bulbs.

FLOWERING

Season Reticulata irises flower in February and March, Junos in April and May, and Xiphiums in June and July.

Cutting The Xiphiums make excellent, long-lasting cut flowers.

AFTER FLOWERING

Requirements Remove faded flowers. Most bulbous irises are best left undisturbed for as long as possible; they can be increased by lifting and dividing the bulbs after flowering when necessary. Juno irises should not be divided until the foliage has died down, and must be handled very carefully. Spanish irises of the Xiphium group benefit from being lifted when the foliage has died down and replanted in September; this helps the bulbs to ripen.

BULBOUS IRIS AT A GLANCE

A varied group of plants with colorful flowers in early spring or in summer. Good for a range of situations.

Month		Recommended Varieties
Jan	flowering	**Reticulata group:**
Feb	flowering	*I. danfordiae*
Mar	flowering	*I. reticulata* "Katharine Hodgkin"
Apr	flowering	*I. histrioides* "Major"
May	flowering	
Jun	flowering	**Xiphium group:**
July	flowering	"Bronze Queen"
Aug	/	"Excelsior"
Sept	plant	"Ideal"
Oct	plant	**Juno group:**
Nov	/	*I. bucharica*
Dec	/	*I. graeberiana*

IRIS—RHIZOMATOUS TYPES
Iris

IRIS WAS THE Greek god of the the rainbow, and this plant is aptly named as there are irises in every color of the spectrum.

WATER IRIS (Iris pseudoacorus) is a tall grower that needs to be planted in water or permanently wet soil.

FEATURES

Irises comprise a very large plant group of more than 200 species. Some grow from bulbs (see the previous two pages): those covered here grow from rhizomes. They have stiff, sword-shaped leaves and carry their colorful flowers on tall, stiff stems in spring and early summer. Iris flowers have six petals; three inner, vertical ones, (standards), and three outer ones, which curve outward (falls). The color range is very varied, covering blue, purple, lavender, yellow, rose, and white; many of the flowers are bicolored, and attractively marked. Rhizomatous irises contain several different groups, the most popular of which are bearded, Japanese and Siberian irises. **Bearded irises** have large, very showy flowers with a short, bristly "beard" on the falls; dwarf cultivars are also available. **Japanese irises** have unusual flat-faced flowers, and **Siberian irises** have delicate flowers with finer petals.

CONDITIONS

Aspect	Rhizomatous irises like a position in full sun, but with protection from strong winds.
Site	Excellent plants for the middle to back of a mixed or herbaceous border. Bearded irises like a slightly alkaline, well-drained soil: Japanese and Siberian irises need moisture-retentive, humus-rich loam.

GROWING METHOD

Planting	Usually sold as container-grown plants in growth. Plant shallowly, with the rhizome barely covered, in late summer.
Feeding	Supplementary feeding is rarely necessary. Ensure moisture-loving types are never allowed to dry out during the growing season.
Problems	Slugs and snails can be troublesome. Use covered slug bait where necessary, or hand pick the pests after dark.

FLOWERING

Season	Flowers are carried in early summer.
Cutting	Make beautiful cut flowers.

AFTER FLOWERING

Requirements	Cut off spent flower stems. Every few years, lift the rhizomes after flowering, cut them into sections each containing a strong, healthy fan of leaves, and replant, discarding the old, woody, worn out portions of rhizome.

RHIZOMATOUS IRIS AT A GLANCE

Stately border plants with fans of sword-shaped leaves and tall, attractively marked flowers in summer.

Jan	/
Feb	/
Mar	/
Apr	/
May	flowering
Jun	flowering
July	flowering
Aug	/
Sept	plant
Oct	/
Nov	/
Dec	/

Recommended Varieties

Bearded irises:
 "Black Swan"
 "Rocket"
 "White City"

Siberian irises:
 "Sparkling Rose"
 "Caesar"
 "Perry's Blue"

Japanese irises:
 "Rose Queen"
 "Moonlight Waves"

IRIS UNGUICULARIS
Winter iris, Algerian iris

THE FULL BEAUTY of this iris can be seen in close up. Many iris have fine veining or feathering on their petals.

A LARGE PATCH of Algerian iris gives a great lift to the garden in winter. Even if flowers come singly their appearance is still a joy.

FEATURES

This beardless, rhizomatous iris is different to all others in its group because it flowers throughout the winter. The beautiful little fragrant flowers rarely exceed 8in in height and may be hidden by the stiff, grassy foliage. They are ideal for cutting and taking indoors, where their sweet scent may be almost overpowering at times.

The flowers of the species are deep lavender with creamy yellow centers deeply veined in violet. There are some cultivars available, including a white form, one or two varieties in particularly deep shades of blue, one in a pale silvery lilac, and a dwarf form. A large single clump of this iris is effective but in the right position it could be mass-planted to good effect.

I. UNGUICULARIS AT A GLANCE

A low-growing iris valuable for its sweetly scented flowers which appear throughout the winter.

Jan	flowering
Feb	flowering
Mar	plant
Apr	/
May	/
Jun	/
July	/
Aug	/
Sept	/
Oct	/
Nov	flowering
Dec	flowering

Recommended Varieties

"Abington Purple"
"Alba"
"Bob Thompson"
"Mary Barnard"
"Oxford Dwarf"
"Walter Butt"

CONDITIONS

Aspect   Needs a reasonably sheltered position because of its flowering time. The rhizomes must be exposed to a summer baking if plants are to flower well, so a position in full sun is essential.

Site   Grow in beds or borders where it will be able to spread—plants can be invasive. Soil must be well-drained. If it is very poor, dig in quantities of well-decayed manure or compost ahead of planting time.

GROWING METHOD

Planting   Plant rhizomes in spring with the top at or just below soil level. Container-grown plants in growth can also be bought and planted virtually year-round in suitable weather.

Feeding   Supplementary feeding is generally unnecessary. Water the plants in spring and fall if conditions are dry, but do not water in summer.

Problems   Slugs and snails will often attack the flowers. Use slug pellets if necessary.

FLOWERING

Season   Flowers are produced any time from late fall through winter.

Cutting   The flowers make a lovely indoor decoration.

AFTER FLOWERING

Requirements   Cut off spent flowers and tidy up foliage when necessary. Little other attention is required. Crowded plants can be divided in spring.

IXIA
Corn lily

EACH TALL SPIKE of corn lily produces dozens of flowers. These are still producing blooms despite the many fading and falling ones.

PALEST TURQUOISE FLOWERS make this lovely corn lily (Ixia viridiflora) a favorite although its corms are not always easy to buy.

FEATURES

This plant produces starry flowers in a stunning range of colors including white, cream, yellow, orange, red, cerise, and magenta. Hybrid varieties are the most popular, but the sought-after *I. viridiflora* has duck-egg blue flowers with a dark center. The narrow, grass-like foliage may be 12–20in high while the wiry-stemmed flower spikes stand clear of the leaves. Corn lilies are a great addition to the garden. Being quite tall they should be planted toward the back of a bed or among other bulbs and perennials. Although colors can be mixed, a better effect is obtained by planting blocks of one color.

IXIA AT A GLANCE

A rather tender plant with masses of colorful, starry flowers on slender stems.

		Recommended Varieties
Jan	/	
Feb	/	"Blue Bird"
Mar	plant 🖐	"Mabel"
Apr	plant 🖐	"Rose Emperor"
May	flowering 🌿	"Venus"
Jun	flowering 🌿	
July	flowering 🌿	
Aug	/	
Sept	/	
Oct	plant (indoors) 🖐	
Nov	/	
Dec	/	

CONDITIONS

Aspect Prefers full sun all day but with shelter from strong wind.
Site A good border plant in reasonably mild districts. In colder areas it can be grown in containers on a sheltered patio or in a conservatory. Needs well-drained soil.

GROWING METHOD

Planting Plant corms in the open garden in spring, about 2in deep and 3–4in apart. Plant in pots for the conservatory in fall.
Fertilising Apply balanced liquid fertiliser in early spring to increase the size of the blooms. In dry conditions, water if necessary in spring when the shoots are growing strong.
Problems No specific pest or disease problems are usually experienced, though corms may rot in overwet soil.

FLOWERING

Season Flowers from late spring to mid-summer.
Cutting Flowers can be cut for the vase but will probably give better value in the garden.

AFTER FLOWERING

Requirements In all but the mildest gardens, lift the corms when the foliage has died down and store them in a dry place for replanting in spring.

LACHENALIA ALOIDES
Cape cowslip

STIFF FLOWER SPIKES of yellow and red tubular bells are the feature of Lachenalia aloides.

CAPE COWSLIPS need a cool room to grow well. In the right conditions they make excellent winter-flowering house plants.

FEATURES

Also known as "soldier boys" because of their upright, neat and orderly habit, this bulb is grown as a house plant to produce its colorful bell-like flowers in midwinter. The rather stiff leaves grow to about 6in high and are dark green, often spotted with purple. The 8–12in spikes of 20 or so tubular flowers stand well above the foliage and remain colorful for several weeks. Individual blooms are yellow or orange-red, marked with red, green, or purple; they are often a deeper color in bud, becoming paler as the flowers open. There are several different varieties with subtly varying shades to the flowers.

LACHENALIA AT A GLANCE

A tender bulb grown as a house or greenhouse plant for its spikes of yellow or orange tubular flowers in winter.

		Recommended Varieties
Jan	flowering	**Recommended Varieties**
Feb	flowering	
Mar	flowering	*Lachenalia aloides:*
Apr	/	"Aurea"
May	/	"Lutea"
Jun	/	"Nelsonii"
July	/	"Quadricolor"
Aug	plant	
Sept	plant	*Lachenalia bulbifera:*
Oct	/	"George"
Nov	/	
Dec	/	

CONDITIONS

Aspect	Needs a very brightly lit spot; will stand direct sun for part of the day.
Site	Grow on a bright windowsill in a cool room, or in a cool greenhouse or conservatory. Lachenalia does not like dry heat.

GROWING METHOD

Planting	Plant bulbs in late summer or early fall, growing six to a 5in pot. Set them just below the surface of the compost.
Feeding	Apply high potash liquid fertiliser every 14 days or so from when the buds appear. Water regularly while plants are in flower.
Problems	Overwatering or poorly drained compost will cause the bulbs to rot.

FLOWERING

Season	Flowers appear between midwinter and early spring.
Cutting	Not suitable for cutting.

AFTER FLOWERING

Requirements	Cut off spent lachenalia flower stems. Continue to water until early summer, then gradually stop watering and allow the pot to dry out until the following fall, when the bulbs can be shaken out and repotted in fresh compost.

LEUCOJUM
Snowflake

THE WHITE BELLS with their fresh green dots at the end of each petal make Leucojum vernum *particularly evocative of spring.*

PREFERING SHADE and moist soil, spring snowflake is one of the easiest bulbs to grow. This plant is typical of an established clump.

FEATURES

Easily grown snowflakes have clusters of white, bell-shaped flowers, each petal bearing a bright green spot on its tip. Foliage is a rich, deep green and bulbs multiply readily to form good sized clumps in a few years.

There are three types of snowflake; spring snowflake (*Leucojum vernum*), summer snowflake (*L. aestivum*), and fall snowflake (*L. autumnale*). The spring snowflake flowers in February or March, while the summer snowflake, despite its name, usually flowers in late spring. Spring snowflake reaches a height of about 8in; summer snowflake up to 24in, and fall snowflake 6in, with very fine, narrow foliage. The flowers have a passing resemblance to snowdrops, but are easily distinguished by their rounded, bell shape and taller growth.

LEUCOJUM AT A GLANCE

Delicate looking plants with white bells tipped with green, appearing in spring or early fall. Hardy.

Month	Activity		Recommended Varieties
Jan	/		
Feb	flowering	🌱	*Leucojum aestivum:*
Mar	flowering	🌱	"Gravetye Giant"
Apr	flowering	🌱	
May	flowering	🌱	*Leucojum autumnale:*
Jun	/		"Cobb's Variety"
July	/		"Pulchellum"
Aug	/		
Sept	plant 🖐 / flower 🌱		*Leucojum vernum:*
Oct	plant 🖐		"Carpathicum"
Nov	/		"Vagneri"
Dec	/		

CONDITIONS

Aspect Grows well in sun but also happy in shade or in dappled sunlight. Fall snowflakes prefer an open, sunny position.

Site Low-growing species are excellent for rock gardens or the front of borders; taller summer snowflakes toward the middle of a border. Spring and summer snowflakes prefer a moisture-retentive soil enriched with organic matter: fall snowflake needs light, free-draining soil.

GROWING METHOD

Planting Plant bulbs 3in deep and 4–8in apart in late summer or early fall.

Feeding An annual mulching with decayed manure or compost after bulbs have died down should provide adequate nutrients. Keep the soil for spring and summer snowflakes moist throughout the growing season.

Problems No specific problems are known.

FLOWERING

Season Spring snowflake flowers between midwinter and early spring; summer snowflake mid to late spring; and fall snowflake in September.

Cutting Best enjoyed in the garden.

AFTER FLOWERING

Requirements Remove spent flower stems. Divide crowded clumps when the foliage dies down, and replant immediately.

LILIUM
Lily

THIS BURNED ORANGE HYBRID shows the characteristic dark spotting in its throat. Lilies make excellent cut flowers.

WHITE LILIES are traditionally symbols of purity. Lilium regale is one of the most popular species, and its flowers are very strongly scented.

FEATURES

Lilies are tall, stately plants that carry a number of large, trumpet-shaped blooms on each flowering stem. Flowering stems may be anywhere from about 2ft to over 6ft high. There are 80–90 species of lily and many hundreds of cultivars, so it is difficult to outline their requirements concisely. Lily flowers are often fragrant and the main color range includes white, yellow, pink, red, and orange—many have spotted or streaked petals. A quite small range of lily bulbs is usually available in garden centers in fall and these should be planted as soon as possible after their arrival: lily bulbs have no tunic or outer covering and so can dry out unless they are carefully handled. For a greater range of species and hybrids you will need to contact specialist growers and mail order suppliers. Many lily enthusiasts belong to societies devoted to learning more about the enormous range of types available and their cultivation.

Types Some of the more popular species grown are *L. auratum*, golden-rayed lily, which has white petals with gold bands; *L. candidum*, Madonna lily, which is pure white; *L. martagon*, Turk's cap lily, with fully recurved, dark red petals with dark spots; *L. regale,* the regal lily, with white flowers that have purple backs to the petals and a yellow base; *L. speciosum* which has white petals with a deep pink center and reddish spots; and *L. tigrinum*, tiger lily, dark orange with black spots and revurving petals. As well as the species, many hybrid varieties are grown, which are classified into a number of groups. Among the most popular are the Asiatic hybrids, short to medium height, with upward-facing flowers produced early in the season; and the Oriental hybrids, which are taller and more refined, with nodding, strongly scented blooms. Asiatic hybrids are ideal for pots and are available pot-grown throughout the summer.

CONDITIONS

Aspect The ideal situation is a sunny position with a little dappled shade during part of the day. They need protection from strong wind.

Site Lilies grow well when mixed with other plants that will shade their roots, in a bed or border, or in containers. Plant them where their perfume can be appreciated. Soil must be well-drained with a high organic content. Dig in copious amounts of well-rotted manure or compost a month or so before planting.

GROWING METHOD

Planting Plant 4–9in deep and 9–15in or so apart in fall or early spring. Bulbs must not be bruised or allowed to dry out, and they should be planted as soon as possible after purchase. Apply a layer of compost or manure to the soil surface as a mulch after planting. Your stock of lilies can be increased by bulb scales, bulbils or offsets, according to type: see page 11 for more details on propagation.

THE GOLDEN-RAYED lily of Japan, Lilium auratum, *carries its attractively speckled, reflexing flowers late in the summer.*

MASSES OF BLOOMS, with buds still to open, make this yellow lily a great asset for the summer garden.

Feeding   If the soil contains plenty of organic matter these plants should not need a lot of feeding. Apply a slow-release granular fertiliser as growth starts and after flowering. Water regularly during dry spells but avoid overwatering which may rot the bulbs.

Problems   Most problems with lilies result from poor cultivation or unsuitable growing conditions. Gray mold (botrytis) can be a problem in cool, humid conditions, especially if plants are overwatered or if air circulation is poor. The small, bright red lily beetle and their larvae can cause a lot of damage in some areas:

control them with a contact insecticide and clear away plant debris in which the adults overwinter.

FLOWERING

Season   Lilies flower some time between early summer and fall with many flowering in middle to late summer. Flowering time depends on the species and, to some extent, the conditions.

Cutting   Lilies make wonderful and very long-lasting cut flowers. Cut them when flowers are just open or all buds are rounded and fully colored. Don't cut right to the bottom of the stem— retain some leaves on the lower part. Change water frequently and cut off spent flowers from the cluster to allow the other buds to develop fully.

AFTER FLOWERING

Requirements   Remove spent flower stems as they finish blooming. Remove only the flowering stem and leave as much foliage as possible. Don't be in a hurry to cut back yellowing growth too soon: allow the plant to die back naturally and mulch with chipped bark for the winter. Bulbs are best left in the ground for several years. When they are lifted they must be divided and replanted at once, as having no tunic on the bulb means they dry out very quickly. If they can't be planted at once, store them in damp sphagnum moss or peat.

LILIUM AT A GLANCE

Stately plants with trumpet-shaped, usually intensely fragrant flowers on tall spikes.

		Recommended Varieties
Jan	/	
Feb	/	"Apollo"
Mar	/	"Barcelona"
Apr	/	"Casa Blanca"
May	/	"Corsage"
Jun	flowering	"Enchantment"
July	flowering	"Green Dragon"
Aug	flowering /plant	"Mrs R. O. Backhouse"
Sept	flowering /plant	"Orange Triumph"
Oct	plant	"Shuksan"
Nov	plant	"Tamara"
Dec	/	

MORAEA
Peacock iris, butterfly iris

IT IS EASY to see how this pretty bulb got its common name of peacock iris. Iridescent blue spots are sharply defined against the white petals.

THE FOLIAGE of peacock iris looks unpromising, as it is sparse and grass-like, but the "floating" flowers are worth waiting for.

FEATURES

Of the 120 species of *Moraea*, most come from South Africa with others native to tropical Africa and Madagascar. Few are in cultivation but it is worth seeking out this unusual plant from specialist bulb growers. All grow from corms and some, such as *M. spathulata*, grow only a single leaf, which may be 8–20in high. Flowers are like those of irises, with three showy outer petals and three smaller, rather insignificant inner ones. The commonest species is *M. spathulata*, with bright yellow, summer flowers on 2ft stems. *Moraea aristata* has white flowers with a large blue blotch at the base of the outer petals, while *M. villosa* bears flowers in a range of colors with a blue blotch on the petals. Plant peacock iris in groups for the best effect.

MORAEA AT A GLANCE

An uncommon bulb with iris-like flowers, often strikingly marked. Needs a warm, sunny position.

Month		Recommended Species
Jan	/	
Feb	/	*Moraea aristata*
Mar	/	*M. bellendenii*
Apr	plant 👆	*M. gawleri*
May	/	*M. spathulata*
Jun	flowering ❁	
July	flowering ❁	
Aug	flowering ❁	
Sept	/	
Oct	/	
Nov	/	
Dec	/	

CONDITIONS

Aspect   Moraea needs full sun all day.
Site   A warm, sunny, and sheltered position is necessary. This corm needs well-drained soil with plenty of decayed organic matter incorporated into it before planting. Moraea also makes an attractive plant for the conservatory or home when grown in containers. Use John Innes or soiless potting compost.

GROWING METHOD

Planting   Plant corms 2in deep and 8in apart in spring.
Feeding   Performance is improved by applying a balanced fertiliser as flower buds appear. Container-grown plants should be liquid-fed every three weeks or so through the growing season. Water in dry conditions, but take care not to make the soil too wet or the corms will be liable to rot.
Problems   No specific pest or disease problems are known for this plant.

FLOWERING

Season   Flowers throughout the summer.
Cutting   Not suitable for cutting.

AFTER FLOWERING

Requirements   Cut off spent flower stems unless you want to obtain seed from them. In fall, lift the corms and store them in a dry place over winter, ready for replanting the following spring.

MUSCARI
Grape hyacinth

THE FEATHERY *violet heads of* Muscari comosum *"Plumosum" make this showy variety quite different from other grape hyacinths.*

ROYAL BLUE *grape hyacinths here border a garden of daffodils and pop up from among the groundcover of snow-in-summer.*

FEATURES

Vigorous and easy to grow, grape hyacinths have blue flowers of varying intensity. There are several species and named varieties available, including the double "Blue Spike" and the feathery "Plumosum." *Muscari aucheri* (*M. tubergenianum*) is known as "Oxford and Cambridge" because it has pale blue flowers at the top of the spike and is dark blue at the base, reminiscent of the English universities' uniform colors. Grape hyacinths·are a great foil for other bright spring-flowering bulbs such as tulips or ranunculus. Flowers are lightly scented and are carried on a stem about 4–8in tall. This plant gives the most impact when planted in drifts: in large yards where there is space it can easily be naturalized in grass or under deciduous trees.

MUSCARI AT A GLANCE

Pretty, easy-to-grow, little bulbs with short spikes of intense blue bells in spring.

Jan	/	Recommended Varieties
Feb	/	
Mar	flowering	*Muscari armeniacum:*
Apr	flowering	"Blue Spike"
May	flowering	"Early Giant"
Jun	/	
July	/	*Muscari azureum:*
Aug	/	"Album"
Sept	plant	
Oct	plant	*Muscari comosum:*
Nov	/	"Plumosum"
Dec	/	

CONDITIONS

Aspect　Best in full sun or dappled sunlight such as is found under deciduous trees.

Site　Useful on rockeries, in the front of borders, and for naturalizing under trees, but the plants can be invasive. Muscari needs well-drained soil, preferably with plenty of organic matter incorporated before planting.

GROWING METHOD

Planting　Plant the bulbs about 3in deep and 4in apart in late summer or early fall.

Feeding　Supplementary feeding is not usually necessary, but a light sprinkling of general fertiliser after flowering helps to ensure good growth. Watering is not normally necessary unless the weather is exceptionally dry.

Problems　No specific problems are known.

FLOWERING

Season　Flowers appear in early to mid-spring.

Cutting　Although not often used as a cut flower, it lasts in water quite well if picked when half the flowers on the stem are open.

AFTER FLOWERING

Requirements　Remove spent flower stems if required. Bulbs can be divided every 3–4 years in fall, replanting immediately. The foliage appears in the winter, long before the flowers.

NARCISSUS
Daffodil and narcissus

MODERN HYBRID DAFFODILS come in a wide range of forms, including double-flowered varieties and varieties with split coronas.

SUNSHINE YELLOW, this group of smaller growing daffodil cultivars lights up the late winter garden.

FEATURES

Daffodils are probably the best known and most widely grown of all bulbs and to many they are the true indicator of spring. They look wonderful mass-planted in the garden or naturalized in grass, but they also make great pot plants and excellent cut flowers. The best-known color is yellow, but there are also flowers in shades of white, cream, orange, and pink. The trumpet, or cup, is often a different color to the petals and may be bicolored. There are many species and cultivars and the genus *Narcissus* has been divided into 12 different groups, depending on the form and size of the flowers. The height varies from 3–20in, depending on variety.

Trumpet	The trumpet (cup) is at least as long as the petals, and there is one flower per stem.
Large cupped	Cup is shorter than, but at least one-third of, the length of the petals. One flower per stem.
Small cupped	The cup is less than one-third of the length of the petals; flowers usually carried singly.
Double	Double or semi-double flowers carried single or in small groups. The whole flower may be double, or just the cup.
Triandrus	Two to six pendant flowers with reflexed petals per stem.
Cyclamineus	Slightly pendant flowers with long trumpets and strongly reflexed petals, usually one per stem.
Jonquilla	Several flowers per stem, with short cups. Sweetly scented.
Tazetta	Half hardy. Very fragrant flowers in clusters of 10 or more per stem. Early flowering.
Poeticus	Small red or orange cup and broad white petals, usually one or two per stem. Often strongly fragrant. Late flowering.
Wild	A varied group containing the species and natural varieties found in the wild.
Split cupped	The cup is split to varying degrees for at least one-third to half its length.
Miscellaneous	Hybrids that do not fit into any of the other divisions.

CONDITIONS

Aspect	These bulbs grow best in a sunny spot or under deciduous trees where they will receive sun in the early spring.
Site	Grow narcissi in beds and borders, on rockeries, or in containers for the patio or in the home. Soil must be well-drained, ideally with some well-rotted organic matter dug in a month or so before planting.

GROWING METHOD

Planting	Planting depth will vary greatly according to the size of the bulb. Plant so that the nose is covered to twice the height of the bulb, in September or October. Plant as early as possible for the best results.

1.

2.

5.

6.

7.

3.

4.

8.

9.

DAFFODILS

There are many daffodil cultivars with wonderful variety in form and color. Yellow is most common color but some have white or pinkish petals or cups.

1. "Flower Record" displays the characteristics of N. poeticus, which is in its breeding.

2. Bright, clear yellow "Meeting" is a fine example of modern double daffodils.

3. "E. E. Morbey," dating from the 1930s, has a particularly pretty center to its orange cup.

4. "Ice Follies" has white petals. The flared lemon cup fades as it ages.

5. Simplicity of form and white purity make "Mount Hood" a classic variety.

6. Reddish-orange inner petals on double-flowered "Tahiti" make it a very showy addition to the garden.

7. The yellow and white center of "White Lion" demonstrates another style of double daffodil.

8. Soft, pretty "Mrs Oscar Ronalds" has a long pink cup and white petals.

9. "King Alfred," raised about 1890, is possibly the most widely grown of all yellow daffodils.

THE ESSENCE OF SPRING BEAUTY is captured in this drift of mixed daffodils and delicate white blossom. As the planting has been kept to the edge of the lawn, the grass can be mown while still allowing the bulb foliage to die down naturally.

Feeding   Feed with a balanced fertiliser in early spring. Plants can be given a liquid feed after the flowers have faded. Watering may be necessary in very dry spells, particularly when flowering has finished.

Problems   Basal rot can occur in storage; destroy bulbs with any sign of softening or rot at planting time. Similar symptoms can be caused by stem eelworm; these bulbs should also be destroyed by burning. Narcissus fly lays eggs near the necks of the bulbs; these hatch into larvae that tunnel into the bulb and weaken or destroy it. Bulbs in light shade are less susceptible to attack. Pull soil up round the necks of the bulbs after flowering to discourage egg laying.

FLOWERING

Season   Depending on area and variety, flowers may be carried anywhere from midwinter to early summer. Bulbs indoors may be brought into flower for Christmas or earlier; specially treated bulbs are available to ensure early flowering.

Cutting   This excellent cut flower should last a week with frequent water changes, or with the use of proprietary cut flower additives. For longest vase life pick daffodils when the buds are about to burst open or as soon as they are fully open. Cut, don't pull, the stems as low as possible. Cut off any white section at the base of the stem. Don't mix daffodils with other flowers until they have spent a day in a vase on their own as their slimy sap may reduce the vase life of other blooms.

AFTER FLOWERING

Requirements   Spent flowers should be removed before they set seed. Allow foliage to die down naturally; do not tie the leaves in clumps. Where bulbs are naturalized in grass, do not mow the grass until at least six weeks after the flowers have faded. Premature removal of leaves will have a detrimental effect on growth and flowering the following season.

If drainage is good, bulbs may be left in the ground and clumps can be divided after flowering every three years or so. Bulbs grown indoors in pots can be planted out in the yard after flowering, where they should recover in a season or two.

NARCISSUS AT A GLANCE

Well-known spring-flowering bulbs in a wide variety of flower forms and sizes. Most types are very hardy.

Month	Activity		Recommended Varieties
Jan	flowering		
Feb	flowering		"Carlton"
Mar	flowering		"Cheerfulness"
Apr	flowering		"February Gold"
May	flowering		"Irene Copeland"
Jun	/		"King Alfred"
July	/		"Minnow"
Aug	plant		"Peeping Tom"
Sept	plant		"Pipit"
Oct	plant		"Thalia"
Nov	/		*N. bulbocodium*
Dec	/		*N. canaliculatus*

NERINE
Nerine, Guernsey lily

THE GUERNSEY LILY, Nerine sarniensis, *needs to be grown in a conservatory or greenhouse except in very mild areas.*

TALL AND ELEGANT, these bright pink nerines appear as the summer garden fades away in fall.

FEATURES

Nerine bowdenii brightens the fall garden, producing its heads of bright pink flowers before the leaves appear. It is easy to grow and flowers last well when cut. Bulbs should be planted where they can be left undisturbed for several years; they flower best when crowded and after a dry summer. They can also be grown in containers. Flower stems grow 12–18in high and the deep green, strappy leaves from 8–12in long.

The Guernsey lily (*N. sarniensis*) has bright red flowers, and other species and cultivars of nerines may be red, white, pink, or apricot, but only *N. bowdenii* is hardy enough to grow outdoors in this country.

NERINE AT A GLANCE

Heads of funnel-shaped pink flowers appear on leafless stalks in autumn. Needs a warm, sheltered position.

Jan	/		Recommended Varieties
Feb	sow 🖐		*Nerine bowdenii alba*
Mar	sow 🖐		*Nerine bowdenii:*
Apr	plant 🖐		"Mark Fenwick"
May	/		"Pink Triumph"
Jun	/		"Wellsii"
July	/		
Aug	plant 🖐		*N.* "Corusca Major"
Sept	flowering 🌿		*N.* "Fothergillii Major"
Oct	flowering 🌿		*N. undulata*
Nov	flowering 🌿		
Dec	/		

CONDITIONS

Aspect   Nerines require full sun and a warm, sheltered spot.

Site   A useful plant for borders, especially under the shelter of a south-facing wall. The soil should be free-draining and moderately fertile. In cold areas and with the more tender species, grow bulbs in pots of John Innes potting compost.

GROWING METHOD

Planting   Plant in middle to late summer or in mid-spring, 4in deep and 6in apart. In containers, plant with the neck of the bulb at or just below soil level.

Feeding   Can be grown successfully without supplementary fertiliser. However, if you wish, you can give weak liquid fertiliser every couple of weeks when flower buds appear until growth slows down. Water regularly while in active growth but keep the bulbs dry during the dormant period.

Problems   No specific problems are known.

FLOWERING

Season   Flowers appear during early fall.

Cutting   Nerines last well as cut flowers with frequent water changes.

AFTER FLOWERING

Requirements Cut off spent flower stems. Outdoors, mulch the planting site for winter protection.

POLIANTHES TUBEROSA
Tuberose

"THE PEARL," a double-flowered cultivar, is the variety most often available to home gardeners.

PINK-TINGED BUDS open to the heavy-textured cream flowers, so prized for their characteristic strong perfume.

FEATURES

Tuberose is known for its heavily perfumed flowers—tuberose oil is used in perfume production. A double form known as "The Pearl" is the most widely grown. It can be grown in a sunny, sheltered border, but is often more reliable when grown as a conservatory or house plant, especially in cooler areas. The scent can more easily be appreciated under cover.

A flower spike 2ft or more high appears from the basal leaves in summer and early fall. The waxy flowers have a heavy texture and are white with a pinkish tinge at the base. Tubers that have bloomed once will not reflower the following season—new tubers must be planted each year.

POLIANTHES AT A GLANCE

Valued for its intensely fragrant, creamy white flowers that are carried on tall spikes in late summer.

Jan	/	
Feb	/	
Mar	plant ☝	**Recommended Varieties**
Apr	/	*Polianthes tuberosa:*
May	/	"The Pearl"
Jun	/	
July	/	
Aug	flowering 🌿	
Sept	flowering 🌿	
Oct	flowering 🌿	
Nov	/	
Dec	/	

CONDITIONS

Aspect Prefers full sun and shelter from strong wind.
Site Grow in a warm, sheltered border, or in containers for the conservatory, house, or greenhouse. Use either John Innes or soiless potting compost.

GROWING METHOD

Planting Plant 2in deep, or 1in deep in containers.
Feeding When growth appears, liquid feed with a balanced fertiliser every 14 days through the growing season. Water sparingly to start with, but keep the plant moist at all times when in growth.
Problems No particular problems are known.

FLOWERING

Season Flowers should appear during late summer or in early fall.
Cutting Makes an excellent cut flower. Cut spikes for the vase when two or three of the lower blooms are fully open. Removing spent flowers from the spike as they fade will help to prolong the vase life.

AFTER FLOWERING

Requirements Tubers are usually discarded at the end of the season. Offsets are produced, and these may sometimes be grown on to flower in two years or so, but they are often disappointing.

RANUNCULUS ASIATICUS
Ranunculus, Persian buttercup

TAFFETA-LIKE PETALS are ruffled and folded closely together around the dark eye of this vibrant scarlet ranunculus.

RANUNCULUS FLOWERS last well in a sheltered, sunny yard and close planting will produce a wonderfully colorful display.

FEATURES

One of the brightest and most colorful of all spring-flowering bulbs, ranunculus can be massed in mixed colors or blocks of single color in the yard or in containers. Left in the ground they may give several seasons, although they are often treated as annuals. However, the woody, oddly shaped tubers can be lifted and stored like other bulbs.

The many-petalled flowers of ranunculus come in bright yellow, cream, white, reds, and pinks, and stems of some strains may reach 18in in height. Although there are single flowered varieties, double or semi-double types are by far the most popular. They are usually sold as color mixtures, but separate red and yellow forms are sometimes available from specialist suppliers.

Ranunculus blooms make very good cut flowers, lasting well in the vase.

RANUNCULUS AT A GLANCE

Brightly colored, many-petalled, poppy-like flowers are carried above attractive ferny foliage in summer.

Jan	/	
Feb	/	**Recommended Varieties**
Mar	planting 🖐	"Red form"
Apr	planting 🖐	"Yellow form"
May	/	"Accolade"
Jun	flowering 🌺	
July	flowering 🌺	
Aug	flowering 🌺	
Sept	/	
Oct	/	
Nov	/	
Dec	/	

CONDITIONS

Aspect	Prefers full sun all day with shelter from very strong wind.
Site	Ideal for beds, borders, and containers, where they will make a colorful display. The soil should be well-drained, ideally with plenty of compost or manure dug in a month or so before planting.

GROWING METHOD

Planting	Plant the woody, tuberous roots 1–2in deep and about 6in apart, with the claws pointing down, in early spring. Soaking the tubers in water for a few hours before planting gets them off to a good start.
Feeding	Liquid feed with a balanced fertiliser every two weeks from when the flower buds start to appear. Keep the soil moist when the ferny leaves appear, particularly during bud formation and flowering.
Problems	Usually trouble free, though powdery mildew may occur in hot, dry seasons. Spray with a general fungicide if necessary.

FLOWERING

Season	Flowers throughout the summer.
Cutting	Cut flowers early in the morning and change the water frequently to prolong vase life.

AFTER FLOWERING

Requirements	Cut off spent flower stems. When the foliage has died down completely, tubers can be lifted, cleaned and stored in dry peat in a frost-free place until the following spring. After three seasons tubers are best replaced.

SCHIZOSTYLIS COCCINEA
Kaffir lily

THE EXTENDED FLOWER spikes give the appearance of a small gladiolus, though the individual flowers are more delicate.

THE RICH ROSE flowers of Schizostylis "Tambara" *are displayed to great effect against evergreen shrubs in the late fall garden.*

FEATURES

The beautiful, scarlet or pink, gladiolus-like flowers of schizostylis add a very welcome splash of color to fall borders, coming as they do right at the end of the season. The tall, grassy leaves form a clump from which 2–3ft spikes of flowers rise, bearing some 8–10 open, star-shaped blooms. There are several named varieties in a range of pink and red shades: "Major" has large, deep red flowers, "Viscountess Byng" is a delicate pink, and "Tambara" is a rich, rosy pink. "November Cheer" is one of the latest-flowering varieties. Schizostylis is not suitable for cold, exposed yards, but grows and spreads rapidly where conditions suit it.

SCHIZOSTYLIS AT A GLANCE

A valuable late fall-flowering plant for the border, with colorful scarlet or pink, gladiolus-like flower spikes.

		Recommended Varieties
Jan	/	
Feb	/	"Jennifer"
Mar	plant	"Mrs Hegarty"
Apr	plant	"November Cheer"
May	/	"Sunrise"
Jun	/	"Tambara"
July	/	"Viscountess Byng"
Aug	/	
Sept	flowering	
Oct	flowering	
Nov	flowering	
Dec	/	

CONDITIONS

Aspect   A sheltered spot in full sun or light shade suits this plant.

Site   Suitable for the middle of the flower border; in cold districts they do well as pot plants in a conservatory or greenhouse. Moisture-retentive, fertile soil is required.

GROWING METHOD

Planting   Plant in spring, 2in deep and 12in apart. Pot-grown plants are available for planting in summer and fall. Rhizomes can also be planted in 8in pots of soilless or John Innes compost in a sheltered position outdoors, being brought into a cool conservatory or greenhouse before the first frosts for flowering inside.

Feeding   Keep the soil moist at all times. Feed pot-grown plants with high potash liquid fertiliser every 14 days from early summer until flower buds form.

Problems   No specific problems are generally experienced.

FLOWERING

Season   Flowers from late September into November.

Cutting   The flower spikes are excellent for cutting, lasting well in water. Pick them when the buds start to show color.

AFTER FLOWERING

Requirements   Cut down faded flower stems. Protect the crowns with a mulch of chipped bark, straw, or dry leaves over winter. Overcrowded plants can be divided in fall.

SCILLA
Squill

A STARBURST *of bright blue flowers topped with golden stamens makes up the pretty inflorescence of* Scilla peruviana, *the Cuban lily.*

THE SIBERIAN SQUILL, Scilla siberica, *makes its appearance in early spring. "Atrocoerulea" has particularly rich blue flowers.*

FEATURES

The most familiar scillas are the dwarf varieties that flower in early spring. They include *Scilla siberica* (Siberian squill), which has clusters of nodding blue bells about 6in high, and *Scilla mischtschenkoana* (*S. tubergeniana*), which has starry, pale blue flowers with a deeper blue stripe on the petals. This species grows only 2–4in high. *S. bifolia* grows to 2–6in, with a spike of 15 or more star-shaped flowers in blue, pink, or white. Leaves of all these species are elongated and strap shaped. *Scilla peruviana*, the Cuban lily, is quite different—a tall, early summer-flowering bulb with densely packed, conical heads of purple-blue flowers.

SCILLA AT A GLANCE

Mainly dwarf bulbs with starry or bell-shaped blue or white flowers in early spring.

Jan	/	
Feb	flowering ✿	**Recommended Varieties**
Mar	flowering ✿	*Scilla bifolia:*
Apr	flowering ✿	"Rosea"
May	flowering ✿	*Scilla siberica:*
Jun	flowering ✿	"Alba"
July	/	"Spring Beauty"
Aug	plant ✋	*Scilla peruviana:*
Sept	plant ✋	"Alba"
Oct	plant ✋	*Scilla peruviana elegans*
Nov	/	*S. p. venusta*
Dec	/	

CONDITIONS

Aspect — Tolerates full sun but the flowers will have better, longer lasting color if they are grown in semi-shade.

Site — Grow in beds and borders, in almost any kind of soil as long as it drains well. Soils enriched with organic matter will give better results.

GROWING METHOD

Planting — Plant the bulbs about 2–4in deep and 6–8in apart in late summer or early fall.

Feeding — Apply a balanced fertiliser after flowering in early summer. Water during dry spells before and during the flowering season.

Problems — No specific pest or disease problems are known for this plant.

FLOWERING

Season — The flower spikes appear during late spring and early summer.

Cutting — Flowers can be cut successfully for indoor decoration.

AFTER FLOWERING

Requirements — Faded flower spikes should be cut off just above ground level. Clumps will usually need to be lifted only every 4–5 years unless they are very congested. Divide crowded clumps in late summer, replanting immediately to avoid drying out of the bulbs.

SINNINGIA
Gloxinia

THE VELVETY *texture of trumpet-shaped gloxinia flowers shows up well here on the variety "Blanche de Meru."*

"GREGOR MENDEL" is one of several fully double-flowered varieties. The heavy heads of bloom may need supporting with thin canes.

FEATURES

Gloxinias are tender plants suitable for growing in the home, greenhouse, or conservatory, where they will make an impressive, colorful display. The large, showy, brilliantly colored flowers are trumpet-shaped, often with speckled throats. Both flowers and leaves have a velvety feel and appearance: the large leaves are mid-green and oval.

Flowers are produced in abundance on well-grown plants, and are available in many colors, from white through pink and red to deepest blue and violet. The edges of the petals may be ruffled, or frilled with a contrasting color; there are several double-flowered varieties.

SINNINGIA AT A GLANCE

A showy house plant with colorful, velvety-textured flowers. Minimum temperature 60°F (zone 11).

Jan	plant	**Recommended Varieties**
Feb	plant	
Mar	plant	"Blanche de Meru"
Apr	/	"Mont Blanc"
May	/	"Princess Elizabeth"
Jun	flowering	"Gregor Mendel"
July	flowering	
Aug	flowering	
Sept	/	
Oct	/	
Nov	/	
Dec	/	

CONDITIONS

Aspect Choose a bright position, but not one that is in direct sun or the foliage will be scorched.

Site Gloxinias are house plants requiring average warmth; they dislike hot, dry air and benefit from standing on a dish of moist pebbles for increased humidity. Moisture-retentive soilless potting compost should be used.

GROWING METHOD

Planting Start the tubers off in moist peat or compost in a frost-free position in spring, potting them up individually when the shoots start to grow. Tubers must be planted with the dished side up, level with the surface of the compost—not buried.

Feeding Apply high potash liquid fertiliser every 14 days during the growing season. Keep the compost only just moist until growth has started, then water more freely. Take care to keep water splashes off the leaves and flowers, and never waterlog the compost.

Problems Hot, dry air causes the leaves to shrivel and flower buds to fall before opening. Overwatering leads to rotting of the roots.

FLOWERING

Season Flowers throughout the summer.

Cutting Not suitable for cutting

AFTER FLOWERING

Requirements Gradually reduce watering until the leaves have died back, then store the tubers in dry compost in a cool but frost-free place. Repot in fresh potting compost in spring.

SPARAXIS TRICOLOR
Harlequin flower

HARLEQUIN FLOWERS *come in a veritable kaleidoscope of colors, with the patterned throat revealing yet more colors and patterns.*

THE STRONG, BRIGHT COLORS *of harlequin flowers are shown to best advantage when they are planted in an open, sunny spot.*

FEATURES

This showy, easy-care plant has bright flowers of yellow, red, pink, orange, or purple carried on stems that can be anywhere from 6–18in high. Many of the brightly colored flowers have a darker purple or deep red area in the center and a yellow throat. Harlequin flowers hybridise readily, often producing seedlings that have interesting color variations. These are bulbs that thrive in dry, warm areas of the yard. They look their best when mass-planted but can also be grown in containers, where they should be crowded together for best effect. The flowers cut well for indoor decoration. Harlequin flower bulbs increase rapidly by offsets.

SPARAXIS AT A GLANCE

Very brightly colored, star-shaped flowers are carried on slender stems in early summer. Not suitable for cold, exposed yards.

		Recommended Varieties
Jan	/	
Feb	/	Usually supplied as a
Mar	/	color mixture
Apr	/	
May	flowering	
Jun	flowering	
July	/	
Aug	/	
Sept	/	
Oct	/	
Nov	plant	
Dec	/	

CONDITIONS

Aspect Needs full sun all day for best results.
Site Sparaxis needs a sheltered spot in a reasonably mild area to do well; in cold gardens it is best grown in containers under cover. Soil must be well-drained and moderately fertile.

GROWING METHOD

Planting Corms should be planted 3in deep and 3–4in apart in mid-fall. Mulch the planting area with chipped bark or leafmold for winter protection.
Feeding In very poor soil apply a balanced fertiliser in early summer after flowering. Mulch the soil in late winter with well-rotted organic matter. In dry seasons, water when the foliage emerges and as buds and flowers develop if necessary.
Problems No specific problems are known.

FLOWERING

Season Flowering should be abundant in late spring and early summer.
Cutting Sparaxis makes a good cut flower for the home and should last well in water.

AFTER FLOWERING

Requirements Allow foliage to die down naturally, then lift the corms and dry them off until it is time to replant in fall. Any cormlets that have formed can be removed when the corms are lifted and replanted separately.

SPREKELIA FORMOSISSIMA
Jacobean lily

THE SCULPTURED LINES of Jacobean lilies need to be appreciated at close quarters. Growing them in containers is a perfect solution.

THE DARK CRIMSON of the flowers tends to recede into the deep green foliage but still gives a lovely rich glow.

FEATURES

The rich crimson flowers of Jacobean lily are carried singly on stems 12–18in high and the foliage, which is about the same height, appears with or just before the flowers. This plant is sometimes called the Aztec lily and is in fact native to Mexico where it occurs in open, sunny places, often in poor soil. The unusual shape of the flower gives rise to another common name, orchid amaryllis, and the exotic-looking flower could easily be mistaken for an orchid. Unfortunately it is suitable for gardens in mild areas only; in less favored climates it must be grown as a greenhouse or conservatory plant. Formerly much more widely grown than it is today, it deserves to become more popular.

SPREKELIA AT A GLANCE

An exotic-looking, rather tender plant that needs greenhouse conditions in cooler areas. Minimum temperature 45°F (zone 11).

Jan	/	Recommended Varieties
Feb	/	Only the straight species
Mar	/	is grown—no cultivars or
Apr	plant ✍	varieties of this plant are
May	/	available.
Jun	flowering 🐛	
July	/	
Aug	/	
Sept	/	
Oct	/	
Nov	/	
Dec	/	

CONDITIONS

Aspect Grows best in full sun with wind protection. Indoors it likes a bright position.

Site Suitable for a sheltered border in mild areas, or containers in a greenhouse or conservatory. Outdoors, soil must be well-drained and enriched with compost or manure. Use John Innes potting compost for containers.

GROWING METHOD

Planting Plant bulbs in spring, 2in deep and 8in apart. In containers, plant with the neck of the bulb just above the compost surface.

Feeding Give a high potash liquid feed every two or three weeks throughout the growing season. Water container plants regularly until the foliage starts to die down.

Problems No specific problems are known.

FLOWERING

Season The showy flowers appear in early summer.

Cutting Can be cut for the vase but usually better enjoyed on the plant.

AFTER FLOWERING

Requirements When the leaves die down, lift outdoor bulbs and keep them in a cool, dry place. For container-grown plants, allow the compost to dry out when the leaves die down, then keep the bulb dry in its pot until spring when watering will start it into growth again.

STERNBERGIA LUTEA
Fall daffodil, lily-of-the-field

MOST SCHOLARS today believe Sternbergia lutea *is the plant referred to in the Bible as "the lily of the field."*

SHORT IN STATURE but big on impact, lily-of-the-field is one of the most delightful of bulbs, especially so as it blooms in fall.

FEATURES

Clear, bright yellow flowers, rather like crocuses, appear on 6in stems from their surround of shorter, dark green, strappy leaves. The foliage persists until spring when it dies down to remain dormant until the following fall. Ideal for the rock garden, these plants also show to advantage when planted in the yard in good-sized groups where they can be left to multiply. This is a bulb that could be naturalized in turf but the area would have to be well-marked to avoid cutting off the emerging growth in fall, and the grass could not be mown for several months. Lily-of-the-field can be grown in containers but they are more successful in the open ground.

STERNBERGIA AT A GLANCE

A crocus-like bulb with flowers appearing in late summer and fall. Needs very well-drained soil to thrive.

Month		Recommended Varieties
Jan	/	
Feb	/	*Sternbergia lutea:*
Mar	/	Angustifolia Group
Apr	/	
May	/	*Sternbergia clusiana*
Jun	/	
July	plant 🖐	*Sternbergia sicula*
Aug	plant 🖐	
Sept	flowering 🌺	
Oct	flowering 🌺	
Nov	/	
Dec	/	

CONDITIONS

Aspect   Prefers full sun: a summer baking of the dormant bulbs is necessary for good flowering in the fall.

Site   Suitable for a rockery, raised bed, or a sunny, reasonably sheltered border. Very well-drained soil is essential for this plant. Well-rotted organic matter can be dug into the bed ahead of planting.

GROWING METHOD

Planting   Plant bulbs in summer about 5in deep and the same distance apart.

Feeding   Supplementary fertiliser is generally not needed.

Problems   The main problem encountered is rotting of bulbs due to heavy or poorly drained soil. Improve drainage by incorporating sharp sand into the planting area.

FLOWERING

Season   The small, bright golden flowers appear in fall.

Cutting   These flowers are not suitable for cutting.

AFTER FLOWERING

Requirements   Ensure the plants are allowed to remain dry once the foliage has died down in early summer. The site may need protection from excessive summer rain with a cloche or similar. Do not disturb established plants unless it is essential.

TRITELEIA
syn. *Brodiaea laxa*

"QUEEN FABIOLA" is probably the most widely planted of the triteleias. The paler center gives definition to the flower form.

BLUE FLOWERS are always a favorite, and the violet-blue, starry flowers of these triteleias fill a sheltered pocket in the garden.

FEATURES

These pretty bulbous plants are native to Oregon and California. There is some confusion over their correct name; they are often listed as brodiaea, with some species as dichelostemma. *T. laxa* is the most popular form. Flower stems may be 18–24in or so high with the strappy leaves growing to about 12in. The starry flowers are carried in loose clusters and are pale or violet blue with the most popular cultivar, "Queen Fabiola," producing deeper violet-blue blooms with a pale center. The foliage dies back in spring while the plant is in bloom, and the corm remains dormant from midsummer until winter.

TRITELEIA AT A GLANCE

Dainty clusters of tubular blue blooms are carried on slender stems in midsummer. Well-drained soil is essential.

Jan	/	
Feb	/	**Recommended Varieties**
Mar	/	*Triteleia hyacinthina*
Apr	/	
May	flowering 🌿	*Triteleia ixioides*
Jun	flowering 🌿	*Triteleia laxa:*
July	flowering 🌿	"Queen Fabiola"
Aug	/	
Sept	plant ✍	*Triteleia peduncularis*
Oct	/	
Nov	/	
Dec	/	

CONDITIONS

Aspect   An open, sunny but sheltered site is necessary.
Site   Grow this plant in the flower border or in containers. The soil must be light and very well-drained; triteleia cannot stand waterlogging. It can be grown in containers of sandy potting compost where the garden soil is heavy.

GROWING METHOD

Planting   Plant corms 3–4in deep and 4–6in apart in fall.
Feeding   A balanced or high potash fertiliser can be given when the flower buds appear, but normally no feeding is necessary. Plants in containers can be liquid-fed every two weeks. Watering is not normally necessary; the soil should be allowed to dry out while the corm is dormant during the summer.
Problems   There are no specific pest or disease problems known for this plant.

FLOWERING

Season   Flowers appear from early to mid-summer.
Cutting   Blooms last particularly well as a cut flower.

AFTER FLOWERING

Requirements   Flowering stems can be cut off when they are past their peak, or left to set seed. Plants resent disturbance, so should be left alone once planted.

TULIPA
Tulip

THE POINTED PETALS of these goblet-shaped, bright lipstick-pink tulips will open to form a starry shape.

A NATIVE of Crete, pale pink Tulipa saxatilis *needs a sunny, warm position with perfectly drained soil in which to grow.*

FEATURES

There are more than 100 species of tulips and many hundreds of hybrids. Most modern garden tulips are the result of extensive breeding programs that began in the late sixteenth century in Europe and are continuing to this day. Tulips were fashionable at that time as more and more species were introduced to Europe from Turkey, Iran, and central Asia. Tulip species range in height from about 6–24in but the greatest number of hybrids are probably in the range of 12–16in. Tulips look their best in mass plantings of one color but they can, of course, be mixed. They make very good container plants and are delightful cut flowers. Some of the most charming are the dwarf types that do particularly well in rock gardens and are also very suitable for containers.

Tulip bulbs are widely available in garden centers in late summer and early fall, but to get a wider choice it is often best to obtain catalogs from specialist bulb growers who run mail order businesses. Many of the species tulips are only available from specialist growers. With careful selection it is possible to have a tulip in flower from early to very late spring.

Like daffodils, tulips are split into a number of divisions according to their flower form and time of flowering.

Single early	Cup-shaped single flowers, up to 16in in early to mid-spring.
Double early	Fully double flowers up to 16in in early to mid-spring.
Triumph	Conical then rounded, single flowers up to 20in in mid to late spring.
Darwin hybrid	Large, single flowers of varying shape, up to 24in in mid to late spring.
Single late	Single, blocky, or square-shaped flowers up to 30in in late spring and early summer.
Lily-flowered	Single, waisted flowers with pointed petals, up to 24in in late spring.
Fringed	Single flowers with very finely cut petal edges, up to 24in in late spring.
Viridiflora	Single flowers with green bands or streaks on the outside, up to 20in in late spring.
Rembrandt	Single flowers with a broken pattern of feathering or streaking caused by a virus. Up to 30in in late spring.
Parrot	Single flowers with very strongly frilled and curled petals, up to 24in in late spring.
Double late	Large, fully double flowers up to 24in in late spring.
Kaufmanniana	Single, often bi-colored flowers of a waterlily shape, up to 10in in late spring. Leaves may be mottled.
Fosteriana	Large, single, wide-opening flowers up to 20in in early to mid-spring.
Greigii	Large, single flowers up to 14in in mid to late spring. Leaves streaked and mottled.
Miscellaneous	Any other species, varieties and hybrids.

1.

2.

3.

6.

7.

TULIPS
(*TULIPA*)

*Tulips, with their wide range of forms
and colors, are divided into fifteen
horticultural groups.*

*1. From a crimson bud "Leen van der
Mark" opens to reveal a crystalline
white center.*

*2. A fully opened "Bokassa Red" shows
its deep scarlet petals tipped with gold.*

*3. "Judith Lyster," a single late tulip, is
rich cream merging to watermelon pink.*

*4. Goblet-shaped "Bokassa Rose" is
deep rose pink with a yellow center.*

*5. "Kees Nelis" is a bright, two-tone
tulip in primary red and yellow.*

*6. No two parrot tulip flowers are
identical as this flamboyant
"Flaming Parrot" proves.*

*7. "Princess Victoria" is a heavy-
textured tulip that is more weather
resistant than some other varieties.*

*8. "Angélique," a pale pink ruffled
beauty, is best grown in pots so it can be
protected from weather.*

*9. "Monte Carlo" is a bright gold,
fully double tulip with a light scent.*

5.

8.

9.

THE BIZARRE FORM of parrot tulips is exemplified by this dark crimson flower. People either love these forms or hate them.

THE BURGUNDY of these full-blown tulips will appeal to lovers of the unusual but they may be hard to incorporate into the garden scheme.

CONDITIONS

Aspect Tulips need full sun for at least half the day, with some wind protection.

Site Grow tulips in beds and borders, on rockeries or in containers. Soil should be well-drained with a high organic content. Add lime to acid soils.

GROWING METHOD

Planting Bulbs should be planted in late fall. Planting depth varies according to the size of the bulbs; usually 6–8in for the larger types and 4in for the smaller species. Space them 4–8in apart.

Feeding Apply liquid fertiliser as soon as buds appear and again after flowers have faded. Water regularly in dry spells, especially once the buds have appeared.

Problems Tulip breaking virus, causing streaking of the flowers, is carried by aphids. Remove affected plants and keep aphids under control. Tulip fire disease is a type of botrytis or grey mold. It causes small brown spots on flowers and leaves; stems may rot and gray furry growth may develop on the damaged areas. Destroy plants infected with this disease and avoid planting tulips in the same spot for a couple of years. Spraying with a general fungicide may control early infection.

FLOWERING

Season Tulips flower somewhere between late winter and late spring, depending on variety.

Cutting If cutting blooms for the house, choose those that are not fully open and cut them early in the morning. Change vase water frequently.

AFTER FLOWERING

Requirements Remove spent flower stems and dead foliage. Tulips may be left in the ground for two or three years, or the bulbs can be lifted when the foliage has died down, cleaned and stored in a cool, dry, airy place. Dwarf tulips tend to be left in the ground, but other varieties usually perform better if they are lifted and replanted every year. If you do not want to lift them annually, make sure the bulbs are planted deeply.

TULIPA AT A GLANCE

Well-known flowers in a very wide range of colors, sizes, and forms, flowering between late winter and late spring.

Jan	/		Recommended Varieties
Feb	flowering		"Peach Blossom"
Mar	flowering		"Apeldoorn"
Apr	flowering		"Clara Butt"
May	flowering		"China Pink"
Jun	/		"Burgundy Lace"
July	/		"Spring Green"
Aug	/		"Texas Gold"
Sept	/		"Angelique"
Oct	/		"Ancilla"
Nov	plant		*Tulipa fosteriana*
Dec	plant		*Tulipa greigii*
			Tulipa tarda

WATSONIA
Watsonia

THE VIVID PINK FLOWERS of watsonia make it a most desirable plant, but it is not commonly grown in gardens.

WATSONIA FLOWERS are displayed well-clear of the upright foliage and so are ideal for planting at the back of a border.

FEATURES

Although there are many species of watsonias in the wild, they are not commonly cultivated plants. The stiff, sword-shaped leaves are similar to those of a gladiolus: the flower spike, growing to over 39in carries tubular flowers in various shades of pink and red, violet, magenta, and orange. Watsonia is ideally placed toward the back of a mixed border. In all but very warm districts the corms should be lifted in fall and stored in a dry place until it is time to replant them the following spring.

The usual species offered is *W. pillansii* (also known as *W. beatricis*), which has orange-red flowers. The slightly more tender *W. borbonica* (*W. pyrimidata*) has rich pink blooms.

WATSONIA AT A GLANCE

An unusual bulb with tall, stately spikes of pink or red flowers, good for the back of the border.

		Recommended Varieties
Jan	/	
Feb	/	
Mar	/	"Stanford Scarlet"
Apr	plant 🖐	"Tresco Dwarf Pink"
May	plant 🖐	
Jun	flowering 🌸	Watsonia borbonica
July	flowering 🌸	ardernei
Aug	flowering 🌸	
Sept	plant 🖐 (warm areas)	
Oct	/	
Nov	/	
Dec	/	

CONDITIONS

Aspect   Watsonia needs full sun and a warm, sheltered position.

Site   These tall plants are good for the back of a border. They can also be grown in pots in a greenhouse. Any well-drained soil is acceptable, but growth will be better if well-rotted organic matter is dug in before planting.

GROWING METHOD

Planting   Plant corms in mid to late spring, 4in deep and 12in apart. In warm, sheltered areas, corms can be planted in fall 6in deep and mulched with chipped bark or dry leaves.

Feeding   Apply a long-acting fertiliser such as general fertiliser in early summer. Watering is necessary only in prolonged dry spells.

Problems   Generally free from pest or disease problems when grown in an open, sunny position.

FLOWERING

Season   Watsonias flower in midsummer.

Cutting   Stems can be cut for the vase. They should last well with frequent water changes.

AFTER FLOWERING

Requirements   Except in very warm areas, lift the corms after flowering, when the foliage starts to die down. Clean them, allow them to dry, and store in a cool, airy place until the following spring.

ZANTEDESCHIA
Arum lily, calla lily

ARUM LILIES have long been favorites with flower arrangers for their texture and sculptural shape, which adds form to an arrangement.

PURE WHITE FLOWERS and decorative leaves are features of arum, which are quite easy to grow in a variety of conditions.

FEATURES

Arum lilies are greatly prized for their beautiful waxy flowers, pure white with a golden central spadix. The arrow-shaped leaves are deep green, and the whole plant can grow up to 39in high. Several species are suitable for growing only in a greenhouse or conservatory, but *Z. aethiopica* can be grown outside in reasonably sheltered yards. It likes moist, boggy conditions, and often grows best beside a pond or water feature: it can be grown as a marginal plant in up to 12in of water. *Z. elliottiana*, the golden arum, and *Z. rehmannii*, the pink arum, are good greenhouse or conservatory plants.

ZANTEDESCHIA AT A GLANCE

A rhizomatous plant grown for its beautiful waxy white flower spathes. Needs greenhouse conditions in some areas.

Jan	/	**Recommended Varieties**
Feb	/	Zantedeschia aethiopica:
Mar	/	"Crowborough"
Apr	plant	"Green Goddess"
May	/	
Jun	flowering	
July	flowering	
Aug	/	
Sept	/	
Oct	/	
Nov	/	
Dec	/	

CONDITIONS

Aspect — Can be grown in full sun or light shade. It should be sheltered from strong wind.

Site — *Z. aethiopica* can be grown on the fringe of a pool or in a border in moist, humus-rich soil. Other arum species need rich but free-draining soil and are grown in a greenhouse or conservatory in containers.

GROWING METHOD

Planting — Plant rhizomes 6in deep and 18in apart in spring.

Feeding — Apply liquid fertiliser as buds appear and continue to feed every 14–21 days while plants are in bloom. Keep the soil moist at all times while the plants are in active growth during spring and summer.

Problems — Leaf spot can cause dark blotches on all parts of the plant and may cause premature leaf drop. It often occurs where conditions are too cool and damp. Destroy affected parts and spray with a suitable fungicide.

FLOWERING

Season — Flowers in early summer.

Cutting — Flowers are excellent for cutting.

AFTER FLOWERING

Requirements — Remove flower stems as they fade. Mulch outdoor plants with dry leaves for winter.

ZEPHYRANTHES
Zephyr lily, rainflower

ZEPHYR LILY shows how even the simplest of flowers can be very beautiful. The green throat and yellow stamens emphasise the purity.

A BROAD BORDER of zephyr lily gives a star-studded performance in the fall garden.

FEATURES

With its starry white flowers and shiny green, grass-like foliage, zephyr lily is a bulb for mass planting in sheltered yards. It is quite easy to grow and can remain undisturbed for years where conditions suit it. It can be planted in borders or on a rockery, and it can also be grown very successfully in containers. The crocus-like flowers are carried in late summer or fall, especially after showers of rain, which accounts for its common name of rainflower. *Zephyranthes candida* is the species suitable for growing outdoors in Britain; it generally reaches a height of 8–10in. *Z. grandiflora* (also called *Z. rosea*) has lovely rosy pink flowers but is only suitable for cultivation in a greenhouse or conservatory, as is the yellow flowered *Z. citrina*.

ZEPHYRANTHES AT A GLANCE

An attractive, low-growing plant with crocus-like flowers in fall.

Month		Recommended Species
Jan	/	
Feb	/	Zephyranthes candida
Mar	/	
Apr	plant 🖐	Z. citrina
May	/	
Jun	flowering 🌱 *	Z. flavissima
July	flowering 🌱 *	
Aug	/	Z. grandiflora
Sept	flowering 🌱	
Oct	flowering 🌱	
Nov	/	
Dec	/	

* indoors

CONDITIONS

Aspect Grows best in full sun.
Site Grow in beds or borders or in pockets in a rockery. Needs a well-drained but moisture-retentive soil. Growth will be improved if soils contain some humus.

GROWING METHOD

Planting Plant in spring, 2in deep and 4in apart. For greenhouse cultivation, plant 5 bulbs in a 5in pot in loam-based potting compost.
Feeding Supplementary fertiliser is generally not needed. Spread a mulch of well-decayed manure or compost around the bulbs in spring. Water in dry spells during spring, but stop watering when the foliage starts to die down.
Problems No specific problems are usually experienced with this plant.

FLOWERING

Season Flowers appear from late summer into fall, or in mid-summer in the greenhouse.
Cutting Flowers are not suitable for cutting.

AFTER FLOWERING

Requirements Spent flower stems may be cut off but this is not essential. No special treatment is needed as the bulbs are best left undisturbed for several years. If you wish to lift and divide a clump this is best done in spring. Greenhouse plants should be allowed to dry out when the leaves die down, and started into growth again by plentiful watering the following spring.

INDEX

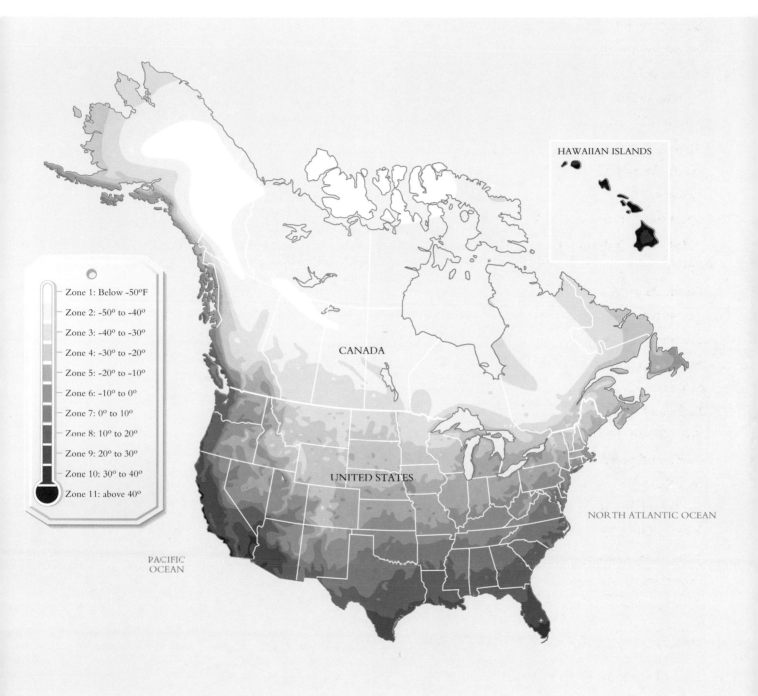

HAWAIIAN ISLANDS

Zone 1: Below –50°F
Zone 2: –50° to –40°
Zone 3: –40° to –30°
Zone 4: –30° to –20°
Zone 5: –20° to –10°
Zone 6: –10° to 0°
Zone 7: 0° to 10°
Zone 8: 10° to 20°
Zone 9: 20° to 30°
Zone 10: 30° to 40°
Zone 11: above 40°

CANADA

UNITED STATES

NORTH ATLANTIC OCEAN

PACIFIC
OCEAN

Published in the United States and Canada by Whitecap Books

First published in 2000 by Murdoch Books UK
Ferry House, 51–57 Lacy Road, Putney, London, SW15 1PR
Reprinted 2001

ISBN 1-55285-074-9

This work is a compilation of:
A Gardener's Guide to Annuals, A Gardener's Guide to Perennials
and A Gardener's Guide to Bulbs (Murdoch Books UK Editions)

Distributed in Canada by Whitecap Books (Vancouver) Ltd,
351 Lynn Avenue, North Vancouver, BC V7J 2CA;
Telephone (604) 980 9852, Facsimile (604) 980 8197
or Whitecap Books (Ontario) Ltd, 47 Coldwater Road, North York, ON M3B 1YB;
Telephone (416) 444 3442, Facsimile (416) 444 6630
Distributed in the USA by Graphic Arts Centre Publishing,
PO Box 10306, Portland, OR 97296-0106, USA;
Telephone (503) 226 2402, Facsimile (503) 223 1410

COMMISSIONING EDITOR: Iain MacGregor
PROJECT EDITOR: Anna Nicholas
AMERICANIZATION: Prima Creative Services
JACKET DESIGN: Axis Design
MAP DESIGN: Julian Osbaldstone
PRODUCTION MANAGER: Lucy Byrne
PUBLISHING MANAGER: Fia Fornari
UK SALES & MARKETING DIRECTOR: Kathryn Harvey
INTERNATIONAL SALES DIRECTOR: Kevin Lagden
GROUP CEO & PUBLISHER: Anne Wilson
GROUP GENERAL MANAGER: Mark Smith

Colour separation by Colourscan in Singapore
Printed in China by Toppan Printing Hong Kong Co. Ltd